IFIP Advances in Information and Communication Technology 444

IFIP – The International Federation for Information Processing

IFIP was founded in 1960 under the auspices of UNESCO, following the First World Computer Congress held in Paris the previous year. An umbrella organization for societies working in information processing, IFIP's aim is two-fold: to support information processing within its member countries and to encourage technology transfer to developing nations. As its mission statement clearly states,

> *IFIP's mission is to be the leading, truly international, apolitical organization which encourages and assists in the development, exploitation and application of information technology for the benefit of all people.*

IFIP is a non-profitmaking organization, run almost solely by 2500 volunteers. It operates through a number of technical committees, which organize events and publications. IFIP's events range from an international congress to local seminars, but the most important are:

- The IFIP World Computer Congress, held every second year;
- Open conferences;
- Working conferences.

The flagship event is the IFIP World Computer Congress, at which both invited and contributed papers are presented. Contributed papers are rigorously refereed and the rejection rate is high.

As with the Congress, participation in the open conferences is open to all and papers may be invited or submitted. Again, submitted papers are stringently refereed.

The working conferences are structured differently. They are usually run by a working group and attendance is small and by invitation only. Their purpose is to create an atmosphere conducive to innovation and development. Refereeing is also rigorous and papers are subjected to extensive group discussion.

Publications arising from IFIP events vary. The papers presented at the IFIP World Computer Congress and at open conferences are published as conference proceedings, while the results of the working conferences are often published as collections of selected and edited papers.

Any national society whose primary activity is about information processing may apply to become a full member of IFIP, although full membership is restricted to one society per country. Full members are entitled to vote at the annual General Assembly. National societies preferring a less committed involvement may apply for associate or corresponding membership. Associate members enjoy the same benefits as full members, but without voting rights. Corresponding members are not represented in IFIP bodies. Affiliated membership is open to non-national societies, and individual and honorary membership schemes are also offered.

Don Passey Arthur Tatnall (Eds.)

Key Competencies in ICT and Informatics

Implications and Issues for Educational Professionals and Management

IFIP WG 3.4/3.7 International Conferences
KCICTP and ITEM 2014
Potsdam, Germany, July 1-4, 2014
Revised Selected Papers

Springer

Volume Editors

Don Passey
Lancaster University
Centre for Technology Enhanced Learning
Department of Educational Research
Lancaster LA1 4YL, UK
E-mail: d.passey@lancaster.ac.uk

Arthur Tatnall
Victoria University
City Flinders Campus
Melbourne, VIC 3084, Australia
E-mail: athur.tatnall@vu.edu.au

ISSN 1868-4238
e-ISSN 1868-422X
ISBN 978-3-662-52627-9
e-ISBN 978-3-662-45770-2
DOI 10.1007/978-3-662-45770-2
Springer Heidelberg New York Dordrecht London

Softcover reprint of the hardcover 1st edition 2014

Typesetting: Camera-ready by author, data conversion by Scientific Publishing Services, Chennai, India

Printed on acid-free paper

Springer is part of Springer Science+Business Media (www.springer.com)

Preface

The papers in this book were selected from those presented at the International Federation for Information Processing (IFIP) conference: "Key Competencies in Informatics and Information and Communication Technologies (ICT)," held in Potsdam, Germany, in July 2014. After the conference each author was given an opportunity to improve their paper, based on conference feedback, before publication in this book. All papers were initially peer reviewed for presentation at the conference and the final improved versions were peer reviewed again prior to publication.

While the theme of the IFIP Technical Committee 3 (TC3) education conference was on "Key Competencies in Informatics and Information and Communication Technologies (ICT)," both strands of Working Group 3.4 (Professional and Vocational Education in ICT) and Working Group 3.7 (Information Technology in Educational Management) within the conference focused more specifically through their areas of interest on Key Competencies for Educating ICT Professionals, Key Competencies Learning and Life Transitions, Key Competencies and School Management, and Educational Stakeholders and Key Competencies.

Twelve papers relating to the WG3.4 strand, "Key Competencies for Educating ICT Professionals," were selected for this book.

In the first of these papers, Holvikivi notes that the ICT profession is extremely international, as are ICT students. She describes cognitive differences in multinational study groups and explores ways to overcome some of the differences. Lecomber and Tatnall then examine education and training issues in project management for ICT professionals, considering the place of the two main project management approaches: PMBoK and PRINCE2. Williams, Černochová, Demo, and Younie describe a working model for teacher training in computing through the "Literacy from Scratch Project." Rocchi next examines the theoretical basis and two "mythical" statements regarding computer science as a discipline. Ruohonen, Mäkipää, and Kamaja then investigate issues relating to "offshoring" of software development and competencies, and work practices for dynamic distributed software development in global value networks. A developing country perspective of enterprise architecture skills by Shaanika and Iyamu explores how and where these skills can be developed and what constitutes competency.

Opel and Wellesen present an analysis of real-life working processes, competencies and operational fields for usage in vocational ICT education. Learning styles of students in computer science are discussed by Loay Talib Ahmed Al-Saffar, who also considers necessary changes in teaching methods to reduce student dropout and offer better learning. Haukijärvi presents a case study and evaluation of the eLearning Maturity Model in a university. Vendruscolo and Behar then attempt to identify relevant educational elements in the development of accounting professor competencies in distance education. iPads in education and professional learning with mobile technologies are discussed by Keith Turvey, who notes the potential of these technologies to "disrupt" established practices in ways that require adaptation if educators are to harness their potential. The final paper in this section is by Iyamu, who presents the South African experience on breeding ICT skills for industry.

Papers from the Working Group 3.7 strand focused on the theme of "Information Technology in Educational Management (ITEM)" and brought together findings from research, practitioner, and policy areas that explored three main themes:

- Key competencies, learning, and life transitions
- Key competencies and school management
- Educational stakeholders and key competencies

Within each of the these three main themes, current practice, development, and research outcomes have been highlighted by researchers, developers, and practitioners from across the world, giving a rich picture, not only of the current position and context in a range of situations, but also highlighting key challenges and issues that are worthy of further research exploration and development.

The theme of "Key Competencies, Learning, and Life Transitions" offers a set of seven papers providing complementary perspectives concerned with ways that different groups in life transitions are concerned with using digital skills and competencies, and how these are having impacts upon their needs and practices. Passey provides a contextual picture for the field of life transitions, defining the field for the reader, and generating a framework of factors that influence life transitions, through which to explore research and practice dimensions, both in terms of digital competencies, and in terms of associated features and skills. Rogers focuses on the motivational factors concerned with life transitions, and draws particular attention to the need to reconsider the polarizing concern with seeking intrinsic rather than extrinsic motivation, pointing more to the need to develop adaptability to support those in life transition arenas. Cranmer explores frameworks that identify digital competencies that individuals now need, and considers how those in life transitions between school and college are affected by the need for digital competencies. Lim and Lee Siew Hoong focus on the ways that a specific digital technology is being used to develop knowledge sharing practices within a commercial setting, where employees are concerned with a life transition within their employment practices. Lee Siew Hoong and Lim further consider this life transition arena, relating experiences from how a knowledge management system has been integrated into commercial practice, and the fundamental importance of factors that go beyond digital skills. Passey, in concluding this section, draws on the framework constructed from across the evidence of the entirety of papers in the section, and considers how this framework can be used to explore needs of individuals in specific life transitions, how digital technologies might support them, and what future research is needed to underpin our deeper understanding of the processes where individuals, supporters, and digital technologies work in harmony to generate positive outcomes for all concerned.

The theme of "Key Competencies and School Management" offers a set of five papers providing perspectives concerned with how teachers and managers in schools are handling digital technologies, and implications for their key digital competency and skill needs. Banzato considers how teachers are taking on board practices of digital storytelling with learners, and concludes that while digital skills are necessary, that curriculum concerns may play a larger role in determining use of these practices. Celep and Tülübaş consider, in a different context, the effect that school leadership has on attitudes of teachers to take on board digital technologies, and conclude that the positive effect of leadership in this respect is not as clear as the effect of overarching government or ministerial policies. Celep, Konaklı, and Kuyumcu explore how teachers are taking social networking sites on board in their practices, and conclude that major existing social networking sites are most commonly used in the population they studied, but moving to using these to support curriculum and school communication needs is far from common. Tatnall and Tatnall report on the ways that management information systems are being deployed and used in a single school setting, indicating the ways these are supporting teachers and managers. By contrast, Castro and Soares report on the challenges, issues, and perceived benefits that school managers identify when considering past and future management information systems.

The theme of "Educational Stakeholders and Key Competencies" offers a set of four papers providing perspectives concerned with ways that specific stakeholders in education (students, teachers, managers, and parents) are being involved increasingly in using digital technologies, and implications for their digital competency. Osorio and Nieves explore in the higher education sector how digital competencies are being described in terms of student requirement, but their evidence indicates that using these in the context of other skills that have a longer-term focus on employment are more likely to be successful. Schulz and Jeske take a different perspective, exploring how data analyses from online uses by students can be used to develop ways to differentiate between learning approaches, and the implications that this may have for teacher and student stakeholders. Strickley explores a development that supports other stakeholders – teachers, parents, and students – and indicates how digital technologies are supporting easier access to data and support, which removes stigma concerned with social status or level. Strickley, Bertram, Chapman, Hart, Hicks, Kennedy, and Phillips describe a development that enables parents to have access to indicators when they are seeking schools for their children, and the approaches they have taken in order to enable easier review by that key stakeholder group – parents.

In summary, these papers provide a range of evidence from many countries around the world, but giving a picture overall that indicates:

- Digital technologies are now being considered as a medium to support specific groups with learning needs – for those in life transitions. However, how the

potential range and depth of digital competencies and skills can be developed and handled by those in transition is a question that is yet to be answered.
- A diversity of digital technologies is being adopted and trialled by school teachers and managers for curriculum, communication, and management purposes. However, how the current factors that are preventing more common and wider adoption of these technologies, and the development of digital competencies and skills to support them, is not yet fully known.
- Digital technologies are being developed and adopted by an increasing range of stakeholders. How these developments will take shape in the future, and what their implications will be for the digital competency and skill of these stakeholders (students, teachers, managers, and parents), is not yet known.

Overall, what is clear from this range of papers is that digital skills and competencies alone are not enough to develop future practice; a deeper understanding of associated skills and competencies is needed if the digital technologies are to support those who can benefit from them most.

July 2014

Don Passey
Arthur Tatnall

KEYCIT Committees

Program Committee KEYCIT - Main Conference

Torsten Brinda	University of Duisburg-Essen, Germany (Chair)
Peter Micheuz	University of Klagenfurt, Austria (Co-chair)
Mary Webb	King's College London, UK (Co-chair)
Nick Reynolds	University of Melbourne, Australia (Editor)
Ralf Romeike	University of Potsdam, Germany (Editor)
Yvonne Büttner-Ringier	Kanton Basel Land, Switzerland
Andrew Fluck	University of Tasmania, Australia
Marie Iding	University of Hawaii, USA
Ulrich Kortenkamp	University of Halle Wittenberg, Germany
Joberto Martins	Salvador University, Brazil
Wolfgang Müller	University of Education, Weingarten, Germany
Sindre Røsvik	Volda University College, Norway
Raul Wazlawick	Federal University of Santa Catarina, Brazil

Program Committee KCICTP - WG3.4 Parallel Conference Stream

Arthur Tatnall	Victoria University, Australia (Chair)
Mikko Ruohonen	University of Tampere, Finland
Tobias Ley	Tallinn University, Estonia
Bill Davey	RMIT University, Melbourne, Australia
Barbara Tatnall	Heidelberg Press, Heidelberg, Australia

Program Committee ITEM - WG3.7 Parallel Conference Stream

Torsten Brinda	University of Duisburg-Essen, Germany (Chair)
Don Passey	Lancaster University, UK (Co-chair)
Andreas Breiter	University of Bremen, Germany (Co-chair)
Arthur Tatnall	Victoria University, Australia
Bill Davey	RMIT University, Melbourne, Australia
Adrie Visscher	University of Twente, The Netherlands
Christopher Thorn	Carnegie Foundation, Stanford, USA

Organizing Committee

Andreas Schwill (Chair)
Sabine Hübner, Conference Secretariat
Matthias Knietzsch
Mareen Przybylla
Wolfgang Severin

Table of Contents

Key Competencies for Educating ICT Professionals

Key Competencies, Learning and Life Transitions

Key Competencies and School Management

Educational Stakeholders and Key Competencies

Key Competencies for Educating ICT Professionals

Building Basic Competences for Culturally Diverse ICT Professionals

Jaana Holvikivi

Helsinki Metropolia University of Applied Sciences, Finland
jaana.holvikivi@metropolia.fi

Abstract. The ICT profession is extremely international, and so are ICT students. University students in one study group in Europe may represent ten or twenty nationalities with varied cultural and educational backgrounds. Selection of appropriate teaching methods for diverse students is challenging. This paper describes cognitive differences in multinational study groups, and explores ways to overcome some of the differences through offering online programming courses to support classroom instruction. Currently, online programming tools are widely used in schools and outside formal institutions. This paper shows that they can be efficient also when building professional competencies.

Keywords: ICT education, programming, cultural diversity, online courses, professional competences.

1 Introduction

The student body in ICT departments is extremely international in European universities that offer tuition in English. Students come from many continents with diverse educational backgrounds. The diversity of students poses a number of challenges, simultaneously offering a number of advantages that the universities need to address. The situation has evoked much research and discussion among universities nationally and worldwide, generating a substantial literature on these issues [1]. The main research approach has centered on a limited number of questions: how to recruit efficiently, how to generate income for the institution, how to help students adapt to the new environment, how to teach the correct behavior, and how to provide supporting studies. On the other hand, the contribution of the international student body to universities has been more or less ignored in research. Thus far, only few universities have attempted to modify their core curricula to accommodate a diverse student population [2].

This paper presents a summary of long-term case studies of the capabilities and backgrounds of international ICT students in the Helsinki Metropolia University of Applied Sciences [3], and aims at describing new strategies for developing competences in a diverse group. Moreover, it explores the impact of the emerging trend of global online education. The offering of high profile MOOC's (massive open

D. Passey and A. Tatnall (Eds.): KCICTP/ITEM 2014, IFIP AICT 444, pp. 3–11, 2014.

online courses) by top universities, as well as other online programming and science courses, reaches students in many parts of the world.

First, some characteristics of western academic culture are discussed, focusing on specific cognitive requirements of technology studies. The gap in primary and secondary education between economically developed and less developed countries is exemplified. In the research section, some consequences of the educational disparity for international ICT education are presented. Finally, one solution to improve the current unsatisfying situation by strengthening competencies by online programming courses is discussed.

2 Western Science and Educational Practices

The academic world has largely functioned on the assumption of universality of western science, and the universal nature of human cognition [4]. Accordingly, most of the research that has been published in psychology journals has been conducted by western researchers (96%), using university students as test subjects (in 67% of the cases in American samples). However, the western sample of study subjects has been shown to deviate from other cultural samples in certain cognitive skills such as spatial reasoning and thinking styles, especially analytical thinking.

Similarly, brain studies [5] have been conducted mainly in rich Western countries, partially because of the high cost of the equipment and the high skill level required for research teams. Only in Japan, Korea and China has the technology been advanced enough to conduct brain scans on the local population [6]. The inclusion of eastern populations has revealed interesting results such as brain differences in reading: the use of Chinese characters employs brain areas differently from using alphabetic characters [7], [8]. Moreover, basic mathematical operations are influenced by the language and writing system [9]. Additionally, decision-making and perception seem to be influenced by culture [4].

The dependence of cognitive variation on culture has also been discussed by Margaret Wilson [10] who introduced a theory of cognitive retooling based on the current neuro-scientific knowledge. She argued that culture exercises a profound effect on the cognitive system of perceiving and thinking, and even more importantly, on the functioning of the cognitive system. Cognitive tools are culturally transmitted through education, and the use of cognitive tools shapes neuro-cognitive architecture. In this paper, comparisons of cognitive and study practices of international students are presented.

The situation in Africa illustrates how weak connections to the practical life the education might have [11]. The curricula in African schools are based on western models, as well as most books and materials. Students hardly have access to computers [12]. The content of textbooks might be very remote from the everyday experience of students, adding an extra level of abstraction to the content to be learned. Therefore, students need to operate from two worldviews and often have two or more cultures to contend with, which results for them in rote learning without reaching a de-contextualization of knowledge.

3 Research and Results

The Helsinki Metropolia University of Applied Sciences has educated international students in English since 1994. Our experience has revealed various kinds of challenges that students with developing country background confront when entering the western engineering education system. Our research has extended over ten years, indicating certain changes that have occurred during this period [3]. In the beginning, students mainly came from Russia and China, later increasingly from Africa and South Asia. However, all continents are still represented among the student body. The variety of students ranges from monolingual Chinese and British students to multilingual South-Asian and African students.

3.1 Previous Research and Findings

Most conspicuous difference between developing country students and western students is their capability to combine theory and practice. An overly theoretical approach by developing country students has been revealed in laboratory assignments in nearly all ICT engineering courses that require hands-on work with the equipment, accurate measurements, or program coding. As students themselves report, these tasks are completely new to them, and they have not been trained in laboratory procedures [13]. The early life experience in western countries includes interaction with technical objects whereas children in developing countries tend to have more social interactions. According to a study by Agiobu-Kemmer in 1984, Nigerian Yoruba children spent more time with human beings than with physical objects. The reverse was true with Scottish children who spent more time with physical objects than with human beings. This comparative study indicated that cultural factors influence the way how the early upbringing introduces the physical world [14].

Student basic cognitive abilities also seem to differ in certain respects, in particular in the reaction times and working memory functioning [15]. A simple working memory test was given to groups of different nationalities, and the western and Chinese students performed significantly better in memorizing and in reaction times than African students. Van de Vijver [16] has previously reached somewhat similar results on reaction times. The working memory capacity of international students has not been studied previously, and even though the results of the study were unambiguous and significant, further studies would be needed to understand the phenomenon better.

The teaching methods in many affluent countries consist of little lecturing, and a range of possibilities for project and team work. Engineering study includes lots of practical work in laboratories. Even though students from developing countries find these new study methods appealing, the methods are perceived demanding as they call for more individual effort and need for self-regulation. Team working practices are usually taught in western schools and therefore university students are expected to have some previous knowledge of them. International students are in a less advantageous position in this regard compared to home students. These findings at our university are very similar to findings from other western institutions [13]. However, universities that primarily apply project based learning and team working methods are aware of the effort that is needed to become a productive project member, and try to address it [17].

Developing country students need to alter attitudes in studying and reflection to match teaching methods where individual knowledge building is encouraged, and questioning and criticizing are allowed and even expected.

Students who are accustomed to a lecturing type of teaching and straightforward drilling practice, find also mathematics teaching different. They might be competent in mathematical operations but when they need to concentrate on problem-solving instead of mechanical operations they encounter a new challenge. Their previous education has been concerned with acquiring a fluency in operations, which have been adopted as separate skills. The phase of deep learning has to be achieved next, and construction of sense-making units of knowledge needs still to be developed [18], [19]. The knowledge and competences that have been acquired in home country education are less useful in the pragmatic engineering field where application of knowledge is required. To become a competent professional, the student has to reach the level of de-contextualizing knowledge, where she is able to apply skills in new situations.

3.2 Current Research

One beginning study group consisting of 56 information technology and media students answered an online questionnaire of their study experiences and previous practices in their first study term in October 2013. The survey included questions on the experience of computer use, earlier use of computers in studies, familiarity with various study methods, and cognitive preferences.

The survey was given as an optional task in a study module; however, all students decided to participate. Moreover, they answered nearly all questions though none was indicated as compulsory. The ages of participants ranged from 18 to 34, with an average of 23 years. Nine of the respondents were women. They came from several regions: 8 from Africa (Af), 9 from Eastern Europe (EE), 9 from Western Europe (WE), 15 from South Asia (mainly Nepal, SA), 10 from East Asia (Vietnam, China, EA), and 5 from Middle Eastern (ME) countries. They reported being fluent in 26 different languages.

The survey consisted of multiple choice questions on technology use and understanding, questions on study modes and use of technology in the studies, questions on career aspirations and cognitive practices, and some open questions on the current studies. Respondents were given a link to the online form, which was implemented at Google drive. The form could be filled in at any time. Duplicate submissions were eliminated from the results.

3.3 Results

A few questions explored the time and place where the student started using computer. The background diversity was reflected strongly in the usage of computers before studies. About one third of the respondents had become familiar with computers already before age 10, 24% started using computers at age 11-15, 28 % at age 15-20, and 16% were older than 20 when they started using computers regularly. As could be expected, Africans had a shorter exposure to computers than the other nationalities, whereas western students had been using computers already very young.

Use of computers in school (fig. 1) gave a similar profile as the starting age. Only one African student had used a computer in high school, all others had started computer use at the university level, whereas 67% of European students learnt using computers in primary school and the remaining 33% in secondary school. Among Asian and East European students the distribution was more even.

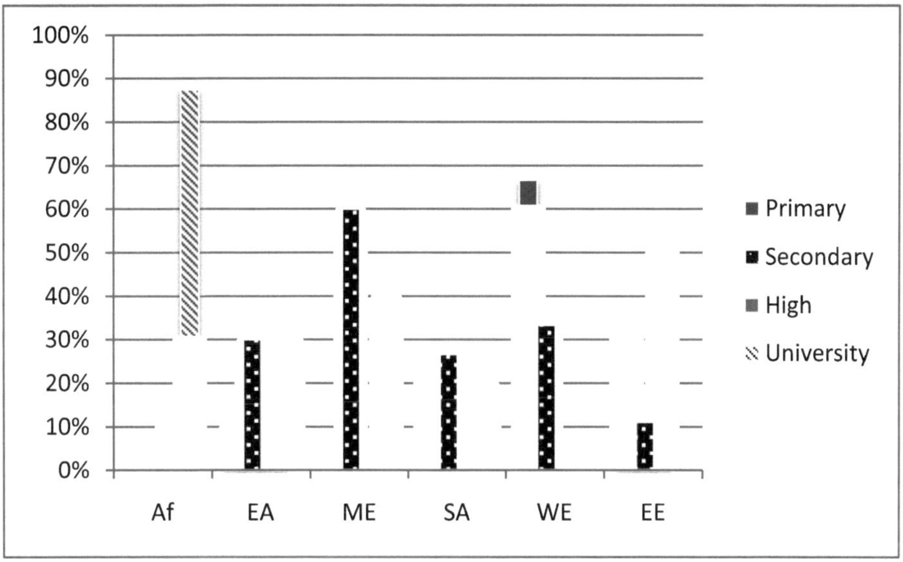

Fig. 1. Use of computers in school by nationality

Previous programming experience or programming studies were not common among the survey population, as half of the students stated that they had not learnt programming before. Only 25% had programming lessons in school, but among East European students this figure was 56%. 30% of respondents had learnt programming on their own; 20% of the students had tried some online courses. (Fig. 2).

According to this study, East European schools seem more science-oriented than others, but in fact the reason might be that students from there have been better informed when choosing their field of study than students from poor countries. Other interviews of East European students indicate that they often have previous studies in ICT, and come to strengthen their career opportunities by a western degree.

Few other questions explored the professional inclination of students. To the question "What kind of job are you interested in?" 60% responded that they were interested in programming as a job. On the other hand, 70% found working in software development attractive.

According to this survey, East European students also had the most traditional study experience and less exposure to varied study methods such as team work, research report writing or giving presentations. They also indicated little interest in natural world. To the statement: "I enjoy learning the names of birds, trees, animals

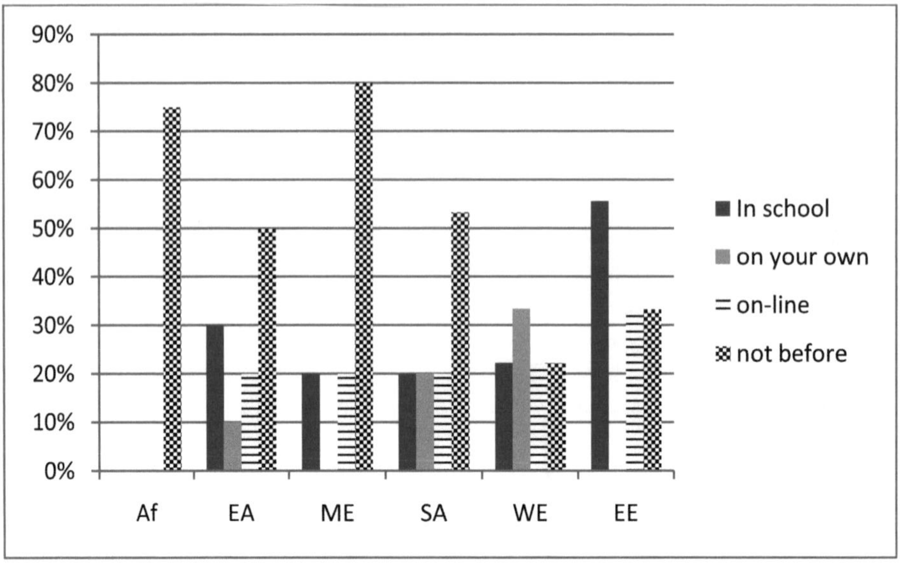

Fig. 2. Previous programming study by nationality

and plants" they gave the second lowest average score, 2,0 (maximum 5). Middle eastern students indicated no interest at all, their average was 1,0, whereas the average in other nationalities was around 3. African and South Asian students had played only little with Legos, which was a shared experience among other nationalities. The frequency of playing word games varied from 2,4 (ME) to 3,8 (SA). (Fig. 3).

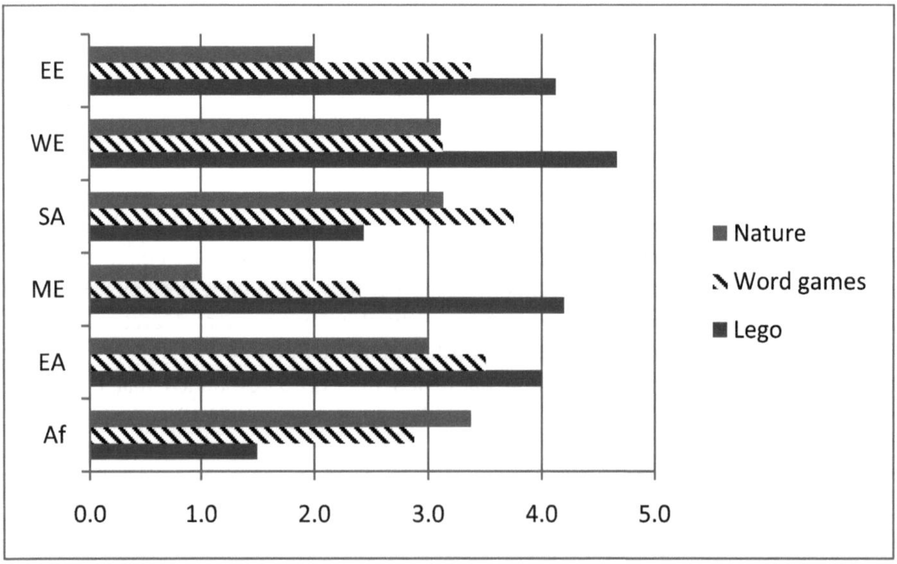

Fig. 3. Childhood hobbies by nationality

3.4 Experiments

All first year students were required to complete an assignment with the online version of MIT's Scratch, at http://scratch.mit.edu/. Scratch is a tool that has been developed for children and it teaches programming structures in an entertaining visual way [20]. The first demo programs show how to create a small animation. When student perceptions of Scratch were inquired in the survey, they were almost exclusively positive. However, approximately 10% failed to grasp the idea and develop anything functional, a couple of students even failed to follow the simple instructions how to start the program. They were among the previously computer illiterate students. In survey responses, two were negative towards Scratch stating that they did not understand it. Student quote: "I think it is useful but I am not being able to use it." On the other hand, there were many enthusiastic comments by programming novices, as well. A student quote: "I've never used Scratch before and I think this program is perfect for those who just doing their first steps in programming. It is clear, funny and easy, I wish I could study it at school." In sum, Scratch was an appropriate tool for beginners also on this level of study, and for a diverse group of students. In fact, it would have been unexpected to get an opposite result, as Scratch is used worldwide in schools, outreach programs, and even at universities. Moreover, experimenting with Scratch seemed to have a positive effect on learning in the C-programming course that followed in the next term.

In our previous research, we tried to replace more demanding programming languages with Javascript as the first language to learn [21]. When the Ville online tool became available, we asked two international groups of third year students to practice Javascript programming in the Ville programming environment. The Ville environment has been developed by University of Turku, at http://ville.cs.utu.fi. In fact, it includes a choice of several programming languages as well as mathematics, language studies, etc. This environment has a visual, user-friendly interface, which allows completely self-guided practice [22]. Most students in our experimental groups had no previous experience with online tools, despite a substantial percentage of Europeans including French and German exchange students. They had taken at least one programming course, though. After the practice, students were asked how they liked the environment for coding practice, and the response was very positive. Around 70 students in two groups completed the required practice that included 60 tasks and took 8 to 20 hours to complete. Only 15 students failed, which was a reasonably good result for these groups.

4 Conclusion

Both Scratch and Ville are based on extensive research on learning and programming. They rely on visualization of programming structures, and automatic interpretation of code. Based on the three experiments conducted in this study, the selected online programming courses can be recommended to any group of international students. The great advantage is the large amount of simple tasks that can be completed on one's own pace. Drilling practice that the online coding systems offer seems to suit almost every student. More advanced students might become bored, but at that point they do not need the practice anymore. On the other hand, if students fail the simple practice, they obviously should not choose programming as a career. Students who come from developing countries, might have a poor idea of ICT profession, and have chosen it based on its importance. Their aptitudes in this regard are checked first when they start university studies. Therefore, some drop-out percentage is natural.

Developing ICT competences in culturally diverse groups requires approaches that allow different starting levels and individual practice times. The online courses in programming that were used in this research have reached a maturity level where they can be considered as a valuable option for all students.

References

1. Leask, B.: Special issue on Internationalization of the Curriculum and the Disciplines. Journal of Studies in International Education (2013)
2. Aydarova, O.: If Not "the Best of the West," Then "Look East": Imported Teacher Education Curricula in the Arabian Gulf. Journal of Studies in International Education 17, 284–302 (2013)
3. Holvikivi, J.: Culture and cognition in information technology education. Dissertation series, vol. 5. SimLab publications, Espoo (2009)
4. Henrich, J., Heine, S.J., Norenzayan, A.: The weirdest people in the world? Behavioral and Brain Sciences 33, 61–83 (2010)
5. Chiao, J.Y., Cheon, B.K.: The weirdest brains in the world. Behavioral and Brain Sciences 33, 88–90 (2010)
6. Hansen, P., Kringelbach, M.: The Neural Bases of Reading. Oxford University Press, Oxford (2010)
7. Chen, C., Xue, G., Mei, L., Chen, C., Dong, Q.: Cultural neurolinguistics. Prog. Brain Res., 178–159 (2009)
8. Yang, J., Wang, X., Shu, H., Zevin, J.: Brain networks associated with sublexical properties of Chinese characters. Brain and Language 119, 68–79 (2011)
9. Tang, Y., Zhang, W., Chen, K., Feng, S., Ji, Y., Shen, J., Reiman, E.M., Liu, Y.: Arithmetic processing in the brain shaped by cultures. Proc. Natl. Acad. Sci. USA 103, 10775–10780 (2006)
10. Wilson, M.: The re-tooled mind: How culture re-engineers cognition. Soc. Cogn. Affect. Neurosci. 5, 180–187 (2010)
11. van Fleet, J., Watkins, K., Grebel, L.: Africa Learning Barometer (September 17, 2012), `http://www.brookings.edu/research/interactives/africa-learning-barometer`
12. Ang'ondi, E.K.: Teachers Attitudes and perceptions on the use of ICT in teaching and learning as observed by ICT champions. In: Proc. 10th IFIP World Conference on Computers in Education, Torun (2013)
13. Holvikivi, J.: From theory to practice: Adapting the engineering approach, In: Proc. of International Conference on Engineering Education, Turku (2012)
14. Lee, Y.-T., McCauley, C.R., Draguns, J.G.: Personality and Person Perception Across Cultures. Lawrence Erlbaum Ass. Inc., Mahwah (1999)
15. Holvikivi, J.: Cultural variation in perception and coding in IT students, In: Proc. 10th IFIP World Conference on Computers in Education, Torun (2013)

16. van de Vijver, F.J.R.: On the meaning of cross-cultural differences in simple cognitive measures. Educational Research and Evaluation 14, 215–234 (2008)
17. Dalsgaard, F., Du, X., Kolmos, A.: Innovative application of a new PBL model to interdisciplinary and intercultural projects. International Journal of Electrical Engineering Education 47, 174–188 (2010)
18. Bereiter, C.: Education and Mind in the Knowledge Age. Lawrence Erlbaum Associates, London (2002)
19. Hakkarainen, K., Palonen, T., Paavola, S., Lehtinen, E.: Communities of networked expertise: Professional and educational perspectives. Elsevier, Oxford (2004)
20. Maloney, J., Resnick, M., Rusk, N., Silverman, B., Eastmond, E.: The scratch programming language and environment. ACM Trans. Comput. Educ. (2010)
21. Holvikivi, J.: Conditions for Successful Learning of Programming Skills. In: Reynolds, N., Turcsányi-Szabó, M. (eds.) KCKS 2010. IFIP AICT, vol. 324, pp. 155–164. Springer, Heidelberg (2010)
22. Laakso, M.-J.: Promoting Programming Learning. Engagement, Automatic Assessment with Immediate Feedback in Visualizations. University of Turku, Turku (2010)

Project Management for IT Professionals: Education and Training Issues

Angela Lecomber[1] and Arthur Tatnall[2]

[1] Victoria University and See Differently, Australia
[2] Victoria University, Melbourne, Australia
Angela@SeeDifferently.com.au, Arthur.Tatnall@vu.edu.au

Abstract. Information Technology Project Management is becoming an increasingly important skill for all IT professionals and one that can be imparted through either education or training. This paper begins by looking at what is involved in project management and the two main approaches to project management: PMBoK and PRINCE2. We outline a core postgraduate subject in IT-based degrees at Victoria University and how this attempts to handle both concepts and practice, and a PRINCE2 training course. The paper then examines the issues involved in each of these approaches and the benefits and drawbacks of each.

Keywords: IT Project Management, PMBoK, PRINCE2, Education, Training, Agile.

1 Introduction: Projects and Project Management

A Project can simply be considered as any temporary endeavour with a one-time objective to create a unique product, service, or result [1]. It is distinguished from activities undertaken in business as usual which are repetitive, permanent or semi-permanent. Unlike business as usual where general management is centred on repetitive and stable tasks, projects are the means by which change is introduced. Projects involve a team of people with different skills working together on a temporary basis to introduce change that will impact others outside of the team [2].

The skills and knowledge of managing projects such as erecting pyramids, building cathedrals, creating aqueducts, building roman roads and conducting military campaigns has been passed down from father to son and kept within exclusive circles for generations from earliest times. Project management can be thought of as being like the art of cookery, which was also passed down from mother to daughter with good recipes kept within family circles from earliest times. Project management and cookery have this common denominator in that they are both an art and a science: both have evolved over time and both represent best practice which has worked; both require adaptation to the environment and will change according to customer needs.

The 'science' part of project management has been captured and documented well. Two forefathers of project management: Henry Gantt and Henri Fayol were very influential contributors. The latter set out the following management functions [3]:

D. Passey and A. Tatnall (Eds.): KCICTP/ITEM 2014, IFIP AICT 444, pp. 12–24, 2014.

organising, staffing, directing, and controlling. Project Management can thus be defined as the planning, delegating, monitoring and control of all aspects of the project including the motivation of those involved, to achieve the project objectives within the expected performance targets for time, cost, quality, scope, benefits and risks [2]. In other words, the project manager oversees specialist work on the project to ensure that the unique product, service or result is delivered fully to the agreed scope, time, cost, quality and benefit expectations of the customer who commissioned the project. The realisation of benefits, even if these are not financial, is the whole point of the project and why a customer would have commissioned it. In addition, the project manager would manage the risks that could potentially affect the project objectives as well as being focussed on the benefits that the project would achieve as a result of the creation of the new product, service or result.

1.1 Problematic Definition of Successful Projects

The definition of 'success' is problematic. For example, the project that built the Sydney Opera House was considered a failure as it cost more than planned, yet the Opera House is an icon of Australia and a huge success. Conversely, the project that built the Concorde aircraft was considered to be a huge success, yet Concorde is no longer in existence due to heating, structural and costs of operation. It is therefore problematic to categorically attribute failure or success to a project. The label really can only be made on hind-sight and sometime after the desired product, service or result has been realised and when the benefits can be assessed.

According to PWC Global Survey [4], "Poor estimates during project planning are the largest contributor to project failure". The key reason is the lack of common understanding of what the project is meant to deliver when the project is being defined [5]. There are often unrealistic expectations in the early phase of the project, which is characterised by wild enthusiasm. All too often customer's expectations are not aligned with the project team's understanding of what the project entails, resulting in dissatisfaction when the project is complete. Another cause of failure is the lack of communication between members of the project team and the project board, sponsoring committee, customer and especially to the people (users) to whom the project is being delivered. Another deficiency characteristic of poorly managed projects is the inability to manage changes due to issues that impact the project.

1.2 IT Projects

Project Management applies to many different domains, but in this paper we will consider its use only in relation to projects involving information technology. One justification for the need to change IT project management practices is to improve their success rate.

There are many examples to choose of IT project failure and how IT projects could have been handled better, but we will look at only a single report by the Victorian State Ombudsman [6] in November 2011 on the development of some eGovernment systems in Victoria. These projects were chosen for consideration by the Ombudsman as they were seen to be complex, high-risk, large budget projects across various agencies in the Victorian public sector [7]. The failed projects investigated were: Link (Victoria Police), HealthSMART (Department of Health), Myki (Transport Ticketing Authority), RandL (VicRoads), Client Relationship Information System (Department of Human Services), Ultranet (Department of Education and Early Childhood Development), Integrated Courts Management System (Department of Justice), Property and Laboratory Management (Victoria Police), HRAssist (Victoria Police) and Housing Integrated Information Program (Office of Housing) [6, 7].

What the Ombudsman found was that all these projects had been poorly managed and did not achieve their intended outcomes: "On average, projects will have more than doubled in cost by the time they are finished." [6 :4]. Singling out poor project management, the report further noted that: "... despite the extensive guidance and literature available, agencies are making the same mistakes around planning, governance, project management and procurement that our offices have observed and reported on for some years." [6 :3]

Information technology project failure is seen by the literature to be anything from slight cost or time overruns to total abandonment. This can include situations such as: when the project does not deliver the benefits the customer expected, investment costs exceed the benefits of doing the project, the project does not meet all the client's or stakeholder requirements, it does not meet all design specifications or quality standards, it over-runs its cost or does not meet its scheduled project finish date, it has some aspect of its project technology not operating properly, it is not fully used or it collapses completely [8].

In addition, to the lack of common understanding or scope definition, lack of communication and inability to manage changes to the project, the Victorian Ombudsman's report pointed to the lack of clear accountability and responsibility as a key reason for project failure [6].

2 IT Project Management Education and Training

The importance of developing appropriate project management skills in ICT professionals is now widely acknowledged and is included in the Bodies of Knowledge of the major IT professional societies around the world. The Core Body of Knowledge for IT Professionals (CBOK) of the Australian Computer Society (ACS) describes six knowledge areas: ICT problem solving, professional knowledge, technology resources, technology building, services management and outcomes management [9]. Project management is involved is part of the last knowledge area 'outcomes management' which involves:

> "... an understanding of the factors required to successfully manage systems development projects. Topics include: team management, estimation techniques, cost/benefit analysis, risk analysis, risk management, project scheduling, quality assurance, software configuration management, project management tools, reporting and presentation technique." [9 :24]

All of the internationally used Information Systems Model Curriculum guidelines give significant weight to teaching IT project management. For example, the IEEE Computer Society's Software Engineering Body of Knowledge [10] makes frequent mention of the importance of project management. Similarly the ACM Computer Science Curricula [11] and the Association for Information Systems Model Curriculum and Guidelines [12] make frequent reference to both Project and Change Management. The Project Management Institute produced the fifth edition of the Project Management Body of Knowledge (PMBoK) [1], but this is not specific to IT projects.

3 Project Management Approaches: PMBoK versus PRINCE2

There are a number of accepted approaches to project management, the Project Management Body of Knowledge (PMBoK) and PRINCE2 being two of the most important. Although several other approaches (and often no set approach at all) are used in some situations, in order to keep this paper to a reasonable length we will concentrate on just PMBoK and PRINCE2.

3.1 PM Body of Knowledge Equates to 'How to Do' and 'Why to Do'

The Project Management Institute's PMBoK [1] divides project management into ten knowledge areas and then describes what work needs to be done in each: project integration, project scope, project time, project cost, project quality, project human resources, project communications, project risk, project procurement and project stakeholders management. The latter was recently added in the latest edition published in 2013.

PMBoK is a body of knowledge of good practice and offers guidance to address a knowledge area. Although there are process groups and data flow diagrams, these can be highly interpretable. This theory is rarely understood until a student actually runs a project and relates it back to the theory for guidance. Even then, successful project outcomes typically happen when a student is managing a project under the guidance of a skilled and experienced project manager. Of course, there are those who may argue that it is not necessary to have guidance from an experienced practitioner to be successful as there are 'born' project managers where the skills are innate and they are naturally good at this. This may apply for those whose skills are innate but even 'born' project managers can still learn from a skilled practitioner and reference the PMBoK to improve their practice.

To use the cookery analogy, some individuals are 'born' cooks and really don't need a cookery course. However for most people, learning to cook is necessary. It is not a natural skill. Similarly, project management is not a natural skill for most people. However even the best of us can still improve with learning from others and best practice to get even better results.

The converse is also true: there is no guarantee that someone who completes a commercial cookery course can produce good food. Their work is really improved through practice in the kitchen: learning under an experienced head chef. Similarly, there is no guarantee that a person who completes a project management course can produce a project output or result that satisfies the client. If however, they are under the guidance of an experienced project manager, then there is a greater likelihood of producing a satisfactory output and benefit to the customer. This view is corroborated by the ACS ICT Body of Professional Knowledge:

> "…ICT is a practical science [13] and practical work as in project work or industry placements, is required at some point in programs of study so that learning of applied skills and knowledge can be fully developed." [9 :7]

To use the cookery analogy, the body of knowledge is compendium of how to cook rather than a recipe book. Just like those cookbooks (particularly old ones) that have sections on 'kitchen and meal planning', 'kitchen equipment', 'methods of cooking', 'entertaining', 'sauces' and 'batters' for example, so the PMBoK can be viewed in a similar way. The PMBoK provides the theory or lens to view the project and make sense of the practice. This is very much in the same way that a student having done study of commercial cookery only really learns to turn out good food in a kitchen when under the supervision of an experienced head chef. The commercial cookery course provides the knowledge of how to cook and the theory of why things are done in certain ways but does not guarantee that the student really can turn out a good meal.

3.1.1 PRINCE2 Equates to a 'What To Do'

PRINCE2 (PRojects IN Controlled Environments 2) is described as a process-based methodology for project management [2]. Even when a project is temporary, unique and introduces change, it is still a process but one that is underpinned by principles. Although each project is unique, there are similarities between projects and hence similar processes that need to be followed. PRINCE2's core structure is that it is made up of seven principles (business justification, learn from experience, defined roles and responsibilities, manage by stages, manage by exception, focus on products and tailor to suit the environment), seven themes (business case, organisation, plans, progress, risks, quality, change) and seven processes (Starting up a project, Initiating a project, Directing a project, Controlling a stage, Managing stage boundaries, Managing product delivery, and Closing a project).

It is significant that PRINCE2 is principles-based because processes are subject to the vagaries of the particular environment into which it is applied. There can be defects and therefore having a sound understanding of the underpinning principles of the processes assists in the efficient tailoring and application of the methodology to the unique project.

To use the cookery analogy, if PRINCE2 is viewed as a process-based methodology, it is like a recipe book with step by step activities that can be followed with specific descriptions of the documents and the fields required. It is prescriptive. It is a 'what to do'. However, the principles that underpin the steps are important and are like annotations in the recipe book that guide the cook and state the principles for example: 'Knead the dough till it is elastic and adjust the water accordingly'. So for a project it is like stating 'In planning, ensure there is a product focus rather than activity focus and undertake the product based planning till a level of definition that a team member is then able to build the output from'.

However, PRINCE2 can be burdensome and misunderstood. The problem is due to a lack of knowledge of how to apply or tailor PRINCE2 to a specific project environment.

3.1.2 Difference between PMBoK and PRINCE2

A whole paper could be submitted about the differences between the two approaches and there are a plethora of discussions on this. Siegelaub [14] provides a concise comparison. Briefly, PMBoK is a body of knowledge and good practice. It is not a methodology. It is not principles based and it is highly interpretable.

PRINCE2 on the other hand is a methodology. The difference between these means that the former is highly interpretable whereas the latter is prescriptive with process activities, with each activity having recommended actions with corresponding templates provided for each action.

However, the elegance of PRINCE2 is the fact that it is principles-based. This distinguishes it from PMBoK that does not have any defined principles underpinning the knowledge areas. By having principles at its core, PRINCE2 provides a unified reference for a project manager to assess the extent the principle is being applied rather than blindly mandating documents and activities to follow. This is a common trap in template driven methodologies.

The advantage of PRINCE2 is that it can co-exist with any delivery approaches for IT development be it Waterfall or Agile [15]. It is limited by not specifying activities to manage procurement and not having a Change Management Strategy that manages the people impacted by the change. It is sometimes seen as overhead in governance [16].

4 Delivery Modes: Education vs. Project Management Training

The focus of this paper is to examine IT Project Management Education vs. Training for IT Professionals. The fundamental difference between education and training is that in education the focus is to provide learning that lasts. "*Education can be described as what remains after one has forgotten what one has learnt in school*" (Albert Einstein). However with training, people are shown what to do rather than really ensuring that they understand the underlying theory. Training does not allow for reinforcing, monitoring and encouraging which are necessary to ensure that real learning is acquired [17].

According to the Kirkpatrick Model, training alone is not enough, there needs to be strategies in place to ensure that what is taught can be effectively translated into skills and behaviours in the workplace. The Kirkpatrick model consists of four levels: (1) Reaction (experience during training), (2) Learning (the acquisition of knowledge, skills, attitude, confidence and commitment during the training) (3) Behaviour (mentoring and support that occurs post training in the workplace) and (4) Results (extent that targeted outcomes are achieved from the training) [17].

If the reader reflects back on personal experiences of training in, for example, how Excel training was conducted, it might have been that they were shown every Excel function. This leads to some level of frustration (due to lack of skill and experience) and little 'sticks'. It would have been better to have been taught some simple Excel skills with easy exercises to practice, followed by an explanation of what Excel is capable of and a list of functions that could be accessed when required.

4.1 Training Providers

The type of training provider has a bearing on the delivery mode for training. There are three types of training providers in Australia in the area of project management:

- Registered training organisations (RTOs) registered by the Australian Skills Quality Authority (ASQA) which offer the Certificate IV, Diploma and Advanced Diploma of Project Management. These can include Universities but more typically are independent training providers.
- Accredited training organisations (ATOs) overseen by the international APMG and the Global Certification Institute (not an exhaustive list) who accredit project management best practice methodologies such as PRINCE2 on behalf of AXELOS (the UK consortium who own the Intellectual Property). It is significant that Universities cannot be ATOs and therefore are not able to offer PRINCE2 training.
- Project Management Institute (PMI) registered training provider. These support the attainment of the Project Management Institute (PMI) Project Management Professional (PMP).

Delivery modes for these providers include face-to-face training, online training or a blend of these.

RTOs can deliver face-to-face classroom courses in project management and complete these in as little as four days with some homework that results in the award of the Certificate IV in project management. The Diploma takes longer and the shortest length of time could be two months which usually requires students to submit evidence from real projects that they have worked on.

ATOs can deliver face-to-face training which leads to the award of the PRINCE2 Foundation qualification in three days and the Practitioner qualification in a further two days after the award of the Foundation.

PMI registered training providers offer a short five day coaching session to prepare students for a PMP exam. However the award of the PMP is subject to a number of requirements other than the exam which includes evidence of current experience in managing projects.

Unlike the PMP and the Certificate IV and Diploma of Project Management, there is no minimal entry requirement for PRINCE2. It therefor provides more accessibility to anyone wanting to learn project management and offers an excellent starting point and clear methodology that provides real value to novice. However it is the delivery and assessment method that can pose problems in terms of real learning.

4.2 Outdated Course Material

The accreditation system for training providers rather than the methodology can result in outdated material that does not support the aims of learning. The restrictions imposed by the accreditor for courses such as PRINCE2 stifles the ability to update courseware regularly so the same material gets churned out year after year and material is not updated regularly enough to meet the learning needs of the students. The system does not easily encourage changes to the material once it is endorsed because it costs the ATO time and money to change courseware (there is a fee payable to the accrediting body to review the revised material). Therefore good educators who intuitively would like to update material after the course from lessons learned are not able to. This is where any course under the AXELOS umbrella that awards qualification in PRINCE2 falls short.

Courseware under the ASQA authority suffers less from this. It is far more easily updated and kept current due to the lesser restrictions imposed. Courses only need to demonstrate mapping to competency levels and performance criteria. Only samples of actual courseware are necessarily reviewed (rather than the full suite of material as with AXELOS) for consistency and there is freedom for the trainer and the RTO to create new versions of courseware without necessarily incurring costs (other than their time). This means that material is likely to be current and meet the changing needs of learners. This reflects a model that fits more closely with education.

Online material is in danger of being ‘dated’ unless the training provider is willing to pay for updates to their online courseware. Online courses are ‘price sensitive’. So it is unlikely that the training provider will want to spend money and erode profit to update material as they know that their customer (the learner) has no way of knowing if the material is current. This is particularly concerning since trends published by a leading training provider sponsored by Computer Weekly state the trend in 2014 is for IT professionals to adopt online methods due to the lack of commitment by organisations to provide training to staff and if they do, the cheaper option is selected. Project professionals have a choice: they can either take the training or they can let their skills calcify [18]. According to the article, training today is shifting, faster and faster, to the Internet accessed by desktops, laptops, tablets, and mobile devices. Delivery is dispersed in ‘chunks’ of video components, webinars, and online modules. Notwithstanding the question of online learning versus classroom learning, the question is how up-to-date is the material and how well has it met the learner’s needs?

4.3 Limitations due to the Delivery Method

PRINCE2 training courses do not equip participants with practical skills to create a project plan and to discuss issues and risks that would typically occur on a Diploma of Project Management course or one based on PMBoK delivered by an RTO or University. Furthermore, PRINCE2 training courses do not focus on techniques such as learning to use scheduling software like Microsoft Project. Whilst it is beneficial to be unencumbered by not having software to learn on a course, it does mean that PRINCE2 qualified practitioners need to undertake separate training to learn these techniques.

4.4 Assessment Methods

The method of assessment has a bearing on the quality of the experience during training and the learning that actually happens. Students present different learning styles with some preferring written assignments and essays whilst others prefer verbal assessment and practical case studies to work with.

The assessment method for PRINCE2® is objective testing (multiple-choice). This has merits in ensuring there is correct understanding of the concepts. The exam questions are tested and moderated from a comprehensive question bank. It is a good examination method, but the PRINCE2 Practitioner examination is based on full PRINCE2. This full methodology does not provide much value to those with little experience or opportunity after the course to apply the skills.

This is particularly obvious with those new to project management who are typically assigned small low risk projects in the work place that might not require the full application of PRINCE2 to manage them. According to Ferguson [16], these individuals may not have the knowledge or experience to tailor PRINCE2 to their projects. This could lead to an ad-hoc approach to small projects with potentially poor outcomes [16]. Hence a weakness of the standard offering for PRINCE2 training does not provide skills in using 'light' PRINCE2 which is more applicable to small projects. There is a need for 'Light PRINCE2' as a course in order to provide a simple methodology to enable the many IT Professionals who have not had the experience nor the support to know how to apply the principles lightly.

On the other hand, the assessment methods for courses under ASQA accreditation allow flexibility to cater for different learner styles. Course accreditation with ASQA requires that material caters for all learning and special needs (for example when English is not the first language). Typically these include short quizzes, case-studies worked on in class, a final written examination and the submission of a body of evidence (records of assessment) of practical work carried out by the project manager to demonstrate competency. The assessment methods are competency based on PMBoK, with students required to demonstrate attainment of performance criteria against each of the competencies stated for the qualification. For example the Diploma of Project Management requires attainment of ten competencies to match the ten knowledge areas.

In summary, training is limited in delivering the behavioural indicators that make up a successful project manager. Chaves [19] cites his organisation (a financial services company with $100 billion in assets), opting for education rather than training in achieving the competencies required on IT projects. The students work collaboratively dissecting past projects and learning from on the job examples of project success and challenge. This approach together with a project management office offering standard templates, processes and access to mentors was found to provide much better outcomes, increased quality and reduced rework in project delivery [19] than standard project management training courses.

5 A Postgraduate Course on IT Project Management at Victoria University

In designing a university course, a holistic approach should be taken so that the core body of knowledge areas and ICT role specific knowledge are planned into schemes of work. Ultimately the aim is to ensure that the students are supported and mentored. A degree of practical work underpinned by theory is required. One of the underlying tenets to designing a course is that "information is not knowledge" and that "the only source of knowledge is experience" (Albert Einstein). The objective for learning is to design a course that both internalises the learning and provides practical changes in behaviour in the workplace.

This is supported by the ACS ICT Profession Body of Knowledge that suggests that when designing a university course "structure should scaffold advanced knowledge on top of programming fundamentals and project management topics from the ICT Knowledge Area of the CBOK." [9 :15]

The teaching of IT project management lends itself particularly well to practice reinforcing theory and this subject is based on belief in the value of integrating both theory and the practical component of any Information Systems course. This idea is not new and was articulated well by Little and Margetson over 20 years ago. They suggest that:

> "No amount of learning about something will, alone, prepare a student adequately to practise a particular skill or to make use of knowledge in a sensible, appropriate, and effective way. This is even more so when the learning in question concerns the design, development, and operation of computer-based information systems." [20 :131]

Hosseini [21] identified challenges of teaching Management Information Systems concepts to students, saying that the abstract nature of concepts around development and management of IT systems make these concepts difficult to teach in the classroom and that as they often lack a practical frame of reference students often miss the various nuances of IT issues, especially at a managerial level. Before this, Piaget [22] proposed his model of 'cognitive information processing' that argued that in order for a person to understand some new concept or piece of information, this new information must be integrated into the person's own schemata of knowledge and be somehow linked to what the person already understands or knows so that they can see how it all fits in with their view of reality. Piaget named this personal view of reality a 'logico-mathematical structure'.

IT Project Management involves a lot more than just project planning and scheduling. It is also concerned with controlling the on-going project during its whole life, and reporting on project progress. Our research and discussions with students has shown that, despite some problems currently inherent in the use of project management software, it is quite possible to provide students with useful project management skills through the use of this software. Several of the assignments are based on the use of adequate size, dynamic and on-going case studies and involve students using Microsoft Project for planning, scheduling, monitoring, controlling and reporting [23].

5.1 Course Content

The subject Information Technology Project Management is a core subject in the masters-level information systems related courses at Victoria University. It concentrates on both the management of IT projects and the use of computer software in the management of these and other projects and aims to show how knowledge of the appropriate application of such skills is vital to Information Systems professionals and managers in the performance of their many functions in an organisation. Subject content [24] includes: Project management fundamentals, Project management methodologies (including PMBoK and PRINCE2), Project management software tools, Defining the problem – the project goal, project charter, Developing the project plan and schedule, Monitoring and control of the project once it has commenced, Building the project team, management of conflict, Implementation difficulties, Risk assessment and project failure, Innovation and the management of technological change, Cost control, Reporting on project status and Software engineering project case studies.

Assessment is based on a number of assignments related to a real project. As the course is conducted over twelve weeks, so is the duration of the project. It is usually one involving the implementation of an ERP system in a small business. The project is initiated in the first week of the course, controlled and delivered in the final week to time, cost, quality, scope and benefits when the students submit their closure report and on the same day sit a short final objective testing examination.

Students have to produce a Project Charter (containing a business case and a clear statement of scope), then plan the project (using Microsoft Project), manage the issues and changes in the project from week to week as provided by the lecturer at each session (project monitoring and control using Microsoft Project), create a benefits review plan for the project and finally report on the project once it has delivered its output to customer satisfaction.

In addition, throughout the course students present a seminar paper and work on syndicate exercises based on real case studies of project management implementations. The methodology introduced to the students is both PMBoK and a lighter version of PRINCE2. Rather than present the two approaches as competing with each other, the focus is on skills and an appreciation of the real value of the application of PMBoK and PRINCE2 in the workplace. There is no pressure to learn PRINCE2 by rote in order to pass an exam but to demonstrate its value in working on the project.

The Victoria University course seeks to inculcate real learning in IT Professionals or those aspiring to be. It offers real learning opportunities compared with the standard offering of a PRINCE2 training course.

6 Conclusion

Increasingly organizations use project management to drive their business objectives [4]. Outcomes in terms of project management skills, knowledge and confidence are a function of both the method of delivery and methods of assessment. Clearly project management courses that provide real projects for participants to work with throughout the course and case studies in which they are able to constructively build their knowledge will have more value to the IT professional than bland objective testing. The former works on a deeper level and enables skills to be practised in a safe environment. This is what the Masters in IT Project Management at Victoria University aims to do.

The PRINCE2 training delivery mode does not allow time for IT Professionals to really internalise how to apply the principles to their workplace. Although the PRINCE2 course and examination is based on a scenario, the problems that an IT Professional faces in the workplace requires on-going support and mentoring that is not provided by the course once the PRINCE2 qualification is achieved.

The Victoria University course is refreshed each year with new perspectives keeping up with the latest developments in project management. After all, project management is both an art and a science and needs to keep current with the latest developments year by year in the business world.

References

1. Project Management Institute, A Guide to the Project Management Body of Knowledge, 5th edn. Project Management Institute, Newton Square (2013)
2. APM Group Ltd. PRINCE 2 (2012), `http://www.prince-officialsite.com/` (January 2013)
3. Fayol, H.: Industrial and General Administration. In: Coubrough, J.A. (ed.) Sir Isaac Pitman & Sons, London (1930)
4. PWC Price Waterhouse Coopers. Insights and Trends: Current Portfolio, Program and Project Management Practices: The third global survey on the current state of project management (2010), `http://www.pwc.com` (February 2014)
5. Tayntor, C.: Project Management Tools and Techniques for Success. CRC Press, Florida (2010)
6. Victorian Ombudsman, Own motion investigation into ICT-enabled projects. Victorian Ombudsman, Melbourne (2011)
7. Tatnall, A., et al.: Major eGovernment Projects in Health, Education and Transport in Victoria. In: Lux Wigand, D., et al. (eds.) 6th Bled eConference, eInnovations: Challenges and Impacts for Individuals, Organizations and Society, Bled, Slovenia, pp. 48–63 (2013)
8. Tatnall, A., et al.: The Ultranet: An eGovernment Project Management Failure? In: Lux Wigand, D., et al. (eds.) 26th Bled eConference, eInnovations: Challenges and Impacts for Individuals, Organizations and Society, Bled, Slovenia, pp. 32–47 (2013)
9. Australian Computer Society, The ICT Professional Body of Knowledge. Australian Computer Society, Sydney (2012)
10. Bourque, P., Fairley, R.E. (eds.): Guide to the Software Engineering Body of Knowledge. IEEE Computer Society, USA (2014)
11. Association for Computing Machinery and IEEE Computing Society. Computer Science Curricula 2013: Curriculum Guidelines for Undergraduate Degree Programs in Computer Science (2013), `http://www.acm.org/education/CS2013-final-report.pdf` (February 2014)
12. Gorgone, J.T., et al.: MSIS 2006 - Model Curriculum and Guidelines for Graduate Degree Programs in Information Systems. Communications of the Association for Information Systems 17(1) (2006)
13. Strasser, S.: Understanding and Explanation. Duquesne Institution Press, Pittsburgh (1985)
14. Siegelaub, J.M.: How PRINCE2 Can Complement the PMBOK Guide and Your PMP. APMG White Paper (2011)

15. Measey, P.: Agile and the Best Management Practice Framework. Best Management Practice White Paper. UK Stationery Office (2013)
16. Ferguson, C.: PRINCE2 for Small Scale Projects. Best Management Practice White Paper. UK Stationery Office (2011)
17. Kirkpatrick, D., Kirkpatrick, J.D.: Training Programs:The Four Levels. Berrett-Koehler Publishers, United States (2006)
18. ESI Viewpoints, Top Ten Project Management Trends for 2014. In: Computer Weekly (2014)
19. Chaves, R.: Education versus Training. Project Management Network, p. 21 (April 2006)
20. Little, S.E., Margetson, D.B.: A Project-Based Approach to Information Systems Design for Undergraduates. The Australian Computer Journal 21(2), 131 (1989)
21. Hosseini, J.: Application of Bloom's Taxonomy and Piaget Model of Cognitive Processes to Teaching of Management Information Systems Concepts. Journal of Information Systems Education 5(3) (1993)
22. Piaget, J.: Understanding Causality. Norton, New York (1974)
23. Tatnall, A., Shackleton, P.: IT Project Management: Developing On-Going Skills in the Management of Software Development Projects. In: Software Engineering: Education and Practice. IEEE Computer Society Press, Dunedin (1996)
24. Victoria University, Victoria University College of Busines 2014 Handbook. Victoria University, Melbourne (2014)

A Working Model for Teacher Training in Computing through the Literacy from Scratch Project

Lawrence Williams[1], Miroslava Černochová[2], G. Barbara Demo[3], and Sarah Younie[4]

[1] MirandaNet Fellowship, London, UK
[2] Charles University in Prague, Czech Republic
[3] Department of Informatics, University of Torino, Italy
[4] De Montfort University, Leicester, UK
lawrencewilliams@mirandanet.ac.uk,
Miroslava.Cernochova@pedf.cuni.cz, barbara@di.unito.it,
syounie@dmu.ac.uk

Abstract. From September 2014, classroom teachers in the United Kingdom are required to move away from teaching ICT, towards new Programmes of Study in Computing, including computer programming. This chapter presents a developing international working model for teacher training, designed to support this major change in focus. Conceived at Brunel University, west London, ideas for the development of computer coding in the classroom were swiftly shared with colleagues at Charles University in Prague, at the University of Torino, Italy, and with De Montfort University, UK. Based on the MIT Scratch program, teacher trainers and classroom pupils are introduced to elementary block-coding, through a highly creative cross-curricular teaching and learning project called "Literacy from Scratch". This centres on the cross-curricular production of animated narratives, together with the pupils' own art work, for Sprites and Backgrounds. The project has successfully engaged pupils in computer coding from the ages of 5 through to 14 in the UK, and to 16 in Italy.

Keywords: Computing, teacher training, key competencies, creativity.

1 The Background to the Literacy from Scratch Project (Lawrence Williams)

From 1st September 2014, teachers across the UK are required to begin teaching a new subject called Computing. ICT and digital literacy remain a part of this new curriculum, but there is now a new agenda involving the teaching of algorithms, programming and development, data and data representation, hardware and processing, communication and networks, as well as the former legal requirement to maintain some aspects of the teaching of information technology.

My personal concern was that this new material might be taught in schools as a very dry, and somewhat unnecessarily academic addition to the curriculum, and might not ignite the enthusiasm of our pupils. My hope, on the other hand, was that, using

D. Passey and A. Tatnall (Eds.): KCICTP/ITEM 2014, IFIP AICT 444, pp. 25–33, 2014.

Scratch to develop the new subject of Computing, the whole approach might lead teachers back to the formerly highly-regarded creative, collaborative, and cross-curricular approach that had been sadly lost to our UK primary schools through the introduction of our National Curriculum, during the early 1990's.

Accordingly, I set out to link the newly designated Computing skills agenda with basic Literacy, by devising a new cross-curricular project called Literacy from Scratch. The original aim was for pupils to create very simple narratives, using Scratch, and then to animate their story's characters (or Sprites). I had done this kind of literacy work before, very successfully, using ICT tools. Starting at Key Stage 3 (with pupils aged 12 and 13 at Bishop Ramsey School, Ruislip Manor, London)) I was later able to move the Scratch project down through Key Stage 2 (ages 7 to 10) and finally to much younger pupils, aged 5 years, at the Swaminarayan School in Neasden, London. The basic concept was that by focussing the pupils' attention on story-telling, a skill well-understood by all of our Primary teachers, the coding aspect of Scratch becomes the tool by which the narrative is enabled to unfold. The project is not, therefore, in the first instance, actually about computational thinking, but about narrative, and artistic creativity. Once the pupils are fully engaged in this well-established creative process, however, they find that the only way to present their story effectively, using Scratch, is by ensuring that all of their coding is functioning correctly. It makes for a very positive start to the process of introducing Computing into the school curriculum both at Primary and lower Secondary level. This process is recorded in detail on my supporting website for teachers at: www.literacyfromscratch.org.uk

There are substantial support materials on this site for teachers wishing to engage in the project, including examples of both pupils' and teachers' work, together with lesson plans and wider schemes of work. These materials have been produced for the project in Prague, as well as in London.

Parallel to this initiative, my colleague, Mirka Černochová, who had been teaching ICT courses at the Charles University in Prague, started to develop the Literacy from Scratch project with teacher colleagues in a local Czech primary school. Under Korunovacni Head Teacher, Tomas Komrska, pupils there effectively developed their Computing and literacy skills alongside their art and Czech/English language lessons. In counter-response to this very welcome innovation in art, we in London subsequently began to develop our pupils' artistic skills, too, as part of our narratives. The complementary teaching and learning styles are posted at: http://www.literacyfromscratch.org.uk/pedagogy/

"Literacy from Scratch" is a response, therefore, to the United Kingdom government's initiative to develop computer programming skills (formerly called Computer Science, now called Computing, and known as "informatics" elsewhere) in both the Primary phase of education (pupils aged 5 to 11) and the Secondary phase (aged 11 to 18). The project has several related aspects: it involves the reworking of Primary and Secondary Initial Teacher Education (ITE) programme, through which Postgraduate students are taught how to use the MIT Scratch programming language, to create sustained and animated narrative work. And it supports developments of innovative approaches to ICT teacher education in the Czech Republic. Whole-school in-service training courses are another aspect currently being developed.

Both our children, and their teachers in the UK, have already learned basic digital literacy. However, it is high time to master much more than just how to operate a computer. It is time to learn why and how to use computers for solving problems; to understand what a computer can really do to serve pupils in their learning and discovering; for acquiring knowledge and skills; how to protect themselves from the various risks lurking in a digital world; how to behave in the right way in such a huge cyberspace. In some countries, criticism of teaching focused merely on computer-user skills' development (using PowerPoint, and Word) has begun, and has been met, in the UK, by the introduction of this new Computing curriculum.

The international Literacy from Scratch team embraces Seymour Papert's ideas about children learning with computers: *"Learning-by-making"* (Papert and Harel, 1991) and Stager's: *"technology as building material, hard fun, learning to make, taking time – proper time for the job. You can't get it right without getting it wrong."* (Stager, 2007). We believe that it is very important to regard, and to introduce, Computing as a compulsory school subject, and that computational thinking is vital for children's mental development.

Merely attaining ICT literacy as an aim for school education belongs firmly in the past. It is essential to teach our children many skills: to be able to formulate problems, and to select appropriate computer tools and applications; to encourage them to be able to decide independently on the appropriate use of digital technology for problem-solving; to determine whether the problem is solvable using computers; how to collect and analyse data; how to automate data-processing and data-mining. It is, therefore, necessary to focus development on the ability to ask questions; to look for and discover links and contexts; to find relations between different phenomena or events; to inquire about what depends on what, and what does not relate to what; to explain results, and put them into contexts in relation to other facts. Equally, importance must be given to teaching pupils to be able to identify errors in their ways of working, and the processes they use, and to verify the correctness of applied methods and actions. The integration of computational thinking into the curriculum is an opportunity to develop further pupils' logical thinking. It would be a mistake if we were to develop these abilities of children entirely in subjects merely about computers, or about computer science, or as a part of a more general computing competency.

The Computing initiative, begun in the UK, has opened up a huge amount of professional discussion in the world, directed at the same ends. First to develop this project beyond the UK have been teachers in the Czech Republic, and in Italy, as follows.

2 The Czech Perspective (Miroslava Černochová)

As part of a recent Brunel – Charles University Erasmus agreement, and in harmony with the Brunel working model, the Charles University, Faculty of Education in Prague ICT (teacher trainers) decided to adopt, and to adapt, the UK teaching approach to Computing in education, and to develop profound links between ICT education and Art and Language education, using the "Literacy from Scratch" model.

The Czech Republic is one of the EU countries which implemented ICT as a compulsory education area (subject) into a curriculum for Primary education (aged in 6 to 11) and Lower Secondary School (aged in 11 to 15). In Primary Education the ICT curriculum is concentrated on three main topics: *Introduction into work with a computer*, *Searching information and communication*, and *Information processing and utilization*. ICT education for lower secondary education is focused on two topics: *Searching information and communication*, and *Information processing and utilization*. ICT concepts and ICT user skills development predominate in the curriculum. There is no demand to develop concepts and knowledge from informatics/computer science. It depends on conditions in schools, on school management, and on ICT teacher professionalism how, in reality, ICT teaching is designed. Textbooks for ICT subjects are unavailable. The Ministry of Education of the Czech Republic doesn't co-ordinate the situation related to textbook publishing, though some teachers do write textbooks, or produce teaching materials themselves.

In the Czech Republic, there are not many ICT teachers of primary or lower secondary schools who pay attention to introducing programming, and to teaching children how to develop algorithmic thinking. A huge research project, organised by a team of researchers from the Faculty of Education at Charles University in Prague, has come to the conclusion that the majority of the Czech Lower Secondary School teachers don't distinguish between ICT and Informatics, and they have no idea what to teach within ICT as a subject. They prefer to teach how to use MS applications (such as Word, Excel, etc.) and how to search for information on the Internet. They "don't appreciate the importance of teaching programming, algorithmic thinking, or databases, …." (Rambousek et al., 2007). There are two reasons for such an approach of the Czech teachers to teaching ICT in schools: firstly, the curriculum for Primary or Lower Secondary Schools is focused on fundamental ICT user's skill-development and their searching for information ability, and secondly, 18% of ICT teachers in Czech Lower Secondary Schools are not qualified and competent to teach ICT/Informatics.

The Faculty of Education in Prague educates, among others, ICT (ITT) teachers who will specialise in schools in the teaching of compulsory ICT Education. The MA degree study in ICT teacher education is focused mainly on the pedagogical aspects of ICT education. In the final semester, ICT (ITT) teachers are given an opportunity to manage a complex project in schools, based on a close collaboration with teachers, and to explore links across the Primary curriculum. Therefore, the idea of "Literacy from Scratch" could well be implemented at the Faculty of Education to great advantage.

Seeing the possibilities, an ICT (ITT) teacher decided to participate in the "Literacy from Scratch" project, designed by Lawrence Williams at Brunel University, and realised it at ZŠ Korunovační. He introduced its main idea to the school management and teachers. He organised a seminar for ICT teachers about programming in Scratch in order to create animated narratives.

The project contributes to developing interdisciplinary (or cross-curricular) relations between Czech/English language and literacy (animated stories), CICT Education (the development of algorithmic thinking) and Art Education (the design of

Sprites, Backgrounds, and four sequences of a story). It fits very well with the education for pupils Year 3 to 7 (age 8 to 13). ICT teachers incorporate its idea into the school curriculum, in accordance with a methodology concerning how to develop key competencies, both in computer literacy and in language literacy.

This project will continue in 2014/15 within a framework of research aimed at determining the impact of story-telling and programming in Scratch on pupils' understanding of how computer programs and a computer work. It will contribute to an effort to design and verify some approaches to the conceptual development of the principles of computer programming in Scratch in primary and lower secondary school aged pupils. This process will also be undertaken in the UK, linking the skills developed in Literacy from Scratch to the new Progression Pathways, created largely by Mark Dorling, and specifically designed to map this. See: http://community.computingatschool.org.uk/resources/1692

The project, based on a story-telling method, will be applied also in another Czech provincial basic school with children aged in 10-11 who will learn how to program Lego Mindstorms robots in Scratch. It is designed to contribute to the conceptual development of pupils' creativity. The project will enable pupils to extend their mental space, and contribute to a process of being aware, and developing an understanding of various complex content including creativity, technical and algorithmic thinking, imagination, and art design.

In addition, this more artistic, rather than literary, approach to story-telling adopted at the Korunovacni School has fed back into the Key Stage 1 curriculum work (for pupils aged 5 to 7 years) undertaken in London. An important part of the second year of the UK project development has involved Scratch stories being created by 5 and 6 year old pupils, but with much more emphasis on creating their own Sprites and Backgrounds for the stories, following the artistic Czech developments of the model. See: http://www.literacyfromscratch.org.uk/pupils/ks1.htm

The project was presented at the WCCE Conference in Poland in July 2013, where the creative aspects of the project were noted by G. Barbara Demo, from the Informatics Department at the University of Torino, Italy.

3 The Italian Perspective (G. Barbara Demo)

The international collaboration between the university departments in Torino, Italy, and Brunel, United Kingdom centres on the development of the project "Literacy from Scratch". The project was first designed in the UK to engage pupils in valid computer programming work, at an elementary stage, through creative story-telling. In Italy, the compelling problem with respect to Informatics in schools is in-service teacher training, a problem mirroring the situation in the Czech Republic. Accordingly, an international workshop was arranged in Torino, in order to explore how the project might be developed. The pedagogical methodology characterizing the project is based on a set of training sessions allowing a gradual approach to both programming and the basic principles of computing. Narrative work produced using Scratch has proved to be very appealing for users, and the development of the project in local primary and secondary schools in Torino, with the work supported by the

Informatics Department of Torino University, has been very successful. Outcomes are posted on the linked web sites: www.literacyfromscratch.org.uk and http://t4t.di.unito.it/ (following T4T-2013, a virtual environment Moodle).

This section of the chapter concerns the activities related to Computing in Italy and describes how the interest which began at a presentation at the 10th WCCE, World Conference on Computer in Education, in Torun (Poland), 2013 (Williams and Černochová, 2013), became the seed for a cooperation between university departments in Torino, Italy, and the Brunel, United Kingdom. At WCCE 2013, the presentation of Lawrence Williams began with the full screen projected show of a "Solar System" story. It was amazing, because of its images and wonderful music. But it was impressive especially because those who usually teach an introduction to computer science, and to programming, are computer science specialists. Thus they tend to engage in completely different activities that are frankly not so appealing. Of course, an activity of the type, "Let's add up a set of integers and find their average" cannot capture the same level of attention for many reasons: it is short, and the images you can add are not inherent in the activity, etc. Besides, the Scratch code to build a story like the "Solar System" story is not difficult to understand, at least compared with some other programming languages which are less suitable for an introductory activity. Indeed, a captivating and original story can be implemented with very few commands, used in a repeated pattern, to produce the whole story. This aspect is important for someone new to programming, but is even more important if we think of a story-telling activity in a primary school, because the focus of the learning, for the pupil, is not on the actual coding. Rather, the pupil is developing a narrative, with characters and dialogue, and the coding is merely the tool for presenting the story in an entertaining way. This means that when difficulties arise, the pupil wants to overcome them in order to complete their story, rather than simply getting some abstract coding to work correctly. Secondary pupils in London, for example, frequently worked through school Break and Lunch times in order to complete their projects. One student in Italy decided to include dialogue in Russian!

The WCCE 2013 presentation convinced us that the story-telling direction was worthy to be investigated for introducing in-service teachers to computer science. The first in-person group meeting happened during the 2013 workshop Teachers for Teachers, where one of the activities was based on integrating Lawrence Williams' UK experience in story-telling using Scratch, with the activities developed in schools by Italian teachers, together with university researchers. T4T workshops are offered yearly, and involve hands-on activities based on the co-operation between university researchers and teachers in all education levels. The main concern of the collaboration is to face the challenge of finding ways to introduce computing in schools appropriate to the ages of the students involved, as well as to the teachers' competences. Indeed, nowadays we face a very peculiar time for informatics education. Till now, Informatics has been taught to students at university level, in technical schools or in vocational schools specializing in computer science. Today, Informatics is going to be taught to:

- schoolchildren who are much younger than previous students, and who have teachers not specialized in Informatics (sometimes knowing very little of it)
- students in secondary school who will not specialize in computer science

To face this new situation, an original pedagogy in Computing must be devised through a common project carried out by researchers in pedagogy and in computer science, because both qualifications are needed. Also, best practices already present in schools for several years must be taken into account, because some teachers have done excellent activities for a development of informatics in education. Alessandro Rabbone, for example, is a teacher involved in both T4T 2012 and again in T4T 2013. This is because for almost thirty years he has introduced computer science both to his pupils in primary schools, and to his colleagues from different types of schools.

The T4T project is encouraging the development of the informatics skills of the teachers involved, and others are coming to subsequent meetings. The success of T4T can be seen in several activities begun in the area which the Informatics Department of the University of Torino is proposing. The most appreciated aspect of the project is its pedagogical methodology, with the decision to focus on hands-on activities involving story-telling as an introduction to computer science, following the UK and Czech models.

The introduction to computing competencies of the T4T-2013 workshop has been attended mainly by primary and middle school teachers, but also by professors of non-scientific disciplines in secondary schools: art, history, and literature professors were present. Professors of scientific disciplines are still missing, probably because most of them consider that digital literacy is already sufficiently well-established in education. In general also, history of philosophy professors seem to be far from paying attention to basic informatics principles, though their discipline should be conditioned by the digital culture. Further developments of T4T activities are underway, and others are planned in order to reach out to these missing teachers.

For further steps toward enriching computing competencies, the Scratch project of facilitating telling stories described in the paper by Demo and Williams, 2014, is exploited by presenting the experiences of the pupils' everyday lives as Scratch stories", in activities under development described in the report "Telling our own stories". By means of these activities, one can realize how expressing some behaviour in Scratch is close to the way one normally would describe his/her own behaviour in everyday life. In so doing, we naturally come to express daily life through branching and interactive stories thus progressing abilities in programming competencies. This idea is currently being developed at Brunel University.

The T4T collaboration around story-telling using Scratch deserves a concluding remark. The common approach turns out to integrate two directions and motivations of activity, each one characterizing the university departments involved:

- developing a narrative, with characters and dialogue, using a tool for presenting the story in an entertaining way, and making possible the implementation of the planned story in a relatively easy way, and in a short space of time, from the very start of using the new tool.
- proposing a first approach to programming, producing meaningful and entertaining results, the narratives easily provide, faster than with other programming environments, a natural basis for computer science.
- The several kinds of computing activities using Scratch for teachers and students in different types and levels of schools are described in the proceedings of the ISSEP Conference in Istanbul September 2014 (Demo and

Williams, 2014). This paper is about introducing 8-9 to 16 years old students to several aspects of computing such as: algorithmic thinking, problem structuring, introduction to algorithms, properties particularly relevant to understanding algorithmic complexity.

We are currently trying to enlarge the working group. Indeed, other projects are starting in the Torino area with activities of the same type of those here described. The integration of these efforts will promote a larger spreading of computer science among teachers, and consequently across all phases of education.

4 MESH – A Global Perspective (Sarah Younie)

A further development of the Literacy from Scratch project is through the MESH initiative. See: http://www.meshguides.org/about-mesh/#how-mesh-operates

MESH - Mapping and Managing Educational Specialist Knowhow is an educational knowledge management system with the aim of underpinning professional judgment with evidence. MESH uses an accessible multimedia mindmap approach to present a diagrammatic database of subject-specific research-based knowledge about the teaching and learning of topics across the curricular disciplines. MESH builds upon existing portals and evidence bases for education, with the aim of summarising and making accessible the existing evidence whilst also documenting gaps in knowledge and mapping points of contention. The approach is inspired by the resources available to professionals and academics in other disciplines such as health, but recognises the challenges that education has as 'a discipline across disciplines'. Wikipedia provides an example of how easily searchable a large database can be and that, over time, and through collaborative effort to pool knowledge, a high quality result may be achieved. The Map of Medicine Healthguides is also a well-developed example of software which supports mapping professional knowledge.

Much research-based knowledge is currently buried in theses, held by individual academics and teachers or published in academic journals and reports, which are not easily accessible to teachers. MESH provides a way for teachers to access this knowledge, so that it can be leveraged to improve student outcomes. MESH provides the e-infrastructure to support worldwide collaborative work between those who want to strengthen the educational evidence base and support teaching becoming a strongly evidence-based profession.

Developing research-informed practice is a challenge for educators, not least because published educational research is rarely focused on the knowledge teachers need to improve educational outcomes. MESH is being developed by a world-wide network of educators who want to make this happen. It is currently being developed at Bedfordshire University to support Literacy from Scratch as part of a coherent approach to teaching and learning using Scratch for cross-curricular work.

The present writers all see the collaboration between the various countries involved in developing this whole new model as a vital step in providing support for teachers who are setting out to promote effective, meaningful, and, above all, engaging lessons in Computing.

5 Conclusions

- The Literacy from Scratch web site provides creative Computing materials for teachers of pupils aged 5 years to 14 years.
- The World Ecitizens web site provides an opportunity for pupils to publish and share their creative learning outcomes in Computing.
- MESH provides the pedagogical underpinnings for the project, with papers published and categorised, for easy access and use by teachers.
- In London, Primary teachers are being trained to develop their own skills in Computing, ready to introduce this into their classrooms, by September 2014. This includes the creation of increasingly complex Branching Stories, and interactive resources for their classrooms.
- In Prague, developments are under way, to continue widening the artistic and Computing aspects of the project.
- In Torino, teachers are being supported in developing creative, collaborative, and cross-curricular approaches to their training needs in Computing.

Much remains to be done, but this learning model has begun very successfully. To support this project, there is a new text, "Introducing Computing: a guide for teachers" as well as the Literacy from Scratch web site.

References

1. Barbara Demo, G., Williams, L.: The Many Facets of Scratch. In: Proceedings of the ISSEP Conference 2014, Istanbul (September 2014)
2. Papert, S., Harel, I.: Situating Constructionism (1991), http://www.papert.org/articles/SituatingConstructionism.html
3. Rambousek, V., et al.: Výzkum informacní výchovy na základních školách. 1. vydání. Plzen: Koniáš, 360 s. (2007) ISBN 80-86948-10-2
4. Stager, G.: An Investigation of Constructivism in the Maine Youth Centre. Informatics in Education - An International Journal 6(2) (2007)
5. Williams, L., Černochová, M.: Literacy from Scratch. In: Proceedings of the 10th IFIP World Conference on Computers in Education, WCCE 2013, pp. 17–27. Copernicus University, Torun (2013), For a supporting text for teachers, as a guide to the project, see:
6. Williams, L. (ed.): Introducing Computing: A guide for teachers. Routledge (August 2014), http://www.routledge.com/books/details/9781138022850/
7. The web site with Literacy from Scratch teaching materials is to be found at, http://www.literacyfromscratch.org.uk

Questioning Two Myths in Computer Science Education

Paolo Rocchi

IBM and LUISS University, Roma, Italy
procchi@luiss.it

Abstract. This paper examines two statements regarding computer science as a discipline and its theoretical basis. We shall demonstrate how those statements are questionable and in addition they tend to hide the real root-causes of some significant educational issues. Those statements are very popular in the scientific community and have noteworthy negative effect on the researchers who frequently double their efforts and get around the same problems for years. This work concludes with the claim that experts on computer science education (CSE) should be more attentive to the theoretical aspects of this discipline and should pay more attention to speculative proposals.

Keywords: Theories on computing, computer technology, computer science education, strategies of research.

1 Introduction

In the preliminary stage, we specify that the terms 'computer science', 'information and communication technology (ICT)', 'computing' and 'informatics' will be used as synonyms hereunder.

Since the birth of the digital age, experts made significant efforts to divulge and explain the technology of systems and their use. It seems that pioneering articles appeared in the early 1950s [1].

By the mid-1960s computer science education (CSE) became a very active area due to the wide spread success of computers in businesses and organizations. There was great demand for skilled practitioners and the courses on ICT offered vital services in Western economies. Several research projects started in order to improve didactics of informatics. Also companies and businesses intervened to suggest amelioration of the contents to be taught.

The amount of contributions presented in the last half a century is simply immense. One could quote the hundreds of academic and professional societies on CSE; the thousands of books, publications, and journals specialized on computer education and not specialized; the thousands of occasional and regular events – see the analysis of SIGCSE symposia in [2]. We put forward two remarks upon this enormous global effort.

1) The vivid activity of CSE researchers and the large amount of contributions do not provide proportionally satisfactory outcomes so far. Sometimes experts give the impression of talking around the same topics [3]; the Royal Society talks

D. Passey and A. Tatnall (Eds.): KCICTP/ITEM 2014, IFIP AICT 444, pp. 34–41, 2014.

about the 'vicious circle' of modern computer science education [4]. Pears and others express an opinion amply shared: "decades of active research on the teaching of introductory programming has had limited effect on classroom practice" [5]. Education of software engineering has raised complaints for years [6]. Various studies attempting to delineate core competencies and skills in informatics provide uncertain guidelines rather than unequivocal answers [7] [8] [9].

2) The considerable energy spent to tackle educational issues in informatics cannot be compared with other disciplines. Nothing like this occurs elsewhere. Researchers are not so busy in discussing curricula, roles, skills and professional profiles in other technical areas.

One could ask: 'Why is there such a great difference between didactics of computing and didactics of other scientific fields?'

2 First Myth

Informatics appears as a rapidly changing discipline, which places considerable pressure on CSE and several commentators ascribe the responsibility of the difficulties, which we have pinpointed in 1) and 2), to the subject matter. The following passage summarizes an amply shared viewpoint:

> "Computing has changed dramatically over that time in ways that have a profound effect on curriculum design and pedagogy." [10]

This common judgment unites the vast community of ICT educators whose inferential reasoning can be subdivided into two sentences:

> "Informatics is a novel and fast evolving discipline. Hence, the pedagogy of informatics meets severe obstacles." (1)

The first line is the premise to the second line which exhibits the conclusion. Statement (1) could be defined as the statement of a theorem including the hypothesis and the thesis. Speaking in general, theorems are to be demonstrated; instead nobody substantiates (1) so far; nobody shows how the close necessarily follows from the premise. so far. Authors cite the various versions of (1) without any logical proof [11] [12]. This common belief seems a dogma rather than a statement sustained by logical reasoning.

The first part (i.e. "Informatics is a novel and fast evolving discipline") is established on the basis of facts and is true beyond any doubt. However the end point (i.e. "hence the pedagogy of informatics meets severe obstacles") is not so evident.

A proof is required to demonstrate a theorem; an example is sufficient to disprove it. Here we present two examples to show how assertion (1) is arbitrary. In particular, we shall examine two innovative and fast evolving scientific sectors which do not raise severe educational problems.

A] In the late 1960s, driven by the growing public awareness of a need for action in addressing environmental problems and the arrival of more severe laws and regulations, environmental science (ES) came alive as an active field of scientific investigation. ES includes instructions in biology, chemistry, physics, geosciences, climatology, statistics, and mathematical modeling [13]. One could deem environmental science more complicated than informatics and in addition ES is fast changing because of the novel and multi-disciplinary technologies required to investigate and to solve large-scale environmental problems. However, educators in environmental science are not so pressed by educational problems as teachers in computing. Prerequisites to ES courses are the lessons of physics, chemistry, biology, geography and other matters. Specialized topics are placed after the introductory lessons. Environmental phenomena are often large scale yet the ES laboratory does not seem as awkward and tricky as computing drilling. Teachers update the courses without special struggle [14].

B] Environmental science probably seems far different in kind and somewhat incomparable to informatics. The second sector – electronics – is closer to computer systems and probably the reader feels it as a more fitting example.

The advances in the development of the electronic market appears remarkable even to common people. It may be said that electronics drags the advance of computer science [15]. Despite its rapid growth and evolution, the study of electrical devices does not result in pedagogical issues similar to those occurring in computing. Usually, the courses of electronics begin with fundamental principles – say Faraday's law of induction, Kirchhoff's equations, the Ohm's law, the Maxwell's formulas etc. – and proceed toward specialized topics.

Electronics does not give rise to severe educational problems regarding the subject contents. Teachers are not so much stressed to 'find a way to present' a certain topic. Students do not undergo disorientation and a sense of groundlessness so frequent in computing. They progressively enrich their culture and arrive at precise professional competencies.

The Association for Computing Machinery (ACM), the Institute of Electrical and Electronics Engineers (IEEE) and other organizations published several reports for experts who prepare courses on computing. This vivid activity is absent in the electronic domain. No organization felt the need to promote the publication of curricula or guidelines similar to those cited above. Experts arrange and optimize the lessons in electronics as technology advances without special efforts.

The reader perhaps objects that informatics has developed so much that now we face different sub-disciplines. The ACM/IEEE Curricula [10] holds:

"The scope of what we call computing has broadened to the point that it is difficult to define it as a single discipline." (2)

One can reply that also electronic experts have inaugurated several new areas such as nanoelectronics, photonics, robotics, power electronics, quantum electronics, and spintronics which do not subvert the didactical curricula. New specialist subject matters substitute the obsolete ones or are appended at the bottom of the pedagogical pathways without great discussion [16]. The new topics give substance to new professional figures and do not raise lively debates comparable to the discussion occurring in CSE.

Concluding, the cases of electronics and environmental science make evident how an advanced and rapidly evolving technology does not oppose necessarily dramatic pedagogical difficulties. *Statement* (1) *sounds like a generic and untrustworthy myth.* Practical evidence demonstrates that *statement* (1) *is false* and results in repeated and prolonged misunderstandings.

3 Doubled Efforts

At this stage it is natural to ask the following question:

What is the substantial difference between computer science and electronics (and even environmental science) from the didactical viewpoint?

The answer appears to be self-evident as soon as one looks closely at the structure of the two disciplines.

Electronics has shared principles that guide and give order to the entire didactical process, no matter the process is running in a high school, a college or a university. Electronics is based on general laws, models, equations and universal properties that constitute its logical frame and inspire the didactical material. Instead, *informatics does not have a solid theoretical frame of reference.*

Factually "teachers need to know more than just their subject. They need to know the ways it can come to be understood, the ways it can be misunderstood, what counts as understanding: they need to know how individuals experience the subject" [17] and the theoretical basis of electronics provides the principal aid to the educators' complex activity. The fundamentals cast light into the entire area which one explains to students without extraordinary efforts. One can arrange the various topics and sub-topics in a rather straightforward manner. A teacher can proceed from general statements to particular cases. By contrast, *informatics is a science not equipped with an exhaustive and amply shared theoretical base.* The courses of electronics may be defined as 'theory-driven,' informatics cannot be defined as such; instead usual courses of informatics are 'practice driven,' 'competency-driven,' 'example driven,' or 'programming driven.'

In consequence of fundamental theory shortage, researchers in computing education have a double job to do: they tackle the usual pedagogical issues and in addition they are required to compensate for the lack of a general and logical reference. Experts in CSE counterbalance the missing cultural basis, and arrange the subject contents and the targets. They also establish the importance of the various topics, the sequel of the lessons and their logical relationships. They take on several other 'structural' issues.

This double job becomes stressing in a particular manner when there is something to update. The change of a detail can result in dramatic consequences. One can quote the dispute about the substitution of the language Pascal with Java or C++ [18]. By contrast, novelties do not overthrow the educational systems of electronics. Any didactical update complies with the theoretical order already established. If a technical solution, an instrument or a work method evolves, the didactical process is not completely redesigned but rather, just the intended part varies.

Educators of informatics – lacking an exhaustive theoretical frame – prevalently illustrate technical solutions. A teaching process – even if optimized and updated – turns out to be provisional when it is based on specialist topics because specialist solutions change. Only general principles can yield a reliable pedagogical pathway. Researchers on CSE spend most of their time with specialist topics that are transitory and cannot ensure a logical order to the overall matter. Hence, not only education specialists do a double job, in addition they are doomed to failure. They spend much energy but create doubtful cultural 'buildings'.

The lack of shared fundamentals yield lessons which often seem to exist only in response to a request for help; e.g. request for coding a program, for the use of spreadsheets, and emailing a message [19]. In other words, theoretical omission forces a teacher toward a 'service-orientated activity'. This somewhat obligatory didactical style emerges even in the introductory lessons [20]. The contrary occurs in electronics which is 'theory-driven'. Teachers spend several lessons explaining abstract statements and general equations. Practical skills are gained later.

Concluding, undisputable evidence shows how most significant difficulties in CSE do not derive from the fact that we teach a novel and fast evolving technology, but rather from the fact that *informatics does not have a consistent theoretical basis* and CSE cannot advance as a 'theory driven' activity.

4 Second Myth

Perhaps the reader challenges the ensuing sentences just mentioned:

- Informatics does not have a solid, theoretical frame of reference.
- Informatics is a science not equipped with an exhaustive and amply shared theoretical base.
- Informatics does not have a consistent theoretical basis.

Several experts believe the contrary is true. They claim that computer science is assisted by a large set of abstract references. They cite the Turing theory, the Shannon theory, the theory of graphs etc. and conclude that computer science has a significant mathematical base. The common opinion upon the theoretical foundations of informatics can be summed up in the following terms:

Computer science has a large mathematical base. (3)

This statement is right in the sense that computing has 'several' theoretical bases. However, when one examines each theory, one by one, he can remark that each formal construction gives support to a small technical area, and no theory covers the entire computer domain. For example, Shannon deliberately ignores semantics, and one cannot use the Shannon entropy to qualify the expressive power of a Web page. The various constructions are not connected either logically or causally or by shared characteristics, and thus do not constitute a consistent framework. The theories do not illustrate the body of computing as an organized description of the knowledge of the field.

It may happen that two or more theories revolve around a single subject matter and pursue different targets. For example, a variety of theoretical constructions treat the programming languages: the Turing theory explains imperative programming [21]; functional programming has a theoretical basis in lambda calculus and combinatory logic [22]; data base languages refer to relational algebra [23], and a special theory supports object-oriented programming [24].

Some theories of computer science overlap and one begins by believing it is hard to say which model is more 'basic'. They are often designed with different goals in mind and are not in agreement with themselves. That is why, the numerous and unrelated conceptualizations do not provide a unified guideline to CSE experts.

A mathematical theory should have adept epistemic capabilities, that is to say it should elucidate the why, the when and the how of the phenomena under observation. Unfortunately a small theory – even if correct – has little explicative qualities because of its proper dimension, and in turn the sum of small theories says nothing or very little as the summation of zeros returns zero. Many CSE researchers have gone through this cultural void. The various attempts to ground a didactical pathway on abstract concepts has not yet gained much success [25]. Educators sometimes prefer to develop the lessons on the basis of practice and experience gained. The students are trained to build knowledge by themselves and actively search for solutions to the problems they experience.

One can reasonably conclude that informatics has several mathematical theories but not a single theory, nor the entire set of theories is able to provide the exhaustive logical framework needed by educators. Practical evidence shows how *statement* (3) *is false*, and the lack of thorough support can but provoke the didactical difficulties discussed in this paper.

5 Practical Development and Conclusion

This paper is an attempt to illustrate how the idea that 'Computer science has a large mathematical base' has not ground and it paves the way to the following deceptive notion 'Informatics is a novel and fast evolving discipline. Hence, the pedagogy of informatics meets severe obstacles'. The two sentences are nothing more than false legends whereas the small and pretentious theories put forward in the computer domain are the authentic root-causes of most problems which current CSE literature is discussing. Hence – in our opinion - researchers should enhance their strategies. They should pay greater attention to the investigations conducted to clarify the fundamentals of CS. They should stimulate and even offer assistance to theorists as frequently occurred in the past with success in various domains.

Computer science as a discipline has always struggled with its identity [26][27] and CSE experts are able to provide a significant contribution. For example, the UK Open University has recently inaugurated a debate on the multifaceted notion of information [28].

Lethbridge [29] claims: "Many important ideas in science and technology have been developed and refined by educators, attempting to determine how to explain complex concepts."

Theories are not carved in stone. Old theories may be replaced by new theories that have broader scopes than the old ones. Sometimes an old construction is not to be thrown away; it can just be viewed as an approximation – applicable in certain restricted circumstances – of the new more comprehensive theory. It is therefore, quite reasonable to think that CSE should bring greater attention to innovative visions and theoretical proposals that outline a comprehensive frame [30][31][32]. It is worth mentioning that some ideas have been already used in education with success [33].

In conclusion, the argument discussed in these pages is far from being abstract and avulse from practical consequence; it entails behaviors that are really innovative.

References

1. Hopper, G.M.: The education of a computer. In: Proc. of the ACM National Meeting, pp. 243–249 (1952)
2. Valentine, D.W.: CS educational research: A meta-analysis of SIGCSE technical symposium proceedings. In: Proc. of the 35th SIGCSE Symposium, pp. 255–259 (2004)
3. Huggins, P.: Universities failing to provide adequate background DP. Computerworld 25, 3 (1970)
4. AA. VV. - Shut down or restart? The way forward for computing in UK schools. The Royal Society Education Section (2012)
5. `http://royalsociety.org/uploadedFiles/Royal_Society_Content/education/policy/computing-in-schools/2012-01-12-Computing-in-Schools.pdf` (accessed December 2013)
6. Pears, A., Seidman, S., Malmi, L., Mannila, L., Adams, E., Bennedsen, J., Devlin, M., Paterson, J.: A Survey of Literature on the Teaching of Introductory Programming. In: Working Group Reports on ITCSE on Innovation and Technology in Computer Science Education, pp. 204–223 (2007)
7. Ghezzi, C., Mandrioli, D.: The challenges of software engineering education. In: Inverardi, P., Jazayeri, M. (eds.) ICSE 2005. LNCS, vol. 4309, pp. 115–127. Springer, Heidelberg (2006)
8. Connolly, R.: Criticizing and modernizing computing curriculum: The case of the web and the social issues courses. In: Proc. of the 17th Western Canadian Conference on Computing Education, pp. 52–56 (2012)
9. Dagienė, V.: Informatics education for new millennium learners. In: Kalaš, I., Mittermeir, R.T. (eds.) ISSEP 2011. LNCS, vol. 7013, pp. 9–20. Springer, Heidelberg (2011)
10. De Kereki, I.F.: Work in progress: Transversal competencies contributions to computer science 1 course. In: Proc. Frontiers in Education Conference, pp. S3G1–S3G3 (2011)
11. ACM-IEEE Computing Curricula 2001 Joint Task Force on Computing Curricula (2001), `http://www.computer.org/education/cc2001/`
12. Goldweber, M., Impagliazzo, J., Clear, A.G., Davies, G., Flack, H., Myers, J.P., Rasala, R.: Historical perspectives on the computing curriculum. ACM SIGCUE Outlook, Special Issue 25(4), 94–111 (1997)
13. Tucker, A.B., Wegner, P.: Computer science and engineering: the discipline and its impact. In: Handbook of Computer Science and Engineering. CRC Press, Boca Raton (1996)
14. Enger, E., Smith, B.: Environmental Science, 12th edn. McGraw-Hill, New York (2009)
15. Elstgeest, J., Harlen, W.: Environmental Science in the Primary Curriculum. SAGE Publications Ltd., Thousands Oaks (1990)

16. Morton, D.L., Gabriel, J.: Electronics: The Life Story of a Technology. Johns Hopkins University Press, Baltimore (2007)
17. Mc Shane, E.A., Trivedi, M., Shenai, K.: - An improved approach to application-specific power electronics education: Curriculum development. IEEE Transactions on Education 44(3), 282–288 (2001)
18. Laurillard, D.: Rethinking University Teaching: A Framework for the Effective Use of Educational Technology. Routledge, London (1993)
19. Abelson, H., Bruce, K., van Dam, A., Tucker, A., Wegner, P.: The first-course conundrum. Comm. of the ACM 38(6), 116–117 (1995)
20. Hatziapostolou, T., Kefalas, P., Sotiriadou, A.: Promoting computer science programmers to potential students: 10 myths for computer science. In: Proc. of the Informatics Education Europe III Conference, pp. 125–133 (2008)
21. Bruce, K.B.: Controversy on how to teach CS1: A discussion on the SIGCSE-members mailing list. SIGCSE Bulletin 36(4), 29–34 (2005)
22. Hoare, C.A.R.: An axiomatic basis for computer programming. Comm. of the ACM 12(10), 576–580 (1969)
23. Hindley, J.R., Seldin, J.P.: Lambda-Calculus and Combinators: An Introduction. Cambridge University Press, Cambridge (2008)
24. Molková, L.: Theory and Practice of Relational Algebra: Transforming Relational Algebra to SQL. Lambert Academic Publishing, Saarbrücken (2012)
25. Gunter, C.A., Mitchell, J.C.: Theoretical Aspects of Object-Oriented Programming, Types, Semantics, and Language Design. MIT Press, Cambridge (1994)
26. Golshani, F., Panchanathan, S., Friesen, O.: A logical foundation for an information engineering curriculum. In: Proc. of 30th Annual Frontiers in Education Conference, vol. 12, pp. T3E/8–T3E12 (2000)
27. Demeyer, S.: - Research methods in computer science. In: Proc. of the 27th IEEE International Conference on Software Maintenance, p. 600 (2011)
28. Denning, P.J.: The science in computer science. Comm. of the ACM 56(5), 35–38 (2013)
29. In: Proc. of Workshop 'The Difference that Makes a Difference'. Open University (2011), http://www.dtmd2011.info/ (accessed December 2013)
30. Lethbridge, T.C., Diaz-Herrera, J.D., LeBlanc, R.J., Thompson, J.B.: Improving software practice through education: challenges and future trends. In: Proc. of Future of Software Engineering Congress, pp. 12–28 (2007)
31. Denning, P.J., Wegner, P.: Introduction to what is computation. Computer J. 55(7), 803–804 (2012)
32. Floridi, L.: Philosophy and Computing: An Introduction. Routledge, London (1999)
33. Rocchi, P.: Logic of Analog and Digital Machines, 2nd edn. Nova Science Publishers, New York (2012)
34. Rocchi, P.: Lectures on CS taught to introduce students with different background. In: Proc. of the Informatics Education Europe III Conference, pp. 115–124 (2008)

Competencies and Work Practices for Dynamic Distributed Software Development in Global Value Networks

Mikko Ruohonen[1], Marko Mäkipää[1], and Pekka Kamaja[2]

[1] University of Tampere, Finland
[2] Haaga-Helia University of Applied Sciences, Finland
{mikko.j.ruohonen,marko.makipaa}@uta.fi,
pekka.kamaja@haaga-helia.fi

Abstract. Offshoring of software development (SD) to cost competitive countries (CCC) has gained increased popularity in US and Western Europe since year 2000. Countries, such as India, have dominated the discussion but now it also seems that not just the labor costs matter. In the future, service levels, dynamic competencies building and community-based activities are also needed for managing dynamic distributed software development (DDSD) work. Instead of the one-way migration of RDI operations there are increasingly voices questioning the rationale of moving operations to CCCs. The key driver of this research-in-progress paper is in searching a new frameworks, tools and practices for managing DDSD work and developing SD operations evaluation solutions. The forthcoming practical outcomes described are both the improvements in SD work in the industry level and provision of enhancements for their current SD work performance assessment. Academic results will be discussed with European, US and Indian partner researchers in the context of changing dynamic sourcing i.e. onshore, nearshore, offshore activities in global value networks. The general objectives are to improve ICT-services companies' competencies and tools in i) assessing their SD work operations with more enhanced evaluation systems and ii) make visible practices in managing dynamic distributed sourcing network operations in global value networks.

Keywords: Software development, competencies, distributed work practices, global software engineering, dynamic offshoring

1 Background and Rationale

Offshoring of software development to cost competitive countries has gained increased publicity in US and Western Europe since year 2000. India, China and even Latin America have been mentioned as potential cost competitive countries [1] [2] [3]. Outsourcing of both information technology (ITO) and business and knowledge processes (BPO/KPO) has increased during the last two decades and now provides increasing business opportunities [4] [5] [6]. Cost competitive countries have dominated although it seems that not just the labor costs matter. In the future, service

D. Passey and A. Tatnall (Eds.): KCICTP/ITEM 2014, IFIP AICT 444, pp. 42–51, 2014.

levels, dynamic competencies and community-based activities are also needed for managing dynamic distributed software development work. Cultural fit and suitability of administrative environment are important to notify when making outsourcing decisions [7]. Outsourcing is too often considered one-sided: handing over assets, people, activities and knowledge to third-party management, but it can also be a contract for two-way collaboration to release your own knowledge and learning potential, while also releasing the provider's potential, for mutual gain [8].

India has been a long time the giant of offshoring, but China has also grown. We must also remember that Latin America countries such as Brazil, Mexico and Chile and East European countries such as Poland, Czech Republic and Hungary are growing and competing in this arena. In addition onshoring, i.e. keeping work inside your home country, is still a potential alternative for maintaining responsiveness, quality control and agility. This makes a challenging decision making arena for many software development companies. Strategic offshoring has created different business models which are in a state of flux. Organizations are looking for new managerial practices and comparisons of near- and offshoring models are frequently done.

2 Competencies for Distributed Dynamic Software Development

2.1 Strategy Demands New Competencies

The background of this paper is that software development companies are willing to assess new knowledge for arguing the research, development and innovation (RDI) operations in their home or foreign countries to make a successful combination of onshoring, nearshoring and offshoring settings. Public discussion in many countries has been quite intensive before and after large outsourcing decisions. As it is noted, the low cost resources are not that clear when the impact of the hidden costs due to human resource management complexities or other structural and administrative issues related to business cultures in South and South-East Asian countries are considered.

Consequently the key driver of this research project is in searching new frameworks, tools and practices for managing dynamic distributed software development (DDSD) work and developing operations evaluation solutions. Therefore, the practical outcomes from this project are both the improvements in SD work management in the ICT industry level as well and provision of enhancements on their current performance management of software development. The overall goal encompasses the tools for management in adopting company management practices globally. Also, the optimization of the division of the RDI resources within the multitude of current and potential locations globally is considered.

Pure offshore outsourcing is changing to a more strategic direction which makes both onshoring, nearshoring and offshoring a number of viable ways to implement software development. The process is bi-directional. For example, Indian IT-service giants have during the last years increasingly acquired shared services companies or invested in nearshoring operations in USA, Latin America and Europe.

India seems to be the most attractive country despite the promises of Chinese sourcing markets. Latin America and East European countries are joining the race. The fairly new EU member states are attractive for ICT services and also growing their ITO/BPO services exports. For the whole picture we should remember that the global sales of IT services is plus 1 trillion USD [9] of which US-based companies such as IBM and Accenture normally take 60% market share. It is estimated [10] that total exports of Indian information technology enabled services (ITES) and business process outsourcing (BPO) business on financial year (FY) 2014 is on the level of 84-87 BUSD and the global market share approximately 4-5%. New EU countries are getting increasingly more visibility and growth.

Strategic offshoring has created different business models which are now in a state of flux. Network strategy requires development of value network to face growing and varying needs of customers. Indian companies attempt to move forward in the value chain in order to foster partnership and make customer innovations. Indian ICT service companies, previously known as "body shopping organizations" [11], are now moving to countries with lower salary costs such as Vietnam, investing in Tier II cities such as Pune, Chandigarh, Jaipur in India to get lower costs of operations and better supply of manpower, set up excellence centers in China for using huge potential of Chinese engineering workforce and acquire IT companies from Europe and Latin America to get closer to customers. Indian companies are really networking to be nearer the customer but in the same time making effectiveness in their engineering work development. In addition to that Indian ICT service companies are heading for building vertical-specific service expertise in many industries and upgrading their knowledge in so-called business transformation outsourcing. Traditionally customer intimacy has been the competitive weapon for US and European ICT service companies. This strategy is based on middle-man model in which companies which are culturally nearer to customer can also use the cost-effective offshore sourcing. The third model is to set up your own captive development center i.e. to execute internal offshoring.

2.2 Competencies for Advanced Performance Management

Combining efficiency, productivity and effectiveness assessment makes an integrated framework. The studies of IBM [12] show interesting rationale for the project's performance management research. With eight selected topics researchers have found a clear link between business performance and software development work evaluation. Some challenges in measuring and managing software projects arise due to separate teams focused on development, build, testing, and deployment each having stove-piped processes. This leads to lack of timely information and in-context, objective, and honest assessment and insight into the status of software delivery projects. These challenges result even if all of the project members are co-located and working on a homogeneous environment.

The picture of software development gets more complicated when we add three additional dimensions commonly seen with many software delivery organizations:

- geographical/regional distribution of team members which adds poor communication, language, culture, time challenges and process gaps resulting in reworking,
- crossing organizational boundaries which leads to lack of effective collaboration, weak project governance, lack of domain expertise, poor line of business oversight, security of IP when outsourcing and
- multiple team and heterogeneous infrastructure which adds more challenges to incompatible tools and repositories, unreliable access artifacts, lengthy on-boarding and inflexible tooling integration.

The dynamic distributed sourcing network is also evolving continuously. Therefore, we need managerial decision-making for finding the most successful teams, effective locations to source, combination of talents, balanced levels and a follow-up of product/service life-cycles.

2.3 Multicultural Competencies for Global Software Engineering

In addition to pure labor costs knowledge management, customer learning, managing different modes and lifecycles affect the final outcomes of dynamic distributed sourcing of software development. Multicultural project teams have a higher potential for success than single-culture teams do, but they also have a higher potential for failure. Even highly data-driven projects need to be carefully managed across cultures. We say: "it's the people, not the technologies, that spell or dispel success". Cultural differences in project management can be difficult to navigate, but whether or not you agree with the benefits of globalization, its effects will be felt for a long time to come, especially in the engineering industry. Taking the time to understand how culture affects a project and an organization not only makes smart business sense but also makes our everyday work life smoother and easier--the improved flow is priceless [13].

It is vital to acknowledge the importance of cultural competence in order to act effectively and successfully in foreign cultures or in multicultural organizations. The concept of cultural competence is divided in knowledge, mindfulness and behavioral skills [14]. Knowledge comprises information about the concept of culture, the ways culture affects behavior and different cultures. Mindfulness means mediating between knowledge and behavior. It means, for example, paying attention to our own assumptions of different cultures, breaking free of stereotypes and readiness to adjust our opinions of others. Acquiring behavioral skills means extending the set of possible behavioral ways and knowing in which situation and in which culture to use each one. Increasing cultural competence is a continuous process that can take considerable time. A good starting point for increasing cultural competence is offered by different cultural typologies.

One of the most widely accepted cultural typologies is presented by Hofstede [15] [16] [17]. He distinguished cultures based on the differences in what they value and found five dimensions: power distance, uncertainty avoidance, individualism-collectivism, masculinity-femininity and long-term orientation. Trompenaars and

Hampden-Turner [18] have identified seven dimensions by which cultures can be differentiated. Five of these dimensions depict relationships among people: universalism-particularism, individualism-collectivism, specific versus diffuse, neutral versus affective and achievement versus ascription. The other two dimensions are time perspective and relationship with the environment. House et al. [19] have presented nine dimensions in the GLOBE study of 62 societies, which help to understand the influence of cultural differences on leadership of organizations. These are power distance, uncertainty avoidance, human orientation, institutional collectivism, in-group collectivism, assertiveness, gender egalitarianism, future orientation and performance orientation.

The advantage of these models lies in their power to make sense of different cultures even if one does not have first-hand experience of a specific culture. However, the risk arises, that the models tend to simplify different cultures too much. For example, when we consider a country like India with many languages, castes and different living environments, it becomes evident that there is not a single homogenous Indian culture. According Jacob [20] most countries are culturally heterogeneous consisting of several sub-cultures, which diminishes the value of cultural typologies describing whole nations. Instead of force-fitting countries in different classes, Jacob suggests the concept of crossvergence, which means "fusing together management practices of two or more cultures, so that a practice relevant to a heterogeneous culture can be assembled". As Jacob (ibid) states, the success of cross-cultural managers is not defined by their knowledge of different culture typologies or ability to classify cultures, but more in their ability to find out what kind of leadership behavior best fits the culture and their ability to develop their own managerial skills according to that. More generally speaking, Fontaine [21] gives two general focus areas for management in terms of cross-cultural management: understanding the past of the culture and shaping the future culture. As important as it is to understand the past of the culture, as we have seen in the number of studies concentrating on that, the more important it is to find ways to shape the future.

3 Research Settings: Questions, Approach, Results

The general objective of the project is to improve ICT-service (focused on software development) companies' competencies and tools in i) assessing their software development work operations with more enhanced evaluation systems and ii) make visible work practices in managing dynamic distributed sourcing network operations in global value networks. This will improve ICT software sector to understand the changing sourcing environment of software development and service, detect their competencies in executing this work in different project and work settings and enable dynamic sourcing with multiple sites. The forthcoming results would be:

1. integrated framework for evaluation software development operations efficiency, productivity and effectiveness indicators (financial, quality and organizational measures)

2. creation of managerial practices for dynamic distributed software development sourcing networks and
3. comparison guidelines for evaluating multiple sourcing sites and locations both in Finnish/European and international offshore settings.

The final goal is that the Finnish/European ICT and software industry can use these evaluation, work alignment and managerial practices for more agile and effective sourcing location management. This will make sourcing decisions more visible and easier to implement and provide agility for operations. Our research questions are:

1. How to find meaningful performance areas and create usable measures beyond traditional financial measures?
2. What are the topical areas for integrated evaluation framework and multisite sourcing management?
3. What are the competencies needed for creating and using implementable managerial work practices for multisite/location management?

Outsourcing research in the context of work organizational management is a research field which needs both knowledge from information systems/software development (IS/SD) research, organizational development and work process management research. Evaluation and performance management literature is also needed in this project.

Our methodological approach in this project will be design/action research with participating companies [22] [23]. In design research researchers and company representatives are both creating new artefacts and evaluating them. It involves interplay of theoretical backgrounds and empirical investigations to produce viable, practical outcomes.

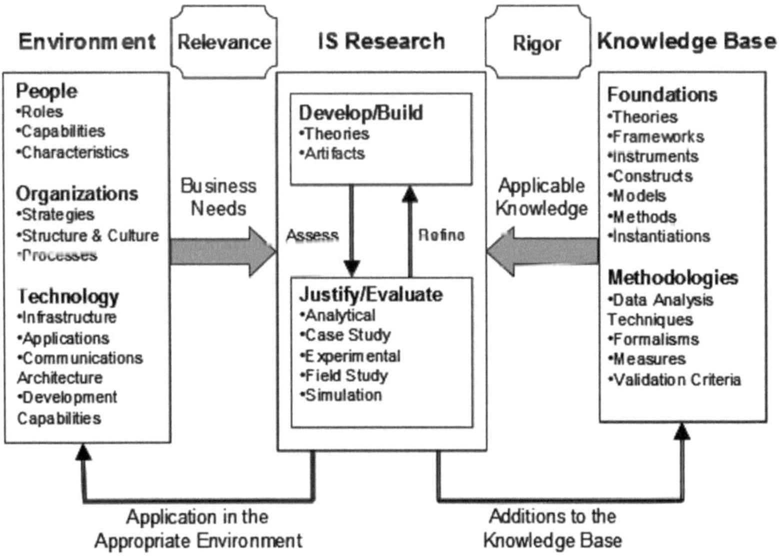

Fig. 1. Information systems research in design research [22]

4 Participating Companies; Minicase Descriptions

4.1 Minicase 1: New Ways of Managing Productivity – Case C PLC

Our first company, Case C, is an international software and *services* company specialized in telecommunications industry. The headquarters is located in Finland and in addition to that it has offices in 16 other locations in Asia, Europe, Middle-East and Australia. Net sales of the C group was 82.7 MEUR and the personnel approx. 700 employees on Y2013.

Since 1986 case C has helped more than 290 service providers across 86 countries to meet over one billion subscribers' communications and infotainment needs. C's service fulfilment, mediation, charging and policy control, and predictive social analytics products with implementation and professional services enable service providers to automate customer interactions and other business decisions for creating revenue, reduce costs and lessen churn.

The starting point in the DD-SCALE project of C is *the increased interest in improving the monitoring of the capabilities involved in the efficiency monitoring practices. Secondly, the company is seeking solution to monitor the site specific efficiency figures that would increase the capability of managing the distribution of C's global research, development and innovation (RDI) resources.*

C's solutions are built within its global RDI network. Various metrics are collected from sites, teams and programs, which are shared in multiple dashboards. RDI productivity is an area, where only limited metrics are available. The case company aims to get more fact-based information and tools from the DD-SCALE project for monitoring and managing productivity of the teams. A key strength of this project is data normalization across multiple companies.

4.2 Minicase 2: Advanced, Large Scale SD Work Evaluation – Case S PLC

The second company, Case S, is a large telecom network software and technology company with the full year sales of S 11.2 BEUR on Y2013. The number of employees is plus 20 000. Company claims to be as one of the world's top three mobile network infrastructure vendors serving more than 90 of the world's 100 largest tele-operators.

Case S's research interest in DD-SCALE project is the development of RDI efficiency analytics. So far the company is using a key performance indicator (KPI) approaches in evaluation of its RDI efficiency and the more conventional financial reporting, too. Case S has not only offshored activities but is also onshoring a n umber of IT development resources from local service companies.

However, the monitoring of less visible factors, which are more intellectual in nature, escapes beyond the current system efficacy. In addition to that, the multitude of the complexities outside the company's borders in S's ecosystem imply factors influencing on company performance but are not currently considered in the S's performance analytics. The more far-reaching vision of the results of the DD-SCALE project is improving the decision making methodology of the distribution management of new sites globally. The current methodology would benefit from the findings in improving the software design work performance metrics.

4.3 Minicase 3: Common Innovation System Boost – Case A PLC

The third organisation, Case A, is a part of a global leading company in power and automation technologies with high market positions in selected main business areas. A Group has more than 150 000 employees in about 100 countries with 29 BEUR in revenues on Y2012. A Group is organized in five global divisions. The participating partner, case A, is the Collaborative Production Management software business (CPM).

The main interest of CPM unit in the DD-SCALE project is the overall effectiveness of A's innovation system for CPM software business that needs to be improved to facilitate further business growth of the global business in high growth markets. This means in particular accelerating the idea-to-market deployment speed in the end-to-end process from innovation idea to its actual deployment in the marketplace. The overall innovation system covers multiple A business units addressing the various industrial markets and the common software platform technology development unit at the corporate level, which is fulfilling the common technology needs of all the target markets. The distributed organization and global nature of business make this challenge particularly interesting.

4.4 Minicase 4: Organisational Development in a Multisite Environment – Case N

The fourth and last company, Case N, is 25 years old company, specialized in the B2B software business providing solutions for ship design and operations The company has approximately 175 employees and offices and/or representatives in 8 countries such as Japan, Korea, China, Singapore, India and Romania. More than 95 % of its 18 MEUR turnover comes from exports and their business operations are truly global. The company has grown steadily and is expanding both geographically and in sales development. The RDI resources are located in three countries: Finland, India and Romania. Since March 2014 case N is owned by a Japanese company and taken out of the stock exchange.

Starting point for the DD-SCALE project in the case N is linked to the continuous development of organization. Creation of the most efficient organizational forms demands enhanced fact-based metrics. Especially, a more accurate and reliable performance reporting of different RDI sites and teams is needed.

Compared to the other business functions, software development is more collaborative in nature. This is seen especially in commonly used modern process frameworks for software engineering. Currently the most favored way to organize the software development is based on agile methods such as SCRUM..

Therefore, the focus of N in the DD-SCALE project is centered on the research of the collaboration and performance of software engineering teams in the multisite IT-organization such as case N. That means, for example, key performance indicators to monitor and determine the most efficient form of the organizations and distribution of work to maximize the overall performance of the company.

5 Conclusive Remarks

Our collaboration network of both research and educational institutes and global-scale software development organizations gives us an excellent viewpoint to both evaluate current situation and create new models and approaches for practice. Collaboration is ensured through active working with case companies and investigating on-going and background research. As it is noted by Prikladnicki and Audy [24] communications, methods, culture, and process details are just some of the facets of the unique characteristics of global software engineering environments. In the next ten years many of software development companies need to find their own competitive position in the evolving software markets, create a pattern of work practices capable for distribution of work, format new managerial practices for performance management in global value networks and promote innovations in open environments

Acknowledgments. The authors would like to express their gratitude to TEKES - the Finnish Funding Agency for Technology and Innovation and participating companies for commitment and start of the DD-SCALE research project and fostering collaboration in the ICT industry.

References

1. Ruohonen, M.: Nearshoring or Offshoring – Comparing ITO and BPO practices between India and Europe. In: Proceedings of the 6th CISTM Annual Conference on Information Science, Technology & Management, New Delhi, India (2008)
2. Ruohonen, M.: Offshoring from Brazil or India – A European View. In: Proceedings of the 7th CISTM Annual Conference on Information Science, Technology & Management, Gurgaon, India (2009)
3. Adelakun, O., Ruohonen, M.: Demystification of Latin Americas Offshore Outsourcing Destination. In: Proceedings of the 8th CISTM Annual Conference on Information Science, Technology & Management, Tampere, Finland (2010)
4. Lacity, M.C., Willcocks, L.: Global information technology outsourcing: In search of business advantage. John Wiley & Sons (2001)
5. Lacity, M., Willcocks, L., Cullen, S.: Global IT Outsourcing: 21st Century Search For Business Advantage. John Wiley & Sons (2008)
6. Saxena, K.B.C., Ruohonen, M., Bharadwaj, S.S.: Strategic Outsourcing of Engineering Processes Using Agile Methods. In: Proceedings of the 8th CISTM Annual Conference on Information Science, Technology & Management, Tampere, Finland (2010)
7. Walsham, G., Robey, F., Sahay, S.: Foreword: Special issue on information systems in developing countries. MIS Quarterly 31(2), 317–326 (2007)
8. Oshri, I., Kotlarsky, J., Willcocks, L.: Managing Dispersed Expertise in IT Offshore Outsourcing: Lessons from Tata Consultancy Services. MIS Quarterly Executive 6(2), 53–65 (2007)

9. Gartner: IT Spending Forecast, Q4 2013 Update (2014), http://www.gartner.com/technology/research/it-spending-forecast/ (checked February 11, 2014)
10. The Hindu Business Line (2014), http://www.thehindubusinessline.com/industry-and-economy/info-tech/indian-it-exports-to-grow-1214-in-fy14-nasscom/article4407167.ece (checked February 11, 2014)
11. Heeks, R.: India's Software Industry: State Policy, Liberalization and Industrial Development. Sage Publications (1996)
12. Reddy, A., Ryman, A.: Software development and delivery performance measurement and management: Optimizing business value in software. IBM (2009), https://jazz.net/library/article/432/ (checked February 11, 2014)
13. Hudson, V.F.: The human touch: Cohesive cross-cultural teams begin with savvy relationship management. Industrial Engineer. Institute of Industrial Engineers, Inc. (IIE) (2007), http://www.highbeam.com/doc/1G1-169311055.html (checked February 11, 2014)
14. Thomas, D.C., Inkson, K.C.: Cultural intelligence: People skills for global business. Berrett-Koehler Publishers, San Francisco (2004)
15. Hofstede, G.: Culture's consequences. Sage Publications (1980)
16. Hofstede, G.: Cultures and organizations: Software of the Mind. McGraw-Hill, London (1991)
17. Hofstede, G.: Culture's consequence: International differences in work related values. Revised edition. Sage Publications (2001)
18. Trompenaars, F., Hampden-Turner, C.: Riding the Waves of Culture: Understanding Cultural Diversity in Global Business. Irwin (1998)
19. House, R., Hanges, P., Javidan, M., Dorfman, P., Gupta, V.: Culture, leadership, and organizations: The GLOBE study of 62 societies. Sage Publications (2004)
20. Jacob, N.: Cross-cultural investigations: Emerging concepts. Journal of Organizational Change Management 18(5), 514–528 (2005)
21. Fontaine, R.: Cross-cultural management: Six perspectives. Cross Cultural Management: An International Journal 14(2), 125–135 (2007)
22. Hevner, A.R., March, S.T., Park, J., Ram, S.: Design science in information systems research. MIS Quarterly 28(1), 75–105 (2004)
23. Jones, C.: Software Engineering Best Practices: Lessons from Successful Projects in the Top Companies. McGraw-Hill (2010)
24. Prikladnicki, R., Audy, J.L.N.: Managing Global Software Engineering: A Comparative Analysis of Offshore Outsourcing and the Internal Offshoring of Software Development. Information Systems Management 29(3), 216–232 (2012), doi:10.1080/10580530.2012.687313

Developing Enterprise Architecture Skills: A Developing Country Perspective

Irja Shaanika and Tiko Iyamu

Namibia University of Science and Technology, Windhoek, Namibia
inshaanika@gmail.com, tiyamu@polytechnic.edu.na

Abstract. Through different approaches, organisations strive to evolve their competitiveness, as well as their addressing their operational and strategic needs. Some organisations employ Enterprise Architecture (EA), to bridge the gap between the business and IT, and to providing strategic goals. However, there exists scarcity of EA Skills in many developing countries. This could be attributed to the uniqueness of the discipline. The skills are instrumental in the development and implementation of the EA. What is even more challenging is that EA skills cannot be developed from any training facility, due to its nature of specialisation and seniority of the specialists. The limited training facilities contribute to the scarcity of EA skills in many developing countries, which have impact skill and transfer, and other resource developmental factors. This study therefore explored how and where EA skills can be developed, and what constitute the competency. The study was carried out in Namibia, using the survey technique, in the data collection. Some of the findings include education and training, leadership, and political implications on EA skill development.

Keywords: Information Technology, Enterprise Architecture, Skill, Competency, Training and Education.

1 Introduction

Organisations face challenges of business processes and information technology (IT) infrastructures change due to the driving factors, of globalization, technology explosion, and rapid growth on organizational structure [1]. In an attempt to addressing the challenges, some organisations employed approaches, such as the Enterprise Architecture (EA), to guide and manage their business and IT challenges. Over the years, the EA has increasingly become an important discipline for the management and governance of both business and IT processes and activities [2].

Many organisations consider the EA approach to be of importance to their processes and activities. The approach is often used to translate business vision and strategy into business and technical requirements, periodically. It is argued that EA assist organisations, to create, communicate and improve the key requirements, principles and models, that describes the current and future state of the enterprise in an evolutionary manner [3]. However, the use of EA depend on how it is understood, defined and scoped [4].

D. Passey and A. Tatnall (Eds.): KCICTP/ITEM 2014, IFIP AICT 444, pp. 52–61, 2014.

Individuals including organisations define the EA differently. The definition is informed and guided by their objectives, and understanding. The definition is critical because it shapes how EA is developed and implemented. Iyamu [5] argued that lack of understanding leads to incompatibility and confusion about the views on the definitions, objectives, process and phases that are required for the development and implementation of the EA.

The EA is a discipline in the field of IT. It is considered to be a unique and highly specialised area of the IT field. It is applied from both operational and strategic perspectives, in many organisations. According to Hiekkanen, Korhonen and Mykkänen [6], EA is used as strategic tool, to holistically address the gap between the business and IT units in many organisations. Some organisations employs EA for governance and management of business and IT processes and activities. Due to the uniqueness and the specialised nature of EA, the skills are scarce to find. In Walrad et al. [7], they emphasically argued that EA skill are not easily available.

Many organisations have not been able to develop and implement the EA primarily because they do not have skilled personnel. What is even more challenging is the availabilty of the training facilities (places). Very few institutions of higher learning offer EA as a course, in the World, and very limited in Africa. The skills are mainly developed through trainings which are offered by professional bodies, such as The Open Group Architecture Framwork (TOGAF), and Gartner Inc. As a result, many organisations as well as researchers are puzzeled by how and where to develop such skills [8], [9], [7]. This has made some organisations to consider developing the skills internally. Erosa and Arroyo [10] argued that some skills, which are of technical nature could be best developed through experience but others are best arquired during proffesional studies.

Skill is defined as the ability to take what you know and apply it to create a desired output [7]. Most oftenly, institutions of higher learning are regarded as organisations for creating and equiping graduates with necessary skills, and foundation preparing them for industries. According to [11], institutions of higher learning are the cradle of learning, theorising, and research; hence they could be used as platform for developing EA skills. In this regard, the development of EA skills is lacking in the Africa continent. This is the main motivation for this study, which objectives were to understand and examine how EA skills could be developed, and the impact.

However many organisations are challenged by how and where to develop EA skills. The article presents the findings from an investigation on why EA skills are needed in the organisations. The research question was why is EA not deployed in the organisations? This includes understanding what is needed to develop such skills as well as the implications of not having EA.

2 Enterprise Architecture and Training

The EA is defined as "the organising logic for business process and IT infrastructure, reflecting the integration and standardisation requirements of the company's operating model" [12]. The purpose of an EA is to provide guidance for business process and their associated information systems toward achieving the organisation's goals according to [1].

In many organisations, the business strategy and IT strategy are often disjointed [13]. Gøtze [9] argued that in many enterprises, IT department do not develop IT strategy in accordance to business strategy, which result in effortless IT planning. This is attributed to the root source, for lack of alignment in some organisations. Alignment is managed at a senior level (in accordance to structure) in many organisations. Some organisations identify the need to make use of the EA as a bridging tool between business strategy and IT strategy [13]. EA is therefore used and managed by senior employees in the organisations that deploy it. According to Iacob, Jonkers and Quartel[14], closing the gap between the business and IT maximises alignment, thus reducing duplications and inconsistences among business processes and IT activities. Business and IT are distinct disciplines influencing each other and their coordination is necessary for organisation goals achievements [14]. Therefore, EA intention is to enable organisation in addresing and achieving the balance between business effeciency and IT [15].

EA promotes the belief that an enterprise, as a complex system, can be designed and managed in an orderly manner, to achieving better overall performance [16]. Such performances shape organisation's competitiveness and sustainability. [17] pointed out that EA helps in the communication of key elements that explains the operations and strategic intent of an organization. As such, the implementation of EA helps organisations to innovate and engineer change through stability and flexibility [18]. However, the development and implementation continue to be a challenging process in many organisations. According to [15], EA experiences both technical and non-technical challenges. While Kaisler et al.[3] identified that the challenges are rarely technical, but they arises from factors, such as political, project management, and organizational issues, and weaknesses.

The development and deployment of EA is carried out through its domains, which include business, information, application and technical architectural, and guided by the organisation's goals and objectives [17]. It is through the analysis of the domains' relationships that EA becomes a valuable management tool [19]. According to Iyamu [20], the development and implementations of EA is based on how the organisation defines and understand the concept. Hence the skill-set is crucial.

The definition and understanding of EA is based on the product of organisation EA skills. [21] argued that due to different approaches that are applied by EA, including their tailoring and adaptation to specific domains, highly skilled personnel are required. Wagter et al., [8] defined EA architects as professionals with competencies that are responsible for the creation of organisational strategies. According to Wagter et al. [8], competences represent a dynamic combination of knowledge, expertise, attitudes and responsibilities. An enterprise architects develops IT strategy and enable decisions for for designing and developing and deploying IT to support the business process [22].

The EA is developed and implemented holizontally or vetrically, using the enterprise domain approach, respectively. Steghuis and Proper [23] differentiated between EA architect and domain architects, stating that EA architects covers the breadth of business and IT, and the domain architects focus on the specific aspect of the enterprise, such as business, information, application and techical. Gøtze [9] categorised enterprise architects into core, implicit, and applied. The artects form enterprise achitecture team that is capable of conducting gap and business requirement analysis at various levels of the enterprise[8].

EA enable an overview picture of how IT supports the different business processes, and how they support the operating model that is choosen to facilitate organisational activities [10]. Across the organisation, a common understanding is required between IT and business operating models. Enterprise architects provide such understanding by translating and transforming knowledge across the organisation boundaries. This includes the boundaries between organisations and vendors, and between business and IT [9]. Hence architects have crucial roles in finding the relevant varieties for the different contexts, often in the form of principles, standards, patterns, and policies.

Relevance and context are attributed to the rapid changes in organisations. Change in business environments causes business to change its processes, services and products, for competetiveness [24]. Changes also influence the IT artefacts in the organisations, as new systems are bought, developed or reused, to refocus on new competitveness. Khan and Zedan [24] argued that business and IT continue to change, and EA is used as a supporting tool. Thus [20] asserts that EA is an agent of change, in the quest for competitiveness. It formalizes the organisation and its information systems to manage the risks that are related to changes [25]. To keep up with the accelerating pace of technology, enterprises should employ the EA [9]. [10] Also argued that enterprises should not just be concerned with business and IT alignments, but also assure employees competecies are aligned with such strategies.

Enterprise architect therefore, need to know how the organisation businesses operate and how decisions are made, and how knowledge is applies when modeling the enterprise architecture [7]. Modeling is essential to describing and understanding EA [3]. [25] elaborated that knowing how enterprise works is important for architects, in order to be able to identify the strengths and weakness of the organisation, and lead gaps recongnition .

3 Research Methodology

The study was carried in Namibia, where it was considered to be esscsntial due to the limited number of EA skills in the country, as at the time of the study. Based on the objective of the study, which was to the development of the EA skills and the impact of such skills, the qualitative research method was applied.

The semi-structured interview technique was employed in the collection of data, for two main reason: richness and flexibility. The technique was selected primarily because it enables the gathering of rich data, through insightful view and opinion from the participants [26]. The semi-structured interview technique allows flexibility during data collection, this include instant probing of participants answers. According to [27], the interviewer has the flexibility to rephrase and restructure the questions, during the interviews. For emphasis sake, we cite [26], who explained that the interviewer may ask additional questions in response to what he or she considered to be significant statement from the interviewee.

A total of ten information technology (IT) specialists were interviewed. The ten individuals, irrespective of their affiliate (employer), are labelled PAS01 to PAS10. This was to respect and maint confidentiality. The interviewees were from different organisations in the country. The interviewees were selected based on their interest in EA, and their availability. A guide, such as the use of the same questions and format, was used in the interview sections, this was to maintain uniformity and consistency.

The data was interpretively analysed. The interpretivism approach was followed primarily because it allows the researcher to analyse interviewees' subjective reasoning [26]. The core idea of interpretivism is understanding the subjective meaning of persons [28]. To attain this, the researcher uses his or her skills as a social being to try to understand how others understand the world around them [29].

4 Enterprise Architecture Skills and Competency

Enterprise architecture skilled personnel holds the positions of architects, in the forms of Enterprise Architect or domain Architect, such as Information Architect. Their roles and responsibilities defers, but are not entire independent of each other. However, organisations sometimes differ in the tasks that they assign to the architects. According to one of the interviewees, an IT manger from a financial institution, *"we need architects to be able to utilize our resources effectively within organisation (PAS03)". We need architects to carry out that function primarily because they are the most highly specialised people within the IT department.* Another participant, who is employed in one of the Government ministries at the time of the study emphasised that *"because they are specialist individual in their domains, they bring in high level of focus and concentration into the organisation (PAS01)".*

As depicted in Figure 1 below, the Enterprise Architects focus on the entire organisational needs, while the domain Architects concentrates on the areas of their specialisations. A manager briefly explained the role of technical architects: *"The architects are needed to provide guidance on technological artefacts, as well as the guidelines through which they are aligned with organisation objectives (PAS09)".* Similar to the role of technical architects, the business architects are responsible for the strategic modelling of processes and activities. In the view of business managers with one of the mining companies in Namibia, *"we need business architects to define the structure of process flow in the organisation, and build performances measurement model PAS04)".*

Architectural process is required across the entire units of the organisation that deploys the EA. The need often focuses on unique and critical areas of the organisation. One of the participants, who manage software development in an insurance company, opined as follow: *"We need architects to help us with references in terms of maturity, and they also have the capability to analyse risks. They can see beyond the normal view of organisational operation (PAS02)".*

Due to the significant of the EA to the organisations, it is critical to have knowledgeable personnel in the field, thus, creating knowledge hub. Many of those who participated in the study believe that the development of architects should be at the institutions of higher learning. This could be attributed to the wide scope, which range from software development and implementation, business and systems analysis, business applications, project management, to networking and operating systems. According some of the participants: *"If it was not in higher institution, I would probably have no idea, and I would have not known what exactly enterprise architecture is actually all about"; and PAS10 - I think that the development of architects can start in institutions of higher learning, and continue into organisations".*

Many organisations are faced with strong competition from their competitors, making case for approaches, such as EA, which enable and support competitiveness. Thus, however, require developing and leveraging EA skills, appropriately. EA skills provide an organisation with understanding of how business strategy should be supported by IT). Such understanding is fundamental in defining the relationship between business and IT units, and how their alignment can enhance business competitiveness.

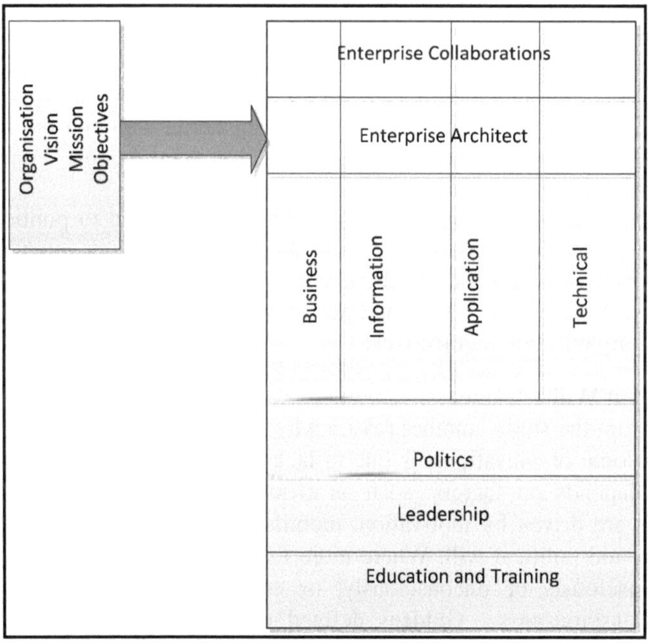

Fig. 1. EA Skill Development

The importance, including the roles and responsibilities of architects in the organisations seems to be well understood. But yet, many organisations do not employ the approach in their operations. The fundamental question is what this study seeks to examine, "why is EA not deployed in the organisations"? Based on the analysis, which was interpretively carried out, the factors hindering the deployment of the EA in organisation include lack of education and training (skilled personnel), lack of technical leadership, and lack of political will by many organisations.

The factors, as shown in figure 1, are discussed as follows:

i. Education and Training

The shortage of skills was attributed to lack of education or training, or both. The skills cannot be developed based on experience alone. Education of enterprise architecture are provided through institutions of higher learning. This is because of the theorised nature of the course offered by the institutions. Training are considered to be hands-on excercises. Training of EA is often offered by professional bodies, such as TOGAF and Gertner Inc.

Due to the specialised nature of the field, the Architects needs both education and training to equip themselves. The edication provides them with the knowledge and skill to be, and act as architecs. The training enhances their competence in the field of specialisation, as enterprise architect or domain architect. The education and trainings enabled the architects to be technical leaders in the organisations.

ii. Technical Leadership

Based on the highly skilled and levels of specialisation nature of the Architects, they are relied upon in the organisations, supposedly so. As such, they should provide Leadership, to guide, motivate, and mobilise colleagues and other employees in the organisation. Also, through their leadership roles, the architects are expected to create the vision and culture of architecture in the organisation. Through the leadership, it would be easier and more flexible to govern and manage people, complexity, and document processes and activities within the organisation.

Some of the leadership components and could be attributed to political will. It is sometimes difficult to disassociate leadership from political interplay. This is attributed to the role of a leader, to drive and lead in the network that the actor finds his or herself. You cannot be an architect f you cannot lead the people towards achieving the organisation's objectives.

iii. Political Will

Empirically from the study, another reason why the EA approach is not considered or employed in some organisations, is due to lack of political will to do so. Enterprise architecture depends on factors, such as efficiency and effectiveness to succeed. These factors are driven by motivation, mobilisation and resources, which manifest from politics, and political will. Where more than one person is involved, politics is involved, consciously or unconsciously, or even so, what Giddens refers to as practical unconsciousness. Giddens defined practical unconsciousness as "What actors know (believe) about social conditions, including especially the conditions of their own action, but cannot express discursively; no bar of repression, however, protects practical consciousness as is the case with the unconscious" [30].

The deployment and exercises of the EA processes and activities can be political. This is primarily because of the roles and responsibilities which are associated to it. To some extent, they are made powerful, and take away some functions from certain individuals and groups in the organisation.

Institutions of higher learning need to begin to introduce Enterprise Architecture as a course, at both undergraduate and postgraduate levels. As revealed in this study, the curriculum of the course should encompass components, such as technical, Leadership, and Politics know-how.

5 Conclusion

Enterprise architecture is considered to be a field that require highly skilled and compeent personnel, due to to its role in the organisation. The EA is intended to bridge the gap between the business and IT units, as well drive the strategies of the organisation from both bsiness and technology perspectives. The roles of the EA require the personnel to be highly skilled, through education and trainings.

As revealed in the study, EA skills and are not easily accessible or available. The skill is beyond technical know-how, which includes non-technical factors, such as leadership and politics. As such, the developers of education and training of the EA curriculum need to take into cognisance, this include non-technical factors.

The findings from this study should boost the confidence levels of managers of business and IT in organisations, particularly in Africa, where EA skills are lacking in a significant high proportion. The study exposes the managers to learn some critical factors, thoughs and beliefs about EA. It hereby make them know what are required, to develop and implement EA in their organisations. The study also reassures sponsors and investors on the significant of the EA in organisations.

References

1. Cekerekil, S., Mticahit, G., Emin, B.: An Agile Approach for Converting Enterprise Architectures. IEEE, Intanbul (2013)
2. Osterlind, M., Johnson, P., Karnati, K., Lagerstro, R., Valja, M.: Enterprise Architecture Evaluation using Utility theory. In: 17th IEEE International Enterprise Distributed Object Computing Conference Workshops, pp. 347–351. IEEE (2013)
3. Kaisler, S., Armour, F., Valivullah, M.: Enterprise Architecting: Critical Problems. In: Proceedings of the 38th Hawaii International Conference on System sciences (2005)
4. Schekkerman, J.: How to suvive in the Junglo of Enterprise Architecture Frameworks (2009)
5. Iyamu, T.: Enterprise Architecture As Information Technology Strategy. In: IEEE Conference on Commerce and Enterprise Computing, pp. 82–88. IEEE Computer Society (2011)
6. Hiekkanen, K., Mykkänen, J., Korhonen, J.: Architects' perceptions on EA use: An empirical study. In: 15th IEEE Conference on Business Informatics (CBI), Vienna, Austria, July 15-8 (2013)
7. Walrad, C., Lane, M., Wallk, J., Hirst, D.: Architecting a Profession. IT Pro., pp. 42–49 (January/February 2014)
8. Wagter, R., Henderik, A.: Proper, & Witte, D. Enterprise Architecture: A strategic specialismα. In: 14th International Conference on Commerce and Enterprise Computing, pp. 1–8. IEEE (2012)

9. Gøtze, J.: The Changing Role of the Enterprise Architect. In: 17th IEEE International Enterprise Distributed Object Computing Conference Workshops, pp. 319–326. IEEE (2013)
10. Erosa, V., Arroyo, P.: Technology Management Competences Supporting the Business Strategy. In: PICMET 2009 Proceedings, pp. 2190–2199. PICMET, Oregon (2009)
11. Yang, Z., Qixial, L.: Innovation Pattern Analysis of The Industry-University-Research Cooperation. In: 2012 International Symposium on Information Technology in Medicine and Education, pp. 274–277. IEEE (2012)
12. Ross, J., Weill, P., Robertson, D.: Enterprise Architecture as a Strategy: Creating a Foundation for Business Excution. Havard Business Press, United States of America (2006)
13. Jin, M., Peng, W., Kung, D.: Research of Information System Technology Architecture. In: 2010 2nd International Conference on Industrial and Information Systems, pp. 293–296. IEEE (2010)
14. Iacob, M.-E., Jonkers, H., Quartel, D.: Capturing Business Strategy And Value In Enterprise Architecture To Support Portfolio Valuation. In: IEEE 16th International Enterprise Distributed Object Computing Conference, pp. 11–19. IEEE (2012)
15. Iyamu, T.: Theoritical Analysis Strategic Implementation of Enterprise Architecture. International Journal of Actor-Network Theory and Technological Innovation 2(3), 17–32 (2010)
16. Rosasco, N., Dehlinger, J.: Business Architecture Elicitation for Enterprise Architecture: VMOST versus Conventional Strategy Capture. In: The 9th International Conference on Software Engineering Research, Management and Applications, Baltimore, pp. 153–157 (2001)
17. Alonso, I., Verdún, J., Caro, E.: The IT Implicated Within The Enterprise Architecture Model. In: Analysis of Architecture Models and Focus IT Architecture Domain, pp. 1–5 (2010)
18. Rouhani, B., Mahrin, M., Nikpay, F., Nikfard, P.: A Comparison Enterprise Architecture Implementation Methodologies. In: International Conference on Informatics and Creative Multimedia, pp. 1–5. IEEE (2013)
19. Xueying, W., Xiongwei, Z.: Aligning Business and IT Using Enterprise Architecture, 1-5 (2008)
20. Iyamu, T.: Enterprise architecture: From concept to Practise. Heidelberg Press, Australia (2013)
21. Antunes, G., Barateiro, J., Becker, C., Borbinha, J., Vieira, R.: Modeling Contextual Concerns in Enterprise Architecture. In: 15th IEEE International Enterprise Distributed Object Computing Conference Workshops, pp. 3–10. IEEE (2011)
22. Armour, F., Kaisler, S., Huizinga, E.: Business and Enterprise Architecture: Processes, Approches and Challenges. In: 45th Hawaii International Conference on System Sciences, p. 4229. IEEE (2012)
23. Steghuis, C., Proper, E.: Competencies and Responsibilities of Enterprise Architects. In: Dietz, J.L.G., Albani, A., Barjis, J. (eds.) CIAO! 2008 and EOMAS 2008. LNBIP, vol. 10, pp. 93–107. Springer, Heidelberg (2008)
24. Khan, M., Zedan, H.: Alignment Strategies and frameworks in co-Evolution of Business and Information Technology. In: International Conference on Information Networking and Automation, pp. 133–136. IEEE (2010)
25. Lakhrouit, J., Baïna, K.: State of the Art of the Maturity Models to an Evaluation of the Enterprise Architecture. IEEE, Rabat (2013)

26. Rowley, J., Jones, R., Vassiliou, M., Hanna, S.: Using card-based games to enhance the value of semi-structured interviews. International Journal of Market Research 54(1) (April 14, 2011)
27. Draper, A., Swift, J.: Qualitative research in nutrition and dietetics: Data collection issues. Journal of Human Nutrition and Dietetics 24(1), 3–13 (2010)
28. Goldkuhl, G.: Pragmatism vs interpretivism in qualitative information systems research. European Journal of Information Systems 21(1), 135–146 (2012)
29. O'Donoghue, T.: Planning Your Qualitative Research Project: An Introduction to interpretivist research in education. Routledge, New York (2006)
30. Giddens, A.: The Constitution of Society: Outline of the Theory of Structuration. Polity Press, Cambridge (1984)

Analysis of Real-Life Working Processes, Competencies and Operational Fields for the Usage in Vocational IT Education - Results of an Empirical Study Based on Job Offers

Simone Opel and Axel Wellesen

University of Duisburg-Essen, Essen, Germany
simone.opel@uni-due.de, axel.wellesen@gmx.de

Abstract. One part of professional IT (information and communication technologies) and CS (computer science) education in Germany takes place in vocational schools. For deeper interlocking of theory and practice, the curriculum is oriented towards the concept of learning fields ("Lernfelder") which are based on real-life working processes. As this concept differs from traditional curricular concepts, teachers only seldom put this concept into practice due to a lack of appropriate teaching material and deeper and valid knowledge on possible underlying working processes. For this reason, the following question arose: What are these working processes? To answer this question, we conducted an empirical study and analysed 100 job offers for computer specialists from online job agencies to explore their task descriptions and the demanded requirements. These descriptions have been assigned to a specially developed categorisation system which made it possible to reference these real-life operational fields and demanded competencies to the curriculum and its learning fields. As a result it appears that most of the described tasks are directly related to the technical aspects of IT Systems. The most demanded requirements have been social skills and good skills in English language. On this basis, a next step in this project will be the development of a general description of all competencies to be gained for the profession of computer specialist during vocational training.

Keywords: Vocational IT Education, Vocational CS Education, Empirical Study, Learning Fields, Operational Fields, CS Working Areas, Working Skills, Working Processes.

1 Introduction

Dual vocational education is a core element of the German educational system (2012: 551.272 new beginners in vocational education ([1], p. 7) vs. 495.088 first-year-students [3]). Dual vocational education consists of practical training at a company and theoretical education at school. In contrast to general secondary schools, the main intention of vocational schools is to teach relevant topics for the students' professional life to support development of working skills and professional action

D. Passey and A. Tatnall (Eds.): KCICTP/ITEM 2014, IFIP AICT 444, pp. 62–67, 2014.

competency ([2], p. 14). Therefore, the curriculum also for the profession as computer specialist ("Fachinformatiker") is oriented towards the concept of learning fields. Learning fields describe the competencies that students should achieve and specific content the students should know ([2], p. 10). For a better integration of theory and practice, each learning field has been based on characteristic real-life working processes. They are supposed to be put into practice by implementing "learning situations". Although this concept leaves room for creative implementation and therefore contains high potential for the development of varied activity-oriented learning situations, the concept is rarely put into practice.

To explore these reasons, Opel and Brinda [5] [7] conducted an study with vocational school teachers. They could show that teachers in general are not familiar with the concept, but open-minded and motivated to implement it. However, they also revealed that "a significant part of the participants in the survey does not really know what it means to implement learning fields into learning situations. "([7], p. 156). The study also revealed that there are publications about the basics of the concept, but only very few about teaching with learning fields. In another interview study among IT and CS Training companies, Opel and Brinda [6] asked for typical working processes in the field of IT and CS. They came to the conclusion that most working processes cover main aspects of different learning fields, which corresponds to the results of the present work. However, the interviewed trainers mentioned that they would like to see more interdisciplinary projects, as well as activity-oriented and self-organised learning methods being put into practice at vocational schools. This could be achieved by consequently implementing the concept of learning fields.

To solve this problem, there is a larger project aiming at the development of a normative competence structure model, exemplary teaching material, tools and guidelines for creating learning situations using the learning field concept as well as a description of competencies the students should gain. Since learning fields are based on real-life working processes, this work contributes to these intentions by acquiring and analysing real-life operational fields, working processes and demanded competencies and how they are weighted in vocational reality.

2 Related Work

To enhance the acceptance of the curricular concept of learning fields, extended co-operation between companies and vocational schools could be useful. Repp et al. [11] discussed a project where apprentices as computer specialists for application development work on real projects from a nearby software company. After designing, realising and testing, the students present the project at the company and hand over the developed software. This way, a close connection with the vocational world can be achieved, which increases the motivation of the students. Furthermore, it offers the opportunity to integrate current technological and organisational developments from companies in vocational schools. Especially in the field of software development, there are chances for activity-oriented implementations of the according learning field by following professional software development process definition and thus represent real-life working processes. In contrast, there are no such implementations of learning fields concerning the field of IT Systems and networks. Instead, topics are treated in separate lessons and not in a wider context. This can cause problems when it comes to transfer the skills to vocational praxis [4].

Another study among over 600 companies and over 1000 apprentices [9] [10] explored IT working processes and education in business practice. The study revealed that lessons in vocational schools need to be improved because apprentices considered the demanded level to be too low. Furthermore, the apprentices criticised the lack of real-life relevance of the curriculum which could lead to a negative image of vocational schools. To improve this situation, the "SEDIKO" project aimed at designing learning fields as well as learning rooms [8]. After analysing and implementing the eleven learning fields, the conclusion was that these learning fields would only partially represent real-life working processes, since each single learning field only represents a part of a working process. The whole process can only be covered by their sum. This leads to the question whether there are learning fields that cover more of the demanded skills and competencies than others – and whether they should therefore be put into focus by vocational teachers.

All these studies confirm that the concept of learning fields seems to have a high potential which is not used consistently. A solution to this problem could be - besides a comprehensive description of competencies needed for the profession of computer specialist - the support of teachers by providing them exemplary material as well as guidelines for designing lessons based on the most demanded real-life working processes and skills.

3 Methodology

For a nationwide overview, we retrieved empirical data from 100 job offers listed in four of the biggest online job agencies: stepstone, monster, jobscout24 and the job market of the Federal Employment Agency ("Jobbörse der Bundesagentur für Arbeit"). Each job offer was analysed according to the demanded requirements and the described tasks. Both aspects were collected in two separate profiles. Requirements represent the competencies directly demanded by the companies. These include personal, operational and professional competencies as well as formal requirements and experience. Tasks represent the vocational operational fields and describe the tasks themselves as well as the area in which they take place (see fig. 1). Based on this data, a categorisation was developed by using an inductive approach. We defined a multi-level category system for requirements and tasks each. The resulting categories have been directly derived from job descriptions by using methods of content analysis and will be described in detail in the next section.

4 Results

To structure the data, we defined three generic terms in the task profile (Systems Administration, Software Engineering, Other) and five in the requirements profile (IT-technical area, Support and Documentation, Soft Skills and Other, Operational Processes and Structures, Formal Requirements). Each of them was further divided into several subcategories (see fig. 1).

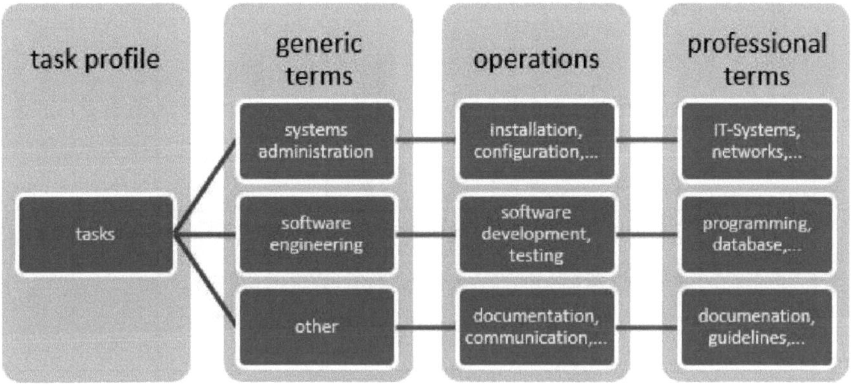

Fig. 1. Example from the task profile

The core elements which structure the generic terms, are operations (e.g. installation, support) or competencies (e.g. the ability to communicate) and professional terms that give a more detailed description of the area in which the operations take place (e.g. installation of software/hardware).

The core elements which structure the generic terms, are operations (e.g. installation, support) or competencies (e.g. the ability to communicate) and professional terms that give a more detailed description of the area in which the operations take place (e.g. installation of software/hardware).

Thus, it is possible to reference the retrieved data with the curriculum and the goals and contents of the learning fields. Each task and each requirement was put into one of the categories by using keywords from their description. Categories that described similar things or could not clearly be divided have been summarised afterwards. At last, the resulting categories were assigned to the eleven learning fields in two steps. The first assignment was based on direct references, which means that the tasks and requirements described in the category had to be directly mentioned in the definition of the learning field. The second assignment was based on indirect references. These represent the previous knowledge that is additionally needed to successfully accomplish the required tasks. Figure 2 shows an excerpt of a matrix which contains the correlation between the three most demanded skills / working processes and the respective learning fields.

The largest number of mentioned tasks with a direct reference to the skills and contents were listed in the learning fields that cover IT Systems in general ("Maintenance of IT Systems", "Simple IT Systems" and "Networked IT Systems"). This emphasises the well-filled categories "user-support", "maintenance and updates", "fault analysis and correction" and "software configuration and administration".

The most frequently demanded previous knowledge in the *task profile* originated from the learning field "Sources of information and working methods". Further learning fields that provide important previous knowledge for a successful accomplishment of the demanded tasks were "Professional English for technical occupations" and "Business processes and operational organisation".

	Categories \ Learning fields	Business processes and operational organisation	Sources of information and working methods	Simple IT-Systems	Professional English	Application development and programming	Networked IT-Systems	Market and customer relationship	Maintenance of IT-Systems
Tasks	SW configuration & administration	b	b	a	b		a	b	a
	Fault analysis & correction		b	a			b		a
	User support		b	b	b		b		a
Requirements	OS & SW-Servers		b	a	b		a	b	a
	General SW skills			a	b		a	b	a
	SW development & testing	b	b		b	a	b		

a: Skill or working process references directly to the skills and contents of the learning field
b: Skills and contents of the learning field are used as previous knowledge for a task or requirement
Dark grey: most frequently mentioned – light grey: least frequently mentioned

Fig. 2. Learning fields and assigned tasks and requirements

According to the direct references to the skills and contents of the learning fields, the results for the *requirements profile* are similar. Differences appeared in terms of previous knowledge. Overall, most of the descriptions in the requirement profile were assigned to the learning field "Market and customer relationships", due to its relevance as previous knowledge. Furthermore, frequently demanded previous knowledge derived from the learning fields "Business processes and operational organisation", "Professional English for technical occupations" and "Sources of information and working methods".

The category "Soft skills and other" was evaluated separately, because its competencies are usually not domain-specific and thus cannot be assigned to a single learning field. The only exception is the subcategory "Knowledge of English", which can be clearly assigned to the learning field "Professional English for technical occupations". The largest number of mentions could be found in this category (demand in 56.0% of all job offers). Of similar importance are the demanded social skills "communication skills" (51.0% of all job offers) and "Ability to work in teams" (44.0% of all job offers).

Overall, the majority of working processes originate from the field of IT Systems in general, whereas the demanded previous knowledge occasionally varies, depending on the branch of business.

5 Conclusion

The question of this study was: What are the real-life working processes of computer specialists? The results show that the main topics all deal with IT systems in general. The most sought-after skills and competencies therefore derive from the learning fields "Networked IT Systems", "Simple IT systems" and "Maintenance of IT systems". The demanded tasks and skills involve installation, configuration, administration and support. The most sought-after previous knowledge can be assigned to the learning fields "Professional English for technical occupations", "Sources of information and working methods" and "Market and customer relationships". It could be valuable for vocational schools to focus on these learning fields in developing learning situations, since they represent the main aspects of the real-life working processes in the field of IT and CS. In addition, the development of social skills must be better taken into consideration across all learning fields.

The next steps will be to connect all data to a normative competence model for vocational computer science education as a general description of all competencies to be gained, furthermore the development of exemplary learning situations based on these results as well as suitable guidelines to support vocational teachers in developing their own lessons.

References

1. BMBF – Federal Ministry of Education and Research (Bundesministerium für Bildung und Forschung). Berufsbildungsbericht 2013 (German), Bonn, Berlin, Germany (2013)
2. CMECA – Standing Conference of Ministers of Education and Cultural Affairs (Sekretariat der ständigen Konferen der Kultusminster der Länder in der Bundesrepublik Deutschland. Rahmenlehrplan für den Ausbildungsberuf Fachinfor-matiker/Fachinformatikerin (German). beschluss der Kultusminsterkonferenz vom (April 25,1997)
3. Destatis – German Federal Statistical Office (Statistisches Bundesamt). Studien-anfänger/-innen (2014)
4. Johlen, D.: Lernfeldübergreifender Zugang zu Betriebssysten und zur Netzwerktech-nik mit den Methoden der objektorientierten Programmirtechnik für die IT-Berufe (German). In: Hubwieser, P. (ed.) Informatische Fachkonzepte im Unterricht, IN-FOS 2003, Garching bei München, September 17-19, vol. P-23, p. 10. GI-Fachtagung Informatik und Schule (2003)
5. Opel, S., Brinda, T.: Learning Fields in Vocational IT Education – Why Teachers Refrain From Taking an Opportunity. In: Knobelsdorf, M., Romeike, R. (eds.) Proceedings of 7th Workshop in Primary and Secondary Computing Education (WiPSCE 2012). ACM, New York (2012)
6. Opel, S., Brinda, T.: Arguments for contextual teaching with learning fields in vocational it schools: Results of an interview study among it and cs training companies. In: Proceedings of the 8th Workshop in Primary and Secondary Computing Education, WiPSCE 2013, pp. 122–131. ACM, New York (2013)
7. Opel, S., Brinda, T.: Learning Fields in Vocational IT Education – How Teachers Interpret the Concept. In: Diethelm, I., Mittermeir, R.T. (eds.) ISSEP 2013. LNCS, vol. 7780, pp. 147–158. Springer, Heidelberg (2013)
8. Petersen, A.: Neue Lernfeld- und Unterrichtsgestaltung in den IT-Berufen. Ergeb-nisse und Erkenntnisse aus dem Meodellversuche und Verbundprojekt SEDIKO (German). Lernen und Lehren (68), 161–167 (2002)
9. Petersen, A., Wehmeyer, C.: Die neuen IT-Berufe auf dem Prüfstand. Erste Ergebnisse der bundesweiten IT-Studie (German). Berufsbildung in Wissenschaft und Praxis (bwp), (6) (2000)
10. Petersen, A., Wehmeyer, C.: Aufgedeckt: IT-Arbeitsprozesse und Ausbildung in der Betriebspraxis (German) (2003)
11. Repp, S., Ziegler, R., Meinel, C.: Lernortkooperation in der IT-Ausbildung – Kompetenzentwicklung in Projekten (German). In: Schubert, S. (ed.) Proceedings of the 2007 German conference on Informatics and Schools (INFOS 2007), pp. 135–146. Köllen, Bonn (2007)

Learning Styles of Students at the Department of Computer Science – University of Potsdam

Loay Talib Ahmed Al-Saffar

Computer Science Dept., University of Potsdam,
Germany and College of Electrical and Electronic Techniques, Baghdad, Iraq
alsaffar.loay@gmail.com

Abstract. This paper is part of a research to understand the learning style preferences of students at the computer science department – University of Potsdam, to be aware of which changes are necessary to be adopted in the teaching methods, in an attempt to make an impact on reducing the dropout rate among students, and to suggest a better learning environment meeting most of the students' learning style preferences. It will present and discuss initial results of using the Index of Learning Styles (ILS) questionnaire developed by Felder and Soloman, which is a 44-item questionnaire for identifying the learning styles according to Felder-Silverman learning style model FSLSM.

Keywords: Learning Styles, Felder-Silverman learning style model, Computer Science, Business Informatics, and Didactics.

1 Introduction

It is generally agreed that different learning styles exist and there is a general acceptance that the manner "in which individuals choose to or are inclined to approach a learning situation" has an impact on performance and achievement of learning outcomes [1]. So incorporating learning styles in teaching plans may make learning easier and leads to better achievement [2]. Researchers have developed many different models for identification of learning styles. In general, a learning style model classifies students according to where they fit on a number of scales pertaining to the ways they receive and process information [3].

There are several different learning style models. In this paper, the Felder-Silverman learning style model (FSLSM) is used; most other learning style models classify learners into a few groups, whereas Felder and Silverman describe the learning style of a learner in more detail, distinguishing between preferences in four dimensions. It is based on tendencies, indicating that learners with a high preference for certain behaviour can also act sometimes differently [2].

According to FSLSM, each learner has a preference on four distinct dimensions: active/reflective (ACT/REF), sensing/intuitive (SEN/INT), visual/verbal (VIS/VER), and sequential/global (SEQ/GLO). Active learners learn by trying things out and working together with others, whereas reflective learners learn by thinking things through and reflecting about them, and they prefer to learn alone. Sensing learners like to learn from concrete material like examples, tend to be more practical, and are careful

D. Passey and A. Tatnall (Eds.): KCICTP/ITEM 2014, IFIP AICT 444, pp. 68–75, 2014.

with details, whereas intuitive learners prefer to learn abstract material, like challenges, and are more innovative. Visual learners remember best what they have seen, whereas verbal learners get more out of words, regardless whether they are spoken or written. Sequential learners learn in linear steps, prefer to follow linear, stepwise paths and be guided through the learning process, whereas global learners learn in large leaps and prefer a higher degree of freedom in their learning process [3, 4, 5, 6].

The Index of Learning Styles (ILS), created by Felder and Soloman, is a questionnaire for identifying the learning styles according to FSLSM, where 11 questions are assigned for each dimension. Each question has two answer choices and the respondent should pick the most suitable one. Each choice represents a preference on a dimension. The preference that scores higher is the dominant preference in that dimension and the difference in scores indicates the strength of the preference. When a dimension is in balance, meaning that the score is between -3 and 3, a student can switch between the preferences depending on the teaching style. In practice this means that no matter which preference is used in teaching, such students will manage. The students that need the teacher's attention are those whose preference is moderate or strong (meaning that the score is between -5 and -11 or between 5 and 11). The more students in that category, the more a teacher should adapt the teaching to meet their needs [4, 5, 6].

The main goal of this research is to understand the learning style preferences of students at the computer science department – University of Potsdam, and look into the differences between students of different study fields at the department who usually take some joint courses.

2 Methodology

Participants were a volunteer sample of students of the computer science department at the University of Potsdam, 135 students covering every academic semester with different study specialties (42% Computer Science, 34% Business Informatics, 16% Teaching Computer Science, and 8% other specialties) participated in filling the ILS questionnaire (A multiple choice questionnaire, see [7]), 116 students filled the questionnaire electronically while 19 students filled a hard copy. 45 female students (33%) and 90 male students (67%) participated in the research. (Figure 1 shows the number of the students participating in the research according to gender in each specialty and figure 2 shows the number of students from each semester)

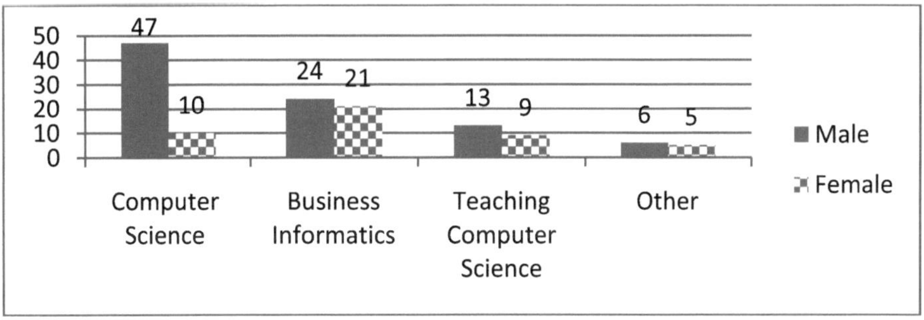

Fig. 1. Number of the students according to gender of each specialty

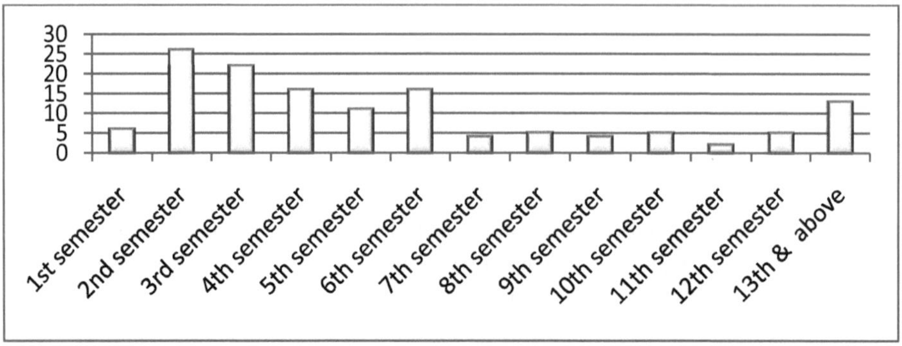

Fig. 2. Number of students from each semester

3 Results and Discussion

From figure 3 which shows the preference of all students one can see that students are more active, sensing and visual while more balanced for the sequential/global dimension. The results, for each of the specialties: computer science, business informatics, and teaching computer science and according to gender are discussed below.

Active/Reflective (ACT/REF) Dimension

Figure 4A shows that female business informatics students are more active learners than the computer science female students, and both of them have no moderate or strong preference towards being a reflective learner. Male students (computer science and business informatics) are more divided between being "moderate or strong active learners" and being "balanced".

The male teaching computer science students are balanced, while the female students have tendency towards being more active learners, see figure 5A.

Sensing/Intuitive (SEN/INT) Dimension

Figure 4B shows that female students (computer science and business informatics) are more sensing learners, while male students (computer science and business informatics) are more balanced with none of the business informatics students being moderate or strong intuitive learners.

The male teaching computer science students are more balanced, and having tendency of being intuitive learner, while the female students are more sensing, see figure 5B.

Visual/Verbal (VIS/VER) Dimension

Figure 4C and figure 5C show that most students are between balanced and moderate visual learners, with computer science students having a little bit more tendency towards being strong visual learners, especially the male students, and the male teaching computer science students share the same tendency.

Sequential/Global (SEQ/GLO) Dimension

Figure 4D and figure 5D show that most of the students are balanced, but computer science students have a little bit more tendency towards being global learners and the business informatics students have a little bit more tendency towards being sequential learners.

Students Opinion

Students who had provided us with a valid email address were sent the personal learning styles results of the first questionnaire together with a second questionnaire to ask them whether they agree with the results they had received. 19% of them responded, see figure 6. Most of them agreed with the results, but in the sensing/intuitive (SEN/INT) dimension students had the biggest doubts whether the results matched their real learning style!

Students who filled a hard copy of the questionnaire (19 students; 9 females and 10 males. 17 of them were business informatics and 2 other computer science students) were asked directly afterwards to give their opinion about their own learning style preferences before giving them the results of the questionnaire. First the students were introduced to each dimension and then they gave their opinion. There were 7 major mismatches for the active/reflective (ACT/REF) dimension (6 male students thought that they are more verbal or balanced while the result of the ILS questionnaire classified them as visual learners), 5 mismatches for the sensing/intuitive (SEN/INT) dimension (4 students predicted to be moderate sensing learners but the result showed them as more balanced), 3 mismatches for the active/reflective (ACT/REF) dimension, and 1 major mismatch for the sequential/global (SEQ/GLO) dimension.

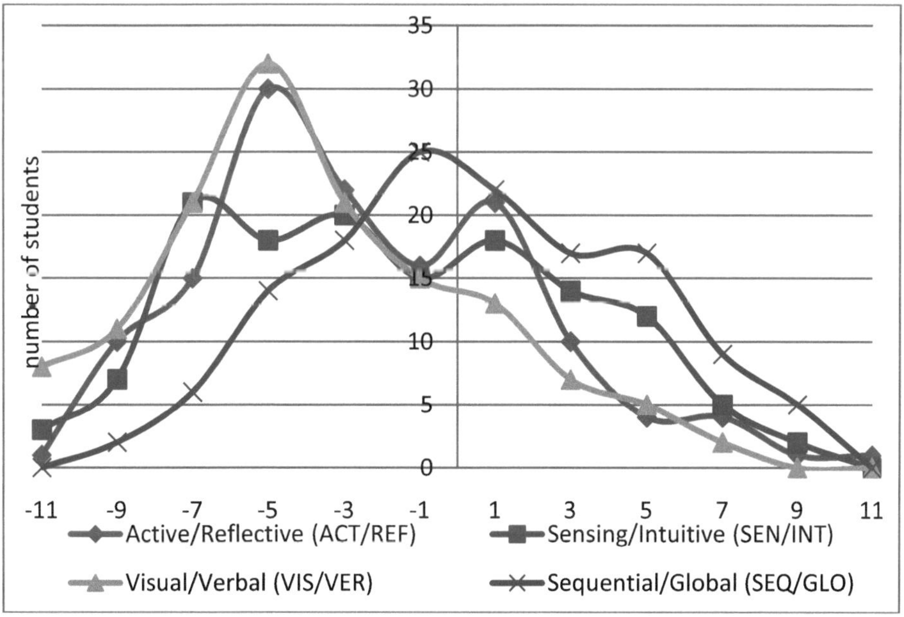

Fig. 3. All four dimensions distribution of the students learning styles

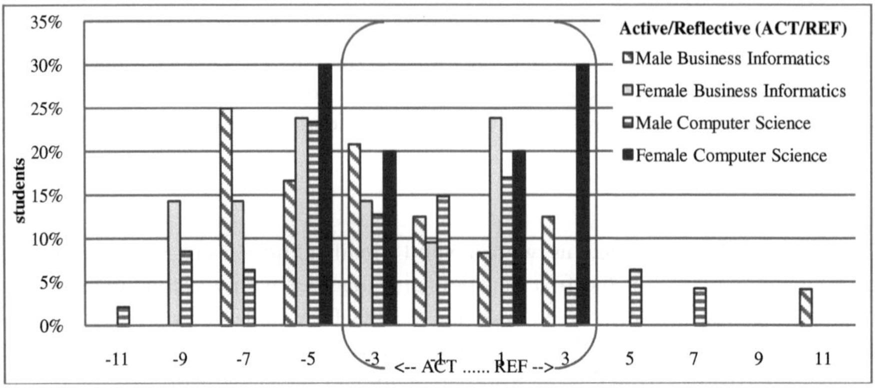

Fig. 4A

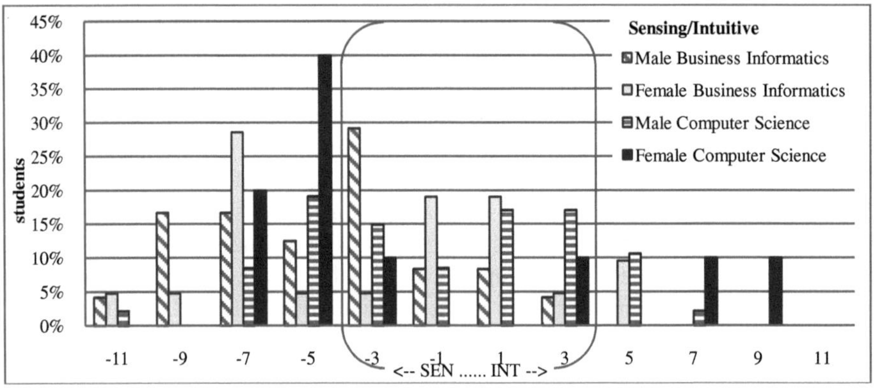

Fig. 4B

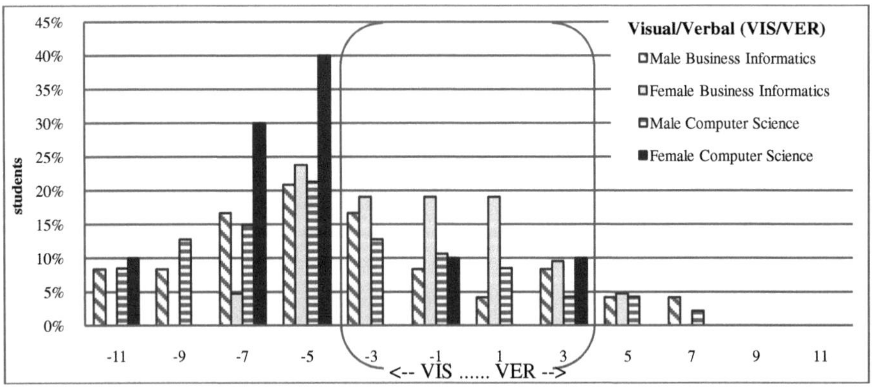

Fig. 4C

Fig. 4. A, B, C and D: All four dimensions distribution of the Business Informatics and Computer Science students, distinguishing between genders

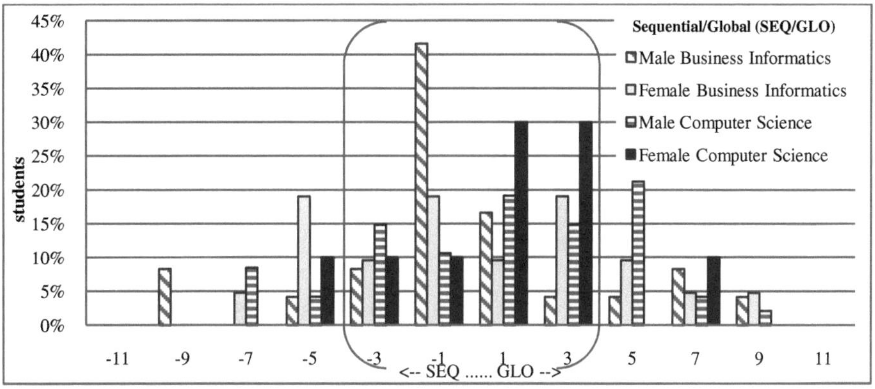

Fig. 4D

Fig. 4. (*Continued*)

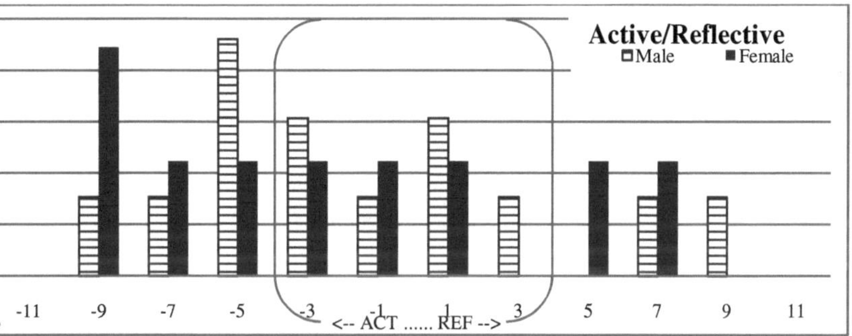

Fig. 5A.

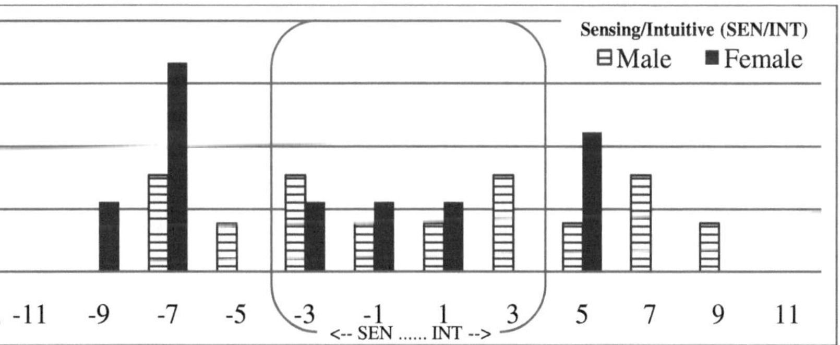

Fig. 5B.

Fig. 5. A, B, C and D: All four dimensions distribution of the teaching computer science students, distinguishing between genders

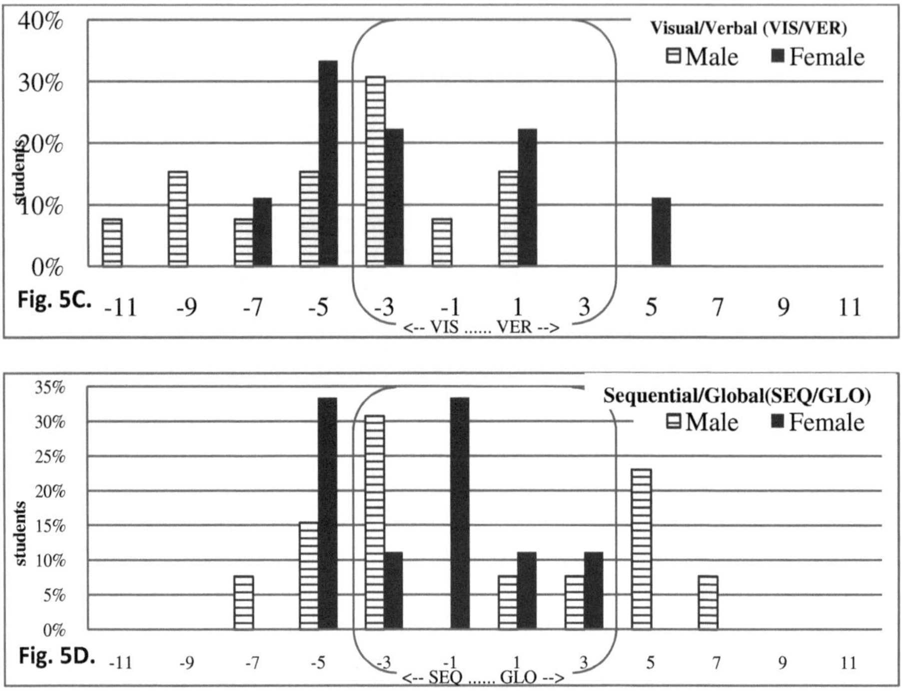

Fig. 5. (*Continued*)

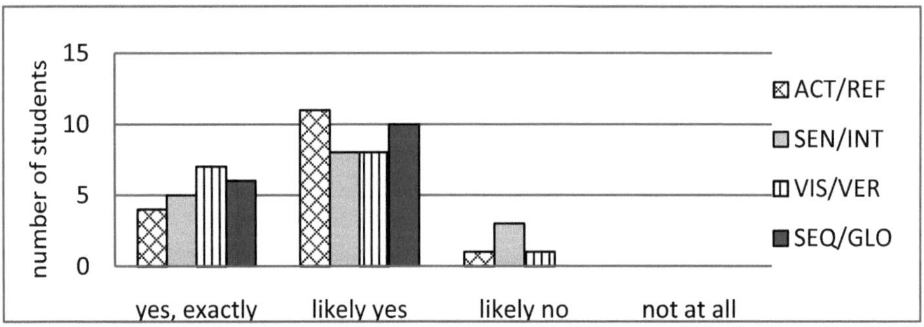

Fig. 6. Students opinion about the results

4 Conclusions

By using the Index of Learning Styles (ILS) questionnaire developed by Felder and Soloman, one can notice differences in the preferences of learning style between male and female students of different study fields at the computer science department, as well as differences between students with different specialties, for example: 'female business informatics students are more active learners than the computer science female students. Computer science students have a little bit more tendency towards being strong visual learners, especially the male students. Male students (computer science and business informatics) are more balanced with none of the business informatics students being moderate or strong intuitive learners, while the male teaching computer science students have tendency of being intuitive learner. And the computer science students have a little bit more tendency towards being global learners while the business informatics students have a little bit more tendency towards being sequential learners.'

Further research should be conducted in this area to look into these differences in a way that reflects positively on the teaching methods of the subjects that embrace all those students who might differ in the way they learn. More investigation in the ILS questionnaire should also be adopted to overcome some of the problems in distinguishing learning styles, for example the visual/verbal (VIS/VER) dimension.

Acknowledgment. I would like to thank Prof. Dr. Andreas Schwill for his advice, help and support.

References

1. Cassidy, S.: Learning Styles: An overview of theories, models, and measures. Educational Psychology 24(4) (2004)
2. Graf, S., Viola, S.R., Leo, T.: Kinshuk: In-Depth Analysis of the Felder-Silverman Learning Style Dimensions. Journal of Research on Technology in Education (2007)
3. Alaoutinen, S., Smolander, K.: Are Computer Science Students Different Learners? In: Proceedings of the 10th Koli Calling International Conference on Computing Education Research, Finland (2010)
4. Derntl, M., Graf, S.: Impact of Learning Styles on Student Blogging Behavior. In: Ninth IEEE International Conference on Advanced Learning Technologies (2009)
5. Felder, R.M., Spurlin, J.: Applications, reliability and validity of the Index of Learning Styles. International Journal on Engineering Education 21 (2005)
6. Soloman, B.A., Felder, R.M.: Learning Styles and Strategies (1993), http://www4.ncsu.edu/unity/lockers/users/f/felder/public/ILSdir/ILS.pdf, Felder, R.M., Silverman, L.K.: Based on Material, Learning and Teaching Styles in Engineering Education. Engr. Education, 78(7), 674–681 (1988)
7. Soloman, B.A., Felder, R.M.: Index of Learning Styles Questionnaire, http://www.engr.ncsu.edu/learningstyles/ilsweb.html

E-Learning Maturity Model – Process-Oriented Assessment and Improvement of e-Learning in a Finnish University of Applied Sciences

Ilkka Haukijärvi

Development Manager, Tampere University of Applied Sciences, Finland
ilkka.haukijarvi@tamk.fi

Abstract. In order to institutionalize e-learning within an institution its significance as an object of continuous process assessment, process improvement and process management must be acknowledged. One of modern higher education institution´s key assets is its capability to develop and sustain social and physical structures and capabilities which enable the development and execution of high quality e-learning. In this article, a case study is presented, during which e-learning related process assessment and evaluation of eLearning Maturity Model (eMM) was carried out in a large Finnish university of applied sciences. The evaluation of the eMM was committed as part of a comprehensive process assessment of the case institution. The eLearning Maturity Model was considered beneficial, although some criticism appeared. It provided a structured, although quite a resource heavy, approach to form a comprehensive and multilevel overview of the institution´s current status of processes surrounding the e-learning. By utilizing the eMM, a more informative basis for future development of processes was formed. Based on the process assessment, the case institution´s capabilities on higher dimensions of capability are generally lower than in lower dimensions. This potentially results in high variation of performance and quality within e-learning.

Keywords: E-Learning Maturity Model, eMM, e-learning maturity, process maturity, process management.

1 Introduction

An institution *(organization)* is dependent on its capabilities and knowledge base in terms of making strategically right decisions. Institutions – whether private or public – have faced an age of digitalization of learning and training. The 'E' has become an essential part of different domains within public and private sector institutions. Ruohonen & Multisilta [1] write that e-business, e-work and e-learning form an integrated entirety, which is to be guided and managed through strategic perspectives. In addition, when developing and deploying e-learning, it is crucial to understand the pedagogic difference compared to traditional learning. In many case, pedagogic approach that supported face-to-face lecturing is transferred to e-learning environment as such. This approach will lead to failure most likely. Strategic development of

D. Passey and A. Tatnall (Eds.): KCICTP/ITEM 2014, IFIP AICT 444, pp. 76–93, 2014.

e-learning should aim for more effective learning of individuals, teams and institutions. Organizational learning is dependent on the level of integration between individual, group, organization and inter-organizational learning processes. Ruohonen & Multisilta [1] state that organizational learning needs to be addressed and a lot of work needs to be done in order to integrate processes for learning in different domains.

Higher education institutions are facing pressures to develop the effectiveness and quality of their operations. The accountability of higher education institutions, also in terms of performance and quality, has seen a significant increase during the last two decades [2]. The development has led to greater utilization of various metrics and process improvement activities on a wide scale. In Finland for example, every university of applied sciences is accountable to the Ministry of Education, and multiple different metrics, mostly quantitative, are being used to determine the performance and further, the annual funding. The mandate and funding of an applied sciences institution is largely based on these metrics and reports. From internal quality assurance and development point of view, both quantitative and qualitative metrics and assessment practices are being utilized in forming a better understanding of how well an institution performs in a given area of assessment. The goals of assessment and evaluation are to form a solid and informative basis for institutional and individual development. The development initiatives and activities are carried out in order to meet the expectations and mutual agreements with key stakeholders. An organisation needs to be managed and developed from strategic perspectives and based on collected information and careful analytics. Explicit objectives need to be set and communicated throughout the organization. Planning, development, assessment, execution and management benefit from structured and rigor approaches, which provide guidance and support for the continuous improvement, but also provide means to enhance the knowledge base of an organisation. A learning organization creates and sustains circumstances that support collaborative construction, open sharing, storing and utilization of knowledge [3].

The role of e-learning has grown essentially during the last two decades. Digitalization of education is considered as a major reforming megatrend in higher education. Many higher education institutions are engaged in studying and utilizing various e-learning solutions. As the role of e-learning is essential part of a modern day higher education institution, assessing the effectiveness of e-learning in a comprehensive manner has become crucial. Institutional assessment and development has a crucial role in ensuring and enhancing the circumstances that support the achievement of desired outcomes. In addition to emphasizing continuous development of e-learning environments and technologies, learning artefacts, learning processes and pedagogies, there should be a complementary emphasis on evaluating institutional processes affecting and defining the circumstances in which the e-learning is developed, deployed and supported.

In this article, a case study is represented, during which an assessment of process maturity was executed in large Finnish University of Applied Sciences. The E-learning Maturity Model CORE version 2.3 by Marshal (2006) was utilized in the assessment. The goal of the study was to form an overview of the case institution´s current state of e-learning process maturity and capability and to collect evidence of the utility of the eMM as qualitative process assessment framework in the local context.

2 Business Process Management – A Theoretical and Practical Framework for Process Development

Within rapidly changing environment, institutions must have capabilities for continuous development. Pressures for change occur from within and from outside the organization. In this kind of environment, the development and assessment of organization´s processes and it´s capability to dynamically reform the resource base play fundamental role in maintaining and developing functionality and competitiveness. Helfat et al. [4] define dynamic capabilities as organization´s ability to create, expand or reform its resource base appropriately – tangible assets, intangible assets, personnel resources and all the capabilities that it owns or has an entitled access to.

The quality of an organization´s processes correlate to the effectiveness of the organization. Business Process Management (BPM) is widely applied and established model for and approach to development of organizations´ effectiveness and competitiveness. The theoretical foundation on which the BPM has been developed on, is the work on statistical process control by Walter Shewhart and W. Edwards Deming and Business Process Re-engineering (BPR) by Michael Hammer [5].

Hammer [5] criticized that the statistical quality approach emphasized too heavily on small scale processes or even work activities, rather than on processes that have real strategic effect in terms of value proposition of the enterprise. Another restriction of the quality approach was heavy focus on eliminating variations and ensuring constant quality within processes or sequences of work [5]. Hammer [5] saw this as restriction since constant quality does not necessarily lead to fulfilling the value proposition – the customer expectations. The absence of greater emphasis on continuous optimization and pursuing for optimal circumstances and fulfilment of the expectations of key stakeholders was seen problematic by Hammer. Hammer´s own work with Business Process Re-engineering has had its impact on the BPM as well. In BPR, processes were defined as end-to-end processes that function throughout the organization and produce value for the customers [5]. End-to-end processes are processes that are crucial and meaningful in terms of the organization´s competitiveness [5]. In the quality approach by Deming and Shewhart the development of processes was continuous activity that based heavily on quantitative metrics, whereas in BPR the development was staged and no clear and defined approach for using pre-defined metrics was introduced. Process planning and design had a large role in BPR, whereas the quality approach relied heavily in assessing the outcomes.

During the last decade, Business Process Management was formed on the basis of quality approach and BPR, introducing a modern approach to the management of processes [5]. In BPM, the development is focused on large scale processes that have essential role in realization of value proposition – defining, designing, assessing and developing these processes as continuous cycle.

2.1 Cycle of Process Management

Careful analysis of systematically collected information on the current state is the basis for development. Information analysis forms the evidence base for planning of development. After planning the development, the changes are realized and effects of the changes are assessed and measured. After these stages, new processes are standardized and implemented throughout the organization [6]. Through careful planning and definition of processes, the probability of achieving higher level process performance grows. In order to manage a massive network of processes, which rely heavily on both physical and social assets, a structured approach to development can be beneficial. Mutafelija & Stromberg [6] state that a structural approach supports planning, guides development and provides a clear framework for assessing development efforts and outcomes.

One example of a structured qualitative process assessment and development framework is the Capability Maturity Model Integrated (CMMI). Key idea of maturity models in general, is that organizations need to develop their capabilities within processes in order to achieve higher level maturity of the processes. This kind of approach provides a comprehensive and holistic approach to assessment and development of processes. Kasse [7] writes that CMMI includes a group of plan, do, check and act –activities which are known to be essential phases in the famous process development PDCA-cycle. CMMI´s purpose is to support continuous process development by providing a structured framework for the analysis of current state, approach to and guidelines for development itself and assessment of development.

Process management cycle of BPM (PMC) has a lot common with the PDCA cycle. The PDCA – plan, do, check, act – is widely recognized and applied process development cycle. The idea is to compare current state of processes with the optimal state and goals. Process management cycle includes multiple different phases as described in Figure 1.

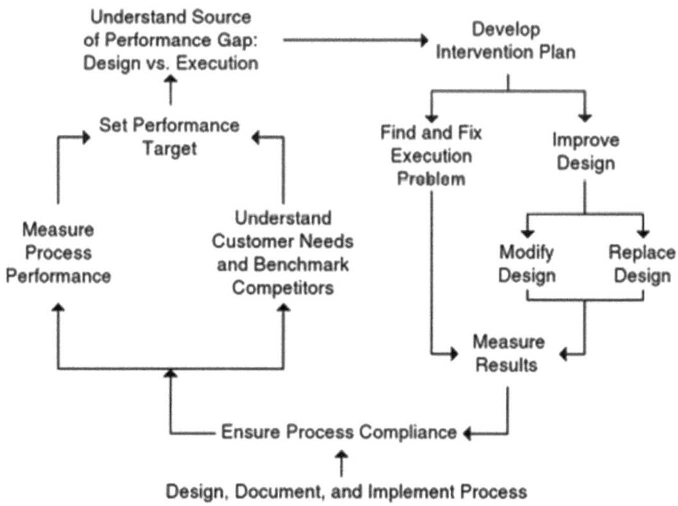

Fig. 1. Process Management cycle as described by Hammer [5]

Defined goals – whether quantitative, qualitative or both – must reflect directly to the planning of process development. Otherwise there is a risk of misdirected development: conflict between development efforts and organizational goals occurs. Thus, it is vital to understand that in the assessment of processes and planning of development, the information of the processes´ capability itself is not enough. Organization´s strategic goals should guide all development.

Failures within processes can occur in two dimensions: processes´ design or processes´ execution. If process is continuously underperforming, most likely the problem lies within design, whereas problems with execution are usually linked to lack of capabilities and insufficient tools. Roots of the problems within execution dimension can be hard to recognize and repair. [5].

Institutionalization of processes is key factor in succeeding at process development. Kasse [6] defines institutionalizing as creation, assessment and deployment of effective, repeatable and long-lasting processes throughout organization. To further specify the definition, Kasse adds that when institutionalizing processes, organization develops practices that provide necessary infrastructural support and enable organization´s continuous learning and evolvement. Lack of institutionalizing can occur in various ways: processes are managed and executed inconsistently, processes are vulnerable to changes in human resource base, process development is not linked to business goals, cost evaluations have no valid history base, lack of commitment to allocation of resources or infrastructure to development [7]. Previously mentioned CMMI includes a certain set of goals – generic goals – which describe the required institutionalizing in order to achieve certain maturity or capability level [6].

3 E-Learning Maturity Model – Description of Key Concepts

Managing and evaluating an institution´s e-learning process maturity and capability demands utilization of systematically collected and analysed information to support and guide further development of the area. From strategic management and planning point of view, this information is critical in order to form a relevant and valid basis to decide about long-term resource allocations and other means of support. According to Marshal [8], e-learning process maturity assessment is a complex area alone, and must involve gathering of information that helps to form broader overview to support strategic planning and development of e-learning, rather than focusing too much into small details.

For this purpose was introduced the first version of the E-Learning Maturity Model by Marshal & Mitchel in 2003. In 2006, the second version of the model was published. The E-Learning Maturity Model (eMM) is a structured quality improvement framework which approaches development through assessment of process maturity and capability [8]. The eMM is based on Capability Maturity Model (CMM) and Software Process Improvement Determination (SPICE) model [8]. The eMM is built on a concept that institutions ability to be effective is dependent on its´ capability to sustainably develop, deploy and support high quality processes throughout institution [8].

In the eMM, there are multiple defined processes within total of five defined process categories *(areas)* (Table 1). The assessment of process maturity and capability is executed through evaluation of a group of practices on five different dimensions of capability. This kind of structure helps approaching wide and complex institutional system holistically with clear vision to the entirety, its´ components and interdependency between them. As Marshal [8] states, eMM´s advantage is that with it a wide and complex area is broken down into categories that can be assessed separately. Thus, an institution does not necessarily have to utilize whole eMM framework when engaging in assessment. Resource allocations can be directed to more narrowed area within the eMM – for example, to a certain process category.

3.1 Process Categories

There are total of five process categories: Learning, Development, Support, Evaluation and Organization. Each category includes multiple processes. See the definition of each category in Table 1.

Table 1. Process categories of the eMM [8]

Category	Definition
Learning (L)	Processes that directly impact on pedagogical aspects of e-learning
Development (D)	Processes surrounding the creation and maintenance of e-learning resources
Support (S)	Processes surrounding the support and operational management of e-learning
Evaluation (E)	Processes surrounding the evaluation and quality control of e-learning through its entire lifecycle
Organisation (O)	Processes associated with institutional planning and management

Processes within the Learning category are executed in order to maintain and protect circumstances that enable effective and high quality learning, despite of the characteristics of technologies or pedagogies applied [8].

Processes within the Development category are executed to ensure effective and productive utilization of resources. Resources are allocated to development of e-learning infrastructure, materials and course production. In addition, the knowledge base formed during history of development initiatives, such as projects and programs, is utilized to the advantage of current and future e-learning development. Processes within Support - category are executed to secure sufficient technical and pedagogical support and sharing of supportive information to use of students and teachers. Processes within the Evaluation-category are executed to provide comprehensive information basis for planning and execution of e-learning strategy and sustainable development of infrastructure and personnel. Processes within the Organisation-category are executed to ensure that development of e-learning technologies and pedagogies are planned based on strategic and operational goals [8]. All development must be linked to institution´s long-term strategic and operational goals – to avoid controversy between strategy based needs and e-learning development. These processes are focused on strategic, administrative and organizational areas of e-learning which set the preconditions to transition from traditional learning towards e-learning [8].

3.2 Practices and Dimensions of Capability

As with the CMMI, briefly referred to earlier in this article, the eMM enables continuous improvement and assessment of quality with defined practices. In addition, dimensions of capabilities provide the holistic view on assessment and development. Capability´s core essence within the eMM is institution´s capability to develop to satisfy the needs of students, personnel and whole organization, and maintain support despite of changes with demand and personnel [8].

Capability within five dimensions is defined through assessment of defined practices under each process. Practices are distributed into specific dimensions and grouped into essential core practices and useful practices within each dimension [2]. The dimensions of capability are: *Delivery (1), Planning (2), Definition (3), Management (4) and Optimization (5).* The eMM provides pre-defined practice statements to help assessment of practice specific capability. Through assessing practices is determined the level of maturity of a process, and eventually, the maturity of a process category.

All the dimensions are interconnected. High capability on higher dimension does not ensure high quality process outcomes if capability on lower dimensions – such as delivery and planning – is low. To further describe the interconnectedness, low capability on higher dimensions causes ad-hoc functionality, unsustainability and unresponsiveness. [8]. There is causality between low level capability on higher dimensions and institution´s inability to proactively manage and continuously improve itself. Assessing merely process outcomes is questionable, as stated in BPM, since there is a complex and interconnected chain between outcomes and phases leading to outcomes. Thus, a holistic approach is needed for developing the whole chain.

Delivery dimension focuses assessment on process´s capability to output desired results on wide scale in an institution. On planning dimension, assessment focuses on how explicit and communicated goals and plans affect and guide processes. Definition dimension is closely related to planning dimension, expanding assessment to more official information guidance, such as standards, formal guidelines and policies which have an effect on process implementation [8]. On management dimensions, assessment is focused on process management and quality assurance. Emphasis on control, measurement and personnel capability is evident. Optimization dimension is dependent on all lower dimensions, meaning that improving capability on this dimension will actualize through improving capability on lower dimensions. Systematic collection and analysis of various types of information and formal approaches to support institutional development and decision making are the emphasis of assessment. As Marshal [8] states, optimization dimension describes how well an institution has adopted culture of continuous improvement.

4 The Study

The original case-study was carried out in 2013. The case institution is among the largest Universities of Applied Sciences in Finland. More detailed institutional information in Table 2. The amount of fully online courses is low compared to the size of the institution. In the year 2013, there were approximately 50 courses which were fully online. From this statistic perspective, the performance was quite low compared to many other similar scale universities of applied sciences in Finland. There are various motivators which endorse transformation towards higher performance and volume in e-learning. Quantitative agreements with the Ministry of Education promote the creation of circumstances that support effective completion of studies. E-learning is one area that has the potential to support more dynamic and effective completion and faster graduation. The results from recent internal inquiries show that there is a demand for higher volume of online courses among the students. In addition, variation of quality between courses has been acknowledged and criticized by the students.

Table 2. Case-institutions describing figures in 2012

Total budget	~72 million euros
Amount of teaching personnel	414
Amount of R&D&I personnel	34
Amount of administration personnel	312
Total amount of personnel	760
The amount youth bachelor´s degree students	8209
The amount of adult bachelor´s degree students	1052
The amount of master´s degree students	453
The amount of teacher education students	699
The amount of specialization studies students	363
Total amount of students in degree awarding studies	9714
Total amount of students in all studies	10776
Amount of fields of education	7
Amount of bachelor´s degree programmes	47
Amount of master´s degree programmes	11
Amount bachelor´s and master´s degrees	1859
Largest fields of education 1. Technology, communication, transport 2. Social services, health and sports 3. Social sciences, business and administration	

Before this study, it was commonly known by experts that the variation of e-learning quality and is very high within the institution. Some educators are experienced with e-learning and provide high quality e-learning. On the other hand, there is great majority that does not utilize the potential of e-learning. With this detail in mind, it is important to note that the results of this study are an overview of the institution, not explicating a single unit´s – such as a degree programme – results. It is safe to assume that some degree programme´s results would stand out notably higher than the overview covered in this study.

For the assessment of the processes, E-Learning Maturity Model CORE version 2.3 was utilized, thus focusing the assessment on essential practices within each process. The aim was to form an overview of case institution´s process capability and maturity, and based on the results, to form an informative basis for future development. In addition, additional purpose of the study was to evaluate the eMM itself. Evaluation of such frameworks is an essential part of the development. Knowledge of different kind of structured approaches to development forms an essential part of the knowledge base related to development.

The assessment of processes and the evaluation of eMM were conducted in small workshops. Various domains of the institution were represented in the workshops: the strategic management, pedagogic development, quality assurance, e-learning technology, e-learning pedagogy and operational management. The researcher´s professional role in the institution was the leader of e-learning support services.

4.1 Evaluation of E-Learning Maturity Model – Summary

In Design Science in Information Systems Research -paradigm (DSISR), understanding and awareness of current issues and correspondent solutions develops during development and utilization of artefacts [9]. The evaluation of eMM in this study is best described as observational evaluation. The evaluation was conducted during the utilization of the artefact, in real higher education environment, for actual purposes. In observational case study, the artefact is studied and analysed in actual business environment [9].

Thorough documentation, systematic monitoring and reporting were partially questioned by the participants. The criticism on formality and control occurred more in discussions with experts who did not work in the field of management and quality assurance. Confrontation between the freedom of expertise and policy based control was evident in some discussions. On the other hand, the majority of formal and systematic aspects were considered very beneficial, for example those addressed to collection and utilization of information to support decision making and development in e-learning. Also, eMM´s dimensional approach to assessment helped participants of different backgrounds to contribute effectively to the study. The participants understood the purpose and aim of eMM´s formal, structured and comprehensive approach to assessment. The framework guided experts to analyze their institution´s processes from different perspectives than they were accustomed to, encouraging – if not forcing – active collaboration of experts from different domains of the institution.

After initial criticism and by developing better understanding of the model, some negative characteristics were eventually considered beneficial. Some informal comparison between other models and eMM, in terms of assessing the state of an institution, was also brought up, even though it was not expected at this stage. In the light of these single coincidental comparisons, eMM was considered a very thorough model that provides tools for addressing issues explicitly in a complex system. It was not necessarily seen as a replacement but rather as a complementary tool. As a maturity model, the eMM also provides a way to measure and monitor development, which was seen as a positive characteristic, although that aspect could not be actualized in the study. The aim was to form an overview of current state and define basis for future development.

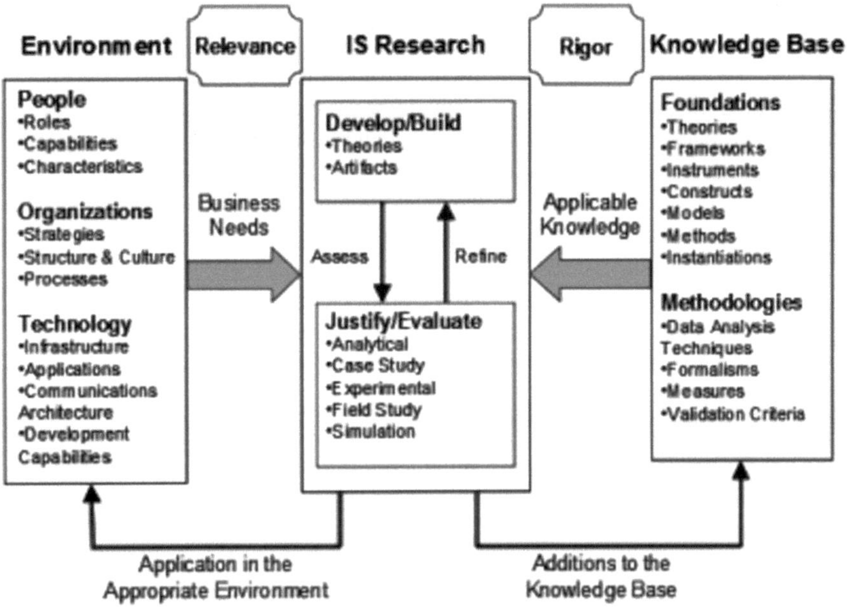

Fig. 2. Information Systems Research Framework by Hevner et al. [9]

During the process of evaluating eMM and assessing the institution´s processes, better understanding was developed on how a structured approach can be beneficial in assessing the current state when it comes to the capability to consistently develop, deploy and support circumstances for high quality e-learning throughout an institution. Consistency and sustainability is supported by strategies, policies, principles, stake holder involvement, formal and systematic top-down and bottom-up quality assurance and enhancement practices. As a disclosure from the discussions, the model was considered beneficial, although very resource demanding to utilize. Further utilization of eMM as a process assessment tool within the institution is expected.

5 Process Assessment – Summary

With the exception of Evaluation category, and partially Development category, lower dimension capabilities are generally higher. On higher dimensions, the lack of systematic collection, sharing and utilization of e-learning specific information in decision making and development is the major factor leading to lower capability. Also lack of formal and defined procedures and policies leads to high variation of process outcomes and therefore to low maturity in many processes. The quotes below do not represent the entire data collected, thus being a narrowed representation of how the maturity was determined. The ratings of the maturity levels are: 4 = fully adequate, 3 = largely adequate, 2 = partially adequate, 1 = not adequate.

Learning category´s strength lies in formal and explicit communication and documentation of learning objectives in curricula and course documentations throughout the institution. Although, there is some variation of quality and amount of course related instructions, such as schedules and communication policies. Also, dedicated modules for information literacy and research skills development is a common practice in the case institution. Interaction between students and teachers is enabled by various communication channels, although response times or the usage of the channels are not monitored systematically throughout the institution.

> "Clear definitions of desired learning outcomes in curriculum and course documentation. Student learning outcomes and quality is monitored and assessed regularly and this information guides further development of courses."
>
> "There can be large variation of quality of the course related information provided in the actual course environment in the learning management system: Some courses include clearly defined instructions on schedules, response times and preferred communication channels, and are aligned with the information provided in the curricula."
>
> "No monitoring of response times in all domains, but clearly defined response times in ICT-support. The monitoring of the use of different communication channels is mostly occasional and informal."
>
> "Assessment practices vary. Institutional policies define the overall type and quality of feedback provided to students. Teachers are provided support on feedback, but this is mostly occasional and not included in common personnel training."
>
> "Feedback given to students is monitored to some degree. Information on student satisfaction on feedback given to them is informally utilized."
>
> "Information literacy skills development is an implicit part of education throughout the studies, and specific training is provided by the library services. Research skills development is enabled with specific course modules built for the specific purpose and through R&D projects which students participate in."
>
> "The information related to the utility and effectiveness of available information sources and tools is utilized in the planning and development of e-learning."

Table 3. Maturity matrix of process category Learning

Learning: Processes that directly impact on pedagogical aspects of e-learning		**D1**	**D2**	**D3**	**D4**	**D5**
L1	Learning objectives guide the design and implementation of courses	4	3	4	3	4
L2	Students are provided with mechanisms for interaction with teaching staff and other students	4	2	1	2	2
L3	Students are provided with e-learning skill development	2	2	2	2	2
L4	Students are provided with expected staff response times to student communications	2	2	2	2	2
L5	Students receive feedback on their performance within courses	3	2	2	2	2
L6	Students are provided with support in developing research and information literacy skills	3	3	4	3	2
L7	Learning designs and activities actively engage students	3	3	3	2	2
L8	Assessment is designed to progressively build student competence	3	3	2	2	2
L9	Student work is subject to specified timetables and deadlines	3	3	3	3	2
L10	Courses are designed to support diverse learning styles and learner capabilities	3	2	2	1	2

Development category´s weakness is the absence of systematization and formalization of processes on a wide scale. This includes such factors as lack of standards, low utilization of explicit plans for the guidance of course development, informal utilization and collection of information within management and optimization. Also inefficient distribution and utilization of produced e-learning resources is evident.

> "Support provided in institutionally defined manner."
>
> "No incentives provided for innovative initiatives in most cases. The quality of planning and development is assessed formatively during some projects."
>
> "Information on effectiveness of support is utilized in development."
>
> "No standards in use for projects. Training provided in various forms for e-learning development. No systematic monitoring of compliance or value of procedures or principles."

"Information on personnel e-learning skills not systematically and formally collected, therefore no explicit linkage between development of principles or standards."

"Utilization of existing e-learning resources is occasional. In addition, these resources or their usage are not systematically evaluated while planning the creation of new resources. No repository in use for the description and wide distribution of resources. Developing are currently."

"Ensuring of accessibility is not an institutionalized procedure. Accessibility is taken into consideration in some projects and initiatives. Accessibility has been recognized as focus of development, and actions have been taken."

Table 4. Maturity matrix of process category Development

Development: Processes surrounding the creation and maintenance of e-learning resources						
D1	Teaching staff are provided with design and development support when engaging in e-learning	4	2	3	2	3
D2	Course development, design and delivery are guided by e-learning procedures and standards	3	3	2	2	2
D3	An explicit plan links e-learning technology, pedagogy and content used in courses	2	3	2	3	2
D4	Courses are designed to support disabled students	2	2	2	2	2
D5	All elements of the physical e-learning infrastructure are reliable, robust and sufficient	3	2	1	2	3
D6	All elements of the physical e-learning infrastructure are integrated using defined standards	3	2	2	2	2
D7	E-learning resources are designed and managed to maximize reuse	2	2	2	2	2

Support category´s reasonably high maturity is based on relatively versatile support functions available to use by personnel and students, and institutionalised approaches to continuous development of such functions. Although, teaching staff´s personal e-learning pedagogical skills development could be more explicit part of strategic personnel capability development planning (HRD). In addition, more systematic approach to management and utilization of support specific information could lead to higher maturity. Library services provide extensive support and information related to essential information databases. ICT-support is built on standardized ITIL *(Information Technology Infrastructure Library)* practices, thus systematic approach to support ticket management is evident, including monitoring of support response times. E-learning technology support and training is continuously provided to teaching staff.

"Support is achievable through a variety of communication channels."

"Key support services utilize feedback largely within the development. Feedback collected from both, the students and the personnel, regarding the effectiveness and service of quality."

"Estimations for needed support resources are required and included in all the investment plans."

"Students´ guide describes all the key support services for students."

"No formal or systematic collection of feedback from teachers regarding the effectiveness and clarity of student support services."

"The handling of student complaints is based institutionalized process and defined policies. Although, information related to the complaints is formally or systematically utilized in the development of e-learning."

Table 5. Maturity matrix of process category Support

Support: Processes surrounding the support and operational management of e-learning						
S1	Students are provided with technical assistance when engaging in e-learning	4	3	3	2	2
S2	Students are provided with library facilities when engaging in e-learning	3	3	4	4	2
S3	Student enquiries, questions and complaints are collected and managed formally	4	4	4	2	2
S4	Students are provided with personal and learning support services when engaging in e-learning	3	3	3	2	3
S5	Teaching staff are provided with e-learning pedagogical support and professional development	2	2	2	2	2
S6	Teaching staff are provided with technical support in using digital information created by students	3	4	3	2	2

Evaluation category´s low maturity is caused partially by the absence of formal and systematic approaches to internal assessment and audit of e-learning courses. In addition, there´s no structured approach to measuring and controlling e-learning course quality, such as quality standards, guidelines and e-learning specific evaluation criteria.

"No information accessible on how personnel feedback is taken into consideration in planning and development of e-learning."

"Personnel feedback not collected systematically regarding their experience with e-learning technologies. Feedback is mainly occasionally and informally delivered."

> "Lack of systematic distribution of knowledge regarding projects, in which e-learning solutions and resources are being developed."

> "Approaches to quality management of projects and initiatives vary extensively, from informal to systematic and formal."

> "No internal reviews or audits of current e-learning courses conducted."

Table 6. Maturity matrix of process category Evaluation

Evaluation: Processes surrounding the evaluation and quality control of e-learning through its entire lifecycle						
E1	Students are able to provide regular feedback on the quality and effectiveness of their e-learning experience	2	2	1	2	2
E2	Teaching staff are able to provide regular feedback on quality and effectiveness of their e-learning experience	2	2	2	2	2
E3	Regular reviews of the e-learning aspects of courses are conducted	1	1	1	1	1

Organization category´s strength is based on institutionalized and strategic, systematic and formal, annual process of planning of development and allocation of resources. The e-learning specific issues could be notably more explicit in the process and in the plans that are defined and undertaken. E-learning development principles have been defined and documented, but not utilized throughout the institution. E-learning specific matters are not explicit in other key institutional principles or guidelines. The lack of systematic assessment of guidelines or principles is also evident.

> "No systematic collection of staff feedback on guidelines or principles. Information received from previous development is normally utilized when developing e-learning strategy and guidelines of e-learning."

> "Teachers participate in defining plans guiding development of e-learning, students much less."

> "Not open and systematic sharing of information on or monitoring of failed development plans."

> "No systematic feedback collection of technology specific aspects of courses. Information of students´ e-learning capability is not collected or shared formally and utilization of this information within development is therefore challenging."

Table 7. Maturity matrix of process category Organisation

Organisation: Processes associated with institutional planning and management						
O1	Formal criteria guide the allocation of resources for e-learning design, development and delivery	4	3	2	3	2
O2	Institutional learning and teaching policy and strategy explicitly address e-learning	3	3	1	1	3
O3	E-learning technology decisions are guided by an explicit plan	3	3	2	2	2
O4	Digital information use is guided by an institutional information integrity plan	2	3	2	1	2
O5	E-learning initiatives are guided by explicit development plans	4	3	3	1	1
O6	Students are provided with information on e-learning technologies prior to starting courses	2	3	1	1	2
O7	Students are provided with information on e-learning pedagogies prior to starting courses	3	3	1	2	2
O8	Students are provided with administration information prior to starting courses	2	2	2	2	2
O9	E-learning initiatives are guided by institutional strategies and operational plans	3	3	3	2	3

The characteristic of non-systematic and informal collection and utilization of information applies to all process categories, in the majority of the processes. Thus, the utilization of e-learning specific information in decision making and planning and execution of continuous development is challenging.

6 Conclusion

Evaluation of current state of processes is the basis for continuous improvement and development. Different kind of approaches on process assessment can be utilized to form an understanding of the gaps between current state and desired state. These approaches may cover both, quantitative and qualitative perspectives on the assessment of process performance.

Desired state of process performance is defined by the understanding of customer expectations and needs. In higher education institution´s case, students and personnel, both, can be regarded as customers when designing and implementing improved processes. Documentation and systematic monitoring of process compliance are mechanisms for ensuring that the process design and actual execution do not differ dramatically.

Systematic and effective utilization of information in management is largely dependent on the availability and quality of the information. Management and development with insufficient information may lead to critically misleading decisions.

For example, allocation of resources between different development initiatives and programs must be based on reliable information and analysis. In order to build capability to more effective utilization of information and more effective creation and utilization of resources, an institution must create structures which support this. For example, processes, practices, tools, skills and policies for collection, sharing and utilization of meaningful information and resources should be promoted. Consistent and careful planning of development projects, and even more so, dissemination of results and best practices help an institution to function more effectively. Also experiences of unsuccessful projects can be of other projects´ interests, as they help to address possible obstacles and risks which current projects can run into. In general, open sharing of all meaningful information and collaboration is one key success factor in organisational learning, and thus, organisational development.

The personnel´s capability is one key aspect in successful development of e-learning. Therefore, enhancing personnel skills should cover e-learning specific aspects as well. To support this, the assessment of e-learning skills should be included in human resource development. Students – whether regarded as customers or not – should also be given a chance to take part in development. Their views are valuable, and help to understand the desired performance and quality of execution. In addition, students have skills that may prove to be beneficial for the development. The strategic management team plays a significant role in the acknowledgement of the importance and opportunities of e-learning: how firm the basis for the development is, depends heavily on the mandate the strategic management team is willing to provide the institution and its developers with.

Assessing e-learning maturity with eMM is an intensive and resource demanding process that benefits from the participation of people from different domains. As with this case study, it was considered beneficial and crucial that representatives from strategic management, quality assurance, e-learning pedagogy, e-learning support and e-learning technology development were involved in the process. Also, student involvement in the process is something to consider carefully in future re-assessments of maturity.

Even though institutional culture would rather promote different kind of approaches to assessing and developing processes, introducing oneself with eMM can widen perspectives on the field. In the case institution, eMM CORE proved its value. Currently, several different scale development initiatives and projects have been planned and started, which can be linked to the results of the study. The purpose is to re-assess process maturity – at least on process categories and processes which were chosen as objects of current development – in 2015. Currently, the strategic management team has acknowledged the ever increasing role of e-learning. This has led to allocation of larger resources for the development of e-learning throughout the institution. Re-organization and re-defining the mission of e-learning department is expected to lead to higher quality processes and higher capability. Initial actions have been taken to develop more effective evaluation practices of e-learning, more specifically e-learning environments, processes and outcomes. Definition of institution-wide e-learning course quality criteria and development of practices and policies for internal evaluation of e-learning courses should lead to higher maturity and capability on evaluation -category.

Future steps of the research will broaden the scope and continue to focus on the quality management and process oriented approaches to organizational development. Business process management as a framework for higher education institution's continuous process improvement is an area that holds interest for further research as well. Performance improvement activities are becoming increasingly more crucial in public higher education, in Finland as well, due to increasing competition and reformed financing policies. Thus, structured and systematic approaches to development are needed more than ever.

References

1. Ruohonen, M., Multisilta, J.: Preface, xiv. In: Nicholson, P., Thompson, J.B., Ruohonen, M., Multisilta, J. (eds.) E-Training Practices for Professional Organisations. Kluwer Academic Publishers, Boston (2005)
2. Marshal, S.: What are the key factors that lead to effective adoption and support of e-learning by institutions? In: HERDSA, Sydney, Australia (2008), http://www.voced.edu.au/node/25701
3. Haukijärvi, I., Nevalainen, T.: Developing a Quality Enhancement Framework for Collaborative Online Courses – Building on Constructivism with a Design Science in Information Systems Approach. In: Proceedings of World Conference on Educational Multimedia, Hypermedia and Telecommunications, pp. 480–489. AACE, Chesapeake (2014)
4. Helfat, C.E., Finkelstein, S., Mitchell, W., Peteraf, M.A., Singh, H., Teece, D.J., Winter, S.G.: Dynamic Capabilities: Understanding Strategic Change in Organizations. Blackwell Publishing, Massachusetts (2007)
5. Hammer, M.: What is Business Process Management? In: Vom Brocke, J., Rosemann, M. (eds.) Handbook on Business Process Management: Introduction, Methods and Information Systems, 1st edn., pp. 3–16. Springer, New York (2010)
6. Mutafelija, B., Stromberg, H.: Systematic Process Improvement using ISO 9001: 2000 and the CMMI. Artech House, Massachusetts (2003)
7. Kasse, T.: Practical insight into CMMI. Artech House, Boston (2008)
8. Marshal, S.: EMM 2.3 Process Descriptions. Victoria University of Wellington, Wellington (2007), http://www.utdc.vuw.ac.nz/research/emm/Publications.shtml
9. Hevner, A.R., March, S.T., Park, J., Ram, S.: Design science in information systems research. MIS Quarterly 28(1), 75–105 (2004)

Accounting Professor Competencies: Identification of Educational Elements in the Education Process of Accounting Professors in Distance Education

Maria Ivanice Vendruscolo and Patricia Alejandra Behar

Universidade Federal do Rio Grande do Sul (UFRGS), Brazil
{maria.ivanice,patricia.behar}@ufrgs.br

Abstract. The aim of this paper is to investigate the elements of teaching skills for professors of undergraduate courses in Accounting Sciences. The professor competencies were studied in order to identify those competencies applicable to the Accounting field. Studies about Accounting Professor training are recent and are tangent to the teacher competencies. They are not dedicated to map them and identify their elements, nor even addressed how to develop them. Hence, it is important to reflect on what skills are necessary for this professor. This is the intention in the continuation of this study in depth.

Keywords: Teaching Skills, Professors Competencies, Distance Education, Accounting Sciences.

1 Introduction

In the current globalized and evolving scenario, Accounting goes through a time of transition that promotes expansions in the functions of accountants, and, consequently, in their academic progress [1,2,3,4]. Similarly to what happens in other areas of knowledge, Accounting suffers the impacts of social, economic, scientific and technological factors and advances, resulting in changes in the practices and methodologies for calculating asset at a global level [5,6,7,8].

Therefore, educational models are also impacted and evolve to include new elements brought by these advances in a significant way when compared to the education from the last century [9]. The professor's role in the training of future professionals acquires a scope that includes theoretical knowledge, pedagogy and professional experience. Thus, the practice of teaching in Accounting is complex [10], due to the relationship between theory and practice, as well as the constant changes brought by the scientific, social, economic and technological developments that have impact on the academic community and to the multiplicity of functions to be performed by the accountant.

The development and inclusion of information and communication technologies (ICT) in Education propel changes in pedagogical models in both types of education. Educational organizations have been making efforts to promote distance education

D. Passey and A. Tatnall (Eds.): KCICTP/ITEM 2014, IFIP AICT 444, pp. 94–105, 2014.

and the incorporation of ICT in traditional didactic teaching methods [11], a worldwide tendency in terms of classroom and distance education [12, 13].

Based on this reality, those involved with the education system, especially professors, need to follow and introduce them in their teaching practices. Consequently, professors are challenged to understand the new dynamics of transformative teaching and learning [14], how to develop skills for the practice of teaching in these circumstances, especially in higher education.

Discussing professor education contributes to the mediation between the new basis of social reality and the demands of skilled professionals to work in organizations in order to respond to evolving challenges of the world of work [15].

Strico Sensu programs are highly targeted to the technical and scientific training, emphasizing content and development research activities, to the detriment of the educational, social and political education of professors [16]. Studies have revealed that the training of professors of Accounting Sciences in Brazil does not contemplate the approach of cognitive theories and the development of professor competencies [17, 18, 19, 16, 20, 21, 10].

Hence it is necessary to reflect on which competencies professors of undergraduate courses in Accounting Sciences are required. What are their elements? What are their specificities for higher education in Accounting? Pedagogical models that are relevant to distance education?

The objective of this bibliography research with qualitative strategy is to investigate the elements (knowledge, skills and attitudes) of competencies of professors of undergraduate courses in Accounting Sciences. The result of this study will support continuing research in order to map the professor competencies in Accounting and to identify mechanisms to develop them through the modality of distance education.

2 Investigating the Teaching Skills

In this section, we investigate the teaching skills in view of different researchers over time, to identify the specificities of their elements (knowledge, skills and attitudes) applicable to the teaching profession in Accounting.

The professor, just like any other professional, has to frame his/her training in two major stages [22]: "(1) preparing to enter the profession, commonly referred to as 'initial training'; and(2) continuing this initial training, updating it, reinforcing it by redirecting or even converting it to - a 'lifelong education' ".

It seems imperative that the development of teaching skills in professor education is an indispensable condition to the curricular competence approach [22].

The term "professor competence" is used in the sense of ability to act with wisdom and awareness of the consequences of his/her attitude. All competence involves at the same time, knowledge, how to do things, values and responsibilities for the results of what has been done [23]. "Competence also means theory and practice to do something, knowledge of the situation - which is required for any worker (and also for the professor)" [24].

Competencies are defined as "a set of interdependent and necessary knowledge, skills and attitudes in order to achieve certain purposes" [25]. Knowledge is considered as the mastery of the knowledge area and pedagogical-didactic aspects. Skills comprise interpersonal relationship, teamwork, creativity, systemic vision, communication, leadership and planning. Attitude refers to commitment, ethics, proactivity, empathy and flexibility [25].

Professors' skills to be developed in their training are intellectual, technical (mastering specific content), educational and political competences [26].

In the context of teaching and learning, competence is defined as knowing how to mobilize resources, expertise, know-how, tools and attitudes to effectively deal with complicated and unexpected situations [27]. The 10 core competencies necessary for teaching are listed below: organize and direct learning situations; manage the progression of learning; develop and evolve the devices of differentiation; engage students in their learning and in their work; work in teams; participate in school administration; inform and involve parents; use new technologies; meet the duties and the ethical dilemmas of the profession; and manage their own training.

Observing the three constituent elements of teaching skills, the key competences for the teaching and research investigated with professors [28] are showed on Table 1.

Table 1. Competencies for teaching and research

Knowledge	Skills	Attitudes
1. Master knowledge area	1. Interpersonal relationship	1. Commitment
2. Didactic-pedagogic	2. Teamwork	2. Ethics
3. Scientific methodology	3. Creativity	3. Proactivity
	4. Systemic view	4. Empathy
	5. Communication	5. Flexibility
	6. Leadership	
	7. Planning	

These competencies constitute the minimum required for quality teaching [29]: communication skills, organizational skills, pedagogical leadership competencies, scientific competencies and competencies of assessment and control.

When addressing the teaching theme, some authors bring the term "knowledges", which is not a synonym for knowledge. The term "knowledges" is not a substance or content enclosed in itself, manifested through complex relationships between professors and their students." [30]. The sources of professor's "knowledge" are [30]: knowledge of the vocational training of Educational Sciences regarding initial and continuing professor training; disciplinary knowledges related to various fields of knowledge of the area; curricular knowledges related to programs (objectives, contents, methods); experimental knowledges developed in the daily work of professors.

Professors must have the ability to analyze complex situations; know how to reflectively decide the best strategies; know how to choose from a wide variety of skills and techniques, learn to critically analyze their actions and results, and know how to learn on a continuous basis throughout their career [31].

Main professor competencies were assigned to the university professor [32]: know how to communicate, in order to facilitate student learning, know how to learn, in order to continually renew their knowledge area in an interdisciplinary way; know how to commit and be closer to the difficulties faced by students, and learn how to take responsibility.

Five characteristics identify professors' work in contemporary societies: knowledge, professional culture, pedagogical tact, teamwork and social commitment [33]: knowledge: the professor's work involves the construction of teaching practices that lead students to learning; the professional culture: the record of practice, reflection on the work and the evaluation exercise are central to the improvement and innovation; it is to understand the meanings of the school, be part of a profession, learn from their more experienced colleagues; pedagogical tact: relationship and communication ability without which the act of teaching is not fulfilled; teamwork: the new modes of professor professionalism imply the strengthening of collective and collaborative dimensions, teamwork, joint intervention in school educational programs; and social commitment: convergence towards the principles, values, social inclusion, cultural diversity.

Analyzing the different approaches of the authors referred to, a consensus about the skills of the university professor could not be identified. However, it is observed, in general, the presence of the three constituent elements of competencies: know (knowledge element), know how to do (skill element) and know how to be (Attitude element).

3 Identifying Elements of Accounting Teaching Competences

According to the Accounting Education Change Commission (AECC) five characteristics are identified in relation to effective teaching [34]:

- curriculum planning and course development : the professor should set appropriate goals, develop a useful structure for conducting courses and programs; conceptualize, organize and properly sequence the topics of the material; integrate the course with other courses, disciplines and related research, and be innovative and conducive to adapt to change;
- use of well-designed materials: it is essential , because they increase the skills of presentation, satisfy course objectives, are consistent with current developments and new technologies in the field of action, create a base upon which continued learning can be built , challenging the students to think, and giving them the tools to solve problems;
- Presentation Skills: stimulate students' interest and their active participation in the learning process, respond to developments in the classroom as they occur , convey mastery of the material, get objectivity on display, instilling professionalism, and engaging students in different learning styles;

- Well-chosen teaching methods and assessment devices: effective teaching methods, for example, experiments, cases, small group activities, vary with the circumstances (class size, the nature of the subject, skill or qualification that is being developed), assessment instruments (exams, projects, papers, presentations, etc.) must be suitable for both goals and the progress of the course, and must have an educational component, which is setting in the student's mind what is most important to learn, to think from a problem, identify weaknesses to be corrected and strengthen the required skills; and
- guidance and counselling: an effective professor guides and advises students as to the appropriate level of study and research, i.e., a freshman student in exploring potential career, a student in the last year to find employment or a student in his doctoral thesis.

A survey with 73 recent graduates of PhD accounting programs in the United States in order to assess the needs of individual development in relation to effective teaching was conducted, taking into account five characteristics identified by AECC. The results of the study showed evidence of accounting professor development based on the recommendations of the AECC. However, despite the fact that respondents agree with the importance of the characteristics (especially curriculum development and presentation skills), they observed that they received little training and that they developed them primarily by self-training [34].

Seeking to characterize the identity of the professional accounting professor, some attributes were identified [18] as follows: the mastering of specific knowledge of their area of expertise in their appropriate initial and continuing education to relativize the knowledge produced by the society, becoming a subject capable of transforming social reality; professors' work that emphasizes the articulation of financial content with other areas of knowledge, surpassing the mere conception of know-how; professionalization that holds direct implications to the formation of professional accountants with a critical profile to the new context; the inclusion of working conditions in the forces in favor of valuing a wage policy and establishing a link in the initial and continuing education career; and understanding of the teaching-research-extension as inseparable aspects of their work.

Three elements are present in the action of accountant professors [18] as follows: (i) organize teaching and learning situations suiting objectives, content and teaching methodologies with the course design, contributing to the quality of education as well as be aware of how to incorporate new technologies to the teaching work; (ii) coordinate research and participate in research groups to produce theoretical and practical knowledge; and (iii) master content and methodologies in order to convert scientific knowledge into curricular knowledge, considering their material conditions and their students.

However, for the teaching profession in Accounting, apart from specific knowledge, others are necessary to the professor: specialized training in the field, general education, didactic teaching, structure and functioning of higher education, education planning, and psychology of learning, teaching and assessment methods and techniques [19]. “For this purpose, it is not enough to know the specific content, professors must be able to know how learning occurs at each stage of human development, the ways of organizing the learning process and the methodological procedures for each content" [35].

This approach is grounded on the epistemological conceptions that professors have to respect the knowledge that underlies these pedagogical act, i.e., expresses a paradigm of educational thought on the understanding that people have of knowledge that empowers professors in pedagogical practices [30].

Table 2. Skills and researched measurable attributes

Competencies	Measurable attributes
Mastering the knowledge area	Have considerable knowledge of the subjects he/she teaches. Conduct research in areas related to the subjects taught
Didactic-pedagogic	Possess fundamental knowledge of teaching and learning concepts. Attend educational didactic courses
Interpersonal Relationship	Establish harmonious and healthy relationship with students. Manage to balance the conflicts that may arise in relation to the students
Teamwork	Cooperate and get cooperation of colleagues in teaching activities with common goals
Creativity	Create innovative solutions in educational activities under their responsibility.
Systemic view	Realize the integration and interdependence between the subject and other subjects taught in an undergraduate course
Reflection	Reflect with students on the relationship between what they are learning and global aspects of science and / or society as a whole
Communication	Listen, process, and understand the different needs of students and provide appropriate feedback
Leadership	Encourage students to achieve personal goals in their learning process. Influence students regarding their personal responsibilities in their learning process
Planning	Know how to elaborate syllabus and courses programs of undergraduate disciplines. Know how to prepare teaching materials to support course activities. Arrange the logical sequence of activities for each lesson taught.
Commitment	Commitment to obtaining positive results in educational activities under their responsibility. Be available to provide out-of-class support to students.
Ethics	Demonstrate respect for students; use a single evaluation criterion for all students.
Proactivity	Have personal initiative to practice concrete actions that contribute to the improvement of the educational process in general.
Empathy	Promote trust and harmony with the students leading to a greater degree of openness to accept their advice and suggestions.
Flexibility	Adapt to new situations when necessary, face new challenges in the educational processes in which you operate. Be willing to revise the teaching process based on results of assessments made. Making self-assessment of your work as a professor.

A study of competencies for the practice of teaching conducted with 267 professors in classroom courses in Northeast Brazil, assumes as its theoretical basis the responsibilities arising from the research [28]. Additionally, two competencies were included in the survey: Commitment and Flexibility [(36]. The measurable attributes are shown in Table 2 [36, 28].

Statistical analysis showed that all competencies achieved an average above 7.9 in the perception of respondents, on a scale of 0 to 10 at the level of perceived importance. The best results were Ethics (9.2), Commitment, Flexibility, Interpersonal Relationship, Planning and Leadership. Didactic-pedagogic competence was in the final position, with an average of 7.9 [36].

Additionally, some important factors were tested for a better professor performance. They are [36]: 1. Title (professors who have *stricto sensu* courses versus those who do not). 2. Employment at the institution of higher education (professors who have more hours *versus* teaching fewer hours). 3. Time experience as a professional in the accounting area (professors who have longer experience as professionals in the accounting area *versus* professors with less experience). 4. Research and extension (professors who have publications or participate in research projects and extension versus professors who did not participate in these projects or do not have publications).

The results of the statistical tests showed that the title factor showed a statistically significant difference (95%) of PhD professors and PhD students in the didactic and pedagogical competence, Commitment and Planning in relation to other professors in the sample. The length of professional experience also proved influential in determining the most competent professors [36].

In another survey of 95 American professors who were certified Accounting PhD, the following skills for teaching accounting were investigated [21]: skills to teach accounting topics; skills to teach various subjects and teaching styles; research skills and publication; the ability to advise students and participate in curriculum development; skills related to the transmission of critical thinking, communication, writing, teamwork, and other non-technical accounting skills; and participation in Professional Continuing Education.

The calculated results indicate that teaching experience was the most influential item in the acquisition of valued skills, after the ability to conduct research in which the preparation made by the doctoral program was the item most influential [21].

Another PhD research, with the aim to investigate the association between professor qualifications and student performance of undergraduate Accounting students [10] considered the qualification in three areas of professor training: Academic qualification, Professional qualification and Pedagogical qualification. It investigated the literature, the factors that constitute the teaching of these skills Accounting and validated by means of the Delphi Technique [10]. Components factors calculated by the author are described: i) Academic qualification: Title: PhD (preparation for research), master, specialist, acting as referee or reviewer of scientific journals, work in HEIs with exclusive dedication, owning publications in scientific journals, participation in associations or bodies of research. Thus, it was found that the academic qualification relates to professor preparation for conducting research on the topics taught; ii) Professional qualification: Acting in the accounting profession; as a consultant, advisor or referee; participation in professional associations or regulatory agencies; development of applied research involving academic environment and the community, participation in university extension projects with community involvement; and iii) Pedagogical qualification: Offering preparation programs for professors, support professor participation in research projects and scientific events; support professor participation in *stricto sensu* courses from other HEIs; promotion of scientific events that include education / teaching; having strict professor training course *stricto sensu, lato sensu* and extension; research projects related to teaching, and teaching experience.

Table 3. Assessment of Competencies of Accounting

Competence	Assessment of Competencies of Accounting
Instructional Skills	States clearly the objectives of the subject / lesson; Presents concepts clearly; Has a thorough mastery of the subject matter; Updated with latest development in the field and can relate subjects to other fields and life situations; Welcomes questions pertinent to the subject matter; Stimulates students' interest in the subject; Encourages students to have a more critical thinking about accounting problems; Encourages creative thinking in solving accounting problems; Gives tests within the subject matter already discussed; Has a good command of the language instruction; Makes use of various teaching aids; Presents lessons using the appropriate teaching strategies and methods like recitation, lecture, demonstration, etc. to ensure the students understanding; and Has good diction, clear and modulated voice.
in management skills	Maintains order, cleanliness and discipline in the classroom; Make the classroom conducive to learning; and Stimulates students' respects to professors and college officials.
in human skills	Shows genuine interest in students; Gives rewards to deserving students; Handles class and students' problem(s) with fairness and understanding; and Inspires students to be self-reliant and disciplined.
in technical skills	Prepares and plans for each class lesson; Lectures and demonstrations are clearly, forcefully and interestingly presented; Has properly balanced theory and practice; Summarizes at the end of each step in a lesson, and gain at the conclusion of the complete presentation; Introduces financial statements and financial information from actual companies; Uses published financial information (such as article in business pages of newspapers, magazines and journals) to reinforce understanding of assignment material; Encourages students interest by showing them how accounting information can be of use in decision-making; and Encourages students to tackle ethical issues in the application of accounting principles and procedures.
in conceptual skills	Stresses fundamental concepts rather than trivial procedures; Explains the accounting concepts at more complex levels as the students gain sophistication and understanding; Uses the experience of students in presenting topics or making use of concepts with which they are familiar; Provides real-world examples at every stage that illustrate the topics consistent with the theoretical treatments; and Cites references to international standards and practices.
in personal and social traits	Conducts himself in a dignified and professional manner; Is well groomed; uses appropriate attire; Is fair and impartial to all students; no favoritism; Has the attitude of respect for the ideas of others; and Is enthusiastic, resourceful and creative (Moves naturally about the room).

A survey with 20 professors and 209 students of Accountancy [14] in the Philippines was carried out. The study aimed to evaluate the skills and teaching skills instruction, management, human resources, technical, conceptual and personal and social characteristics. The skills and abilities assessed [14] are described in Table 3.

The results showed that professors are efficient in the use of teaching skills and management skills. They also possessed human skills and techniques required to ensure the formation of competitive market students [14].

An exploratory study of professors in the areas of Business and Accounting of higher education institution was conducted in Mexico. The research had the purpose of identifying the skills in information technology, and analyze the factors that determine the use of these technologies, for these professors. The results revealed four ICT skills [37]: (i) use of text files and tools, (ii) capabilities in the operating system, (iii) use of database and multimedia; and (iv) preparation of presentations and Internet use. The factors identified by professors in the sample were: Positive view of teaching using ICT, teaching and training in the use of such technologies and availability of infrastructure [37].

Other studies have been conducted taking into consideration students' perception about Accounting professor qualifications and their relevant characteristics. The main results are shown in Table 4.

Table 4. Main characteristics of the professor by the student perception

Authors	Results
[38]	students surveyed prefer professors who have a balance between the emotional and intellectual attributes, while the studies of Lowman highlight professors with intellectual stimulation; the reasons for the good professor are chosen based on the quality of the professor's pedagogic practice and mastery of content; educational and organizational attributes in the intellectual stimulation dimension and attentiveness, interest and helpfulness attributes in the interpersonal dimension; regarding pedagogical practice, professors are well respected, but rarely negatively evaluated, including the ability to challenge students, the forms of evaluation and enthusiasm to teach.
[39]	students considered didactics, followed by theoretical knowledge, as the two most relevant skills out of five skills studied: didactics, relationship, level of demand, theoretical knowledge and market experience.
[40]	students value the mastery of knowledge, didactics / methodology and teaching strategies, attitudes and personal attitudes of professors, but also value teaching that corresponds to the satisfaction of their interests and immediate needs.
[41]	content mastery as a key competence for Accounting professors.
[42]	content mastery, clarity, motivation, readiness to answer questions and be communicative.
[43]	factors for development of teaching skills were: A PhD: Didactic-pedagogical factors, planning and commitment; Influence of teaching experience in terms of time.
[44]	the practice disciplines were perceived throughout the course as the most significant learning, being didactic or teaching methodology, attitudes and personal qualities of the professor the main reasons for the choice of teaching reference.
[45]	students chose mastery of knowledge, teaching and market experience as the most relevant skills to the practice of teaching in the Accounting course.

4 Final Considerations

Analyzing the different approaches of the authors referred to, a consensus could not be identified about the teaching skills of professors. However, it is observed, in general, the presence of the three constituent elements of competencies: knowledge, skills and attitudes.

Studies about Accounting Professor training are recent and tangent to the professor competencies. They are not dedicated to map them and identify their elements, nor even addressed how to develop them. Hence, it is important to reflect on what skills are necessary for this professor. This is the intention in the continuation of this study in depth.

The development of teaching skills in accounting requires additional studies, particularly in relation to distance education, which is still in progress.

On the other hand, universities worldwide have thought of new institutional arrangements, with flexible schedules and more sophisticated pedagogical architectures to meet the demands of a globalized and competitive market. This alternative also meets the increasingly empowered emerging challenges of the profession, including teaching scenario in the Brazilian accounting with a lack of professionals.

Based on the questions presented, it is understood that Accounting professors need to monitor innovative changes introduced in education and incorporate them or adapt them to their pedagogical practice as well as develop new teaching skills to work in this scenario.

References

1. Cardoso, R.L.: Accountant Skills: An empirical study. School of Economics, Business and Accounting. São Paulo's University (2006)
2. Passos, I.C.: Critical Reasoning of Undergraduate Students in Accounting: Application of instructional model Richard Paul. School of Economics, Business and Accounting. São Paulo's University (2011)
3. Miller, W.F., Becker, D.A.: Why Are Accounting Professors Hesitant to Implement IFRS. The CPA Journal 80(8), 63–67 (2010)
4. Ott, E., da Cunha, J.V.A., Cornacchione Junior, E.B., De Luca, M.M.M.: Relevance of knowledge, skills and instructional methods from the perspective of students and professionals in the accounting area: International comparative study. Revista Contabilidade Finanças 22(57), 338–356 (2011)
5. Theóphilo, C.R.: Research in Accounting in Brazil: A critical-epistemological analysis. School of Economics, Business and Accounting. São Paulo's University (2004)
6. Cornachione Junior, E.B.: Technology for education and courses in accounting: virtual collaborative models. School of Economics, Business and Accounting. São Paulo's University (2004)
7. de Sá, A.L.: Fundamentos da contabilidade geral. Juruá, Curitiba (2005)
8. de Iudícibus, S.: Some essay about deep roots of accounting in supporting fundamental principles. Revista de Contabilidade e Organizações - RCO 1(1), 8–15 (2007)

9. Avendaño-Castro, W.R.: Un Modelo pedagógico para la educación ambiental desde la perspectiva de la modificabilidad estructural cognitiva. Revista Luna Azul 36(2), 110–133 (2013)
10. Miranda, G.J.: Relationship between teacher qualifications and student performance in undergraduate accounting in Brazil. School of Economics, Business and Accounting. São Paulo's University (2011)
11. Behar, P.A.: Modelos pedagógicos em educação a distância. Artmed, Porto Alegre (2009)
12. Moore, M.G., Kearsley, G.: Educação a distância: uma visão integrada. Translation by Roberto Galman. 2nd reprint. 1st edn. Cengage Learning. São Paulo (2008)
13. Peters, O.: A educação a distância em transição: Tendências e desafios. Translation by Leila Ferreira de Souza Mendes. Editora Unisinos, São Leopoldo (2009)
14. Del Mundo, G.V., Refozar, R.F.G.: The accounting teachers of Batangas: Their profiles competencies and problems. International Scientific Research Journal (1), 131–166 (2013)
15. Kraemer, M.E.P.: Reflections on the teaching of accounting. Revista Brasileira de Contabilidade 153(2), 65–80 (2005)
16. Andere, M.A., AraúJo, A.M.P.: Aspects of teacher training higher education in accounting sciences: An analysis of graduate programs. Rev. Contab. Finanç 19(48), 91–102 (2008)
17. Nossa, V.: Formation of the faculty training of graduate courses in accounting in Brazil: A critical analysis. Cadernos de Estudos FIPECAFI 21(2), 1–20 (1999)
18. Laffin, M.: Teacher of the accountant: The trajectory of teaching in higher education accounting. Imprensa Universitária, Florianópolis (2005)
19. Gil, A.C.: Didática do Ensino Superior. Atlas, São Paulo (2006)
20. Slomski, V. G.: Know that underlie pedagogical practice professor of accounting. In: VIII Congresso USP de Controladoria e Contabilidade, Anais... São Paulo (July 2008)
21. Marshall, P.D., Dombrowski, R., Garner, M., Smith, K.: The accounting education gap. The CPA Journal 80(6), 6–10 (2010)
22. Gaspar, M.I.: Competencies in question: contribution to the training of teachers. Discursos. Series: Perspectives on education, Lisboa, PT (2004)
23. Braslavsky, C.: Rules, guidelines and criteria for the design of teacher training programs. Revista Iberoamericana de Educación. Buenos Aires 19(1), 13–50 (1999)
24. Pimenta, S.G., Anastasiou, L.G.C.: Docência no ensino superior, 3rd edn., Cortez, São Paulo, SP (2008)
25. Durand, T.: Forms of incompetence. In: International Conference on Competence Based Management, vol. IV. Norwegian School Management, Oslo (1998)
26. Zabala, A.: A prática educativa: Como ensinar. Artmed, Porto Alegre (1998)
27. Perrenoud, P.: Dez novas competências para ensinar. Artmed, Porto Alegre (2000)
28. Pereira, M.A.C.: Competencies for teaching and research: A survey of teachers of chemical engineering. Polytechnic School, São Paulo's University (2007)
29. Bozu, Z., Canto, P.: University teaching in the knowledge society: Teaching skills. Revista de Formación e Innovación Educativa Universitaria 2(2), 87–97 (2009)
30. Tardif, M.: Saberes docentes e formação profissional, 9th edn. Vozes, Petrópolis (2008)
31. Paquay, L., et al.: Formando professores profissionais: quais estratégias? Quais competências? Translation by Fátima Murad and Eunice Gruman, 2nd edn. Artmed, Porto Alegre (2001)
32. Karawejczyk, T.C., Estivalete, V.: University professor: The meaning of their work and develop new skills in a changing world. In: Encontro Anual da ANPAD, vol. 27, ANPAD, Anais (2003)
33. Nóvoa, A.: Professores: imagens do futuro presente. EDUCA Instituto de Educação da Universidade de Lisboa, Lisboa (2009)

34. Swain, M.R., Stout, D.E.: Survey evidence of teacher development based on AECC Recommendations. Journal of Accounting Education 18(2), 99–113 (2000)
35. Kuenzer, A.Z.: Training policies: The establishment of the identity of the teacher Sobrante. Revista Educação & Sociedade 68(special Edition), 163–183 (1999)
36. de Vasconcelos, A.F.: Teachers in accounting: A study on skills for the practice of teaching in classroom courses in Northeast Brazil. Multi-institutional and Inter-Regional Postgraduate Programme in Accounting, Federal University of Paraiba and Federal University of Rio Grande do Norte (2009)
37. Pedraza, N., Farias, G., Lavin, J., Torres, A.: The ICT teaching skills in the areas of business and accounting: An exploratory study in higher education. Perfiles Educativos 35(139), 8–24 (2013)
38. Celerino, S., Pereira, W.F.C.: Attributes and pedagogical practice of accounting professor who has success in the university environment: A view of academics. Revista Brasileira de Contabilidade 37(170), 65–77 (2008)
39. Gradvohl, R.F., Lopes, F.F.P., da Costa, F.J.: da.: The profile of good accounting professor: an analysis from the perspective of students for Graduation. In: Congresso USP Controladoria e Contabilidade, São Paulo. Anais.., vol. 9 (2009)
40. Volpato, G.: Brands of professionals to become teachers-reference. Revista Brasileira de Estudos Pedagógicos 90(225), 333–351 (2009)
41. Gomes, M.E.M., et al.: Attributes and pedagogical practices of accounting professor who has succeeded in the classroom: a study of student perceptions in public HEIs. In: Encontro de Pesquisa Em Administração e Contabilidade, Anais.. Curitiba, vol. 2 (2009)
42. Catapan, A., Colauto, R.D., Sillas, E.P.: Perception of students about the exemplary teachers in public accounting and private HEIs. RIC - Revista de Informação Contábil 6(2), 63–82 (2012)
43. Vasconcelos, A.F., de, C.P.R.N., Monte, P.A.: Fatores que influenciam as competências em docentes de Ciências Contábeis. VEREDAS FAVIP - Revista Eletrônica de Ciências 5(1), 86–101 (2012)
44. Miranda, G.J., Casa Nova, S.P., de, C., Cornacchione Junior, E.B.: The knowledge of teachers-reference in accounting education. Rev. Contab. Financ̦ 23(59), 142–153 (2012)
45. Rezende, M.G., Leal, E.A.: Competencies required of teachers of accounting course in perception of students. Sociedade, Contabilidade e Gestão 8(2), 145–160 (2013)

iPads in Education? A Participatory Design for Professional Learning with Mobile Technologies

Keith Turvey

Education Research Centre, School of Education, University of Brighton, UK
k.turvey@brighton.ac.uk

Abstract. It is recognised in the literature that mobile technologies have the potential to 'disrupt' established practices in ways that require adaptation if educators are to harness their potential. Thus, there is a need for participatory models of research and partnership that give teachers agency over the process of professional development with new technologies at a time when there is increasing pressure for educators to respond to the proliferation of mobile technologies. This paper reports on the development and initial testing of a participatory narrative ecology approach to developing teachers' professional practice with mobile technologies in the UK. A prototype, haptic infographic was developed that teachers and teacher educators could use to story the development of their pedagogical practice as they appropriated mobile technologies in various contexts. The narrative ecology model was developed through a participatory methodology of working with school and university partners in teacher education. The objective was, to explore the model as a participatory approach to developing educators' critical analysis of the process of appropriating mobile technologies for educational purposes and, to capture the subsequent process of pedagogical adaptation. This paper focuses in detail on both the narrative ecology model and how it was used in the case of a secondary school science teacher. The emerging evidence suggests that the process of adaptation to mobile technologies in education is prolonged and complex. Yet in a digital age of rapidly increasing connectivity and converging cultures there is a need for further research into the implications of mobile technologies and how educators can be located as central agents in changing and adapting pedagogical practices. The findings also suggest that participatory narrative approaches offer potential for exploring new designs for pedagogical practice with mobile technologies.

Keywords: Pedagogy, narrative methods, didactic analysis, participatory design, mobile technologies.

1 Introduction

The project was designed to test and develop a model of narrative ecology in educators' professional practice with mobile technologies. A prototype infographic for iPad was designed that teachers manipulate through gestures and use as a prompt for articulating their pedagogical narrative concerning their appropriation of mobile technologies into their practice (Figure 1).

D. Passey and A. Tatnall (Eds.): KCICTP/ITEM 2014, IFIP AICT 444, pp. 106–123, 2014.

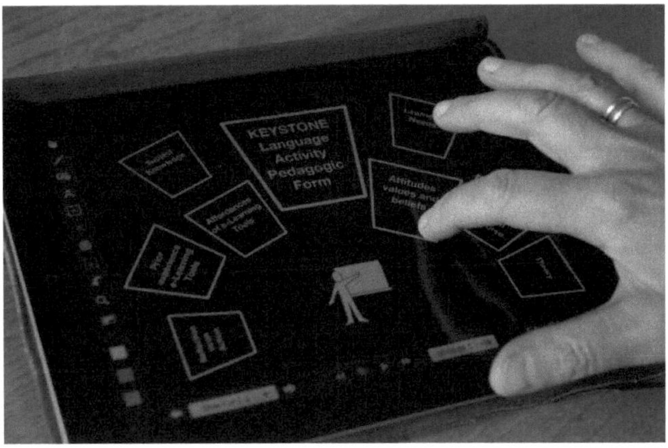

Fig. 1. Narrative ecology iPad infographic – blocks are manipulated (resized and moved) to prompt discussion

The resource was developed and introduced through a participatory model of working with school and university partners in teacher education. The overall objective of the project was to find out how effective the narrative ecology model (Turvey, 2013 [1]) can be in developing educators' critical analysis of the process of appropriating mobile technologies for educational purposes. This is important because I argue there is a need for participatory models of research and partnership in teacher education and development that give teachers agency over the process of professional development with new technologies at a time when there is increasing pressure for educators to respond to the proliferation of mobile technologies and the convergence of social and professional networking practices (Pachler, Bachmair and Cook, 2010 [2]; Turvey, 2012b [3]). The project was also significant in enabling the partnership schools and the School of Education at the University of Brighton to take advantage of the new relationships that are emerging between HE and schools in response recent teacher education reforms in England. The main aims of the project were:

- To form new models for working with partners through participatory research into professional practice, pedagogy and mobile technologies;
- To investigate a narrative ecology framework as a model for critical reflection and development in the appropriation of new technologies in educators' professional practice;
- To develop a prototype interactive iPad resource (Figure 1) to support educators' professional and critical judgements of the integration of mobile technologies in education through dialogue and narrative.

Teachers from three partnership schools were engaged in the project. Their secondary schools (11-16 year olds) had recently launched 1:1 iPad initiatives to support learning and teaching. Similarly, the School of Education, University of Brighton had embarked on a mobile learning project with a number of lecturers in initial teacher education exploring the use of iPads in their professional practice in response to recent higher education policy reports (HEFCE, 2009 [4]; JISC, 2009 [5]).

Thus, the project was timely and provided an opportunity to work with local partners investigating professional practice in the context of newly acquired mobile technologies (iPads). Initial meetings held with representatives from the schools identified a common need to examine how the iPads can be harnessed to support teachers' professional and pedagogical development, and ultimately enrich the learning experiences of students. Thus, the aims of this project were designed around a participatory model of research that could generate empirical evidence, in the form of narrative cases, of the process of mobile technology (iPads) appropriation in educational contexts.

2 Discussion and Literature

It is recognised in the literature that mobile technologies have the potential to 'disrupt' established practices in ways that require adaptation if educators are to harness their potential (Jenkins, 2006 [6]; Baron, 2008 [7]; Pachler, 2009 [8]; Traxler, 2007 [9] & 2010 [10]). A more detailed depiction of the character of such 'disruption' is emerging with research focusing variously on concepts of convergence, mobile learning, personalisation, connectivity, sustainability and indeed the compatibility of emergent mobile learning practices within established contexts of formal education (Traxler, 2010 [10]; Pachler, Bachmair and Cook, 2010 [2]; Crook, 2012 [11]). The emerging evidence suggests that the process of adaptation is prolonged and complex. Yet in a digital age of rapidly increasing connectivity and converging cultures there is a need for further research into the implications of mobile technologies and how educators can be located as central agents in changing and adapting pedagogical practices. The discourses at the interface of macro-level educational policy and the micro-level contexts of professional practice are fertile ground for understanding the complex and unpredictable process of technological appropriation and its implications for education (Castells, Fernadez-Ardevol, Linchuan Qui and Sey, 2007 [12]; Pachler et Ranieri, Manca and Cook, 2012 [13]; Selwyn, 2012 [14]). Processes of technology appropriation are often far less transformative of pedagogical practice in the short term than techno-centric arguments proclaim (Cuban, 2001 [15]; Selwyn, 2012 [14]; Crook, 2012 [11]). However, Jenkins (2008, p.11 [6]) has argued that we are in a 'period of prolonged transition' with regards the implications for new technologies and the way we learn. Similarly, Laurillard (2012, p. 226 [16]) comments 'the difference that marks out the early years of the twenty-first century from any previous period in education is that digital technologies not only enable a change to treating teaching as a design science, they also require it.' Hence, the narrative ecology framework uses participatory narrative methods to place teachers at the centre of this process of teaching as a process of design. In any such pedagogical design process teachers are conceived as active agents (Somekh, 2007 [17]; Pachler, Cook and Bachmair, 2010 [18]).

The narrative ecology model of technological appropriation I will posit for discussion here places the appropriation of mobile technologies within their wider educational and socio-cultural contexts emerging as it does from critique of Activity

Theory (Engeström, 1987 [19], 2000 [20], 2001 [21]) that questions the place of intentionality and individual agency within Activity Theory (Nardi, 1996 [22]; Wertsch, 1998 [23]; Ellis, Edwards and Smagorinsky, 2010 [24]). That is, in the narrative ecology model, digital technologies are not merely conceived of as educational tools mediated by educational and wider socio-cultural contexts, but also as integral items of the expressive life and intentionality of the individual (Goffman, 1959 [25]; Perkins, 1993 [26]); that is, for effective appropriation to occur I argue that technologies need to be conceived as an anthropomorphic extension of teachers' multiple identities within contemporary society. Technology brings I suggest an added layer of complexity and potential disruption to the established professional and socio-cultural ecology of the classroom and is inherently problematic (Turvey and Pachler, Forthcoming [27]). As long as techno-centric arguments dominate this discourse I argue that at best technology will continue to disappoint in terms of realising anything more than a perfunctory role in education and at worst may bring further disruptive unintended consequences.

2.1 The Narrative Ecology Framework

The narrative ecology framework offers a process of participatory research into professional practice with new technologies (Turvey, 2012a [3], 2012b [28], and 2013 [1]). This model is positioned within a significant body of research focusing on teachers' innovation with new technologies (See for example Fisher et al 2006 [29]; Somekh, 2007 [17]; Loveless, 2003 [30] and 2007 [31]). As such it places teachers at the centre of the pedagogical design process with new technologies and offers a useful tool for the synthesis and analysis of technological tools and pedagogical processes. It is an attempt to recognise Klafki's (1995/1958, p.21 [32]) didactic analysis of pedagogy 'as a selection made in a particular human, historical situation and with specific groups of children in mind' but which can also illuminate the macro-to-micro and micro-to-macro imperatives and constraints at play as teachers appropriate technologies into their practice. It is a theoretical tool for developing more rich, 'state-of-the-actual' descriptions of technology-enhanced learning (Selwyn and Facer, 2013 [33]). As Loveless and Williams state (2013, p.158 [34]); 'being ready, willing and able to teach, calls for a reading of the world in which content, context and tools can be orchestrated with skill and purpose.' The German tradition (Klafki, 1995/1958, p.20 [32]) of didactic analysis requires the teacher not just to understand the what (content) and the how (pedagogy) but also the why 'with its attendant past and the anticipated future'.

From these perspectives I argue that the pedagogical appropriation of new technologies is a complex process, predicated on the interdependency of various contextual and autobiographical factors. In the model, these are arranged in an arch structure supporting the concept of a pedagogical keystone (Figure 2). The variable factors identified are; the affordance of the technological tools; teachers' and learners' subject knowledge; learners' needs and teachers' perceptions of learners' needs; teachers' and learners' prior experience of the e-learning tools available; teachers' and learners' attitudes and values; teachers' capacity to reflect in or on action; wider socio-cultural discourse around policy, education and technology and; intrinsically or extrinsically generated theories of pedagogy and practice. These contextual and autobiographical factors are conceived as an ecology creating both resonance or dissonance in the development of the teacher's pedagogical keystone. A pedagogical keystone is defined here as the synchronic interdependency of the contextual and autobiographical factors at play as the teacher goes about their work of designing contingencies for learning. As Postman notes, (1993, p.18 [35]) in an ecological system, change in one variable 'generates total change' to the system as a whole. However, there can be a tendency to regard agents as passive actors settling into new niches as the ecology changes around them. On the contrary, Normak, Pata and Kaipainen (2012, p.264 [36]) define a niche as a 'learning onto-space' where the 'perceived qualities of persons' such as their past experiences and intentionality (autobiographical) are significant factors in the ecology in which they are operating.

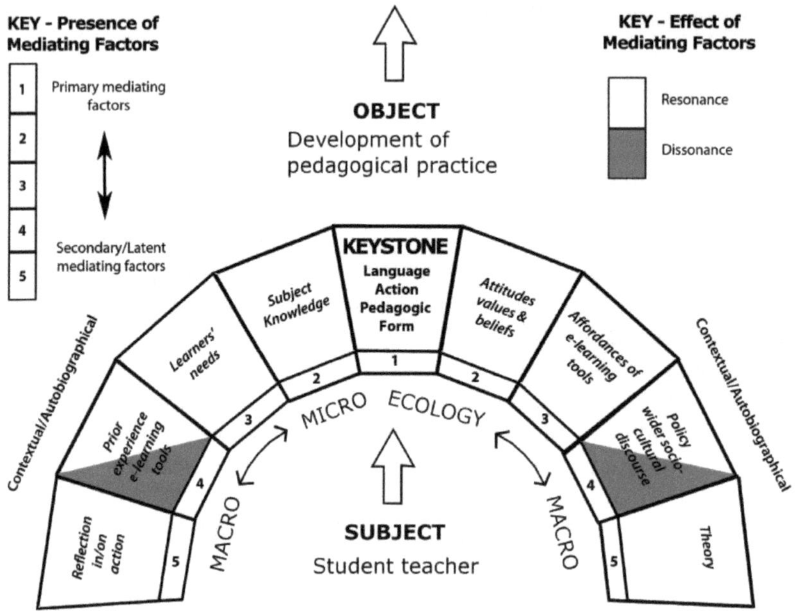

Fig. 2. Narrative ecology theoretical framework

If as discussed earlier, we perceive of the pedagogical process as a design process, the qualities and intentions the teacher brings are vital and live elements within the ecology. A key issue, however, is how such past experiences and intentionality can be captured as they are woven into the teacher's interactions within a dynamic and complex pedagogical ecology incorporating mobile technologies. In the narrative ecology model this complex and dynamic interdependency between the tools, the context and the agent's intentionality and experience is represented through the concept of a pedagogical keystone (Figure 2). Narrative, with its potential to reveal participants' underlying 'organising principles' (Goodson, 2008, p.18 [37]) as they act on the world, is seen as an important methodological device in capturing and characterising the teacher's pedagogical keystone. Narrative methodologies have the potential as Schostak discusses to position subjects as 'expert in their own ways of seeing,' (2006, p.149 [38]). Furthermore, as Pata (2011, p.3 [39]) notes, narratives are useful 'vehicle[s] for meaning making and identity-determination.' That is, narratives can bring deeper meaning to the apparently isolated yet constituent events and activities as they can convey 'what one thinks one did in what settings in what ways and for what felt reasons' (Bruner, 1990, p.119 [40]). Such narrative methods require establishment of trusting and participatory relationships between research participants and researcher so the conduct of the project was important as I discuss now.

3 Conduct

This project was conducted in two phases (Table 1). In phase 1, a day symposium was held at which secondary school teachers and lecturers in initial teacher education were invited to present to colleagues about how they were incorporating the use of iPads into their professional practice. These presentations were video recorded with the permission of participants. At the symposium, the narrative ecology model was also presented to participants and a group discussion was held which was also recorded. The participants were given access to the recordings of the presentations, group discussion and the editable infographic of the model (Figure 1) on their own iPads for use in phase 2 of the project.

During phase 2 a self-selecting sample of 4 participants 2 secondary school teachers and 2 lecturers in initial teacher education agreed to further participation. An in-depth narrative interview was conducted with these participants in which they were supported in using the framework to narrate and discuss their on-going experiences of incorporating the iPads in their professional practice.

Table 1. Methods and data collection

Project Phase	Type of data	Quantity
1	Group Interview Presentations Field notes	8 Participants
2	In-depth narrative interviews Narrative portrayals Participant response and commentary on narrative portrayal Documentary evidence (e.g. published material by schools about their 1:1 iPad projects)	4 Participants

These individual narrative interviews together with the participant's presentation, their contribution to the group discussion from the symposium and any further documentary evidence were then analysed using Nvivo. The 8 variable factors identified in the narrative ecology framework (Figure 2) were applied to the qualitative data. As far as possible the raw data was used for analysis as opposed to transcribing the video and audio footage. That is, footage was coded using the 8 variables from the model directly in Nvivo. This enabled more direct engagement with the raw data and was felt to add to the validity of the interpretations being made as important aspects such as tone remained integral to the raw data. Figure 3 illustrates this process showing the coding applied to one of the in-depth narrative interviews.

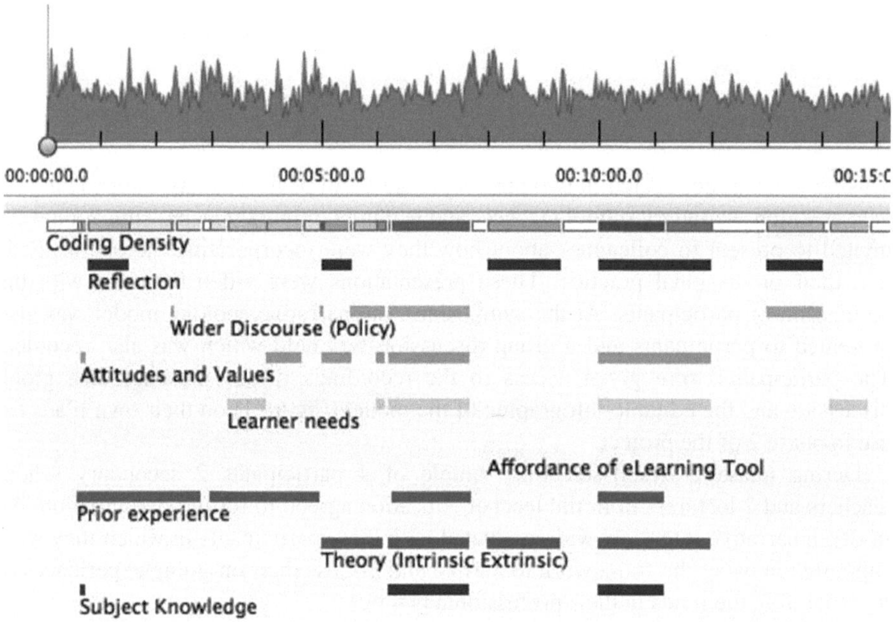

Fig. 3. Narrative ecology coding applied to in-depth interview using Nvivo

When the data had been analysed and coded, an individual narrative summary was constructed. The narrative summary was an attempt to identify from the data, the individual participant's pedagogical keystone or the factors which appeared to take priority and have most influence as they reflected on their appropriation of the mobile technologies into their pedagogical practice. The narrative summary was then shared with the participant for further commentary on the researcher's interpretation and further reflection.

It is acknowledged that this approach does not easily lend itself to broad generalisations about the impact of technologies in education. The aim of the research was to understand and capture in much more depth, the complex qualitative ways in which educators adapt their pedagogical practice when incorporating mobile technologies and what factors appear to guide and influence this. As Crook et al. (2010, p. 53 [41]) note, the 'impact' of new technologies in education is often defined narrowly in terms of examination results and attainment whereas 'the value added may be more than the value measured'. It is argued here too that any narrowly defined impacts of technologies in education are largely meaningless and open to questioning without the rich qualitative factors that characterise dynamic educational contexts and educator experiences. It is beyond the scope of this paper to present and analyse all of the participants' narrative cases. I will therefore focus on the presentation and analysis of one case in depth.

4 Narrative Case: Sam

Sam is a Science teacher in a large secondary school in England (11-16 year olds). At the time of this research she was in her seventh year as a qualified teacher and as well as her role in the science department she had a role as a 'digital leader', providing support to other colleagues with the integration of digital technologies into their pedagogical practice. The school has recently adopted a 1:1 iPad policy providing all students with iPads through a scheme in which parents can purchase an iPad for their child at various subsidised levels depending on financial circumstances. There are also options provided for those families just above the Free School Meal entitlement threshold who are unable to afford to buy a device. The school looked into various strategies such as Bring Your Own Device (BYOD) before adopting their approach and Sam was involved in this process from early on. So as a 'digital leader', significantly involved in the 1:1 iPad project she has already identified herself as open to the aims of this school-wide initiative which were identified as:

- Empower students by encouraging creativity, problem-solving and independence in their learning;
- Provide an increasingly high degree of personalised feedback to students and their families;
- Bring students into closer partnership with teachers in the development of learning pathways and learning materials;
- Systematically share learning materials with students and parents in order to empower their support for learning anytime, anywhere;
- Place our teachers at the heart of a vibrant local and national innovation partnership where skills, knowledge and learning materials are actively shared and developed. [1]

In this narrative portrayal of Sam's current position with regards the wider school iPad initiative and her own professional practice I identify three significant themes that emerged from my analysis of Sam's narrative ecology, namely; prior experience, attitudes and values, recognition of learner needs and agency. These themes overlapped throughout the analysis of the data and also appeared to reveal an underlying open yet pragmatic approach to pedagogical adaptation, as Sam continues to reflect on the implications of the 1:1 iPad initiative for her own pedagogical practice. As might be expected when researching the professional practices and perceptions of experienced teachers such as Sam, the variable themes identified within the narrative ecology framework were often densely populated in the data in

[1] Documentary evidence provided by the school in the public domain.

Sam's case. For example 51.7% (Nvivo) of the source data was coded against the theme of reflection indicating the extent of her capacity to critically reflect on the initiative in question. However, while this capacity to reflect critically was no doubt significant in Sam's case it is the nature of the insights afforded by these reflections that led to the glimpses of Sam's open yet pragmatic approach to pedagogical adaptation in response to the 1:1 iPad initiative in her school. This open yet pragmatic approach revealed itself in the interplay between her prior experiences, her attitudes and values and the ways in which she appeared to adapt her pedagogical practices in ways that were sensitive to learner agency and needs as I will explore now.

4.1 Prior Experience; Attitudes and Values; Learner Agency and Needs

These three themes were often present in the data as was apparent from Sam's initial reflections in the interview when I asked her to tell some of her background and route into the teaching profession. She related that as part of her degree in Human Sciences, which she describes as a course that tried 'to bridge the divide between the arts and science,' she had been prompted to reflect on her development and through this process she states that:

> *'I realised at the end of the degree that I did want to do something to do with education. It had become really obvious to me that what I cared about was how do you get students to really understand and how do they become part of that? How do you make it happen basically?'*

That is, helping students to 'become part of' the learning process or active agents in the process of learning was identified as being important to her on first thoughts of entry to the profession. Another important factor of her prior experience and route into the profession was her work as a learning mentor supporting children with Special Educational Needs (SEN) which she believes continues to influence her approach now as a teacher. For example she related:

> *'I would say that influences my teaching quite a lot because I've come from that background of SEN. I wouldn't say that makes me any better than anyone else at dealing with that, but awareness side of things ...... I find that experience helps me when building good relationships with students.'*

Sam places emphasis on the importance of teachers having 'good relationships' with students here again signposting this aspect of her attitudes and values about teaching and learning in terms of learners' needs but also locating this in her prior experiences as a learning mentor. As Sam began to talk more about her practice, however, she was keen to point out that she was also quite pragmatic in her approach to her pedagogical practice. This was evident when prompted to try and describe what kind of teacher she felt she was as she replied

'I think I kind of go from one extreme to the other from being quite didactic this is what we need to learn about and I can't think of an exciting way to do it or teach it (laughing). I'm just going to tell you (in a teacher voice)... to the more extreme I going to think of something ridiculously creative and I'm going to get you on board.....I guess as a teacher I go from one to the other. I don't always necessarily get them as tied together...'

That is, she sees her teacher identity as a synthesis of these two extremes, the ideal being when she is able to combine aspects of creative teaching which actively engages her students with more authoritative and didactic approaches. Furthermore she offers more evidence that this open yet pragmatic pedagogy she is developing lies in her prior experiences by referring back to her experiences as an Aim Higher learning mentor as she continues:

'I don't want to sound too idealistic or have ridiculous ideas like a PGCE student just coming into it. But I've come into it because of my background as a learning mentor. As an Aim Higher learning mentor the whole purpose was to get children into higher education who might not have thought it was a possibility for them. And the students I was working with in my first place as a learning mentor were on the C/D borderline. So things that were happening in a lesson where they could have understood if you'd just used the right example or just made it applicable in some way to them. It was what the teacher did that could have made a massive difference and I think it's this that made me realise I wanted to be a teacher rather than a learning mentor. The reason I came into teaching is because I saw that...it's like an inequality of access to learning and understanding. And that need to try and address that balance and make it more equal. But they're kind of pie in the sky idealisms that don't necessarily play out day to day.'

The ambiguity in her first sentence is interesting in that Sam is positioning herself as open to innovation and ideals but at pains not to appear naïve. As an experienced practitioner she appears to hold onto certain ideals about the needs of learners and helping them to access knowledge and understanding. The last sentence of this extract clarifies that despite holding such ideals, she recognises them as ideals that are often problematic to realise in practice.

These interview extracts suggest that the way Sam currently positions her professional practice, including her attitudes and values about teaching and learning, together with her perceptions about learners' needs, are located in both her current and prior experiences in becoming a teacher. These themes can be seen as significant nodes within her narrative ecology, which continue to resonate in her on-going narrative of professional identity formation. Furthermore these themes remain significant as Sam relates her on-going experiences of adapting her pedagogy with the introduction of the iPads.

4.2 Pedagogical Adaptation

The ways in which the 1:1 iPad project had begun to impact upon and become appropriated by Sam, and to some extent some of her colleagues in the science department was evidenced through her presentation and contribution to the mobile learning symposium that was held at the University, but also through the school-based interview and observation. During the symposium, after explaining the background information of her school's 1:1 iPad initiative, she went on to share how as a science department they were exploring the use of the iPads in learning and teaching. There appeared to be an early progression in that initially the focus was very much on finding particular apps for specific science topics in order to illustrate difficult concepts. However, Sam went on to say that 'in science one of the most powerful things has just been the camera.' She described how they had explored a range of uses of the iPads but much of this involved visual aspects such as taking microscopic photographs. Similarly, there had been much experimentation with creating short animations of scientific processes with one teacher using animation to model ionic bonding with the children. On my visit and observation I watched another teacher creating a short time-lapse animation of the process of crystallisation as hot wax cooled slowly on a microscope slide. The iPad was set up on an improvised rig to hold it steady over a period of time. However, it was during the interview with Sam that she offered more of an insight into her own interpretations of these pedagogical science initiatives and how her prior experience of her Human Sciences degree influenced this interpretation. For example when asked to describe her own practice with the iPads she relates:

> *'I don't know if we've got any further but I think it requires looking at things from a thinking skills perspective. We've done things like mapping apps to Blooms but I don't think that actually means anything...it's about what's the task not what's the app? So we're using animation a lot and that seems for science particularly a good way in to using iPads........ But if you just say to students OK here's a topic/process....and me as quite a visual person with a science background I can think of oh I would do this with it...I could do that with it...but students are not necessarily bringing that to it as they don't have that kind of experience or maybe their brain doesn't work that way. So we've had to structure the experience. And a more successful way of doing it seems to be where you give them a diagram and maybe some plasticine and they literally do the moving. So it's all there for them and they're just showing the process. So it's pinning down the real specifics.....(Pauses) I would quite like to see that built into students becoming more creative in their own way which is what I had with some Year 11s last year. These two girls who just got it. They had that visual and kind of design perspective on it and they really grasped what they could do with it, how it could look and really ran with it which I think students could get to but maybe it's a step-by-step thing which requires a longer term view, which I haven't really thought about yet.'*

What is particularly interesting about this response is that Sam appears to be recalling her own experiences of her Human Sciences degree, which she described earlier as trying to bring together the 'arts and science' and using this experience to consider how the affordances of the technology can be exploited more effectively in her teaching and the children's learning. In terms of the learners' needs she recognises that they may not have the visual literacy skills to be able to exploit the tools offered by the iPad to illustrate scientific concepts in new ways and therefore has adapted her practice to suit, limiting the resources she makes available to the children to ensure that they can focus on the scientific processes involved rather than becoming inhibited by their potential lack of visual literacy or being overwhelmed by the creative possibilities. Again it appears her approach can be characterised here as pragmatic openness as she is prepared to explore the potential of the tools but recognises the important role she can play in scaffolding the experience for the learners in order to avoid the students becoming more concerned with what she described as 'style over substance'. Furthermore, despite being pragmatic and thinking about how she can adapt her practice to scaffold the learning she sustains the ideal to which she sees herself working whereby children will be able to become more independent and creative in time as she goes on to express further:

> *'The idea is where they're doing the creation themselves of what they've learnt and presenting it for you and themselves as a coherent thing that they've worked out...that's when the penny drops and it's a much stronger experience but then that's where we're talking about the highest level skills and that's not necessarily where most students are going to get to in the course of a 100 minute lesson.....but yeh that's what it would be ideally.'*

That is, she acknowledges that her current approach does not cede as much agency to the learners as it could, due to the constraints of time, the need to remain focused on the scientific subject knowledge and the possible limitation of children's visual literacy, yet she retains the ideal of the learner being able to take greater agency in the process of illustrating and demonstrating their learning and understanding. Again this demonstrates an openness to further pedagogical adaptation but from a pragmatic position. This sense of taking increased responsibility for one's learning is something again that appeared to be echoed in Sam's prior experiences. When prompted to reflect on her own experience of using technologies she recalls her experience growing up around technologies noting that:

> *'Yeh...I'm capable...I'm not any kind of expert with computers...erm..I was thinking about this the other day as I was talking to someone about having a Spectrum when we were young and I was thinking I need to ask my Mum and Dad you know why did they buy one.... It would have been quite expensive ... but they obviously saw this technology and thought wow we're going to get our children a computer and we ended up trying out programming and Basic and stuff... So we always had something and we had the Internet from about 1997 at home and I used to use.. (builds up suspense) Encarta*

(laughs..). But also we had reference books, encyclopaedias and things that I used to use and I'd go between the two. And you know I like...I've got a smartphone. And I use my computer quite a lot but I'm not an expert. I'm not massively technological... I'm quite practical so if I don't know how to use something I look it up and I find out and I work it out. So yeh generally... like I changed the hard drive on my laptop but you know...Google it...figure it out and have a go.'

Thus, Sam's attitudes and values regarding agency in learning as expressed in the desire to move closer towards a pedagogy that affords greater agency to learners is a pattern that can be traced in her own prior experience of using technologies in her willingness and capacity to 'figure it out and have a go'. The significance of this seemed also to resonate further. Learners taking responsibility for their learning and the decisions they make is one of the ways that Sam frames and resolves some of the day-to-day tensions that the introduction of iPads into the classroom has brought. Moreover, some of these tensions resonate beyond the classroom as Sam talked about how she assuages parents' concerns that the presence of the iPads might prove to be too much of a distraction from learning for their children, as she says:

'Like when I'm talking to parents I put it in this way ....like I say if we were in a meeting now, I have a choice and say there are lots of people in the room they have a choice...I could look at my emails but I'm not going to because I'm concentrating on what we're talking about.. I have that choice....There are plenty of adults who wouldn't be able to ignore that and think look I've got to do that now. And this technology is going to be there now forever and we need to help students to develop that ability to say "I'm going to ignore that" and help them to see that it's their responsibility.'

Hence she draws on her attitudes and values built from her own prior and current experiences that learners need to take responsibility for their own learning and the choices they make. Whilst Sam recognises there is a potential tension and disruption to learning as children could become distracted by the technology she is accepting of this tension recognising it as part of the learning process. Indeed, Sam provides yet further evidence of how she is adapting her pedagogy to the inclusion of iPads, using her attitudes and values about learning and agency as a guiding principle in an incident she related both in her presentation at the university-based symposium and her interview. She continues:

'I caught myself almost about to have a go at a student who.......I had some like finger puppets (laughs) and we were talking about a tapir and I was like is it a tapir or is it an ant eater or is it an aadvark? And I was like hang on ant eaters and aadvarks I get confused (laughing)... which is which? We had a little discussion and no one quite knew so we were carrying on and I was talking about what they were going to do and one of them was on their iPad. I was thinking "oh no I'm going to have to have a go" and then I realised "oh no he's looking up...he's just finding out for me". Ant eaters...aadvarks

are they different?.... "Yes they are here we are miss"..... You have to allow a bit more freedom I think...You have to be willing to let go of the reins a little bit.'

Interestingly, although Sam is open and willing to 'allow a bit more freedom' in the pedagogical process she also appears to be pragmatic in adapting her pedagogy to accommodate this freedom yet retain control as she goes on to explain that 'I think I have relaxed a bit in that I think they're on their iPad but you know (pauses).....I look for clues.' The clues she now looks for are the gestures that the children are making as they interact with their iPads as she explain further:

'So today someone was doing this (gestures and acts like someone tilting their iPad) and I said (puts on teacher voice) "I don't think anything I've asked you to do today involves you needing to tip your iPad like that.." And you know it made them laugh because they knew they weren't doing the right thing. But you can sort of tell by gestures if they're doing something they are supposed to or not. But it is disconcerting because the teacher alarm goes off a lot more in my head than it used to. So as you're walking around the classroom, it might be that you've asked them to do something but you haven't stipulated whether it's on paper or iPad then there is that possibility but even if it is on paper....are they looking something up and referring back to it?...... So you think they're not doing what they're supposed to but yeh you have to kind of hold it back a bit until you know for sure because otherwise you are going to jump down their throats for doing the right thing.'

Similarly, Sam describes other strategies involving the interpretation of new gestures describing tapping on the iPad as 'a give-away' because:

'That's a game because yes what else would require you to tap like that other than a game...And then moving it (referring back to comment about tilting iPad)...And generally the kind of focus on the iPad. So if the person next to them is kind of interested....it can mean they're not doing something they're supposed to. Or if they've got it like that (demonstrates a stance of taking a sneaky photo of someone). And also of course you can see their notifications come up and you walk past them and they're being good...they're not touching them so they've got however many notification there.... waiting.'

What these insights into how Sam is creating the space for this new technology in the children's learning show, is how the technology brings new layers of complexity to the pedagogical process. These new layers of complexity need to be negotiated by the teacher and the learners in ways that allow the affordances of the tools to be exploited appropriately in ways that resonate with the educational goals identified. In negotiating these added complexities that the technology brings, Sam's prior experiences appear significant. For example her prior experiences; as someone able to take responsibility for her own learning with technology; as someone with experience and expertise in understanding the visual in the scientific; as someone who began her career working with SEN children trying to help them 'really understand'; as someone of several years teaching experience, all seem significant in enabling her to adapt her pedagogies remaining open to pedagogical adaptation yet sustaining a pragmatic approach.

5 Conclusions

The nature of this in-depth qualitative research limits the extent to which one can generalize from this case. However, it is appropriate to indicate how the evidence from this case fits with the general body of evidence emerging about mobile technology appropriation in education, which was discussed in detail in the earlier sections of this paper.

The evidence from Sam's case concurs with the literature discussed regarding the potential of mobile technologies to 'disrupt' established practices both at the micro and meso level. For example, at the micro level of classroom practice there was clear evidence of Sam adapting aspects of her practice in response to the introduction of the technology. A significant aspect of this concerned adjustments to her behaviour management strategies such as tolerating uncertainty regarding appropriate student behaviours with the iPads during lessons. This had also triggered Sam's development of a wider repertoire of behaviour cues to make sense of the various gestures involved in manipulating the technology, in order to gauge the extent to which students appeared to be on task. Also at the micro level of classroom practice, the introduction of the technology had prompted Sam to consider how to utilize the new opportunities offered by the technology but without losing the focus on the science subject content. Thus in working with the animation facilities, she had acted to limit the resources available to the students in order to ensure the scientific content was addressed. These examples represent specific ways in which the technology can 'disrupt' or challenge established professional practices at the micro level. However, similarly, at the meso level Sam faced the challenge of justifying to parents the use of the iPads in their children's education. From this perspective the introduction of the technology had the potential to 'disrupt' the important relationship between the wider community and the school and as such required Sam to act in order to counter the skepticism of parents and maintain their trust.

Using the narrative ecology model as a participatory tool to story the range of variable factors in Sam's case revealed a complex and rich picture highlighting the interdependency of a range of autobiographical and contextual factors involved in the appropriation of technologies in professional practice. Whilst the technological tool and its potential were significant, the exploitation of its educational value was mediated significantly by Sam's past experiences and current intentions. Her experience of her Human Sciences degree with its study of visual representation in science and her experience of working as a mentor to children with SEN gave another layer of nuance to her pedagogical adaptations in response to the introduction of the iPad. That is, the participatory approach to the use of the narrative ecology model helped to uncover tacit levels of critical reflection on Sam's part. Her ambiguity about limiting the children's resources when using the animation app were tempered by her pragmatic understanding of the need to address the scientific content and the level of visual literacy that would be required if the students were given more free rein. This level of critical reflection on practice – past experiences resonating with Sam's awareness of current limitations whilst remaining open to future potential – appeared to be laid bare through the use of a participatory narrative approach. These findings point to the need to place greater importance on making sense of the complex interdependency of factors at play when mobile technologies are appropriated into professional practice. Significantly, however, these findings are also indicative of the importance that educator and teacher perspectives can play in making sense of the complex ecology involved in pedagogical adaptation. From this perspective, the development of participatory methods would seem to be a priority for further research into this field.

Acknowledgements. The author would like to thank the Education Research Centre, School of Education, University of Brighton for the funding of this project. Thanks are also due to colleagues from the local partnership schools and the School of Education who took part in the mobile learning symposium and committed their time to participate in this project.

References

1. Turvey, K.: Narrative ecologies: Teachers as pedagogical toolmakers. Routledge, London (2013)
2. Pachler, N., Bachmair, B., Cook, J.: Mobile Learning: Structures, Agency, Practices. Springer, New York (2010)
3. Turvey, K.: Questioning the character and significance of convergence between social network and professional practices in teacher education. British Journal of Educational Technology 43(5), 739–753 (2012b)
4. Higher Education Funding Council England.: Enhancing learning and teaching through the use of technology: A revised approach to HEFCE's strategy for e-learning, London (2009)
5. JISC.: Effective Practice in a Digital Age, London (2009)
6. Jenkins, H.: Convergence culture: where old and new media collide. New York University Press, New York (2006)
7. Baron, N.S.: Always on: Language in an online and mobile world. Oxford University Press, Oxford (2008)
8. Pachler, N.: Research methods in mobile and informal learning: some issues. In: Vavoula, G., Pachler, N., Kukulska-Hulme, A. (eds.) Researching Mobile Learning: Frameworks, Tools and Research Designs. Peter Lang Publishing, Oxford (2009)
9. Traxler, J.: Defining, discussing, and evaluating mobile learning: The moving finger writes and having written. International Review of Research in Open and Distance Learning 8(2), 1–12 (2007)
10. Traxler, J.: Sustaining mobile learning and its institutions. International Journal of Mobile and Blended Learning 2(4), 58–65 (2010)
11. Crook, C.: The 'digital native' in context: Tensions associated with importing Web 2.0 practices into the school setting. Oxford Review of Education 38(1), 63–80 (2012)

12. Castells, M., Fernandez-Ardevol, M., Linchuan Qiu, J., Sey, A.: Mobile Communication and Society: A Global Perspective. MIT Press, MA (2007)
13. Pachler, N., Ranieri, M., Manca, S., Cook, J.: Editorial: Social Networking and Mobile Learning. British Journal of Educational Technology 43(5), 707–710 (2012)
14. Selwyn, N.: Ten suggestions for improving academic research in education and technology. Learning, Media and Technology 37(3), 213–219 (2012)
15. Cuban, L.: Oversold and underused: Computers in the classroom. Harvard University Press, Cambridge (2001)
16. Laurillard, D.: Teaching as a Design Science: Building Pedagogical Patterns for Learning and Technology. Routledge, New York (2012)
17. Somekh, B.: Pedagogy and Learning with ICT: Researching the art of innovation. Routledge, New York (2007)
18. Pachler, N., Cook, J., Bachmair, B.: Appropriation of mobile cultural resources for learning. International Journal of Mobile and Blended Learning 2(1), 1–21 (2010)
19. Engeström, Y.: Learning by expanding: An activity-theoretical approach to developmental research. Orienta-Kosultit Oy, Helsinki (1987)
20. Engeström, Y.: Activity theory as a framework for analysing and redesigning work. Ergonomics 43(7), 960–974 (2000)
21. Engeström, Y.: Expansive Learning at Work: Toward an activity theoretical reconceptualisation. Journal of Education and Work 14(1), 133–156 (2001)
22. Nardi, B.: Studying context: A comparison of activity theory, situated action models, and distributed cognition. In: Nardi, B. (ed.) Context and Consciousness: Activity Theory and Human-Computer Interaction. MIT Press, Cambridge (1996)
23. Wertsch, J.V.: Mind as Action. Oxford University Press, New York (1998)
24. Ellis, V., Edwards, A., Smagorinsky, P. (eds.): Cultural-historical perspectives on teacher education and development: Learning Teaching. Routledge, Oxon (2010)
25. Goffman, E.: The Presentation of self in everyday life. Doubleday, New York (1959)
26. Perkins, D.N.: Person-plus: A distributed view of thinking and learning. In: Salomon, G. (ed.) Distributed Cognitions: Psychological and Educational Considerations. Cambridge University Press, Cambridge (1993)
27. Turvey, K., Pachler, N.: 'Problem spaces': A framework and questions for critical engagement with learning technologies in formal educational contexts. In: Rushby, N., Surry, D. (eds.) The Wiley Handbook of Learning Technology. Wiley-Blackwell (Forthcoming)
28. Turvey, K.: Constructing narrative ecologies as a site for teachers' professional learning with new technologies and media in primary education. E-Learning and Digital Media 9(1), 113–126 (2012a)
29. Fisher, T., Higgins, C., Loveless, A.: Teachers learning with digital technologies: A review of research and projects. Futurelab, Bristol (2006)
30. Loveless, A.: The interaction between primary teachers' perceptions of ICT and their pedagogy. Education and Information Technologies 8(4), 313–326 (2003)
31. Loveless, A.: Preparing to teach with ICT: Subject knowledge, Didaktik and Improvisation. Curriculum Journal 18(4), 509–522 (2007)
32. Klafki, W.: Didactic analysis as the core of preparation of instruction (Didaktische Analyse als Kern der Unterrichtsvorbereitung). Journal of Curriculum Studies 27(1), 13–30 (1958)
33. Selwyn, N., Facer, K.: The Politics of Education and Technology. Palgrave Macmillan, New York (2013)
34. Loveless, A., Williamson, B.: Learning Identities in a Digital Age: Rethinking Creativity, Education and Technology. Routledge, London (2013)

35. Postman, N.: Technopoly: The surrender of culture to technology. Vintage Books, New York (1993)
36. Normak, P., Pata, K., Kaipainen, M.: An Ecological Approach to Learning Dynamics. Journal of Educational Technology & Society 15(3), 262–274 (2012)
37. Goodson, I.F.: Investigating the teacher's life and work. Sense Publishers, Rotterdam (2008)
38. Schostak, J.: Interviewing and Representation in Qualitative Research. Oxford University Press, Maidenhead (2006)
39. Pata, K.: Participatory design experiment: Storytelling Swarm in hybrid narrative ecosystem. In: Daniel, B.K. (ed.) A Handbook of Research on Methods and Techniques for Studying Virtual Communities: Paradigms and Phenomena. Hershey, New York (2011)
40. Bruner, J.S.: Acts of Meaning. Harvard University Press, London (1990)
41. Crook, C., Harrison, C., Farrington-Flint, L., Tomas, C., Underwood, J.: The impact of technology: value-added classroom practice. Final report. BECTA, Coventry (2010), http://dera.ioe.ac.uk/1771/

Breeding ICT Skills for the Industries: The South African Experience

Tiko Iyamu

Namibia University of Science and Technology, Windhoek, Namibia
iyamut@polytechnic.edu.na

Abstract. Skilled and competent personnel are required in the use of information and communication technology (ICT), for organisations' competitiveness and sustainability. Many organisations rely on institutions of higher learning to produce ICT skilled personnel for them. However, many of the graduates are said to be incompetent in their roles and responsibilities. In an attempt to close that gap of incompetency, some organisations source for postgraduate candidates. Unfortunately, the gap of ICT skill shortage seems to remain, leading to this study. The study was carried out in South Africa, one of African countries to examine and understand the extent, as well as impact of ICT skills in the country. Different approaches and techniques of research methodology, such as qualitative and quantitative, and interpretivism were applied in the study. As found in the empirical study, the underlying factors in the challenges of ICT skill short in South Africa are the gap between the qualification and competency. Other influencing factors include government interference, organisational need, and curriculum development and transformative scheme.

Keywords: Skill-set, Alignment, Curriculum, Organisational need, Environment trend.

1 Introduction

Human resources, particularly skill set are fundamental to the development and growth of a country's economy. As such, in order for a country, including South Africa to develop sustainability, skill shortage must receive significant attention. This has never been an easy task by any standard, in any environment, and whether in a developed or developing country. An assessment revealed that different sociotechnical factors are involved in the fulfilment of the quest to bridge the gap of skill shortages [1]. Some of the factors often considered are either societal or governmental. Some studies attributed the challenges of skill gap to factors, such as ageing nature of employees which has impact on their growth; none availability of qualified individuals; cultural orientation; lack of retention strategy; and cost implication for trainings and retraining of workers [2], [3], and [4]. In the zeal to reduce skill shortage, there exist misalignment and of interest and requirements. This results to creating more gaps. Hamer [5] argued that the academia and industry expect

D. Passey and A. Tatnall (Eds.): KCICTP/ITEM 2014, IFIP AICT 444, pp. 124–135, 2014.

and produces two very different skills sets, respectively. Harmer therefore proposed that aligning the available skills sets can only result in positive outcomes.

Many organisations in Africa rely on fresh university graduates, and develop them further over time. Some organisations have various development strategies, through which they develop their employees, such as internships and mentorships programs. This is in order for them to gain the necessary skills and experiences as required by the organisation. Hamer [5] argued that internships, mentorship, and other cases in organisations can be used at the universities, but it is critical for the organisations to participate. The Mentorship programs would be a good solution to the skills gap as it assists with skill transfer of knowledge, however, companies still do loses skilled employees for various other reasons [6].

Poverty and previous disadvantage steers from political imbalance also contribute to skill shortage in many countries, Africa in particular. Johnston et al. [7] argued that South Africans that came from previously disadvantage background have poor primary and secondary schooling. In that study, it was argued that such poor background make it difficult for them to succeed in their higher education pursuit, contributing to the skill shortage in the country [7]. This argument could be considered to be fair, and attributed to the challenges some black South Africans uphold when it comes to finding job.

Skills shortage exists in every country, but worst in developing countries. Natarajan [8] presents statistics of global skills shortage: at the time of his study, in the USA there was a skills shortage of 126,000 in the nursing profession; a 615,000 shortfall of IT networking skills in Europe; 40,000 vacancies in the engineering sector also in Europe; and in India there were a shortfall of 500,000 ICT professionals. This could be argued to be relative to the population of the countries. However, the figures are still high, a case of one too many.

Many countries have developed initiatives and emphasis that the universities need to help reduce skills shortage. To skills shortage, the stakeholders from the industries in South Africa argued they notice poor performance by the Universities in the country, which according to them contributes to the high unemployment rate [9]. The assessment by Macgregor [9] has inspired organisations to invest on numerous strategies, such as short term training courses, internship, and mentorship, in addressing the challenges of skills shortage. After few years of such investment by many organisations in the country, fundamental questions are raised: What has been the return on investment of that front? Did the strategies invigorated brain drain? These are some of the questions that need to be answered with time. According to Haskins [10], the South African Institute of Measurement and Control, aim to contribute to addressing the skills shortage in the country, focusing on process control industry. The institute promote synergy between students and industry, and as such, is expected to help provide some statistics in answering the questions, overtime and in perspectives.

Skills are categorised to be either generic or specialised, and carries the ingredients of competency. They are a necessity in organisations' production and reproduction, for competitive advantage and organisational objectives. Haag, Cummings and Phillips [11] explained that companies require skilled people in the field of IT in order to be productive and innovative and thus give the company a commercial advantage over its competition. General skills are the same in many countries, including South Africa. Saunders, *et al* [12] Skills gap focuses on specialized areas such as engineering, medical, nurses, and IT professionals. Leung's [13] list of the Global Knowledge top 10 IT skills in demand as follow: (i) Project management, (ii) Security, (iii) Network administration, (iv) Virtualization – cloud, (v) Business analysis, (vi) Business process improvement, (vii) Web development, (viii) Database management, (ix) Windows administration, and (x) Desktop support.

The paper narrows its focus to ICT which includes software development, network administration and database management. This is primarily because ICT is one the areas where Africans and its organisations are generally challenged in their search for skilled personnel. According to Barker [14], 33.7% of organizations are challenged with recruiting or retaining persons with IT business analysis skills.

2 The Roles of Society and Higher Education

On the other hand, institutions of higher learning, particularly Universities of Technologies pride themselves on having hands on approach in equipping graduates with industries related skills. Universities of Technology are supposed to align their curriculum with Industries' needs. Unfortunately, this is not often the case. This has contributed to unemployment, as some graduates find difficult or impossible to align their skills to job specification. Others are tagged unemployable.

To this extent, some of the organisations sources for skills from institutions of higher learning, for basic and minimum requirements, which are at undergraduate level. Higher skilled personnel, at postgraduate levels, are also sourced from institutions of higher learning, as well as from competitors. However there are still sizeable ICT skill shortages in Africa. This study was carried to understand the factors which causes skill shortages.

This study was undertaken based on the rationale above. The study investigated the skill gap between institutions of higher learning and Industries. The objectives include understanding the factors which influence the academic curriculums and the organisation's requirements, and why curriculums of institutions of higher learning are not in alignment with industry's needs and requirements.

3 Methodology

The approaches and methods that were applied in the study include a mix method of qualitative and quantitative, for data collection; and interpretivism for analysis of the data. The data was collected from the field, of industries which has employed at least 5 fresh graduates in the last 18 months, at the time of this study. Data was also collected from organisations which sought the service of internship students. As shown in Table 1 below, a total of 18 organisations and 117 individuals, at both senior and junior participated in the study. This includes fresh graduates and internship that were also consulted, to get their perspectives on their real-life hand-on experience. The organisations were from 5 different industries.

Table 1. Participants

Industry	Organisation	Participant (Individual)	Senior Employees	Junior Employees	Graduate/ Internship
Financial Institutions	FI-1	11	5	4	2
	FI-2	8	4	1	3
	FI-3	6	3	1	2
	FI-4	5	3	-	2
	FI-5	6	4	2	-
	FI-6	7	3	1	3
Government Institutions	GI-1	9	5	2	2
	GI-2	7	4	1	2
	GI-3	7	4	2	1
	GI-4	7	5	-	2
	GI-5	4	2	1	-
Energy and Mining	EM-1	5	4	-	1
	EM-2	4	2	1	1
	EM-3	4	-	2	2
Telecommunications	TELCOM1	7	3	2	2
	TELCOM2	6	2	4	-
Transport	TP-1	9	4	2	3
	TP-2	5	3	-	2
Total	**18**	**117**	**60**	**26**	**30**

The mixed data of qualitative quantitative were analysed, using the interpretive method, in accordance to the research questions.

4 Factors Influencing Skill Development

As in other countries, ICT qualifications are obtained from Universities and other formal training facilities in South Africa and outside the geographical boundaries of the country. The qualifications are obtained at different, from certificate, diploma to doctorate levels. Some qualifications are considered to be basic requirement in many organisations. This is sometimes attributed to jobs, roles and responsibilities.

Sufficiently, many candidates hold qualifications from Universities and other formal training facilities, yet statistics revels that there is shortage of ICT skills in the country. Irrespective of the number of persons with formal qualifications, and the levels of qualifications, there exists challenge of competency. Many organisations assess the challenge of competency to be more critical. Such organisations had rather have quality than quantity. This has contributed to the continued search for candidates, from the perspective of the employers. This contributes to the unemployment figure.

Qualification does not automatically manifest into competency. It is an equation of Qualification + Competency = Skill. As depict in Figure 1, the skill development is an iterative process, in order to meet organisational needs. As organisational vision and needs change, employees are trained to have certain competency to achieving the objectives.

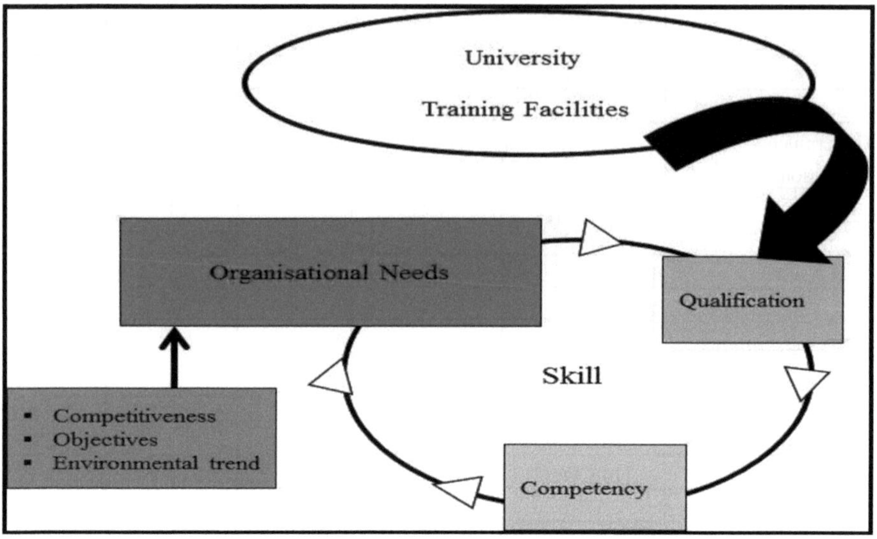

Fig. 1. Skill Development

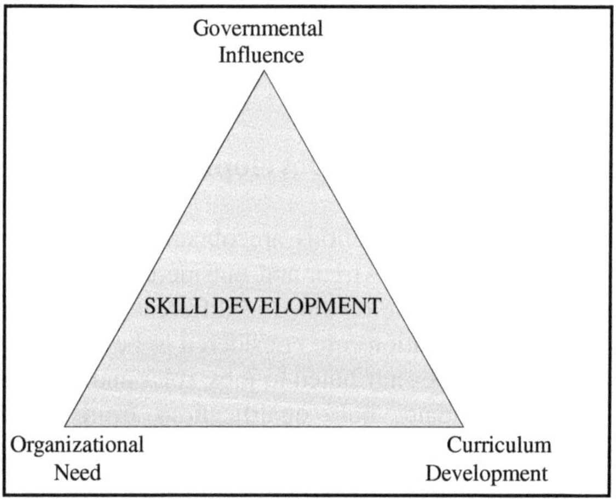

Fig. 2. Factors Influencing Skill Development

There are many factors that influence ICT skills development, from qualification stage to competence level, of individuals and groups. According to Gruba et al [15], there are factors which influence curriculum change. They include industries' viewpoints, competitive advantage (competition amongst the universities), financial pressure, and course accreditation. The factors considered to be most critical include government interference, organisational need, and curriculum development and transformative scheme. These factors are interlinked as depicted in Figure 1 below.

The influencing factors as depicted in Figure 1 depend on each other in the course of developing skills in the country. The factors above are discussed in the remainder of this section.

4.1 Governmental Influence

The government influences are primarily either economic or political or both. The government influence is carried out through policies, rules and regulations. Also, the influence is either direct or indirect.

Some African countries including South Africa who were colonised by the British has based their education system on the Westernization system (Burger, S.a). For example, Australia and South Africa have similar education systems to that of England. African countries kept the colonial education system after their independence, but adapted the system to suit their environmental needs.

Within the context of skill development, South Africa is different to other developing and developed countries primarily because the country has recently had a political shift to a democratic state, which caused the education system to also change and it is still constantly changing. It is taking South Africa years (1994 – 2003) to find a schooling system that is equal for all. Few systems including the Outcomes Based Education (OBE) have been employed. Once the schooling system (foundation) has been stabilised, only then could a fair and equal system be realised.

The introduction of the OBE at the secondary school level, as well as the merger of Universities and Technikons (Polytechnics), brought another type of challenge to the education system in the country. The Traditional Universities including the Universities of Technology in South Africa are now faced with challenges of transforming their curriculum to suit the needs of the organisations, and the country at large. What is even more challenging is the fact that old techniques are being used to teach new initiatives. This has impact on both the educators and the learners.

The South African Department of Education divided its formal education into three sectors, namely: General Education and Training, Further Education and Training, and Higher Education and Training. Also, Sector Education and Training Authority (SETA) was established by the South African government in 2000 in an attempt to address the skills shortages in the country. The main focus of SETA is on quality of qualifications, they ensure that the learners are appropriately equipped and skilled. Through SETA, training centres with appropriate facilities were established across country.

The centres were aimed to assist organisations to train and prepare individuals for employment, so, the unemployment rate in the country could decrease. Therefore, the creation of FET colleges and the partnership with SETA started to address the skills gap in South Africa. The organisation established leaner-ships programs to help alleviate the unemployment rate in the country and give people the opportunity to start their careers.

4.2 Organisational Need

Organisations have their individual goals and objectives, mission and vision for existence. The organisations are in various classified disciplines and industries such as Energy, Financial, Information Technology (IT), Manufacturing, and Transport. The factors which motivate the existence of organisations are enabled, supported and managed by specialized skill sets. The skill sets creates and supports competition and competitive advantage.

It is critical for the organisation and institution of higher learning to have a common understanding of job titles and its roles and responsibilities. For example, business analyst is defined and understood differently by both the organisation and institution of higher learning. As a result, a business analyst is often confused with technical positions such as a systems analyst or IT systems requirement engineer. A business analyst must have some technical experience to be able to translate what the user wants into a technical form that the programmer can understand. A business analyst is defined as an information technology worker who improves the efficiency and productivity of business operations through information systems. According to Evans and Hoole [16], a business analyst translates requirements, design process, manage skills and knowledge, and analyses system development.

4.3 Curriculum Development

Universities, both in developed and developing countries have different timeframes and causes for reviewing their curriculums. This is driven by factors such as societal (organizational need), and sustainability. Programs, whether accredited or not, should be reviewed at least once every five years. For accredited programs, the frequency should coincide with accreditation cycle. This is mainly to respond to rapid changes in the environment.

Industries require specialized skilled people to use the latest technology to give the company a competitive advantage and Institutes of Higher Learning are supposed to be training these specialized skilled people but they are not because Institutes of Higher Learning are not keeping up with Industries changes.

5 Skill Alignment Framework

Neither the universities nor organisation can achieve the goal to improve skill development alone by itself. Collaboration within a framework is needed. The collaboration should be a consortium, consisting of the primary stakeholders, which includes the university, organisations, and government, as revealed above. The roles and responsibilities of the stakeholders should be defined and reviewed overtime in accordance to the political, economy and social factors at the time.

Skills development could be achieved and supported through experiential training or institutions of higher learning (universities). Itin [17] defines Experiential training as the transfer of knowledge, skills, experience, between a teacher who is knowledgeable in that environment and a student. Experiential training could take place at any level, and at any facility, other than the Universities. According to Fletcher [18], students should participate in real activities and experience the real consequences. Some Universities have created a module within their curriculum that allows the students to work in organisation (industry) of their choice but related to their field of study, for a set period of time. This is for the students to gain experience and hands-on practices from their learning at the university.

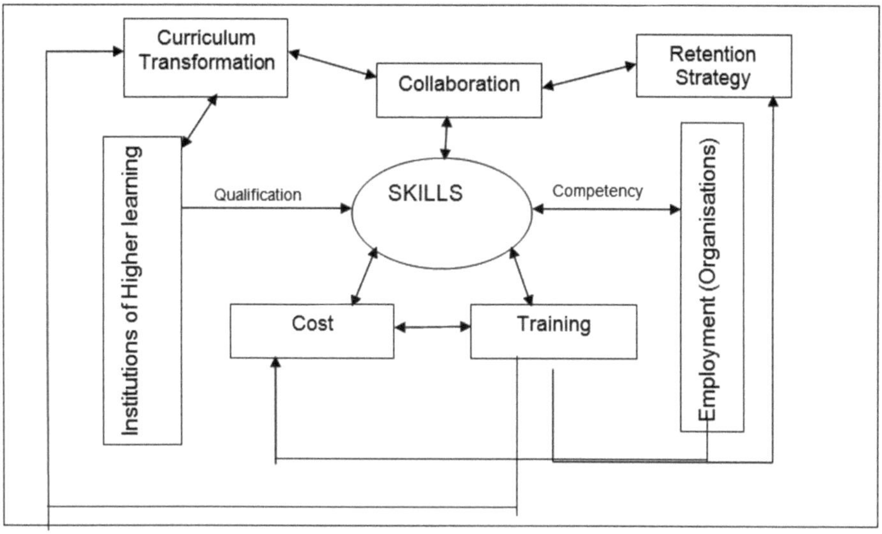

Fig. 3. Skill Development

The skill alignment framework would require all participants (universities, government and organisations) to work together as one entity, to teach and prepare students for employment. As depicted in Figure 2, some of the factors required to carry out these tasks, and achieve the goal involved: cost, training, retention strategy, curriculum transformation and collaboration. The factors are discussed as follow:

5.1 Cost Implication

Cost is essential if the skill development is to succeed. Unfortunately, some candidate takes longer to develop and acquire the necessary skills for employment as required by different organisations. Likewise those that are employed also take longer to develop further. The time and other facilities that are used in the development can be cost prohibitive or scarce. As a result, it becomes a serious challenge for one entity to embark on it alone. Hence collaboration amongst the primary stakeholders is crucial.

On another front, if a limited number of employees is adequately trained for a certain type of job, that company would bc facing a high risk of staff turnover. That would mean that companies will have to offer their employees more incentives and rewards, such as salary increase in order to keep the skilled staff. Otherwise, the employees would leave to pursue other more beneficiary and challenging employment elsewhere. This leads to a higher cost of sustainability for the company. Also, this can be attributed to the company's low return on its investment.

5.2 Training

Continuous training and mentorship are critical in the pursuit to closing the skill gap. Training at various levels from the schooling to working environment with the aid of government and organisations contributes to the reduction of skills shortage in the country. For example, a mentoring program between the Australian Library and Information Association and the Queensland University of Technology was created to help postgraduate students prepare for their careers [19]. The mentorship program was a formulated collaboration amongst: a professional association, the educators, practicing professionals, and the potential employees. The aim was to prepare the candidates for employment in various fields for their career. This was done while the students were still at the University, and about to enter the job market.

Training at any level requires many factors, such as time, cost, and interest. The factors are not easy to come by as seen from afar. They require some political will, social influences and economy implication. It is difficult to separate the factors from one another. Time and cost are invested because there is interest, and interests are pursued with resources, such time and finance. Also, finance is used to acquire resource of interest, which is aimed to save time.

5.3 Retention Strategy

Many companies are reluctant to send their employees for further training, to improve and enhance their skills. This is attributed to the costs involved, as they are sometimes challenged with return on investment. Other organisations are sceptical because they might lose the employees to their competitors. Haskins [10] argued that companies are required to increase their effort to recruit and retain trained workforce, for competitive advantage. According to Saunders et al [12], the importance of training and creation of a learning environment contributes to the success and competitive advantage.

In the process of keeping and holding-on to workforce, many organisations have adopted retention strategies, which involve factors such finance and cost. The retention strategy impacts different levels and area disciplines within the organisation that deploy it. Some of the organisations adopt the mentorship program to identify personnel for retention.

In some organisations, it is argued that the mentorship programs are timely and not a cost effective solution for bridging the skills gap in both short and long terms. Teaching and learning takes and consumes resources and time, which is equated and valued to money. Companies are willing take the responsibility, but the fear of brain drain remains a disturbing factor. It has been of high risk in the last decade. Once the person has gained the necessary knowledge required, they leave the company for better opportunities. If the curriculum in institutions of higher learning is continuously transformed, there little or no need for retention strategy or fear of brain drain.

5.4 Curriculum Transformation

Some countries, as well as universities are expected to take the lead in addressing the skills gap at both short and long terms. One way of doing so is for the universities to be transformative in their curriculum. The transformation of curriculum should be imbibed as a culture, only then, the approach and can survive at a longer term. The aim is for the transformative process to evolve and adapt to the constant environmental changes.

Students are more interested in Universities that could assist them find employment. This conclusion is based on curriculum assessment by the students. Maharasoa & Hay [20] argued that students choose a University based on the courses offered, especially if the student is guaranteed a job at the end of the course. Students are more interested in working towards a chance of being employed than having a degree and being unemployed. This notion could be attributed to one of the reasons why students often would prefer a University of Technology (or polytechnics) to traditional university. The University of Technology (or polytechnics) seem to focus more on what industry needs. For example, some Universities of Technology constitute an advisory board, made of academics and professionals (industry personnel). The primary aim of the advisory board is to guide and advise the university on course contents. Based on the guidance and advice of the board, curriculum of courses are frequently reviewed and transformed.

Another approach through which curriculums could be transformed is continued research on curriculum matters. Currently, there seems to be limited research studies on curriculum matters, particularly in the areas of computing and engineering. Curriculum transformation would help mainly because many institutions of higher learning are sadly not up-to-date with factors of changing social needs, intellectual and technology trends, and industries' competitive need.

The concept of cooperative learning at institutions of higher learning is fundamental to curriculum development and transformation. Cooperative learning is the exposure of students to the industry 'real world' and practical environment. The assessment of students during this period is vital for curriculum development and transformation. It assists the institution to shape and reshape its content in preparation of students.

5.5 Collaborative

Closing the skill gap in any community or the country at large requires collaboration of the primary stakeholders, which include learners, educators, organisations and government. The collaboration is aimed to solidify the empowerment of institutions of higher learning and organisations towards achieving the same goal. It assures the quality of the products, thus improving the attractiveness for employability of the qualified student (graduates).

The role of the government is critical. The roles could be carried out through different means and methods such as policies and programs. For example, the department of Education in South Africa has imposed on all institutions of higher learning (Traditional University and Universities of Technology) to adapt and improve and transform their curriculums before 2014. This is to ensure that the curriculum aligns with the general needs of the country. This policy requires collaboration of organisations, the government and the focal actor, universities. This is aimed to improve poverty alleviation through fostering sustainability and development.

6 Conclusion

Specialised skills are needed in organisations for competitive advantage, and in the country for sustainability, development and growth. The basis and foundation for skills and specialisation are the responsibility of institutions of higher learning. The responsibility is shared. Otherwise, quality and appropriation of the skills become a challenge. Hence collaboration is significantly vital.

Industries employ new workforce (both new graduates and experienced personnel) but are challenged by leadership or mentorship programs which has many implications such as costs and time. As a result, they are retrained. Hence the collaboration with other stakeholders such as the government is critical.

Undertaken of roles, responsibilities and accountabilities of the stakeholders as revealed in this paper would help bridge the skills gap in the country. Partnership is vital, collaboration is critical, and monitoring of the forms of bridging the skill gap is of utmost significant.

References

1. Preston, R.: Beyond 'Talented Shortages' lies a cultural Divided. InformationWeek. ProQuest Computing 1159, 76 (2007)
2. Savvas, A.: More firms report skill shortages. Computer Weekly. ProQuest Computing, 8 (August 8, 2006)
3. Goodwin, B.: Ageism will hit skills, warn suppliers. Computer Weekly. ProQuest Computing, 48 (October 17, 2006)
4. Peckman, S.: Technically Speaking. Tech Directions. ProQuest Computing, 67(5), 2 (2007)
5. Hamer, L.: University – Industry Alliances: A Foundation for Innovative Business and Science Education in Emerging Professional Graduate Programs. Journal of the Academy of Business Education, 24–30 (2007)
6. Klein, K.E.: How to establish a Mentor Program. BusinessWeek (2010), http://www.businessweek.com/smallbiz/contnet/feb2008/sb2008026_636479.htm (accessed March 17, 2010)
7. Johnston, K., Fenn, J., Kretschmer, L., Lennox, G. 2002. A proposed study into why Information Systems graduates struggle to find jobs even though there is a skills shortage in South Africa (2002), http://www.sacla.org.za/SACLA2002/Proceedings/Papers?Johnston_etal.doc (accessed: September 02, 2008)

8. Natarajan, A.: Job shortages or skill shortages? World academy of Art and Science (2009), http://www.worldacademy.org/forum/job-shortages-or-skill-shortages (accessed: February 28, 2011)
9. Macgregor, K.: South Africa: Joblessness amid skills shortage. University World News (2007), http://www.universityworldnews.com/article.php?story=20071101145653965&mode (accessed: August 08, 2010)
10. Haskins, S.: Industry body proactive in confronting skills deficit. Engineering News (2008), http://www.engineeringnews.co.za/article.php?a_id=131326 (accessed: May 29, 2008)
11. Haag, S., Cummings, M., Phillips, A.: Management information systems for the information age, 6th edn. McGraw-Hill/Irwin, New York (2007)
12. Saunders, M., Skinner, D., Beresford, R.: Mismatched perceptions and expectations: An exploration of stakeholders' view of key and technical skills in vocational education and training. Journal of European Industrial Training 29(5), 369–382 (2004)
13. Leung, L.: Top 10 skills in demand in 2010. Global knowledge. (2010), http://www.globalknowledge.ae/knowledge%20centre/white%20papers/microsoft%20white%20papers/top%2010%20skills%20in%20demand%20in%2010.aspx (accessed: February 28, 2011)
14. Barker,C.: Demand for Key IT skills remain high. ZDNet UK (2009), http://m.zdnetasia.com/demand-for-key-it-skills-remains-high-62050081.htm (accessed: February 28, 2011)
15. Gruba, P., Moffat, A., Søndergaard, H., Zobel, J.: What drives curriculum change? In: Lister, R., Young, A. (eds.) Proceedings of the Sixth Conference on Australasian Computing Education - Volume 30 (Dunedin, New Zealand). ACM International Conference Proceeding Series, vol. 57, pp. 109–117. Australian Computer Society, Darlinghurst (2004)
16. Evans, N., Hoole, C.: Promoting business/IT fusion: An OD perspective. Leadership & Organization Development Journal 26(4), 310–325 (2005)
17. Itin, C.M.: Reasserting the Philosophy of experiential Education as Vehicle for change in the 21st Century. The Journal of Experiential Education 22(2), 91–98 (1999)
18. Fletcher, A.: Meaningful student involvement: Student as partners in school change. Common Action, Olympia (2005), http://en.wikipedia.org/wiki/Experiential_education (retrieved: December 6, 2007), (accessed: November 25, 2009)
19. Hallam, G., Gissing, C.: Mentoring fosters personal growth - and membership growth. In: Proceedings World Library and Information Congress: 69th IFLA General Conference and Council, Berlin, Germany (2003)
20. Maharasoa, M., Hay, D.: Higher Education and graduate Employment in South Africa. Quality in Higher Education 7(2) (2001)

Key Competencies, Learning and Life Transitions

Life Transitions, Learning and Digital Technologies – Common Threads and Conceptions

Don Passey

Centre for Technology Enhanced Learning,
Department of Educational Research, Lancaster University, Lancaster, UK
d.passey@lancaster.ac.uk

Abstract. This positional paper opened a symposium within the Information Technology in Educational Management (ITEM) strand of the IFIP KEYCIT conference in Potsdam, Germany, on 2nd July 2014. The key question asked, across the seven papers presented and included as chapters in this book, was: how do digital technologies support life transitions? The argument within this initial positional paper asked a pre-requisite question: what are life transitions, and how might they be connected to digital technologies and learning? Life transitions can occur at different times across a lifespan, and different technologies may be used by those involved, not only according to the age of the learner, but also according to their needs. Temporal shifts as learning technologies develop make their influences on life transitions difficult to generalise or even to monitor; affordances and facilities that learners can use over time, and which they can apply to their life transition needs, change, as digital technologies are diversified. This paper considers features and factors that affect learners in their uses of digital technologies in life transition settings. A framework for exploring the ways learners might use digital technologies within life transitions will be developed; other papers within the symposium explore factors and features in a variety of more specific settings and detail.

Keywords: Life transitions, digital technologies, life transition factors, life transition features.

1 Introducing the Concepts

This chapter asks a central question, which the following six chapters also consider, but from a variety of different perspectives: how do digital technologies support life transitions? Before this question can be tackled, a pre-requisite question needs to be considered: what are life transitions? Across a range of papers presented [1, 2, 3, 4] a number of life transitions are illustrated – moving from one part of the education system to another, from education to work, and from one set of working practices to another. Features of these transitions can be quite different. The nature of the distinct transitions researched will be explored in this paper, as will their relationships with digital skills and the development of digital skills to support specific needs in each distinctive transition.

D. Passey and A. Tatnall (Eds.): KCICTP/ITEM 2014, IFIP AICT 444, pp. 139–149, 2014.

Life transitions could be considered the same as ongoing development, in that transitions are happening very often across the lifespan; in fact, they could be considered as happening continuously in some respects. However, in the context of the studies considered here, life transitions are not defined in the same way as life development. Life development is described as a continuous development across age ranges, through physical, cognitive and social perspectives (see, for example, Bee [5]). In the context of the studies considered here, life transitions are concerned with major shifts or rifts, which are normally outside the control of the individual, are concerned often with major contextual shifts, and may give rise to potential emotional or social or cognitive concerns or issues. Other authors have defined such transitions as transfers (for example, Galton, Gray and Rudduck [6]). An example would be, in a learning context, the move from a primary (first or elementary) school to a secondary (high) school. Although this move happens for the vast majority of learners, many do not experience major issues or challenges, but some do, and these can persist for long periods of time. So, life transitions that are challenging or difficult may never occur for some people. For most of us, they do occur, but probably not too often, but for some of us, they recur or persist or are concerned with major issues or challenges. The concern of many in this respect is that a life transition can occur in ways that do not affect future prospects adversely. While most learners move through a life transition at the age of 11 or 12 years in the United Kingdom (UK), for example, many go on to prosper in terms of their learning. However, studies have shown that learner attitudes, interests and attainments tend to be lowered after this transition [6, 7, 8, 9]. For those where there are these potential adverse effects, are digital technologies able to help and support? But evidence points to the need to consider underlying factors, rather than a superficial concern with continuity alone. As Galton et al. [9] stated:

> *"The dominant assumption has been that continuities in pupils' learning need to be strengthened. But when we tuned in to what Y6 [Year 6] and Y7 pupils were saying it became clear that while continuity matters for some aspects of transfer, discontinuity is also important – especially for pupils. Continuity has been mainly thought about in terms of the curriculum and is currently supported by 'Bridging Units'. However, there can be problems if the transfer school receives pupils from a large number of feeder schools, where the units have been handled in different ways, and if pupils regard them as 'last year's work'. Ironically, while policy makers and schools have given attention to curricular continuity they have thought less about continuity in ways of learning." (p.v)*

This report indicates that if digital technologies are to have an impact on supporting challenging life transitions, then they may need to address more a continuity of ways of learning, and then leading to evolving or developing shifts in learning, rather than necessarily providing a continuity of context or setting.

This paper will consider features and factors that could affect learners in their uses of digital technologies in life transition settings, particularly focusing on those life transitions that might be considered to be difficult or challenging. A framework of the ways learners might use digital technologies within life transitions will be developed.

2 Examples of Life Transitions

Concerning life transitions and learning, there are some clear examples of where challenging and difficult life transitions are recognised:

- Going to kindergarten or school for the first time. This is a shift in context, from an informal (home) to more formal (class group or play) setting, where the form of learning may be quite different, moving from a personally known one-to-one situation, to a personally unknown one-to-group situation, from 'home discourse' to 'play discourse'. The Harvard Family Research Project [10] from their review of practices to support this transition positively, identified the need for kindergartens to have contact with preschool families, contact with preschool children, kindergarten visits, the setting up of appropriate home learning activities, informational meetings, information dissemination and home visits. Although the report did not focus on uses of digital technologies in this context, there are clearly potential ways in which digital technologies could support the communication, information, and forms of learning that are being highlighted here as being fundamental to this transition.
- Transferring from a primary to a secondary school. This is a shift in context, from one formal setting to another, but where the form of learning may be quite different, moving often from a group or project-work focus largely with a single teacher, to a classroom learning situation that focuses on individuals' learning and involving many teachers. A study for the then government department of education in England [11] identified some critical factors to support a transition from primary to secondary school: "developing new friendships and improving their self-esteem and confidence; having settled so well in school life that they caused no concerns to their parents; showing an increasing interest in school and school work; getting used to their new routines and school organisation with great ease; experiencing curriculum continuity" (p.ii). Again, whilst not focusing specifically on the roles of digital technologies, it is clear that there are a range of functions that could support these specific and important factors.
- Moving from school to a training setting. This is again a shift in context, but from a formal to a non-formal (often project or group based), where the form of learning may shift from individually focused and assessed to collaboratively focused and assessed, where the content moves from concepts and knowledge that need to be put into practice, to concepts and knowledge that are within and for practice. Although this transition clearly involves important accommodation to shifts in forms and contexts of learning, there is limited research that has looked at it from a transition perspective. More research has focused on the way that an integrated approach to support a continuity from education to training might work most successfully. For example, the Wolf Report [12] on the state of further education in the UK, emphasised the need for ensuring qualifications fit to business or employment demands, for accurate and useful information about prospects and opportunities, and for simplified systems to be put in place.

- Moving from unemployment to employment. This involves a shift in context, from informal (home) to formal (work-based) settings, where the form of learning shifts from informal (home) or non-formal (group or training) to formal (work-based) practice. A recent report by The Work Foundation [13] indicated that the number of people in the UK who are unemployed is high (and clearly this fact in itself enables a range of attitudes to form within different contexts), that length of time in unemployment is a key issue, that many are poorly qualified, they find it difficult to get an initial foothold, they often lack work experience, and that they are diverse in terms of their position to employment. These key points again are not addressed within the report in terms of how digital technologies might support this group, but there are clear ways in which that might be considered and approached.
- Changing responsibilities within employment. This may not involve a contextual shift, but it does involve potential shifts in terms of forms of learning, from individual to group perhaps, from formal (within the work-place and just-in-time) to formal (project based or training) practice. Even if the form of learning does not appear to shift for the individual involved, the practices themselves that are required may shift, such that the need for a change in the form of learning is not recognised. Examples of these transitions are provided within the symposium papers [3, 4], which explore how digital technologies are adopted by employees within specific companies, and the challenges that they face in moving forward with elements of knowledge management that are introduced to support business needs. The roles of affective and motivation factors are highlighted particularly by these authors.
- Moving from one area of employment to another. This involves a shift in context, but may well also involve a shift in the forms of learning, from formal (within the work-place and just-in-time) to formal (project based or training) practice. An example of this form of transition, where the transition is found to be difficult by some, is where members of the armed forces move to civilian employment. Davies [14] has studied how individuals and groups are supported in these ways, and the roles that digital technologies play. This example is discussed further in a section presented later in this paper.

3 Digital Technologies Accessible to Those in Life Transitions

From these examples, it is clear that life transitions occur at different times across a lifespan, and different technologies might be used by individuals in terms of their need to accommodate both their age and their purpose. Taking the example of the life transition from home to kindergarten, early learners (up to 5 years of age) may well use digital technologies such as Bee-Bot programmable floor robots, Roamers or Pixie Robots, but these are not likely to be used by older learners. However, they also use devices modified specifically to accommodate access and use, such as laptop computers, mobile telephones, photocopiers, scanners and televisions [15]. In this case, technologies accessible to users clearly affect how they can be applied to life transitions; for example, they may well be modelling potential uses that can be applied at later times, rather than using the digital technologies per se to support their life transitions.

Different levels of technology are accessible according to age. Examples are demonstrated by evidence from Ofcom in the UK [16], while data from other sources indicates that levels are different in other countries, however (see, for example, [17]). So, the preponderance of mobile telephones in some countries (such as Japan, for example), might mean that learners are aware of how these devices can be used to support social interaction (communication) purposes, but not necessarily for learning purposes. A shift here is concerned with purpose related to need, which might be apparent to some, but not to many others.

Technologies accessible to individuals also change over time. Mega-changes (about every ten years) and major changes (about every five years) are more hardware related [18], while regular changes are more software related and are concerned with the introduction of new software, upgrades of existing software, and the doubling in the power of computer capacity within an eighteen month period. These changes affect the affordances and facilities that learners can use over time, and how they can apply them to their life transition needs. For example, the facility now to create on-the-spot video recordings means that learners can capture experiences that they can re-run, reflect on, and discuss with others. This means that new forms of learning might be explored in these ways in the future; individuals in life transitions might experience new situations, capture them on video, and then have chance to discuss these with others so that their shift towards those practices might be more easily accommodated. This practice has been reported already in the transitions from primary to secondary school, where pre-recorded video material is used in primary schools to discuss transitional features in moving to secondary schools (see [19]).

4 Changes in Context

Life transitions that involve a change in context can be vitally important for some learners. Learning settings do change for individuals across a lifespan. Early learners initially experience informal, home settings. For some, from perhaps 3 years of age, and for others from about 6 years of age, they experience learning in somewhat more formal kindergarten or nursery school settings, moving to more formal settings from about 5 to 7 years of age, while from about 9 to 11 years of age many learners will experience learning within non-formal club and society settings. More informal settings can again predominate for some learners when they reach 16 years of age or more, when learning happens at home, and non-formal experiences tend to increase as learners work in more specific communities, societies or groups [20]. In training and employment situations, non-formal settings may also arise more frequently, where groups of learners are involved in problem-solving or team endeavour approaches rather than being involved in more formal classroom settings. The roles of attitudes and motivations, behaviours and emotions, clearly can come into play within the contexts of these shifts. For example, take the way that an individual on the autistic spectrum might experience a shift from a more formal to a more non-formal setting, where the need and forms of learning change from individually focused study to collaborative working and outcomes. In a context not concerned with digital technologies, a case study from CareTech Community Services [21], illustrates the importance of time and care in building up positive relationships if young people with autism are to move towards collaborative working with others. The UK National Health Service [22] indicates the need for a 'transition plan' to support this process. For such difficult transitions, it is possible that there are roles for digital technologies in supporting individuals in developing trust and bridging social relationships.

5 Increasing Complexity

Researchers are indicating that life transitions are in some ways changing and that, consequently, different ways to consider these are needed. Wyn [23], in a keynote presentation to the British Educational Research Association (BERA) argued that increased complexity is the case now with life transitions, that more external factors are increasing complexity, with a move from a close context or learning setting (within a defined geographical area with a low number of 'significant others' [24] to a wide geographical area bounded by internet or mobile telephone access with a larger number of potential 'significant others'. Ecclestone et al. [25] argue additionally that life transitions are becoming more drawn-out, so the time frame for some individuals in moving from unemployment to employment, for example, is becoming longer. In the careers context, Hooley et al. [26] argue that the level and form of support is also shifting, and that it is becoming less for some career transitions (at least in some situations). In this respect, therefore, it can also be argued that the context change is not so much a 'location' concern now, as a 'virtual location' concern bounded by access and facility using internet and mobile telephone applications, for example.

Indeed, digital technologies are already being seen to be used differently in different transitions. For example, workers moving to new countries, who may be working in one country with their families in another country, have been shown to use communication technologies to support their social networking [27]. In another context, some teachers have used video-based resources to support learners prior to transition (transfer) from primary school [28], while others have supported video-recorded interviews by learners in a primary school with those in a secondary school.

6 A Specific Example

At this point it is perhaps useful to consider a specific example of a difficult life transition that involves learning and digital technologies. It concerns the transition from employment in the armed forces to civilian employment [14]. In this study, the roles of three key factors were identified and detailed - identity, agency and structure. These were recognised as key socio-cultural concepts for understanding transition:

- Identify – the way an individual perceives themselves with respect to others and their environment, in the present, as well as in the future.
- Agency – the abilities and resources that an individual has to enable them to make a move from one situation to another.
- Structure – the way the individual has to handle the situation, and perhaps break it down into elements that are sequentially managed.

Daniel, Schwier and McCalla [29], in their review of online networks and the role of social capital, highlighted the importance of 'trust, shared understanding, reciprocal relationships, social network structures, common norms and cooperation, and the roles these entities play in various aspects of temporal communities' (p.xx). Interestingly, in a learning context, Luckin [30] describes cognitive elements that are strongly parallel to the concepts of identity, agency and structure:

- a Zone of Proximal Adjustment – how to make sense of what the needs are to move to the next stage of learning.
- a Zone of Available Assistance – identifying what is available to the learner that can be used, and how it can be assessed in terms of usefulness.
- a Zone of Collaboration – how to work with others in order to support a shift in learning.

Those three zones lie within a Zone of Proximal Development [31], but offer more detail about the processes that might be involved than was detailed within the original concept.

In terms of how some members of the armed forces are being supported in moving to civilian employment, digital technologies are being used to 'extend the scope of their on-line presence and identify their own learning opportunities' [14]. This clearly relates to how digital technologies are supporting challenges that individuals face with regard to identify, agency and structure, or to their proximal adjustment, available assistance and collaboration. In the study, Davies [14] indicates that in some instances, the digital technologies provide a vital link, enabling contact, building 'social and cultural capital, social networking and knowledge sharing skills', but he goes on to say that the importance of 'affective and motivational factors is clear'.

7 A Framework to Explore How Digital Technologies Might Support Life Transitions

So, are digital technologies and skills enabling a stabilising or positive impact upon life transitions? What associated skills are needed in developing social and cultural capital, integrated or developed alongside these digital skills? Do digital skills enable individuals to survive situations by empowering and enabling change rather than responding to it?

This paper does not attempt to answer all of these questions. Some of them are certainly the focus of research reported in the five papers that follow. But in this paper, I am making an attempt to identify a form of framework through which to explore how digital technologies might support life transitions. From the previous discussion in this paper, seven dimensions are apparent, when individuals are handling life transitions (often difficult life transitions). These are (in no particular order, and represented more appropriately, perhaps, in Figure 1):

- A digital dimension: concerned with the digital technologies that are accessible to the individual, those that can be used, those chosen for use by the individual and those supporting them, such as social network structures, and for what purpose.
- A learning dimension: the importance of learning continuity, or ways of learning rather than the 'content' of learning, how to develop shifts in learning, the importance of information as well as communication, and having appropriate accurate and useful information about the transition.
- A social dimension: how trust, shared understanding, reciprocal relationships, common norms and cooperation are handled, considering the roles of the home as well as the formal learning environment, integrating concerns of those around the individual, considering how support might work within a given situation, the levels of support that might be accessible, providing links, building social and cultural capital, and knowledge sharing skills.

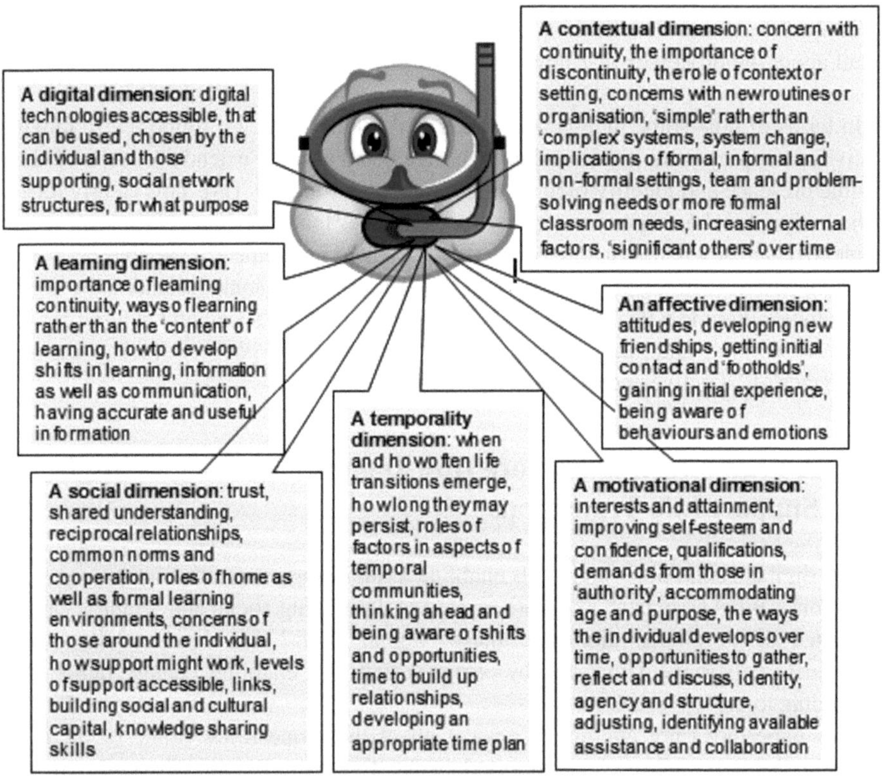

Fig. 1. Factors influencing life transitions

- A temporality dimension: when and how often difficult life transitions emerge, how long they are felt to be likely to persist, the roles trust, shared understanding, reciprocal relationships, common norms and cooperation play in various aspects of temporal communities, thinking ahead and being aware of shifts and opportunities, having time to build up relationships, and developing an appropriate time plan.
- A motivational dimension: the roles of interests and attainment, improving self-esteem and confidence, the importance of qualifications, or demands from those in 'authority', accommodating age and purpose, the ways that the individual develops over time, the importance of opportunities to gather, reflect and discuss, the roles of identity, agency and structure, adjusting, identifying available assistance, and collaboration as needed.
- An affective dimension: the role of attitudes, whether developing new friendships is important, getting initial contact and 'footholds', gaining initial experience, and being aware of behaviours and emotions.
- A contextual dimension: the concern with continuity, or the importance of discontinuity, and the role of context or setting, concerns with new routines or organisation, being involved in systems that are 'simple' rather than 'complex', but being aware that systems do themselves change, being aware of the implications of formal, informal and non-formal settings, whether situations are based on team and problem-solving needs or more formal classroom needs, being aware of increasing external factors, and those who become 'significant others' over time.

8 Conclusions

If digital technologies are to support individuals involved in life transitions (and perhaps difficult life transitions), then those who support and those who are directly experiencing these situations are likely to need to explore the issues presented in this framework, to identify the appropriate means and facilities accessible. The papers which follow will explore some of these key areas further, and the final paper in this section will look at these examples through the framework presented here.

References

1. Cranmer, S.: Digital skills and competencies in schools. In: Passey, D., Tatnall, A. (eds.) KCICTP/ITEM 2014. IFIP AICT, vol. 444, pp. 165–177. Springer, Heidelberg (2014)
2. Leahy, D., Wilson, D.: Digital skills for employment. In: Passey, D., Tatnall, A. (eds.) KCICTP/ITEM 2014. IFIP AICT, vol. 444, pp. 178–189. Springer, Heidelberg (2014)
3. Lee Angela, S.H., Lim, T.-M.: An Exploratory Study on the Use of Knowledge Management System and the Employees' Perception on Organisational Knowledge Sharing and Reuse. In: In Passey, D., Tatnall, A. (eds.) KCICTP/ITEM 2014. IFIP AICT, vol. 444, pp. 205–218. Springer, Heidelberg (2014)

4. Lim, T.-M., Lee Angela, S. H.: Using "Yams" for enterprise knowledge sharing among knowledge workers from the perspective of a task categorisation-knowledge sharing systems fit. In: Passey, D., Tatnall, A. (eds.) KCICTP/ITEM 2014. IFIP AICT, vol. 444, pp. 190–204. Springer, Springer (2014)
5. Bee, H.: Lifespan Development, 2nd edn. Longman, New York (1997)
6. Galton, M., Gray, J., Rudduck, J.: The Impact of School Transitions and Transfers on Pupil Progress and Attainment. DfEE, London (1999)
7. Hargreaves, L., Galton, M.: Transfer from the primary classroom - 20 years on. General Teaching Council for England, London (2002)
8. Ofsted: Changing schools - the effectiveness of transfer arrangements at age 11. HMSO, London (2002)
9. Galton, M., Gray, J., Ruddock, J., Berry, M., Demetriou, H., Edwards, J., Goalen, P., Hargreaves, L., Hussey, S., Pell, T., Schagen, I., Charles, M.: Transfer and Transitions in the Middle Years of Schooling: Continuities and Discontinuities in Learning. DfES, Norwich (2003)
10. Bohan-Baker, M., Little, P.M.D.: The Transition to Kindergarten: A Review of Current Research and Promising Practices to Involve Families. Harvard Family Research Project. Harvard Graduate School of Education, Cambridge (2002)
11. Evangelou, M., Taggart, B., Sylva, K., Melhuish, E., Sammons, P., Siraj-Blatchford, I.: Effective Pre-school, Primary and Secondary Education 3-14 Project (EPPSE 3-14) - What Makes a Successful Transition from Primary to Secondary School? Research Report No. DCSF-RR019. Department for Children, Schools and Families, Nottingham (2008)
12. Wolf, A.: Review of Vocational Education – The Wolf Report. Department for Education, London (2011)
13. Lee, N., Sissons, P., Balaram, B., Jones, K., Cominetti, N.: Short-term crisis - long-term problem? Addressing the youth employment challenge. The Work Foundation (Lancaster University), Lancaster (2012)
14. Davies, P.: Difficult Life Transitions: Learning and Digital Technologies - Discussion Paper and Preliminary Literature Review. Lancaster University, Lancaster (2014)
15. Aubrey, C., Dahl, S.: A Review of the Evidence on the Use of ICT in the Early Years Foundation Stage. Becta, Coventry (2008)
16. Ofcom: Communications Market Report. London: Ofcom. (2012), http://stakeholders.ofcom.org.uk/binaries/research/cmr/cmr12/CMR_UK_2012.pdf (retrieved September 20, 2014)
17. Eurostat: Data in focus 50/2010: Internet usage in 2010 – Households and Individuals (2010), http://epp.eurostat.ec.europa.eu/cache/ITY_OFFPUB/KS-QA-10-050/EN/KS-QA-10-050-EN.PDF (retrieved September 20, 2014)
18. Passey, D.: Strategic evaluation of the impacts on learning of educational technologies: Exploring some of the issues for evaluators and future evaluation audiences. Education and Information Technologies 4(3), 1–28 (1999)
19. Passey, D.: Independent evaluation of the uses of Espresso online digital resources in primary schools: Final Report – School Uses and Learning Impacts. Lancaster University, Lancaster (2011), http://eprints.lancs.ac.uk/40905 (retrieved September 20, 2014)
20. Passey, D.: Inclusive technology enhanced learning: Overcoming Cognitive, Physical, Emotional and Geographic Challenges. Routledge, New York (2013)
21. CareTech Community Services: Supporting adults, http://www.caretech-uk.com/solutions-for-adults/my-needs/autistic-spectrum-disorder.aspx (n.d.) (retrieved August 31, 2014)

22. NHS: Supporting children with autism into adulthood, http://www.nhs.uk/Livewell/Autism/Pages/Thetransitionprocess.aspx (n.d.) (retrieved August 31, 2014)
23. Wyn, J.: Youth transitions in difficult times: Where and how do young people belong? In: Keynote Presentation at the Annual BERA Conference 2013. University of Sussex, Brighton (2013)
24. Berger, P.L., Luckmann, T.: The Social Construction of Reality: A Treatise in the Sociology of Knowledge. Anchor Books, Garden City (1966)
25. Ecclestone, K., Biesta, G., Hughes, M.: Transitions in the lifecourse. The role of identity, agency and structure. In: Ecclestone, K., Biesta, G., Hughes, M. (eds.) Transitions and Learning through the Lifecourse. Routledge, London (2010)
26. Hooley, T., Hutchinson, J., Watts, A.G.: Careering Through the Web. UK Commission for Employment and Skills, London (2010)
27. Cuban, S.: Deskilling migrant women in the global care industry. Palgrave Macmillan, Basingstoke (2013)
28. Passey, D.: Technology enhancing learning: Analysing uses of information and communication technologies by primary and secondary school pupils with learning frameworks. The Curriculum Journal 17(2), 139–166 (2006)
29. Daniel, B., Schwier, R.A., McCalla, G.: Social capital in virtual learning communities and distributed communities of practice. Canadian Journal of Learning and Technology 29(3), 113–139 (2003)
30. Luckin, R.: Re-designing learning contexts: Technology-rich, learner-centred ecologies. Routledge, London (2010)
31. Vygotsky, L.S.: Mind in Society: The Development of the Higher Psychological Processes. The Harvard University Press, Cambridge (1978)

Digital Skills and Motivation in Young People in Transition

Colin Rogers

Department of Educational Research, Lancaster University, UK
c.rogers@lancaster.ac.uk

Abstract. This paper explores the underlying assumptions that are often made concerning the beneficial impact of the use of Digital Technologies in relation to the motivation for academic work, and related forms of engagement. In particular, these claims are assessed in the context of an overarching concern with the motivational characteristics that are most likely to abet the effective transition of young people from one context to another. In this light, relevant theories of motivation are explored together with an assessment of how they might, together, provide a more productive basis for the development of the role of Digital Technology in assisting the making of effective transitions.

Keywords: Transition, motivation, digital technologies.

1 Introduction

This paper is part of a set concerned with the potential beneficial role of Digital Technologies (DTs) in assisting young people to progress through the transitional points in their lives. Other papers in this section will focus upon the nature of transition itself and will help to scope the various ways in which DTs might help. It will be readily apparent that there are a number of ways in which DTs might assist, or indeed hinder, transition. The ability of DTs to package, transmit and provide in timely manner relevant information will be an important part of the process. Providing information is one thing, making effective use of it is another. Information is likely to be accessed and used effectively as a function of the motivation of an individual to do just that. Transitions themselves are likely to be demanding and to present challenges that will require a sufficient degree of motivation to be met effectively. As will be discussed in greater detail below, it has been argued (or perhaps asserted) that DTs have the capacity to influence the motivation of people, young people particularly. Perhaps then DTs can not only provide informational support, but might also have a positive impact on the very nature of the motivation that young people can bring to the transitions they face.

This paper, then, sets out to review and consider the options that might be available to us in considering the role of DTs in influencing the nature of motivation. There is a particular focus on the need to understand the requirements concerning the development of motivational styles that will help to enable young people to manage,

D. Passey and A. Tatnall (Eds.): KCICTP/ITEM 2014, IFIP AICT 444, pp. 150–164, 2014.

in both a fluid and a productive manner the transitions that are a necessary part of study and work. There are, as shall be seen, many claims for the power of DTs to have a transformational impact upon the motivation of students. These claims however are generally based upon a non-theorised construct of motivation and thus the nature of the claims themselves remains uncertain. There are clear indications that a concern with the fundamental nature of motivation is often confused with the more immediate and, sometimes, superficial construct of interest. However, it is also clear that there remains a very considerable potential for the use of DTs in the development of more effective and adaptive forms of motivation. This potential is demonstrated by the clear plasticity of motivational characteristics.

The paper essentially concerns two issues. The first is a broad, and necessarily brief, account of the desiderata in relation to effective forms of motivation in transitional situations. The adopted approach involves the setting out of the key concerns of three important theories of motivation in learning contexts together with a demonstration of the issues that arise when transitions become the main focus. It is more typical for the theoretical focus to be upon a relatively static phase of the educational process. The overview will emphasise the essential plasticity of motivation and thereby the considerable potential for change and growth that such a view allows for.

The second point of focus will be a consideration of the claims that have been made for the motivational benefits of DTs. To anticipate the conclusion, whilst the theoretical potential remains high, the demonstrated gains are limited largely due to the essentially non-theorised ways in which motivation has been construed in the relevant studies.

2 Approaches to Motivation

Three well established theoretical approaches to motivation are introduced here to illustrate the range of concerns that any consideration of the motivational benefits of DTs should address. These theories are not exhaustive of the literature. More importantly they are presented here in the belief that rather than serving as competitors for our allegiance they could represent, in synthesis, a powerful set of tools for considering how DTs might help to develop a beneficial way of developing robustness and adaptiveness in transitional situations.

Self-determination theory [1] highlights the role played by the fundamental human needs of competence, autonomy and relatedness. In as much as these three needs are met by achievement strivings in particular settings, then an individual's motivation for the associated activities will be enhanced. Perhaps more importantly, work associated with this theory has highlighted the importance of, and the limitations of, intrinsic motivation. As an individual's needs are met, so intrinsic motivation is likely to be enhanced. Enhanced intrinsic motivation in turn leads to greater persistence and other adaptive approaches to learning. However, it becomes clear that high levels of intrinsic motivation are relatively rare, as all three sets of needs are unlikely to be simultaneously and unambiguously met in most of the situations we daily encounter.

Therefore other forms of motivation, all essentially extrinsic, are identified. These extrinsic motivational forms range along a dimension of self-regulation. At one end of this dimension is "amotivation" (essentially disengagement) followed by "external", "introjected", "identified" and "integrated" regulation in turn. External regulation finds an individual doing things because they see themselves as being under the control of others. Through the development of integrated regulation an individual imposes a sense of self-discipline in order to carry out activities leading to an outcome which they personally value. They undertake these things, not simply or necessarily because they enjoy them - they may well not – but because they recognise that a "person like them" would wish to achieve what those activities might lead to.

This elaboration of the simple distinction between intrinsic and extrinsic motivation is one that has essential implications for DT related research. The simplistic notion that DTs will enhance motivation through making activities more "enjoyable" and thereby adding to any intrinsic motivation already associated with the task is replaced by a need to seek ways of deploying DTs to develop more self-regulated motivational forms. Crucially this approach can recognise that learning is not, and probably cannot, always be intrinsically enjoyable. Many activities, where engagement is strong with a clear focus on success, will not be enjoyed, but the actor will persist. Self-regulated motivation becomes particularly important when people find that a transition has left them losing some of the enjoyable aspects of the core activity, for example the transition from school to university [2].

A second approach to attend to is that of Future Time Perspective (FTP) [3]. While less well known and, in its entirety, less well researched than the other two theoretical systems discussed here, FTP offers an integration of approaches, concerns and ideas that ought to make it essential reading for those interested in developing motivation through the use of DTs. While ultimately complex, the theory posits a division between two time frames each of which has implications for an individual's motivation. The time frames focus upon both future oriented and proximal self-regulation. The former encompasses the generation of a personal value system stemming from the individual's sociocultural context. When linked to their knowledge of what might be possible, this gives rise to a set of personally valued goals with a matching system of proximal subgoals (the steps that need to be taken to reach the defined goals). These feed through into the proximal system concerned with the regulation of current activity, relevant facets of which include the perceived value of the current task, the link between the value of the current task and the individual's longer term aims, their level of self-efficacy for the present task and the eventual link back to a more enduring self-concept of ability that influences the ongoing development of long-term values and goals.

A key point here is that the individual cannot be isolated from either the context within which they presently work, or the greater context (spatially, temporally and culturally) within which that present context is embedded. In short, school, let alone the use of DTs in school, has its limits when set against the substantial legacy of an individual's sociocultural context. Students' present values, interest levels and self-efficacy levels cannot be separated from their longer-term values, goals and the more enduring aspects of their self-concept. Against such a model, many of the studies claiming motivational benefit for DTs are shown as merely engaging with one very small part of the overall process. More importantly, it is possible to argue that these contributions may be classified as "quick fixes" rather than as attempts to bring about enduring changes in the longer-term motivational characteristics of a person.

The final, and most significant, approach is motivational goal theory [4, 5, 6, 7]. Goal theory has recognised the existence of two primary motivational goals, each of which is found in two varieties. While there are differences in nomenclature and differences of potential importance concerning the use of measuring instruments [8] there is a general consensus concerning the broad definitions of the principal characteristics of learning goals and performance goals. Learning goals provide a focus upon individual progress with movement towards the obtaining of a higher level of expertise being central. Performance goals are concerned with a display of competence with this often, but not always, being demonstrated through relatively high levels of performance in comparison to members of a peer group.

Each of these goals is held to operate in either an approach or an avoidance mode. This second dimension, which together with the first provides the basis for what is referred to as the '2 x 2' model of motivational goals, is more clearly understood in relation to the operation of performance goals. To illustrate: an individual with a strong performance approach goal will be likely to relish opportunities of demonstrating high levels of competence in relatively public ways. They are likely to enjoy the opportunities provided by competition, will be willing to undertake activities in seminar rooms and in school classrooms which allow for the demonstration of competence and will relish the opportunity to receive feedback about their performance. Conversely, an individual with a clear performance avoidance goal will have a more "fearful" approach to their learning and study. In these cases, rather than perceiving the opportunities that success might provide for gaining positive feedback, the focus is likely to be upon the opposite side of the coin. In other words, the opportunities to fail and therefore receive feedback confirming a lack of competence become the focus of attention. Individuals with strong performance avoidance goals are therefore often seen to engage in a range of avoidance strategies each of which can be understood as being designed to protect the individual from the consequences of an anticipated failure. However, at the same time, those strategies risk minimising the learning opportunities present. One example of this concerns the adoption of "effort avoidance" strategies which enable the individual to anticipate being able to explain any actual failure by the absence of effort rather than by the absence of ability. The focus upon this particular defensive strategy owes a great deal to the contribution of Dweck to the development of goal theory and her explication of the differences between incremental and entity views of the nature of ability [9, 10].

The differences between learning approach and learning avoidance goals [11] have received less attention and have probably, to date, been regarded as possessing less practical usefulness. However, the same basic concern is again evident with individuals who are strong in learning approach goals seeking out opportunities to engage in activities that might lead to the demonstration of improvement and learning. Learning avoidance goals are concerned with the again somewhat fearful desire to avoid the demonstration that one has failed to learn or to improve. This is perhaps most readily understood when applied to groups of people whose learning capacity may be challenged through the ageing process or by any onset of some other potentially disabling incapacity. Interestingly, people in the early stages of a transition might also find learning avoidance goals heightened.

Elliot [6] draws attention to the ways in which the goals that have been adopted by an individual will have a critical influence upon the ways in which the nature of success (and thereby failure) are defined. Learning goals define success in terms of progress while performance goals do so in more normative terms. All motivation theories, rather self-evidently, share a concern with people's responses to success and failure. The identification of the role of goals in defining the ways in which success might be understood is therefore highly important. If experiences can shape goals so they will also shape the very meaning of what it is to be successful.

Even for readers lacking in any prior familiarity with these concepts, it is probably apparent that approach goals will generally be perceived as being motivationally beneficial in comparison to avoidance goals. Learning goals would similarly be identified as preferable to performance goals. While there is little equivocation in the literature regarding the limitations of avoidance goals, the advantages of learning goals over performance goals, particularly in respect to higher education, have not always been quite so apparent [e.g. 12]. However the point to be explored here is to do with the changes that are regularly identified in the dominant motivational goal patterns displayed by students as they progress through their years of study, with higher education providing the examples.

3 Motivational Plasticity

Remedios et al. [13] provide an illustration not only of some of the changes within individuals over time that have been observed in earlier research, but also draw attention to the important impact of culture, and indeed a changing culture, upon these trends. Their review of earlier work draws attention to research showing that United Kingdom (UK) university students will be likely to begin their studies with relatively strong learning goals but will see a gradual increase in the relative strength of performance goals as time progresses. They also illustrate how students in other cultures, specifically Russia or the Soviet Union, have been shown to be more likely to maintain the initial levels of learning goals. The work was designed not only to test for the continuation of these trends in the UK but to investigate the extent to which cultural changes in Russia since the dissolution of the Union of Soviet Socialist Republics (USSR) might be associated with changes to the students' motivational patterns. Their results confirm a continuation of the established trends in the UK and also suggest that in post-USSR Russia the motivational trends are now much more like those found in the UK.

With a clearer focus upon the transition into higher education, further illustrations of the way in which context can have an impact upon the motivational characteristics displayed by students can be found in work currently being undertaken by Rogers

[14, 15]. This work is examining the possibility that the '2 x 2' motivational goal model outlined above might not be adequate to capture fully the range of motivational goals employed by students as they enter higher education. This work posits "Performativity" as an additional motivational goal, and also as one which may be of particular importance in helping us to understand some of the difficulties that many students in the UK seem to experience upon moving from school to university.

In England, for those students intending to enter university, the last two years of schooling are characterised by an intense focus upon the qualifications that they will gain as they leave school - the General Certificate of Secondary Education (GCSE) Advanced level, commonly referred to as A-level. Admission into university is dependent upon the grades achieved in these qualifications (A-levels being scored from a top A* to the lowest pass grade of E). High status universities in England will typically be requiring students to obtain three A-levels at or around A-grade standard in order to gain admission.

Consequently, schools find themselves under considerable pressure to give their students the maximum possible support in achieving those grades. Such pressure is argued to lead to an intense form of "teaching to the test" with the provision of a very high degree of learning support and structure. While such teaching strategies have been highly successful in producing a remarkable continuation of year-on-year increases in the proportion of students obtaining those high grades (until the last two years, writing just prior to the publication of the 2014 results), Rogers [14] argues that this leads to the adoption of an approach to learning by students that makes it very difficult for them to develop the characteristics of the "independent learner" that are seen by many as a central part of the full development of graduate capabilities.

For present purposes the concern is to simply illustrate the ways in which various aspects of the culture within which an individual is studying can have a notable effect upon the development of their pattern of motivational goals, their motivational style. Variations in culture can be very much: at the micro level - what is happening in one particular school classroom; at a meso level – the influence of one particular national assessment regime; or at the macro level - changes in a broad pattern of values and expectations coming about as the result of a major social and political upheaval.

In any event the culturally determined environment in which a student is working will impose its own particular set of demands. For some time [e.g. 17, 18] motivation theorists have been suggesting that it is unhelpful to categorise motivational styles as simply good or bad, strong or weak. Instead it has been argued that they are more usefully and productively categorised as adaptive or maladaptive. Some of the key derivatives of this assertion are that:

a) in making any judgement about how adaptive a particular motivational style might be, it will always be necessary to specify what it is that a given style might be adapted to;
b) a style that might be highly adaptive in one situation may well not be in another;
c) when we consider the multifaceted nature of many cultural contexts the precise focus of the adaptation may not be immediately apparent.

As a consequence, although school teachers may genuinely aim to develop the characteristics of independent learning prized in the university context, and of course elsewhere, the pressurised environment in which both they and their students have to work will lead to the adaptive formation of performativity goals. As the transition to university is undertaken, the student is likely to find that those same performativity goals that had served them very well as they worked to achieve their high A-level grades were now no longer adaptive to their new environment and its somewhat different set of concerns. The holder of those goals may well however not be among the first to notice this lack of adaptiveness.

In this light, it might be argued that there is no such thing as the best combination of motivational goals in any absolute sense. Instead there is a need to consider both short-term and long-term consequences of the adoption of any particular motivational style and then strive to develop those styles that are most likely to give an adaptive benefit. The difficulty for a teacher of A-levels in England is that there appears to be a conflict between the benefits gained in the short-term (high grades) and in the long-term (better eventual transition into university). Successful transitions then, from a motivational perspective, are not necessarily about beginning with the "right" type of motivation. They will be more to do with the ability of all parties involved to be aware of, and to appropriately respond to, the changing adaptive demands as the transition is carried out.

As we now shift our attention to a consideration of the impact of DTs upon the development of motivational style, it is clear that the same concerns with the balance of the consideration of the impact of the present context, the observation of any apparent short-term gain, and the prediction of any claimed long-term gain remain. In considering the potential of DTs to enhance motivation we need to be asking clear questions concerning the criteria that we would use to identify change, to assess the desirability of that change and to determine primarily where the adaptive focus of developed motivational styles might lie. There is also a pressing need to highlight the importance of individuals being able to develop insight into and thereby some possible control over their own motivational characteristics.

4 Digital Technologies and Motivational Development

A full review of the claims made by researchers concerned with DTs is beyond the scope of this article. A useful starting point is provided by a review for Becta [19] which indicates the range of impacts illustrated by research. Motivation emerges as the area where positive impacts are most unambiguously and consistently reported. The following captures the claims: "At present the evidence on attainment is somewhat inconsistent, although it does appear that, in some contexts, with some pupils, in some disciplines, attainment has been enhanced. ... The body of evidence on the impact of ICT on intermediate outcomes, such as motivation, engagement with and independence in learning, is greater and more persuasive" (p.4). Results for attainment are qualified; those for motivation are not.

Given the significance that is ascribed to motivation within the learning process [20] the conclusion that DTs may enhance classroom motivation is important. However, without clarity concerning the nature of the evidence base for the claim, including a concern with definition, moves to policy and practice development may be premature.

A representative sample of studies cited by Condie et al. [19] supporting the claim that DTs have positive motivational impact will now be examined. The prime concern will be to examine the models of motivation, both explicit and (more typically) implicit that have been deployed in those studies, alongside a consideration of the methods employed.

5 Forms of Motivational Impact

Motivational enhancement is taken to be an unproblematic concept in the clear majority of the studies covered by Condie et al. and indeed in the review itself. However, it is possible to deduce a number of formulations that authors largely implicitly draw upon. The following are the main examples. Throughout the following discussion the focus is upon the possible impact of DTs upon motivation for the associated subject of study. This is importantly different from the development of motivation for the use of DTs themselves.

Emerging initially from references to the development of micro-computing technology during the 1980s and 1990s, DTs are seen to have an inherent ability to capture and hold attention. This derives from the novelty value or other properties of the DT forms themselves. As engagement with the technology is, apparently, tied to engagement with the associated tasks, DTs can draw in and "hook" students. One form of enhancement I therefore identify as the "hook model". "Hooking" students in this way will be dependent upon the continuing presence of elements within DT platforms that are sufficiently intrinsically interesting to provide the hook. In as much as these are often dependent upon the novelty value and superior "power" of the technology (in comparison to instances used elsewhere by the student) the success of the hook model may be relatively short-lived. These forms of influence will also be dependent upon the level of interest that individual students may show in the technology. So one might expect to find that some students (e.g. boys), are more influenced than others (e.g. girls), by the particular DTs on offer. More importantly, the hook model may be limited to providing an initial motivational impact that is dependent upon a continuing technological presence.

Condie et al.'s review progresses to indicate that current DT school usage is characterised by "collaborative, investigative and problem solving activities" (p.21). The emphasis now shifts from the direct level of interest that students may have in the technology to ways in which the application of technology influences the students' classroom interactions. On occasion, such changes in interaction patterns would be the result of something as straightforward as the DT resource level, with limited resources requiring some degree of sharing. With technological progression, forms of interaction can be more directly influenced by DTs. Interactive whiteboards, one of the more researched technological forms, can promote patterns of interaction within a whole class, while multi-touch technologies can promote smaller group-based interactions (see [21] for an example that postdates the Condie et al. review). Within this approach, any motivational effects of DTs are indirect and may be achievable without the use of those DTs. If increased collaboration enhances motivation, then any way of increasing collaboration may produce the effect. Such broad models of motivational enhancement I refer to as "interactive models".

The "interactive" model can be subdivided. One variant shares elements of the "hook" model. Rather than DTs providing the initial and (possibly) the ongoing reason to engage with the activity at all, it is the collaboration and the consequentially more rewarding interactions with peers that fulfil this function. DTs help to structure the nature of the interactions and, if these become more rewarding, the student becomes more likely to remain engaged with the activity and is thereby held to be more motivated.

A second variant focuses on the cognitive gains that often follow from greater collaboration [e.g. 22]. In as much as the evidence shows attainment gains under conditions of enhanced collaboration, the introduction of DTs, in as much as it enhances collaboration, will thereby enhance attainment. The link to motivation then comes through enhanced feelings of competence and raised levels of self-efficacy. These aspects of the motivational process are discussed further below, but for now I note that DTs would have an indirect influence upon motivation and that it would be a consequence of raised attainment levels rather than a cause.

Finally Condie et al. discuss the nature of the research they have reviewed and the longer-term prospects concerning DTs' impact on learning. They anticipate the point when any particular form of DT's deployment in school will be normal and fully embedded. They intimate that the greatest potential for DTs is, therefore, still in the future. While this will in part have something to do with the development of ever more powerful, mobile and well-designed technological forms, their prime concern is the embeddedment of DTs in a permanently changed set of teaching practices. One may go on to draw upon the self-efficacy literature [23] to suggest that more effective teaching, in as much as it leads to more effective learning, will then enhance student self-efficacy, thus setting up a beneficial cycle influencing students' motivation. Enhanced motivation then plays its part in generating further enhancements in attainment and so forth. Such a model, which I refer to as the "cyclic model" assumes that the impact of DTs on motivation will be long-term, indirect, subtle and ultimately self-sustaining.

From this initial summary, a number of alternative models emerge of the ways in which DTs' use might affect motivation development:

a) DTs' use is seen as something that (some) students will find intrinsically interesting. This intrinsic interest provides a form of motivation that is additional to whatever else motivates the students to engage in the given activity. With all other things assumed to be more or less equal, this increased engagement leads to more effective participation and higher attainment.
b) The use of DTs changes the ways in which students interact with the task and with each other. This in turn makes the activity more intrinsically interesting and

therefore adds to the sum total of motivation to engage. The increased motivation leads to more prolonged engagement ultimately leading to greater attainment.

c) The use of DTs changes the ways in which students engage with each other and with the task. Primarily as a result of these variations in the form, rather than the duration, of task engagement, student attainment in key aspects of the task increases. Increased success eventually raises motivation for further engagement.

The difference between b) and c) above may at first appear subtle, but is of potential significance. The former promotes change through a "more of the same" strategy. The cognitive aspects of the students' work are constant but they may engage for longer and with greater intensity. The latter model, c), highlights changes in the form of student cognition which then lead to more effective learning and higher attainment. If higher attainment also helps to develop and sustain motivation to engage with the task, then a beneficial cycle can be established.

The Condie et al. review primarily discusses motivation as an intermediary variable (operating between initial task presentation and attainment). This is a common way of conceptualising motivation and indeed largely accounts for the perennial interest shown by educators and researchers alike in the phenomenon. Attainment gains during the present phase of education are the prime target. However, it is also possible to conceive of motivation as the target variable. A distinction can thus be made between the potential for DTs to impact upon motivation so to enhance present levels of attainment, or to act as a spur to the development of "better" motivation in the longer term. Short-term attainment gains would not necessarily be a consequence of this latter approach. The longer-term perspective depends upon the adoption of a model of motivation which recognises motivation as possessing elements of a skill – a view established in motivation theory some while ago but not always fully reflected in other literatures that refer to motivation [17]. This is considered to be a vital distinction in the present context. On the assumption that motivation development has adaptive features, then a drive to enhance motivation in order to bring about gains in attainment in the relatively short-term is likely to be associated with motivational developments that also fit with that context. When we are concerned with high stakes (indeed very high stakes) attainment outcomes then the associated motivational characteristics are possibly going to prove to be very deeply ingrained. This raises the possibility of motivational styles developing that are indeed well suited to current concerns but are also poorly adapted to future environments and at the same time difficult to change.

6 The Evidence Base

The above comments suggest that we need to be very careful in considering claims that might be made in respect to the impact of DTs upon motivation. This is particularly likely to be the case when the role of motivation in transition situations is the focus of concern. However, it is also necessary to take a closer look at the evidence base for the claim that DTs might be able to exercise any significant impact upon motivation in the first place. An examination of a sample of the studies that have been implicated in the claim that DTs can have a beneficial impact upon motivation follows.

The Impact2 project [26] provided a focus on the effects of networked technologies. As with the predecessor study [27], the focus of attention was on the influence of DTs on attainment. The project aimed to identify the relationship between degrees of DT use and performance in the National Curriculum at Key Stages 2 to 4 (for students aged 7 to 16 years). Assessing the academic progress made by students revealed a consistent, but often small and statistically insignificant, advantage for those students with higher levels of DT use. Variations across curricula area were identified, and these variations were themselves found to co-vary with age.

Motivational consequences were addressed via information gathered from interviews and observations. A consideration of the claims made from these data show a fit with the categories identified above. DTs are seen as intrinsically interesting - they all "want to go on the computer". The use of DTs is also seen to improve the level of performance and thus increases satisfaction and motivation. In as much as the use of the computer speeds up the process of getting the work done, there is more time available for student reflection. However, it remains unclear as to which of these pathways, and possibly others, were responsible for any actual changes in motivation. More importantly, it is unclear just what "motivation" is taken to be. Finally, it is important to note the marked difference between the claims made for the effects of DTs in respect to attainment and then motivation. While it is unlikely that the Impact2 authors would wish to defend a claim that DTs have uniform and entirely consistent motivational effects across the National Curriculum and age ranges, nevertheless the claims for motivational impact are presented as being much more ubiquitous than those for attainment. With attainment the outcomes are clearly context specific, whereas similar qualifications on the impact of motivation are less evident. In part this is simply a reflection of the relative degree of attention paid by the researchers to each. However, it also reflects the dependency on relatively undifferentiated, undefined and unchallenged teacher perceptions of motivational effects.

Torgerson and Zhu [28], using the Evidence for Policy and Practice Information and Co-ordinating Centre (EPPI-Centre) methodology in their review concerning the impact of DTs on literacy learning in English for 5- to 16-year-olds, offers the overall conclusion that "Policy-makers should refrain from any further investment in ICT and literacy until at least one large and rigorously designed randomised trial has shown it to be effective in increasing literacy outcomes" (p.9). This essentially neutral but cautious conclusion is concerned with the impact on attainment. The authors make the point that some studies (often used by government agencies to support the development of DT usage in schools) are not suited to the making of any causal claims as they only employ observational or correlational data. The impact of other factors that might be associated with "high" ICT use may well be responsible for the positive associations observed.

Torgerson and Zhu [28] include in their analysis, studies that claimed to have investigated the effects of DTs upon reading attitude and attributions. While the review does not explicitly draw out the measured impact of DTs upon motivation, the conclusion is as for attainment effects. There would appear to be no existing study that has targeted the impact of DTs upon motivation that would meet the conditions that Torgerson and Zhu require. Reasons for this will include the lack of clearly agreed measures and definitions.

Further studies add support to the suggestion that students find materials mediated by DTs to be interesting [29], a view clearly shared by parents with regard to engagement in homework [30], and that the use of DTs can provoke teachers to reflect upon their pedagogic practices and so develop more collaborative working [31]. Each of these studies, and the others that they are selected to represent, generally fail to offer any precise definition of motivation. Any unique contribution of DTs to the enhancement of motivation is far from being identified.

According to Condie et al. the "most significant study to date on the motivational effect of ICT on pupils" is a project carried out for the then DfES [32]. According to Condie and Munro, this research is one of very few to draw explicitly upon motivational theory and to attempt to develop a quantitative set of measures rather than relying solely upon teacher or other reports of motivational effects.

The Passey and Rogers' research constructed a multi-dimensional model of "adaptive" motivation drawing upon a number of strands from motivation theory. These included goal theory [7] and self-determination theory [1]. Working from these positions, Passey and Rogers constructed "adaptive" and "maladaptive" motivational profiles. Measurements were obtained of the profiles of students in a number of schools identified as exemplars of 'good DT practice'. Condie and Munro state that "...the forms of motivation associated with [information and communication technologies] ICT use were concerned with learning rather than mere task completion and, when using ICT, pupils perceived their classrooms to be very focused on the process of learning". Passey and Rogers concluded that using DTs helped to draw pupils into more positive modes of motivation and could offer a means by which pupils could envisage success. All of the secondary school teachers involved felt that DTs had a positive impact on pupil interest in, and attitudes to, schoolwork.

A fuller reading of the original research leads to some important caveats. Primarily the Passey and Rogers study was correlational in nature. As such it would fail to meet the requirements set out by Torgerson and Zhu [28]. Nevertheless, the Passey and Rogers model is one of the very few that attempts to go beyond "taken for granted" or "common-sense" definitions of motivation.

This summary of highlighted studies leads to the following observations. There is a generally held, and typically unchallenged, view that the use of DTs in classrooms has motivational benefits. Precisely what this may mean however is another matter. In some cases the implication is that the use of DTs themselves is something that students enjoy and they are therefore willing to spend time engaging with them and thereby with the associated academic work. This means relatively little when it comes to making claims that student motivation for learning any specific aspect of the school curriculum might be enhanced. Nonetheless, DTs may have the capacity to add to the sum total of whatever is motivating students to engage. DTs can also have an impact upon pedagogic practices and may enhance the use of collaborative processes, generally regarded as having positive motivational benefits [22]. In order to achieve these benefits however, the proactive and regulating role of the teacher remains essential. Finally, while motivation is generally undefined, it is considered to be an intermediary variable helping to determine attainment levels as distinct from an objective of development itself.

7 Conclusion

If we are to be able to offer a coherent position on the ways in which DTs may help with the development of more effective motivation in young people experiencing important life transitions, then a clear understanding of the nature of motivation in those situations is needed. Motivation research has tended to concern itself with the nature of motivation in given contexts or to examine the degree of fit with the "far" side of the transition for those characteristics developed on the "near" side. Concern with the process of transition has been limited. Three major theoretical positions in motivation (goal theory, self-determination theory and future time perspective) have been introduced. In short, these three central approaches to the conceptualisation of motivation move us away from conceptualising motivation as something that operates only in the here and now of the particular classroom activity and relocates it as an essential part of the total organic experience of the individual student. Clearly it does not follow from this that only interventions or changes to classroom practice that address all relevant aspects of the individual equally and simultaneously can be recognised as genuine attempts. However, without a consideration as to how any single change in current practice might bring about such longer-term changes we will be left with an inadequate model of practice. Motivation has for some time been conceptualised as a skill [17] that needs to be developed and learned. Typical claims around the impact of DTs have generally deployed a less effective deficit model where the addition of DT inspired elements can make up for the motivational inadequacies of a student. Such approaches can be severely limiting in that they generate a DT (or other "sweetener") dependency that would do little if anything to truly enhance motivation.

A major objective of this review has been to highlight the importance of helping students to develop the skill of motivational self-regulation. As with many other aspects of human behaviour, motivational patterns will be characterised by a degree of adaptiveness to the relevant context. This is a powerful process and one that generally helps to ensure that people will develop appropriate motivational forms. However, if transitions bring about clear changes in relevant situational demands, then the adaptiveness of any particular pattern can be rapidly lost. The effective transition will then be one that will be marked by the re-adaptation of motivation. DTs may well have a role to play in this, but they are more likely to do so through the effective scaffolding of self-regulated change than through the provision of forms of "interest" to carry the student along.

References

1. Deci, E.L., Ryan, R.M. (eds.): Handbook of self-determination research. University of Rochester Press, Rochester (2002)
2. BBC: Teaching 'better at school than university' - survey (2011), http://www.bbc.co.uk/news/education-15150382 (retrieved August 16, 2014)
3. Miller, R.B., Brickman, S.J.: A model of future-oriented motivation and self-regulation. Educational Psychology Review 16, 9–33 (2004)
4. Senko, C., Hulleman, C., Harackiewicz, J.M.: Achievement Goal Theory at the Crossroads: Old Controversies, Current Challenges, and New Directions. Educational Psychologist 46, 26–47 (2011)
5. Maehr, M.L., Zusho, A.: Achievement goal theory: the past, present and future. In: Wentzel, K., Wigfield, A. (eds.) Handbook of Motivation at School. Routledge, London (2009)
6. Elliot, A.J.: A conceptual history of the achievement goal construct. In: Elliot, A.J., Dweck, C.S. (eds.) Handbook of Competence and Motivation. The Guilford Press, London (2005)
7. Pintrich, P.R.: Multiple Goals, Multiple Pathways: The Role of Goal Orientation in Learning and Achievement. Journal of Educational Psychology 92, 544–555 (2000)
8. Elliot, A.J., Murayama, K.: On the measurement of achievement goals: Critique, illustration, and application. Journal of Educational Psychology 100, 613–628 (2008)
9. Dweck, C.S., Molden, D.C.: Self Theories: Their Impact on Competence Motivation and Acquisisiton. In: Elliot, A.J., Dweck, C.S. (eds.) Handbook of Competence and Motivation. The Guilford Press, London (2005)
10. Dweck, C.S.: Self-theories: Their role in motivation, personality, and development. Psychology Press, Philadelphia (1999)
11. Elliot, A.J., McGregor, H.: A 2x2 achievement goal framework. Journal of Personality and Social Psychology 80, 501–519 (2001)
12. Durik, A.M., Lovejoy, C.M., Johnson, S.J.: A longitudinal study of achievement goals for college in general: Predicting cumulative GPA and diversity in course selection. Contemporary Educational Psychology 34, 113–119 (2009)
13. Remedios, R., Kiseleva, Z., Elliott, J.G.: Goal orientations in Russian university students: From mastery to performance? Educational Psychology 28, 677–691 (2008)
14. Rogers, C.G.: Transition, self-regulation, independent learning and goal theory. Psychology of Education Review 36, 26–31 (2012)
15. Rogers, C.G.: The Vernon Wall Lecture: Psychology in education in a political world. Some thoughts on performativity in higher education. In: The British Psychological Society, Education Section Annual Conference, York (2013)
16. Elliot, A.J., Murayama, K., Pekrun, R.H.: A 3 x 2 achievement goal model. Journal of Educational Psychology 103, 632–648 (2011)
17. Ames, C.: The enhancement of student motivation. In: Maehr, M.L., Kleiber, D.A. (eds.) Advances in Motivation and Achievement. Enhancing Motivation, vol. 5, JAI Press, Greenwich (1987)
18. Ames, C.: Motivation: What teachers need to know. Teachers College Record 91, 409–421 (1990)
19. Condie, R., Munro, B., Seagreaves, L., Kenesson, S.: The impact of ICT in Schools - A landscape review. Becta, Coventry (2007)
20. Hattie, J.: Visible learning: A synthesis of over 800 meta-analyses relating to achievement. Routledge, London (2009)

21. Higgins, S., Mercier, E.: Multi-touch technologies and motivation in the classroom. In: BERA Annual Conference, Warwick (2010)
22. Blatchford, P., Baines, E., Rubie-Davies, C., Bassett, P., Chowne, A.: The Effect of a New Approach to Group Work on Pupil-Pupil and Teacher-Pupil Interactions. Journal of Educational Psychology 98, 750–765 (2006)
23. Bandura, A.: Guide for Constructing Self-Efficacy Scales. In: Self-Efficacy Beliefs of Adolescents. Information Age Publishing, Charlotte (2006)
24. Torff, B., Tirotta, R.: Interactive whiteboards produce small gains in elementary students' self-reported motivation in mathematics. Computers & Education 54, 379–383 (2006)
25. Turel, Y.K.: An interactive whiteboard student survey: Development, validity and reliability. Computers & Education 57, 2441–2450 (2011)
26. Harrison, C., Comber, C., Fisher, T., Haw, K., Lewin, C., Lunzer, E., McFarlane, A., Mavers, D., Scrimshaw, P., Somekh, B., Watling, R.: ICT in schools. In: The Impact of Information and Communication Technologies on Pupil Learning and Attainment. Research and Evaluation Series, vol. 7. DfES and Becta, Nottingham and Coventry (2002)
27. Watson, D.M., Cox, M.J., Johnson, D.C.: The Impact Report: An evaluation of the impact of Information Technology on children's achievements in primary and secondary schools. Department for Education and King's College London, Centre for Educational Studies, London (1993)
28. Torgerson, C., Zhu, D.: A systematic review and meta-analysis of the effectiveness of ICT on literacy learning in English. In: Research Evidence in Education Library, pp. 5–16. EPPI-Centre Social Science Research Unit, Institute of Education, London (2003)
29. Livingston, K., Condie, R.: Evaluation of Phase Two of the SCHOLAR Programme Final Report. The Quality in Education Centre, University of Strathclyde, Glasgow (2004)
30. Valentine, G., Marsh, J., Pattie, C.: Children and Young People's Home Use of ICT for Educational Purposes: The impact on Attainment at Key Stages, pp. 1–4. DCFS, Nottingham (2005)
31. Hennessy, S., Deaney, R., Ruthven, K.: Emerging teacher strategies for supporting subject teaching and learning with ICT. University of Cambridge Faculty of Education, Cambridge (2005)
32. Passey, D., Rogers, C.G., Machell, J., McHugh, G.: The Motivational Effect of ICT on Pupils. DfES, Nottingham (2004)

Digital Skills and Competencies in Schools

Sue Cranmer

Department of Educational Research, Lancaster University, UK
s.cranmer@lancaster.ac.uk

Abstract. This paper will compare a range of recently developed frameworks, which identify digital skills and competencies drawn from the United Kingdom (UK), from across the wider European Union, and internationally to include Australia. It will also briefly explore who and what is driving this agenda. The models will be set within the context of recent evidence that highlight the deficits that exist in children and young people's skills and competencies in order to emphasise the need for schools to address this issue. In order to consider the issue more practically, it will explore the digital skills and competencies of one young person who is currently in transition to explore how useful the frameworks are for the development of their skills. It will show the correspondence and divergence between the different frameworks and the composite headings which can be drawn from the content. Examples of these dimensions will be outlined to show how digital technologies, and particularly digital skills and competencies, can influence a specific transition from school to college.

Keywords: Digital skills, digital literacy, disability.

1 Introduction

A central problem of the digital technologies agenda is how to develop young people's skills and competencies to support immediate and longer-term life transitions. Learners need these skills and competencies to support their life transitions. Evidence about schools and what they are doing to develop digital skills is far from clear. There are different models of digital skills and competencies which have emerged in recent years in the United Kingdom (UK) and Europe [1, 2]. Whilst it is not immediately apparent who is driving this agenda, it includes in the UK, for example, the UK Government, and industry [3, 4, 5]. Likewise, this agenda is also being driven forward by government and industry in many other countries [6, 7, 8].

This paper will compare a range of recently developed frameworks, which identify digital skills and competencies drawn from the UK, from across the wider European Union, and internationally to include Australia. It will also briefly explore who and what is driving this agenda. The models will be set within the context of recent evidence that highlight the deficits that exist in children and young people's skills and competencies in order to emphasise the need for schools to address this issue. In order to consider the issue more practically, it will consider the digital skills and

D. Passey and A. Tatnall (Eds.): KCICTP/ITEM 2014, IFIP AICT 444, pp. 165–177, 2014.

competencies of one young person who is currently in transition to explore how useful the frameworks are for the development of their skills. These data are drawn from a small pilot project currently underway, exploring how young people in mainstream schools who are blind or visually impaired use digital technologies – such as the computer and Internet – for learning at school, home and in other environments. In particular, this paper will draw on the data to address the following research questions:

- How far do the frameworks enable understanding of young people's digital skills and competencies?
- How might the frameworks be implemented in practice?
- How do digital technologies support life transitions?

2 Background

'Digital skills and competencies' as a term describes an often expanded multifaceted range of competencies which are difficult to define given the different perspectives and professional disciplines engaged in the field [9]. These skills have variously been called 'digital literacy', 'media literacy', 'computer skills' and 'Internet literacy'.

Debates about what should constitute digital skills and competencies are prolific and the abundance of these debates – also set out in policy – in themselves contest Prensky's notion of 'digital natives' [10]. Prensky argued that 'digital natives', young people born in the last 3 decades who have always been surrounded by digital media: are '...all "native speakers" of the digital language of computers, video games and the Internet' (p.1). As so-called 'digital immigrants', Prensky argued that (older) educators needed to up-skill in order to address new ways of learning in order to engage this new type of learner. Since 2001, much research has contested the view that all young people have an innate capacity to learn how to use digital technologies effectively. A recent face-to-face survey was carried out in the UK by the Princes Trust to explore what they refer to as 'digital literacy' [11]. The survey included 1,378 young people aged between 15 to 25 years of age which also comprised 265 young people classed as NEET (Not in Education, Employment or Training). Whilst the survey found that many young people feel confident in carrying out a wide range of tasks, particularly social activities such as e-mailing friends (66%), accessing social media sites (64%), 12% reported that they do not think their computer skills are good enough to use in the job they want; 10% of NEETS feel "out of their depth" using a computer; and 17% of NEETS believe they would be in work today if they had better computer skills. A larger project, 'EU Kids Online' again carried out a face-to-face survey, in this case with 25,000 9 to 16-year-olds in 25 European countries to understand their online activities, skills and self-efficacy. The data show that children from lower socio-economic status homes are gaining less digital skills and competencies than their more affluent counterparts; younger children in general have less developed skills accompanied by less confidence using them; girls have slightly less confidence about their skills than boys; and the majority of children gauged their skills to be less than their parents (only 36% said it is 'very true that they know more than their parents'). As the authors reported, this finding again debunks the myth of the digital native [12]. These findings could be expanded upon drawing on other international research studies which demonstrate evidence about the level of development of children's digital skills and competencies and whether they are underdeveloped and in turn require intervention in order to address this.

In recognition that a problem does exist, there have been numerous calls and initiatives for the development of young people's digital skills and competencies in schools including from industry in the UK. The Confederation for British Industry has highlighted the need for action in this respect [4], as have the video games and video effects industries [5]. The UK government have recently issued a new curriculum to be introduced in September 2014 for England for both primary (ages 5 to 11 years) and secondary (ages 11 to 16 years) children and young people. Within the curriculum for computing, it is stated that: 'Computing also ensures that pupils become digitally literate – able to use, and express themselves and develop their ideas through, information and communication technology – at a level suitable for the future workplace and as active participants in a digital world' [3, p.204]). More broadly, the European Commission's Europe 2020 flagship initiative Digital Agenda for Europe emphasises the need for young people, workers and all citizens to have '… the skills needed to meet 21st century challenges' [6]. These attributes are seen as important for economic recovery and growth within the European Union. In Australia, the Melbourne Declaration on the Educational Goals for Young Australians [7] states that in a digital age, young people need to be highly skilled: 'Rapid and continuing advances in information and communication technologies (ICT) are changing the ways people share, use, develop and process information and technology. In this digital age, young people need to be highly skilled in the use of ICT. While schools already employ these technologies in learning, there is a need to increase their effectiveness significantly over the next decade (p.5).'

3 Introduction of Frameworks for Digital Skills and Competencies

In light of the developments summarised above, three frameworks for the development of digital skills and competencies have been identified for analysis in this paper. Criteria for inclusion were:

- Must be based on empirical research.
- Must be recent (i.e. developed in the last 5 years).
- Must be broken down into different elements and descriptions of the constituent skills and competencies.
- Must be written in the English language.
- Must be represented in a diagrammatic form for ease of top-level representation.
- Must have the main focus on digital skills and competencies rather than broader elements of 21st-century skills.

In light of these criteria, frameworks from Australia, Europe and the United Kingdom were selected for comparison: two aimed at helping teachers to develop their students' skills [2, 13]; the other aimed at supporting the development of "All citizens" to "create consensus at European level about the components of Digital

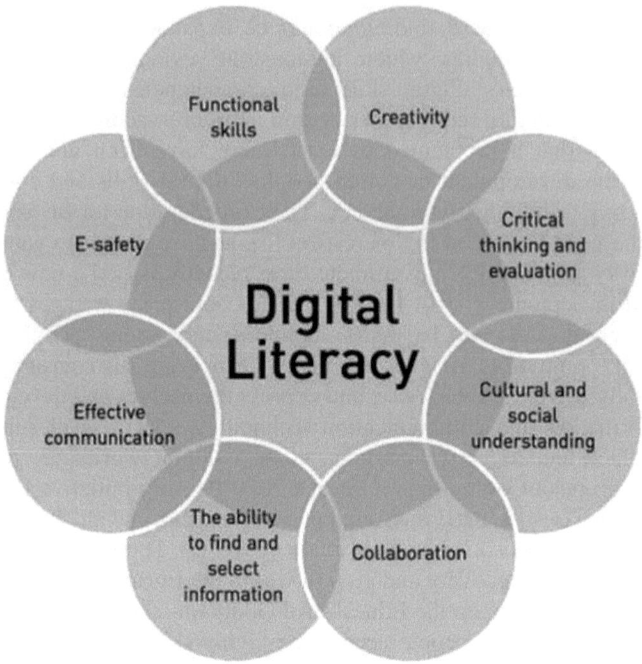

Fig. 1. Futurelab [2]

Fig. 2. Institute for Prospective Technological Studies [1]

Competence" [14, p.7]. Given the large number of models of digital skills and competencies developed, the selection could be expanded upon in a further extended study (see for instance the National Council for Teachers of English in the United

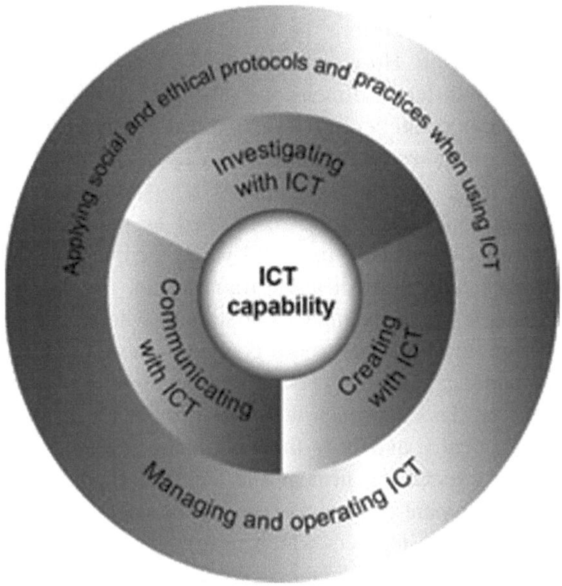

Fig. 3. The Australian Curriculum, Assessment and Reporting Authority [19]

States [15] or BECTA [16] in the UK. The details considered in each of these frameworks were: components of the framework (see Figures 1, 2 and 3); which organisation produced it; when it was produced; who it was aimed at; what its stated purpose was; and how it was produced.

4 Methodology and Methods

In order to consider the frameworks more practically, an individual case has been drawn from an ongoing small-scale study about how young people with visual impairments in mainstream schools use digital technologies for learning. Firstly, the three frameworks were considered straightforwardly by placing them side-by-side to compare and contrast the differences and correspondences. The comparison took place at the level of headings and brief description of content which represent each dimension of digital skills and competencies, as set out in Table 1.

Table 1. The elements of each framework included in the analysis

Framework 1: Futurelab	Framework 2: IPTS	Framework 3: ACARA
Diagram p.19; descriptions and ideas for how teachers can foster digital competencies for learners pp.22-45	Diagram p.5; outline description of different dimensions of digital competencies pp.5-6	Diagram p.5; outline description of different dimensions of digital competencies pp.5-6

The decision was made to explore the frameworks at this level of detail for the purposes of cross comparison. However it should be noted that the IPTS framework in particular sets out the different dimensions of digital competencies in much more detail, and analysis of this could be usefully expanded in further work. Also, the IPTS and ACARA self/student assessment frameworks could be used to evaluate young people's digital skills and competencies in depth.

Data from the individual case being researched as part of the ongoing digital technologies for learning by visually impaired young people project was then drawn upon to look more practically at the different frameworks. The case was selected from the larger project sample as an example of a student who is currently in transition from school to college, to understand more concretely how the selected frameworks appear in terms of understanding and potentially developing young people's digital skills and competencies. This approach therefore provides a means of exploring the frameworks more practically and how they might be implemented in practice. In relation to this student's visual impairment and therefore the relevance of the case to understanding the development of digital skills and competencies, Passey argues that there are differences between learners which need to be recognised so that learning can accommodate '… learner's individual needs, their interests and aptitudes, so they can gain to the greatest possible level' [17, p.103].

The ongoing small-scale study from which this data are drawn is exploring the situation for visually impaired young people in terms of access to digital technologies, uses and how digital technologies influence learning in both formal and out-of-school settings. It is also considering how digital skills and competencies developed by this group of visually impaired young people support formal and out-of-school learning and it is this part of the project which is drawn on here. The research is qualitative in design; and involves 16 participants between the ages of 11 to 18 years. School visits include a semi-structured interview with each young person, observation in the classroom of how they use digital technologies for learning and interviews with the support team. Sixteen detailed case studies will be developed from the data. Where possible, common themes will be drawn out across the sample through adopting a constant comparison approach [18]. Nevertheless, this may not be appropriate because the young people in the sample may have other impairments, which may vary across the group and weaken a cross comparison approach.

'Laura' (a pseudonym) is a 16-year-old girl with a significant visual impairment who lives in the North of England. She was interviewed in May 2014 shortly before taking her examinations and before leaving school in July 2014. She has been selected for this paper as she is currently in transition and making choices about whether to move into the sixth form at the school or outside to a different college. Indeed, during a semi-structured interview she reflected on how her digital skills and competencies could influence her future career. She was also observed in a science lesson using digital technologies. Nevertheless, as this was a revision class, she was mainly using an iPad to access a Microsoft (MS) PowerPoint presentation prepared by her teacher through using the iPad's zoom facility during which the whole class including Laura were being asked questions. This engagement with technology was more limited than if Laura had been, for instance, using the iPad to create content, communicating and collaborating.

5 Comparison of Frameworks

5.1 Dimensions/Headings

Comparison of the three frameworks showed that for the most part, the categories described and the dimensions of each framework can be mapped onto each other (see Table 2). This is perhaps unsurprising given that when considered in detail, it emerged that all 3 were underpinned by international research and analysis of other models. Even so, these similarities also represent a convergence to a large degree of what are seen to be the digital skills and competencies needed by young people today in Australia, Europe and within a specific European Union country, the UK. Where headings do exist which are not reflected in other frameworks, the content within these headings has mainly been conflated under other headings. For instance, the Futurelab framework has a separate category for collaboration. Nevertheless, elements of collaboration have been integrated into the IPTS and ACARA dimensions under the heading of communication.

The order of the headings in Table 2 has been dictated by the dimensions/headings set out in the Futurelab framework (starting from Functional skills on the upper left of the diagram) and then the other frameworks are set out by how they correspond to this. Nevertheless, the diagrammatic form of the Futurelab framework suggests less of a hierarchy than the other two frameworks which have a linear order which could potentially be viewed as a hierarchy of their relative importance. The extent of intentionality for this is unclear.

Given the overall similarities and convergence between the frameworks, it was decided to form composite headings by looking across the headings from the 3 original frameworks to show correspondence. This also allows for consideration of how the dimensions of the frameworks can be used practically to interpret one young person's skills. The paper does not intend to evaluate the usefulness of each framework individually given the extent to which they overlap; however, it will briefly consider how the content described by three of the dimensions/headings may concur or differ across the frameworks.

6 Practical Application of the Frameworks

Table 2 has shown how the content of the dimensions/headings within each framework map onto each other. This section will therefore focus on the practical application of the digital skills and competencies as represented by the composite headings. Three dimensions have been chosen given that this is a short paper, and being selective will allow for more depth in exploration of the issues. Nevertheless, this could be usefully expanded upon. The three dimensions selected have also been chosen where data from the case study of Laura can provide examples of content within each category.

Table 2. The dimensions/headings within the frameworks that map onto each other taking account of the content

	Framework 1: Futurelab	Framework 2: IPTS	Framework 3: ACARA
Dimensions/headings	Functional skills	Problem solving	Managing and operating ICT
	Creativity	Content creation	Creating with ICT
	Critical thinking and evaluation	Information (described as Information management in the diagram)	Investigating with ICT
	Cultural and social understanding	Does not directly map. Elements of the Communication dimension are closest to this.	Does not directly map. Elements of the Applying social and ethical protocols and practices dimension are closest to this.
	Collaboration	Integrated into Communication	Integrated into Communication
	The ability to find and select information	Information (described as Information management within the diagram)	Investigating with ICT
	Effective communication	Communication	Communicating with ICT
	E-safety	Safety	Applying social and ethical protocols and practices when using ICT

6.1 Functional Skills/Managing and Operating ICT/Problem Solving

All 3 frameworks have aspects of this dimension which mainly describes having the appropriate technical knowledge and skills needed to carry out the other dimensions of the frameworks. The IPTS framework is interesting in that it includes that users also need to be able to identify digital competence gaps within this dimension. This is described as: ‘To understand where own competence needs to be improved or updated, to support others in the development of their digital competence, to keep up-to-date with new developments' (p.6). This is an important dimension of the frameworks in emphasising the need to update and develop further technical knowledge and skills.

This dimension is useful for understanding the functional skills which Laura possesses alongside somewhat more extended skills to use digital technologies to overcome visual impairment. She is a competent user of an iPad which she accesses through the built-in accessibility functions. She also uses a laptop with supernova magnification as an assistive technology. She has the functional skills to access a range of devices and software to support her studies. In relation to the need to update and expand knowledge and skills, it is interesting that Laura says that she is able to do most of the things she wants to with digital technologies. Nevertheless, this does not account for other applications and potential uses which Laura might find helpful but does not yet know exist.

6.2 Creativity/Content Creation/Creating with ICT

All 3 frameworks describe creativity as being an essential competence online both in terms of content creation and in having the necessary digital skills and competencies to be actively creative more broadly. For example, in the Futurelab framework, creativity is described in terms of: creating a product or output; thinking creatively and imaginatively; and creating knowledge and knowledge production. The IPTS framework also includes the need to consider copyright and licenses within this dimension, and programming, which the others do not.

In relation to Laura, this category has particular resonance as she said that her favourite subject at school is 'Creative media'. For this subject, she needs to create both films and photographs. She described how she really enjoys going out filming, editing the results in Adobe Premiere Pro and using an optical mouse which enlarges what she is editing in detail. Her interest in the subject combined with having the digital skills and competencies to do this means that her decision about what to do next – whether school or college – hangs on this subject and where best to pursue it. She is as yet undecided. But her ability to do well in this subject (enabled by digital skills and competencies), and to have the skills needed to do so, are crucial in this decision.

6.3 E-Safety/Safety/Applying Social and Ethical Protocols and Practices When Using ICT

There is more divergence between the 3 frameworks in this dimension, immediately signalled by the broader ACARA heading. Nevertheless, all 3 frameworks include the issue of personal safety. The Futurelab model for E-safety puts the onus on critical thinking and what is referred to as 'critical awareness', protecting yourself online personally and in terms of copyright, knowing the risks, cyberbullying; and virus protection. The IPTS dimension is somewhat similar, emphasising safety and security, physical and psychological well-being, risks and threats, protection of personal data, and cyberbullying. It also includes protection of the environment. The ACARA dimension of 'Applying social and ethical protocols and practices when using ICT' is broader and appears to place more prominence on intellectual property rights, storage, digital information security practices; and personal security. It also takes a wider view in the expectation of a developed understanding on the impact of ICT on society and on the benefits and consequences of ICT, setting this dimension within a wider context.

When Laura was asked about online safety, interestingly her immediate response was in relation to having been bullied off-line rather than online. She said that this had happened more at primary school than at the secondary school which she attends now. And she put this down to being the only person with a disability. She said that she had been called 'horrible' names. In relation to transition, she said: '... It just makes you tougher, it makes you in some ways ready for the workplace because it's not going to be all happy and all sweet and everyone is going to be okay with everything'. More positively, Laura said that she had not been bullied much online. On Facebook she only accepts people who she knows face-to-face and who she would like to see her 'timeline'. Also on Facebook if somebody acted in a way that upset her, she said that she could 'block them' suggesting she felt more empowered to do this online than off.

Whilst the issue here for Laura is off-line rather than online bullying, it is included here to show how she feels more empowered online to prevent being bullied compared with being off-line. It is also interesting that she has turned being bullied off-line to positive effect, as in some way being prepared for the workplace. Obviously it is of concern that she anticipates that she may be bullied when she enters the workplace possibly due to her visual impairment. Nevertheless, the way she rationalises how she has been bullied in the past suggests she has a well-developed coping strategy for this.

6.4 How Could Frameworks Be Implemented?

One of the questions that this paper set out to answer was how far the frameworks can be implemented in schools, taking account of the more practical consideration of a specific young person's skills and competencies at the point of transition from school to college or sixth form. The straightforward answer for all students would be to carry out student evaluations as in the ACARA framework, or ask students to self-evaluate as in the IPTS framework, and then to design interventions to address any areas needing further development. Nevertheless, the curriculum in many countries is already tightly packed and this may prevent initiatives designed to develop young people's digital skills and competencies gaining resonance. In the new curriculum for England, for example, it will be important to gauge how far digital skills and competencies will be developed through their stipulation within the curriculum for computing; and how far they can also be embedded across other subjects in the curriculum. In Australia, it will be useful to monitor the impact following the introduction of the ACARA standard. In this, further research will be necessary.

6.5 Skills and Competencies in Specific Life Transitions

A key question for this paper is also how do digital technologies support life transitions? In the case of this paper the question is more one of how do underpinning digital skills and competencies support life transitions. In relation to Laura, there is one clear example where the subject of 'creative media' is influencing Laura's choice of college or sixth form as it is a subject she would really like to continue with. It is also a subject in which the part played by digital technologies, and digital skills and competencies, are fundamental. It would be very useful to relate the findings of this chapter more broadly to studies of transition and particularly research about children and young people's 'resilience' which is known to be important for successful transition [19]. Resilience factors are seen to support transition so that children and young people are able to exhibit '… positive adaptation in circumstances where one might expect, due to atypical levels of stress, a significant degradation in coping skills to take place' (p.1). Indeed, in relation to digital skills, Graham has conceptualised this as 'techno-resiliency to describe the characteristics and strategies through which individuals are able to cope with challenging technology-related circumstances [20]. Further work is needed to understand how digital technologies and the underpinning skills and competencies needed to use them can support transition. This would seem to be highly relevant in the debate about how digital competencies and skills are needed both to equip young people for changes in their lives as well as in order to be able to adopt newer technologies.

7 Conclusions

This paper has compared a range of recently developed frameworks and shown how the dimensions contained within them often converge. It has also sketched out previous studies which highlight the deficits that exist in some children and young people's skills and competencies. The current study could usefully be further expanded through looking in detail at a much larger sample of frameworks and explore these in relation to a larger sample of young people in transition. In an extended study, it would also be useful to set the frameworks within their cultural context in terms of why particular dimensions and elements of each framework have been given the emphasis they have. For example, Futurelab's E safety description appears to draw heavily on current concerns in the UK about children's online safety and the risk of online grooming and sexual predation, and exposure to pornography, rather than for instance, the ACARA framework which places more emphasis on intellectual property and the wider consequences of ICT on society. It would be useful to understand the trends and concerns within each country which may be traceable into the frameworks themselves. It is also clear that the frameworks alone do not ensure implementation, and given that in Australia and the UK, for instance, emphasis on the development of these skills appears to be growing in terms of further inclusion in curricula, further research would be helpful to understand how these developments work in practice.

Acknowledgements. The author would like to thank the tutors and young people who kindly participated in the study about how young people with visual impairments in mainstream schools use digital technologies for learning. Also, to thank Professor Don Passey for generously sharing ideas and giving much support in developing this paper and other projects.

References

1. Ferrari, A.: Digital Competence in Practice: An Analysis of Frameworks. Institute for Prospective Technological Studies, Seville (2012), http://ftp.jrc.es/EURdoc/JRC68116.pdf (retrieved August 30, 2014)
2. Hague, C., Payton, S.: Digital literacy across the curriculum. Futurelab, Bristol (2010), http://www2.futurelab.org.uk/resources/documents/handbooks/digital_literacy.pdf (retrieved August 30, 2014)
3. Department for Education (DfE): The national curriculum in England. Framework document. Reference: DFE-00177-2013 (2013), http://www.gov.uk/dfe/nationalcurriculum (retrieved August 30, 2014)
4. Confederation for British Industry: First steps: A new approach for our schools – ambition (noun) a desire and determination to achieve success. CBI, London (2012), http://www.cbi.org.uk/media/1845483/cbi_education_report_191112.pdf (retrieved August 30, 2014)
5. Livingstone, I., Hope, A.: Next Gen. Transforming the UK into the world's leading talent hub for the video games and visual effects industries: A Review. Nesta, London (2011), http://www.nesta.org.uk/library/documents/NextGenv32.pdf (retrieved August 30, 2014)
6. European Commission: Europe 2020 Strategy (2010), http://ec.europa.eu/europe2020/index_en.htm (retrieved August 30, 2014)
7. Ministerial Council on Education, Employment, Training & Youth Affairs (MCEETYA): The Melbourne Declaration on the Educational Goals For Young Australians (2008), http://www.curriculum.edu.au/verve/resources/National_Declaration_on_the_Educational_Goals_for_Young_Australians.pdf (retrieved August 30, 2014)
8. Partnership for 21st Century Skills (P21): Framework for 21st Century Learning, http://www.p21.org/about-us/p21-framework (retrieved August 30, 2014)
9. Meyers, E.M., Erickson, I., Small, R.V.: Digital literacy and informal learning environments: an introduction. Learning, Media and Technology 38(4), 355–367 (2014)
10. Prensky, M.: Digital natives, digital immigrants. On the Horizon 9(5), 1–6 (2001)
11. Princes Trust: Digital Literacy Survey (2013), http://www.princes-trust.org.uk/pdf/DIGITAL_LITERACY_2013B.pdf (retrieved August 30, 2014)
12. Sonck, N., Livingstone, S., Kuiper, E., de Haan, J.: Digital literacy and safety skills. EU Kids Online, London School of Economics & Political Science, London (2011), http://eprints.lse.ac.uk/33733/1/Digital%20literacy%20and%20safety%20skills%20lsero.pdf (retrieved August 30, 2014)
13. Australian Curriculum Assessment and Reporting Authority (ACARA): Information and communication technology (ICT) capability, http://australiancurriculum.edu.au (retrieved August 30, 2014)

14. Ferrari, A.: DIGICOMP: A Framework for Developing and Understanding Digital Competence in Europe. Institute for Prospective Technological Studies, Seville, Spain (2013), http://ftp.jrc.es/EURdoc/JRC83167.pdf (retrieved August 30, 2014)
15. National Council of Teachers of English: 21st-Century Literacies. A policy research brief. National Council of Teachers of English, Urbana, IL (2007), http://www.ncte.org/library/NCTEfiles/Resources/Magazine/Chron110721CentLitBrief.pdf (retrieved August 30, 2014)
16. BECTA: Digital literacy. Teaching critical thinking for our digital world. BECTA, Coventry (2010), http://tinyurl.com/k5rgdru(retrieved August 30, 2014)
17. Passey, D.: Inclusive technology enhanced learning: Overcoming Cognitive, Physical, Emotional and Geographic Challenges. Routledge, New York (2014)
18. Strauss, A.: Qualitative analysis for social scientists. Cambridge University Press, Cambridge (1987)
19. Newman, T., Blackburn, S.: Interchange 78. Transitions in the Lives of Children and Young People: Resilience Factors. Scottish Executive Education Department, Edinburgh (2002), http://www.scotland.gov.uk/Resource/Doc/46997/0024005.pdf (retrieved August 30, 2014)
20. Graham, R.G.: Techno-resiliency: An Exploration of Professional Practices in the Field of Technology-Enriched Teaching and Learning. Lancaster University, Lancaster, Unpublished PhD Thesis (2014)

Digital Skills for Employment

Denise Leahy and Diana Wilson

Trinity College Dublin, Ireland
denise.leahy@cs.tcd.ie

Abstract. How are digital skills developed for those involved in life transitions to employment? Digital skills are developed over time. Some of these skills are developed in formal education, others in informal and non-formal education settings. Digital skills are acquired over time through educational and social use of technology, through formal instruction, informal self-learning and learning from peers. Our world today requires digital skills to enable an individual to succeed in finding, evaluating and creating information for further and higher education, training and employment. This paper examines the need for these skills, some European initiatives and the frameworks which define the skills.

Keywords: IT competency, frameworks, IFIP, CEN, basic ICT skills.

1 Introduction

Technology is changing the way people live in today's "Information Society". Work is global, personal communication is immediate and information is available at all times of the day and night. Digital skills are needed to understand and cope with these changes as a person moves through the various stages of life. As the European Union (EU) has stated, "Information and communication technologies profoundly and irreversibly affect the ways of working, accessing knowledge, socialising, communicating, collaborating - and succeeding – in all areas of the professional, social, and personal life of European young people and citizens" [1]. The Digital Agenda for Europe [2] recognises the need for digital skills for innovation and growth in Europe and notes that the skill requirements are constantly changing: "In a competitive and rapidly changing world, workforces need to be capable of continuously adapting to shifting job requirements and organisation procedures related to new skill-intensive technologies" [3].

Unemployment in the EU reached 10.7% by December 2013, yet the number of "digital jobs" is growing at a rate of 3% per annum [4]. A recent IT Skills Audit [5] estimated an excess of over 4,500 unfilled jobs in the ICT sector in Ireland and a 2014 report from LERO, the Irish Software Engineering Research Centre, predicted that thousands of Irish software jobs could be lost as a result of the growing IT skills shortage. As technology touches all levels of society and business, e-leaders with digital skills (e-skills) are needed at every level in an organisation [6]. According to Accenture [7], "Every Business Is a Digital Business"; it could be argued that every employee needs digital skills. In 2011, EU commissioner Neelie Kroes said, "You

D. Passey and A. Tatnall (Eds.): KCICTP/ITEM 2014, IFIP AICT 444, pp. 178–189, 2014.

are nowhere without digital skills in the 21st century"[1]. But what are these skills? There have been several frameworks developed to address this issue and to help employees identify skills gaps in supporting a life transition. This paper examines the different definitions of the skills, and the skills' frameworks that have been developed to help understand what is needed during major changes in a person's life.

2 The Need for Skills

2.1 The World of Work Is Changing

The concept of a 'job for life' has disappeared. Both employment and organisations are becoming increasingly precarious; many jobs have become contractual, part-time or flexible and the average lifespan of a company has fallen since 1960 from 76 years to 15 years [8]. The acquisition of digital skills can give people entering, or re-entering the workplace greater choice and job security. More importantly, the decreasing cost of technologies and learning how to use them opens up new opportunities for self-employment and entrepreneurship that had previously been denied (e.g. Arduino, Raspberry Pi, 3D printers).

A person needs to demonstrate a large variety of "complex cognitive, motor, sociological, and emotional skills" [9, 10] to take benefit from technology and the Information Society. Without these skills there is a danger of being excluded. It is important that people know how to use technology safely and securely. Using the Internet often involves entering personal details on a web page and putting pictures on a social networking site that can expose a person's privacy and can involve the person being "tagged", thus allowing the searching for all pictures which may be held in any system worldwide. This "tagging" is growing and likely to grow further – "Recently, with the popularity of social networking websites, we observe a massive number of user-tagged images, referred to as *"social images"*, that are available on the web" [11]. There are implications for the future, for employment prospects, future careers and personal privacy. Global positioning systems (GPS) and geographic information systems (GIS) are very useful in finding routes to unfamiliar places, but these location-based technologies can also identify where the user is at any moment as he or she moves around.

"Cloud computing" is a term used often but most people do not know that they are actually using cloud computing. With cloud computing some or all of the software and hardware services can reside on the Internet and the person using the computer need not know where. According to Hayes [12], "As software migrates from local [personal computers] PCs to distant Internet servers, users and developers alike go along for the ride." Cloud services can be accessed by any user (client) interface, for example telephone, tablet, any mobile device, monitor, computer or any intelligent device. Large organisations are using the cloud to reduce costs by using information technology (IT) resources only when they need them as an "on demand" service. This service has been likened to the switching on of electricity [13]. There are security

[1] http://europa.eu/rapid/press-release_SPEECH-11-836_en.htm

issues in using the cloud. Companies must consider the reliability, the service levels and the security of data and systems in the cloud; individuals must be aware of the security and privacy of their data. It is vital that people are aware of privacy issues when they are using technology in their daily and business lives, in what Moran *et al.* [14] refer to as "the personal information cloud, i.e., the working set of information that is relevant to the individual and his work".

2.2 Teachers

Teachers need to understand technology and its use in education. Teachers must have a basic knowledge of technology and must be able to use e-learning tools to create course content, to set assessments, to enable collaborative work and to design the administrative functionality required for their specific class. This usually involves the use of a learning management system and a content management system. Students need to know how to access the classes, register online, communicate with teachers and other students and download material as required. They all need to know when technical help is needed. Awouters *et al.* [15] believe "Teaching and learning with [information and communication technologies] ICT requires specific competencies for teachers and lecturers" and "using a Virtual Learning Environment like Blackboard or Moodle demands more didactical than technical skills. Especially e-learning and blended learning is too demanding to let teachers learn to use these tools only by experimenting." John and Wheeler [16] discussing the needs of learners in the classroom identify the change that technology brings - "There is a need, for example, for students to engage with digital media in a number of ways, transcending those which are required to learn from paper-based text or images".

Bawden [17] expresses concern that teachers have not taken up the challenges of technology and asserts that "Information literacy and digital literacy are central topics for the information sciences. They are associated with issues as varied as information overload, lifelong learning, knowledge management and the growth of the Information Society. Naturally, they have been much discussed in the literature, but not, perhaps, as much as their importance deserves; in particular, they have not impinged much on the practitioner." While there have been positive developments since 2001, in particular the rise of Massive Open Online Courses (MOOCs) such as Coursera and the Khan Academy, these issues have not yet been resolved.

The management in educational establishments must also understand the needs - "Teachers who want to change need an innovative environment to act in. Therefore also management has to change." Another consideration might be the measurement of the e-skills achieved so that the effectiveness of the teaching can be measured and gaps in the process can be discovered; this is included as a priority in the Digital Agenda [18].

2.3 Information Literacy

Information literacy enables the individual to be discriminating in the information available to him or her. So much data is available online and it is necessary to be able to evaluate the accuracy and integrity of such data - "IT literacy... must also capture the notion of information literacy – the ability to assess the validity of various sources of information" [19]. The European Union agrees: "In the global information and knowledge society, the ability to communicate competently in all old and new media, as well as to access, analyze and evaluate the power of images, words and sounds, is a fundamental skill and competence for every young European citizen. These skills of media literacy are essential for our future as individuals and as members of a democratic society" [20].

2.4 Lifelong Learning

Technology can facilitate learning at any time, any place and throughout one's life. Lifelong learning is becoming accepted as a necessity in personal and working lives. Included in the European Union's "Key Competences for Lifelong Learning" are the needs for competencies in "learning to learn" and "digital competence" where it is stated "Competence in the fundamental basic skills of language, literacy, numeracy and in information and communication technologies (ICT) is an essential foundation for learning". As technology is used more in education and in everyday lives, there is a need to continue to develop skills in this area. Lifelong learning can be facilitated and made more accessible with technology. Information literacy, as part of digital literacy, is necessary for participation in learning.

The European Union recognises the need for lifelong learning and talks of the "triangle of lifelong learning", this triangle being education, research and innovation. The European Centre for the Development of Vocational Training [21] stresses the importance for society - "Lifelong learning supports creativity and innovation and enables full economic and social participation." This is not a new idea; Kilpatrick said in 1918, "We of America have for years increasingly desired that education be considered as life itself and not as a mere preparation for later living. The conception before us promises a definite step toward the attainment of this end. If the purposeful act be in reality the typical unit of the worthy life, then it follows that to base education on purposeful acts is exactly to identify the process of education with worthy living itself" [22].

2.5 Technology Acceptance

Companies must overcome the potential barriers to the use of technology. People will use technology if they think it will help them and people will use technology if they find it easy to use. Davis [23], investigating why people accept technology, defined "perceived usefulness" as "the degree to which a person believes that using a particular system would enhance his or her job performance" and "perceived ease of use" as "the degree to which a person believes that using a particular system would be free from effort". This "Technology Acceptance Model" (TAM) was developed in 1989. Today, people have little choice but to accept technology, therefore digital literacy is vital to understand how technology can help and how to use it. In business, digital literacy is vital to ensure the success of new systems. The King and He [24] research asserts that the TAM is a reliable predictor for the successful implementation of computer systems in business. Applying the findings to digital literacy, it could be argued that digital literacy knowledge and skills address many of the issues identified and that the TAM can be applied to the use of technology in personal lives. If a person is comfortable and confident in using technology, he or she will use it. If not, the technology will be avoided or could be used incorrectly. This has implications for business in the future.

When introduced to new technology, people adopt the technology at different speeds, from those who are enthusiastic about technology and keen to adopt it to those who are slow to take it up. The Diffusion of Innovations model [25] was first used to describe farmers' attitudes in the United States towards the adoption of science and technology. However, it has been used since 1962 to describe the adoption of modern technology in business. In his research, Rogers identifies five different levels of adoption. "Innovators" are the first people to adopt an innovation; they will take risks and may fail. Usually these people are young, wealthy and are close to other innovators. "Early Adopters" are "more discrete in adoption choices than innovators" and will follow the innovators in adopting a technology. "Early Majority" people adopt an innovation some time after the innovators and early adopters. "Late Majority" people will adopt an innovation after the majority of society and "Laggards" are the last to adopt an innovation. This model is normally applied to the take-up of new or "leading edge" technology by business. Nevertheless, the model could be applied to the adoption and acceptance of technology by the ordinary citizen. Having digital literacy can increase the adoption rate and the quality of decision making, making individuals more critical of new technology and its mode of application, and understanding when it is time to be innovative and when it is time to disengage from an intrusive or exploitative innovation.

An issue which must always be considered when adopting technology is the dependence on this technology and the risk that basic skills of living could be lost. It is important to understand the "prudent" use of technology; as Prensky [26] says "Digital wisdom is a twofold concept, referring both to wisdom arising *from* the use of digital technology to access cognitive power beyond our innate capacity and to wisdom *in* the prudent use of technology to enhance our capabilities."

2.6 e-Leadership

The European Union describes e-Leadership as "the capabilities needed to exploit opportunities provided by ICT, notably the Internet; to ensure more efficient and effective performance of different types of organisations; to explore possibilities for new ways of conducting business/administrative and organisational processes; and/or to establish new businesses."[2] It could be argued that the skills required to be an e-leader can be found not only in an Information Society environment but also in all ***areas*** of business and all ***levels*** within an organisation.

[2] http://ec.europa.eu/enterprise/sectors/ict/files/eskills/insead_eleadership_en.pdf, p10

3 Digital Agenda

EU policy suggests that the Information Society can improve the lives of citizens, improve productivity, promote innovation and create a better society [27]. There have been several initiatives designed to promote the use of technology to improve lives, opportunities for citizens and Europe's position as a technology leader. The eEurope "An Information Society for all" initiative endorsed in 2002, aimed to bring every citizen into the digital age, create a digitally literate Europe and ensure that the process was inclusive by 2005 [28].

The Action Plan to deliver eEurope 2005 was launched at the Seville European Council in June 2002 and was endorsed by the Council of Ministers in the eEurope Resolution of January 2003. It addressed public services, e-business and of broadband access. It concluded in 2005 and was followed by i2010 (European Information Society in 2010) with the objective of ensuring "that Europe's citizens, businesses and governments make the best use of ICTs in order to improve industrial competitiveness, support growth and the creation of jobs and to help address key societal challenges" [29]. According to the i2010 High Level Group, the "take up of ICT is expected to impact on the economy and more in general on society" [30].

Replacing the i2010 initiative is the Digital Agenda as part of EU 2020. The Digital Agenda is one of seven initiatives in the EU 2020 growth strategy, which has initiatives grouped into three target areas - "Smart growth", "Sustainable growth" and "Inclusive growth" [31]. These initiatives include actions on education, youth, business/innovation, climate and inclusion. The EU has defined goals for the Digital Agenda and produces a scorecard demonstrating how each country and the EU in total are performing against these goals.

There is concern in the EU that a large part of the population is still unable to take advantage of opportunities offered by knowledge of technology, in particular people from disadvantaged groups such as the elderly or people with disabilities. The EU has declared its intention to ensure that "Every European (is) Digital" by 2015 and has an employment target for 2020 of 75% of the working-age population in employment. The working population is defined as those aged between 20 and 64 years. In order to reach the target an "Agenda for new skills and jòbs" initiative was launched in 2010 [32] and digital literacy and e-skills have been included among the priorities of the initiative. These skills will be included in lifelong learning policies and actions will be taken in the areas of education and teacher training.

The Digital Agenda promises to "promote the take-up and use of the Internet in order to ensure inclusion in the digital society, namely through the extensive use of equipment and digital content and tools in education and learning, by enhancing digital literacy and skills and by improving accessibility for all, especially for persons with disabilities". Actions 57 to 68 of the Digital Agenda aim to increase e-skills and make digital literacy and competences a priority for the European Social Fund. These actions include addressing the competences of ICT users and practitioners, making digital literacy skills a priority and increasing lifelong learning and on-line education.

4 Digital Skill Frameworks

Digital skill frameworks can allow a person to understand the scope of digital skills and how they relate to soft skills. These frameworks are useful to allow a person to understand, and sometimes measure, their digital skills; examples include the European Computer Driving Licence (ECDL) (see www.ecdl.org); for ICT professionals there are the Skills Framework for the Information Age (see www.sfia-online.org) and the European e-Competence Framework (see http://www.ecompetences.eu/) and for organisations there is the IT-CMF Framework (see www.ivi.com). Many training and educational organisations use the frameworks to provide training, testing and certification [33]. In the United Kingdom, the Confederation for British Industry (CBI) has undertaken surveys to identify digital as well as other skills required by employers [34].

4.1 ECDL

ECDL, as a deliverable, was "one of the successful projects" within the European Union in 1997 and was reported as such to the European Commission at the end of the project evaluation. The programme has developed over the years in terms of numbers of users, contribution to skills and even contribution to the economy in some countries. In Greece, the ALBA industry study [35] looked at the cost of digital "illiteracy" with 140 people and found that they spent between 48 and 148 minutes per week trying to sort problems with office software. After ECDL training, the time spent on these problems was halved for word processing and spreadsheets and was reduced by over 90% for presentations and databases.

AICA, the Italian Computer Society, did a study in 2003 with Bocconi University [36] examining the cost of "digital ignorance". The study, using Italian 2003 pay rates, found that the cost of ignorance was over €2,200 per annum per employee. The Irish "Impact Report" [37], examining the people in the office sector in Ireland who had taken the ECDL programme, calculated that ECDL had generated "cumulative productivity saving of €186.9 million and currently generates annual productivity savings of €62.3 million for Irish employers in this sector."

4.2 Other Definitions of Digital Skills

Three other frameworks that consider definitions of digital skills are considered here. The Joint Research Centre, Institute for Prospective Technological Studies (IPTS), produced a report in December 2013 [38] which assessed the frameworks in existence at that time. The research examined the knowledge, skills and attitudes required to be digitally competent and produced descriptors of digital competence.

The Microsoft Digital Literacy curriculum[3] has five parts. These are: Computer Basics; The Internet; Cloud Services and the World Wide Web Productivity

[3] http://www.microsoft.com/about/corporatecitizenship/citizenship/giving/programs/up/digitalliteracy/eng/curriculum4.mspxthe

Programs; Computer Security and Privacy; and Digital Lifestyles. Microsoft also provides certification at a professional level which includes the Microsoft Certified Application Specialist (MCAS) and the Microsoft Office Specialist (MOS).

The Global Digital Literacy Council (GDLC) created an e-skills standard called Certiport IC³ (Certiport Internet and Core Computing Certification). According to the GDLC web site[4], "You don't have to be focusing on a career in computers to benefit from IC³. Today, virtually any career or field of study requires the use of computers."

4.3 ICT Professional Skills

While all people need basic digital literacy skills, the skill needs for ICT practitioners are more comprehensive. Much work has been completed in creating a skills definition for the ICT practitioner. This includes the *European Certification of Informatics Professionals* (EUCIP) created by the Council of European Professional Informatics Societies (CEPIS); the *Skills Framework for the Information Age* (SFIA) created by a consortium in the United Kingdom (UK) which includes the British Computer Society and e-skills UK and the definitions created by Career Space in 1999 [39].

The framework (SFIA) has five areas, defined by the different capabilities required by an IT professional. The higher level skill areas are - Plan, Build, Run, Enable and Manage. There are 36 e-competences within these five skill areas. This framework was created by the European Committee for Standardisation CEN [40] to help a practitioner check his or her skills and identify gaps. CEPIS has recently used this framework to assess the skills of IT practitioners in Europe. According to CEPIS [ibid], "It is a reference framework of ICT competences that can be used and understood by everyone involved".

The original framework was created by CEN and published in 2008. It is now available as version 3.0 and claims "The European e-Competence Framework is a component of the long term e-skills agenda of the European Union supported by the European Commission and The Council of Ministers" [41]. The framework is available in English, French, German, and Italian and claims to comprise an agreed set of competences for ICT practitioners and managers and it "provides a European basis for internationally efficient personnel planning and development".

5 Summary

There is a need for digital skills in all areas of employment. Computer awareness is necessary for all employees and technical skills are a requirement for those involved in developing and maintaining systems. E-leadership is a relatively new term, but is vital for competitiveness for companies operating in today's global business environment.

---

[4] http://www.certiport.com/portal/desktopdefault.aspx?page=common/pagelibrary/About_partners_GDLC.htm

Much work has been done to develop frameworks to define the competencies needed. The following skills appear in some form in the frameworks examined:

Technical skills
: Technical skills range from being comfortable with technology to reaching the level of an IT practitioner. They all appear in some form on the skills' frameworks.

Information handling
: Information handling is an important part of digital literacy. The frameworks identify basic skills, from being able to locate and evaluate information to being able to create and synthesise information.

Communication
: The basic use of communication technologies is sending email and texts. Using social networking tools, collaborating and networking are also needed as part of a digital literacy definition.

Work-related skills
: The skills required will depend on the industry in which the person works and the level of seniority of the person in the organisation. For teachers, skills in IT are becoming vital, as a tool in teaching and as a subject to teach.

Personal attributes
: A person needs to demonstrate a large variety of "complex cognitive, motor, sociological, and emotional skills". Chief amongst these, perhaps, is the ability to anticipate and exploit rapid change to fulfil personal potential and for societal benefit.

Personal attitudes
: A person's attitude to technology will affect how he/she will use it. Most frameworks identify the need for acceptance of technology, the awareness of ethical and security issues and the ability to be critical, creative and innovative with technology.

According to the Organisation for Economic and Co-operative Development (OECD) [42] there is a worldwide demand for competent and skilled ICT practitioners and a demand for digitally literate people in all organisations and walks of life. "At the same time … [as the need for practitioners], the portfolio of basic skills needed to navigate ICT-rich environments and function effectively in our connected societies has expanded." With the rapid development of advanced automation and the increasing computerisation of non-routine tasks, including what is regarded as 'knowledge work', these skills will continue to evolve and will require on-going re-evaluation.

References

1. European Commission: Survey of Schools – ICT in Education: Benchmarking Access, Use and Attitudes to Technology in Europe's Schools (2013), https://ec.europa.eu/digital-agenda/sites/digital-agenda/files/KK-31-13-401-EN-N.pdf (retrieved September 20, 2014)
2. European Commission, A.: Digital Agenda for Europe (2010), http://ec.europa.eu/information_society/digital-agenda/index_en.htm (retrieved September 20, 2014)
3. CEDEFOP: Research Paper No 21, Skill mismatch: The role of the enterprise. Luxembourg. Publications Office of the European Union (2012)
4. Eurostat: Unemployment statistics (2012), http://epp.eurostat.ec.europa.eu/statistics_explained/index.php/Unemployment_statistics (retrieved September 20, 2014)
5. Fastrack to IT: Skills Audit (2013), http://www.fit.ie/index.php?page=ict-skills-audit (retrieved September 20, 2014)
6. Leahy, D., Dolan, D.: E-skills for e-leadership. Paper presented at IT-Star, Bari, Italy (2013)
7. Accenture Technology Vision 2013: Every Business Is a Digital Business (2013), http://www.accenture.com/SiteCollectionDocuments/PDF/Accenture-Technology-Vision-2013-Executive-Summary.pdf (retrieved September 20, 2014)
8. Innosight: Creative Destruction whips through Corporate America (2013), http://www.innosight.com/innovation-resources/strategy-innovation/upload/creative-destruction-whips-through-corporate-america_final2012.pdf (retrieved September 20, 2014)
9. Talja, S.: The social and discursive construction of computing skills. Journal of the American Society for Information Science and Technology 561, 13–22 (2005)
10. Eshet, Y.: Digital literacy: A new terminology framework and its application to the design of meaningful technology-bases learning environments. In: Proceedings of ED-MEDIA 2002, World Conference on Education and Multimedia, pp. 498–498 (2002)
11. Wu, L., Hoi, S., Jin, R., Zhu, J.: Distance metric learning from uncertain side information with application to automated photo tagging. In: Proceedings of the 17th ACM International Conference on Multimedia. ACM (2009)
12. Hayes, B.: Cloud Computing. Communications of the ACM 51, 7 (2008)
13. Carr, N.G.: The big switch. Rewiring the world, from Edison to Google. W. W. Norton, New York (2008)
14. Moran, T.P., Zhai, S.: Beyond the Desktop Metaphor in Seven Dimensions. MIT Press, Cambridge (2007)
15. Awouters, V., Jans, S., Ruben, J.: E-learning Competencies for Teachers in Secondary and Higher Education. International Journal of Emerging Technologies in Learning IJET 4, 2 (2009)
16. John, P., Wheeler, S.: The Digital Classroom, harnessing technology for the Future. Routledge, London (2008)
17. Bawden, D.: Information and digital literacies: a review of concepts. Journal of Documentation 572, 218–259 (2001)

18. Digital Agenda: Communication From The Commission To The European Parliament, The Council, The European Economic And Social Committee And The Committee Of The Regions: A Digital Agenda for Europe (2010), http://eurlex.europa.eu/LexUriServ/LexUriServ.do?uri=CELEX:52010DC0245R%2801%29:EN:NOT (retrieved September 20, 2014)
19. Perez, J., Murray, M.: Computing for the masses: extending the computer science curriculum with information technology literacy. Consortium for Computing Sciences in Colleges 24, 220–226 (2008)
20. Elearning Europa: Approaches to Media Literacy and e-Learning (2002), http://www.elearningeuropa.info/directory/index.php?page=doc&doc_id=998&doclng=6 (retrieved September 20, 2014)
21. CEDEFOP: Joint progress report on the implementation of the Education and Training 2010 work programme: Delivering lifelong learning for knowledge, creativity and innovation (2008), http://www.cedefop.europa.eu/EN/news/7091.aspx (retrieved September 20, 2014)
22. Kilpatrick, T.: The Project Method. Teachers College Record, pp. 319–334 (1918), http://historymatters.gmu.edu/d/4954 (retrieved September 20, 2014)
23. Davis, F.D.: Perceived Usefulness, Perceived Ease Of Use, And User Acceptance of Information Technology. MIS Quarterly 13, 3 (1989)
24. King, W.R., He, J.: A meta-analysis of the technology acceptance model. Information & Management 43(6), 740–755 (2006)
25. Rogers, E.: Diffusion of Innovations. The Free Press of Glencoe, New York (1962)
26. Prensky, M.: From Digital Immigrants and Digital Natives to Digital Wisdom (2009), http://eric.ed.gov/?id=EJ834284 (retrieved September 20, 2014)
27. ETSI: Human Factors HF; Multimodal interaction, communication, and navigation guidelines. European Telecommunications Standards Institute, ETSI Guide 202 191 v1.1.1 2003-08 (2003)
28. An, E.U.: information society for all (2002), http://ec.europa.eu/information_society/eeurope/2005/index_en.htm (retrieved September 20, 2014)
29. EU i2010: A European Information Society for growth and employment (2005), http://ec.europa.eu/information_society/eeurope/i2010/index_en.htm (retrieved September 20, 2014)
30. EU i2010: High Level Group, Benchmarking Digital Europe 2011-2015 (2009), http://ec.europa.eu/information_society/eeurope/i2010/docs/benchmarking/benchmarking_digital_europe_2011-2015.pdf (retrieved September 20, 2014)
31. EU2020: Flagship initiatives for EU 2020 (2011), http://ec.europa.eu/europe2020/tools/flagship-initiatives/index_en.htm (retrieved September 20, 2014)
32. EU: Agenda for new skills and jobs (2010), http://ec.europa.eu/social/main.jsp?langId=en&catId=958 (retrieved September 20, 2014)
33. Ferrari, A.: Digital Competence in Practice: An Analysis of Frameworks. Seville, Spain, Institute for Prospective Technological Studies. European Commission (2012), http://ftp.jrc.es/EURdoc/JRC68116.pdf (retrieved September 20, 2014)
34. Confederation for British Industry: Building for growth: business priorities for education and skills – Education and skills survey (2011), http://www.cbi.org.uk/media/1051530/cbi__edi_education___skills_survey_2011.pdf (retrieved September 20, 2014)

35. ALBA: IT skills, the business gain (2010), http://www.ecdl.org/media/Alba%20Study%20Summary_Final.pdf (retrieved September 20, 2014)
36. AICA: The Cost of Ignorance (2003), http://www.ecdl.org/files/2009/for-employers/docs/20090311041919_Cost%20of%20Ignorance.pdf (retrieved September 20, 2014)
37. O'Donnell, S.: The ECDL in Ireland: Impact Study. Itech Research, Dublin, Ireland (2003)
38. IPTS: DIGCOMP: A Framework for Developing and Understanding Digital Competence in Europe (2013), http://ipts.jrc.ec.europa.eu/publications/pub.cfm?id=6359 (retrieved September 20, 2014)
39. SFIA Foundation: The SFIA Foundation, http://www.sfia-online.org/about-us/sfia-foundation/ (n.d.) (retrieved September 20, 2014)
40. CEPIS: Professional e-Competence in Europe, Identifying the e-Competences of European IT Professionals (2011), http://portal.ecdl.org/media/eComp_Brochure_Final1.pdf (retrieved September 20, 2014)
41. EU: A common European framework for ICT Professionals in all industry sectors (2009), http://www.ecompetences.eu/ (retrieved September 20, 2014)
42. OECD: Skills for the Digital Economy (2013), http://skills.oecd.org/developskills/documents/skillsforthedigitaleconomy.html (retrieved September 20, 2014)

Using "Yams" for Enterprise Knowledge Sharing among Knowledge Workers from the Perspective of a Task Categorisation-Knowledge Sharing Systems Fit

Tong-Ming Lim and Angela Siew-Hoong Lee

Sunway University, 5 Jalan Universiti,
Bandar Sunway, Selangor, Malaysia
tongmingl@sunway.edu.my

Abstract. Emerging digital technologies play a key role in the development of enterprises. Their uses demand a transition on the part of knowledge workers, however. Web 2.0 is an emerging communication technology that supports collaborative knowledge sharing in corporate learning paradigms, changing tailor-made, expensive and high learning curve digital systems to simple but well-accepted ones [1, 2]. These platforms revolutionise how participants share, communicate and create knowledge in a corporate setting [3]. The use of Web 2.0 to support Knowledge Sharing (KS) has been extensively investigated [4, 5]. Studies that use a task-technology fit model on systems such as decision support [6] and eLearning [7] demonstrate that a good fit between tasks and digital technologies is able to improve performance of knowledge workers. This research reports the outcomes on the fit between task categorization and knowledge sharing systems. The task categories and Web 2.0 functions used in knowledge sharing practices were consistent. The outcomes highlighted that intuitive design, ease of use and a low learning curve were able to elicit both tacit and explicit organizational knowledge. Text analysis demonstrated that new knowledge was created, exchanged and shared. The study concluded that knowledge sharing activity and the fit between Web 2.0 functions and task categories were consistent and significant.

Keywords: Knowledge sharing, task categorization, knowledge sharing systems, text mining, Web 2.0.

1 Introduction

The use of social computing systems for knowledge creation and sharing has shown a sharp increase according to Alexa (alexa.com) in the last two decades. Many social computing platforms such as Facebook and Xanga have been used extensively for both personal and commercial reasons to publish leisure, lifestyle, technical and engineering related journals. Recent studies also show that Weblogs have been adopted for teaching and learning, knowledge creation and sharing, customer satisfaction and retention exercises by many companies worldwide. One of the most recent developments is the adoption of weblogs as the most preferred knowledge

D. Passey and A. Tatnall (Eds.): KCICTP/ITEM 2014, IFIP AICT 444, pp. 190–204, 2014.

management system due to its ease-of-use and social phenomenon [3]. In the last five years, researchers have started to shift their focus from people-centred or motivational-centred research to technological features-centre research work in their quest for a more manageable and measurable knowledge creation and sharing goal.

The discovery of hidden knowledge in social media systems such as Facebook and Twitter has become an important source of knowledge for companies and non-profit organizations. Research conducted in the last few years has shown that design of new products and launching of marketing campaigns were crafted and based on feedback and comments mined from unstructured data posted by customers. Understanding customers' needs and critiques before investing into commercial activities saves a large amount of money and the outcomes harvested from the investment are more encouraging. However, mining text information is not an easy task. Text data is ill-structured and hence proper tools are required. In addition, the amount of data produced by Web 2.0 systems are usually dynamic and this makes text mining a challenging task indeed. In this research, an enterprise microblogging system, Yammer, is chosen and implemented for a shared services company. An enterprise microblogging system runs behind the firewall. Compared to Twitter, which is a public microblogging system exposing the 'twitts' to their followers openly, an enterprise microblogging system requires that the participant belongs to a specific company domain. This research identified the usage pattern and communication topics from the posts by employees of a case study company.

The participating company in this research uses Yammer to contribute and share knowledge; topics of discussion among participants were mined and the tasks category–knowledge sharing system fit was studied. Based on the microblog entries, topics of discussion and communication behaviour were investigated too. The concept map that links between topics allows the researchers to draw a more accurate and interesting picture of knowledge contributed and shared among participants. Based on the analysis, the text mining tool also shows the fit between features of an enterprise microblogging system to different categories of task carried out by the participants when they communicate and share knowledge.

Even though most of these companies realize the need to be strategically competitive in a globalized commercial environment, tacit knowledge is one of the important assets to retain. However, many companies have even understood and adopted the process of conversion between tacit and explicit knowledge [8]. In view of the need to properly understand the challenges faced by these companies and the adoption of Web 2.0 platforms such as Weblogs, this research intends to investigate the features and functions of Web 2.0 used to carry out participants' tasks, while their posts provide evidence of enterprise knowledge sharing activity. These outcomes allow a better understanding of the fit between different categories of task and Web 2.0 functions toward the exchange activity of knowledge among participants. Alejandro *et al.* [9] pointed out that technologies are facilitators within collaborative learning spaces for learners. In addition, Kaiser *et al.* [4] also highlighted those technological features of weblogs such as blogrolls, permalinks and trackbacks which essentially are the keys promoters for successful knowledge creation and sharing by quoting the Open Source Software (OSS) case in his study. The research objectives of this project are: to explore whether collaboration and communication promote strong engagement; whether knowledge can be mined from posts; and whether Web 2.0 functions and task categories fit facilitates better than knowledge activities.

2 Web Technologies

Social computing systems such as Facebook and Twitter are new technology enablers for many young and technical savvy users. Since Coakes *et al.* [10] and Bausch *et al.* [11] coined the term 'web' and 'log' or 'weblog' in December 1997, weblog technology has evolved from a first generation which features first-person dairies. Second generation weblog technology features weblog community features such as "permalinks" with improved word processing features. Third generation weblogs would consists of Bulletin, commentary, individual profiles, Eprops, Permalink, Skins, Syndication, Blogring, Chatterbox and Archival elements. Comparisons between all these weblogs are shown in Table 1.

Table 1. Weblogs and their features

Types of Weblog	Features and Usage
Bulletin	Disseminating messages
Commentary	Allowing members to add comment on weblogs
Individual Profiles	Allowing community members to read what the author has blogged about
Eprops	Is a way of letting the author know you like his/her post. Some websites offer unlimited Eprops
Permalink	Individual permanent URL to their weblog post
Skins	Readymade templates for users to change blog outlook
Syndications	Notification features where it prompts the readers about their favorites weblogs being updated
Metro/ Community/Blogring	A group of webloggers from the same geographical region or shared or similar interests
Chatterbox	Allowing real time interaction between webloggers and visitors
Private Blogs	Blogs which are only accessible to certain people

3 Related Works

Related works on knowledge sharing, text mining, knowledge sharing on Web 2.0 sites and task-technology fit are reviewed and discussed.

3.1 Text Mining

Zhong *et al.* [12] found that modern computational technology approaches such as the Natural Language Processing (NLP) technique are used to mine the meaning behind text documents so that they are easily understandable. This approach allows the text mining engine to discover relationships and patterns that exist in text files. Microsoft is one of the companies that use text mining to conduct their analysis for their online reporting application, NetScan. According to Mailvaganam [13], the NetScan software uses a combination of reporting, Online Analytical Processing (OLAP) and Data Mining applications to analyze the posts from Usenet. Microsoft uses NetScan to analyze their Usenet posts, frequencies, e-mail addresses of posters, trend analysis, values of the messages posted and eventual creation of a better search engine for the company. NetScan analyzes the posts to obtain meaningful information. In order for NetScan to perform this, it uses text mining features to achieve its objective. This feature allows NetScan to classify and cluster the Usenet posts and generate a predictive model using a decision tree technique to evaluate the posts that are useful. Hence, it is apparent that text mining can be used to determine the usefulness of the content of a system with proper analysis.

3.2 Knowledge Sharing

A range of studies have been carried out by researchers by considering people factors [14, 15, and 16] in the quest for more effective and successful knowledge creation and sharing in an organizational environment. However, recent research [8, 17, 18, 19, 20, 21, and 3] also find that social computing systems such as weblog have been very successful in improving knowledge creation and sharing among bloggers.

3.3 Task-Technology Fit

IP, Fun and Wagner [18] looked at social networking systems as a medium for young people and organizations, interviewing 33 young bloggers using a fit model to evaluate their needs and the technology features offered by weblogs. There is clear evidence which shows that social computing is shifting away from traditional technologies such as email. The latest social computing development such as Web 2.0 has shown progressive impact on organizational computing. Commercial organizations intend to take advantage of the webloggers' social computing skill to address their customers' as well as organizational information processing and knowledge management needs. The author suggested grouping the users into four categories based on their usage intensity. The author found that different groups of users would use a different set of weblog's features. The author used Task-Technology and Needs-Technology Fit models to explain the relationship between different groups of users and their needs using these two models. With this, the author attempted to relate to the organizational needs of users for knowledge creation and sharing. Other Task-Technology Fit studies reviewed include Zigurs *et al.* [16], Maruping *et al.* [22] and Goodhue *et al.* [23].

3.4 Knowledge Sharing on Web 2.0 Sites

Yang and Chen [3] found four contingency factors based on two cases: Microsoft Longhorn Blogosphere (Case A) and the European Research Institute (Case B), using weblogs as the social networking tool to study knowledge creation and sharing activities for organizations as a novel social and organizational phenomenon. The authors also strongly believed that creation and sharing of knowledge in organizations is more of a social phenomenon rather than an individual and cognitive process. The four contingency factors are: process of implementation (CF1); the rule of membership (CF2); the type of work supported by ICT (CF3); and the distribution of knowledge (CF4). Figure 1 shows that considering intrinsic and extrinsic motivational stimuli with the two cases studied, information obtained can be used to explain the four contingency factors. The results in Figure 1 concluded that successful weblog implementation can be achieved in a corporate setting for the purpose of knowledge creation and sharing through a set of stimuli strategies with the application of the contingency factors in a technology-mediated environment.

Alejandro *et al.* [9] compared several information technological tools that offered the most efficient way of knowledge construction in the education world. Construction of knowledge through social interaction helps students to create and manage the new knowledge that is being delivered to them. His comparisons on several commonly used ICT tools in education covered: clickers, collaborative editing, Facebook, Google Jockeying, Instant Messaging ,Social Bookmarking, Videobloging, Virtual Meeting, Virtual Worlds and Wikis. He concluded and recommended that Virtual Meeting, virtual worlds and wikis were still the few best tools to be used in education.

Du and Wagner [8] also strongly agreed that learning with weblogs is able to enhance and create active learning among students. Students are able to perform better by uploading their coursework in public to be criticized by other students; hence this has improved student performance. Du and Wagner's [8] research also found that active learning is able to form knowledge sharing and collaboration group work among students. Their investigation on the effectiveness of weblog and its impact on the performance of different learner levels has concluded that a web based learning log can be a predictor of learning performance and this enhances a traditional learning log.

Other works reviewed also demonstrated that weblogs are a collaborative distributed tool which promotes constructivism learning among bloggers. Ras *et al.* [20] showed that using weblogs promotes knowledge sharing and learning in information spaces where journals are maintained through weblogs as an input for both an experience base and information element base learning from experiences. Hsu *et al.* [17] interviewed 212 bloggers in their work and based on the theory of reasoned action, the authors found that the model proposed by them had evidently shown factors such as ease of use, enjoyment, knowledge sharing (altruism and reputation) that were positively related to attitude toward blogging. Social factors and attitude toward blogging also significantly influenced a blogger's willingness to continue to blog.

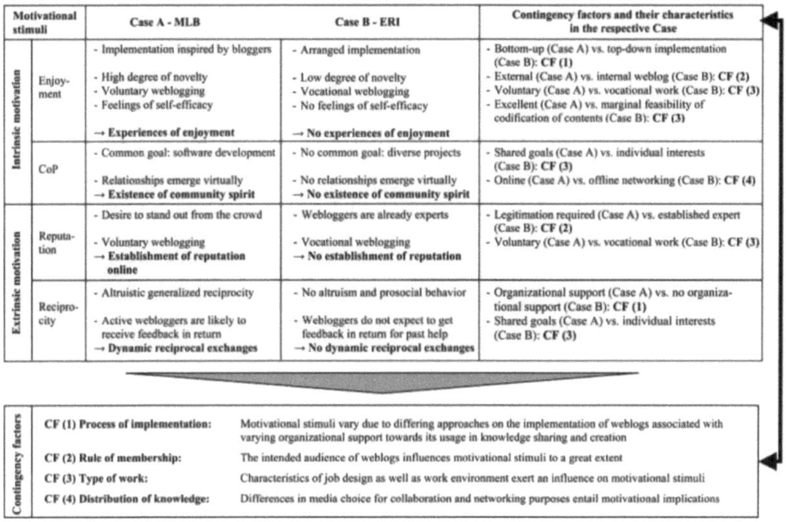

Fig. 1. Intrinsic and extrinsic motivational stimuli with the two cases

4 Research Methodology

The research reported here was conducted using two approaches: microblog entries were collected from a chosen group of employees who were involved in a project for a 30-day period in the case company; and text analysis was used to analyse the microblogs. This was followed by an interview session conducted with the participants of a chosen project on their tasks and Web 2.0 system's functions that they used as they exchanged and shared knowledge with their peers to carry out their project activities.

First of all, an active project that consists of members from all the departments that participated in the project was identified. This was followed by a briefing to set the objectives appropriately. Yammer was chosen to be implemented for a period of 30 days by all the members of a project team. Training and features of Yammer were also provided. All the entries and comments posted by participants were extracted into a Microsoft (MS) Excel file. The MS Excel file contained the raw post data. In this research project, the SAS Text Miner system was used to analyse the microblog entries so that unstructured text that consisted of the employees' opinions could be identified and analysed. By analysing these entries, the text mining software was able to identify topics of discussion, importance of these topics, related sub-topics and knowledge generated by participants from their discussions and problem-solving activities. The outcomes of the text mining allowed ease of knowledge retrieval from topics of importance and easy-to-understand topic linked maps visually highlighted knowledge contributed and shared by the employees on Yammer. During the interview session with all the project participants, a list of related questions on task categories and Yammer's functions were asked.

5 Yammer Microblog: Text Mining and Analysis

SAS Enterprise Miner software was used to carry out text analysis. Figure 2 depicts the patterns of the post entries of the employees on the Yammer microblogging system. The visual output of their usage patterns is shown in the form of a bar chart indicating frequency of post by author. Figure 2 also shows the frequency of entries posted by different authors. The chart shows that one of the project members, Phoebe Than, is the most active participant among all the other participants in the microblogging space. She has posted the most entries in this exercise. She had contributed a total of 61 entries. One of the possible explanations is the fact that she is the project manager of the chosen project and she is very supportive of the use of microblogging system as a tool to update status and share knowledge with her other peers. She had taken the initiative to devote herself and her time to willingly share a lot of information pertaining to the chosen project with other members on the chosen social networking platform. Her contribution as a knowledge creator and sharer also ensured that the research project yielded the anticipated outcome.

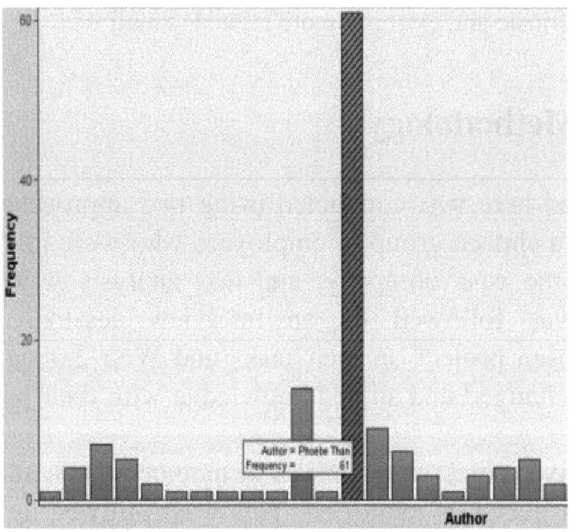

Fig. 2. Author with the highest frequency of postings

In Figure 3, different terms and their frequency from the posts are illustrated. Every box in the diagram is a term measured by its frequency and the weight of the term within every post being made. The box which is highlighted shows the term "+server" has the highest frequency count. In this example, it has a total of 52 counts that appear in the data collected from the entire test period. However, the weight of the term is only 0.56547 which shows that the importance of this term is at an average level. The higher the weight the more importance the term has from the entire corpus of the posts. This shows that the entries posted in the project are mostly related to the issue on "server". A question that one may need to answer in the future work is to study the low weightage value for terms that were identified as terms of slightly above average levels from the participants.

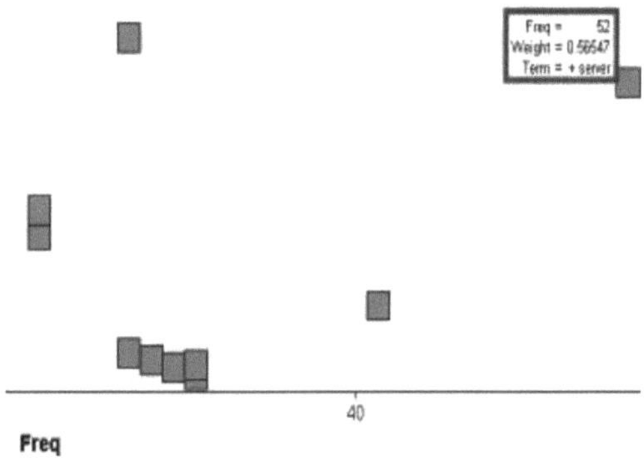

Fig. 3. Terms with the highest frequency

In Figure 4, the term "license" has the highest weight with a value of 0.9. This means that the importance of this term is the highest among all other terms being talked about among members of the project although the frequency of this term is only five in the entries posted by the users. This means that the current project is currently handling "license" or legal issues. It is consistent with the findings of the interview content conducted at the end of our research work.

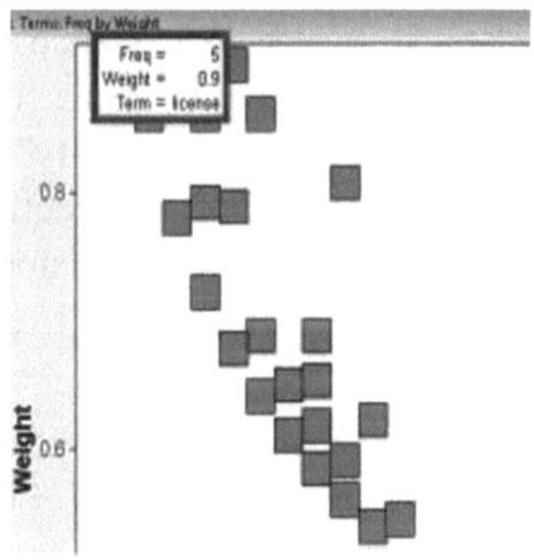

Fig. 4. Terms with the highest weight

In Figure 5, a concept map is used to show the topics which are related to the term "ITSSC". Related topics of discussion could be expanded into a second level of the map to understand the sub-topics. For example, in Figure 5, the term "setup" is expanded and it shows that "setup" is relevant to the infrastructure department and it is also related to the setup of "server". Furthermore, the term "Putra" when it is expanded, shows that it is related to "Sunway", "Project" and "Hotel". This explains that several topics of discussion among participants are all related to the Putra Place project. Furthermore the lines that connect between any two terms were presented using different thickness. The lines connecting the "Putra" and "Hotel" is the thickest which means that the frequency of discussion communicated by project team

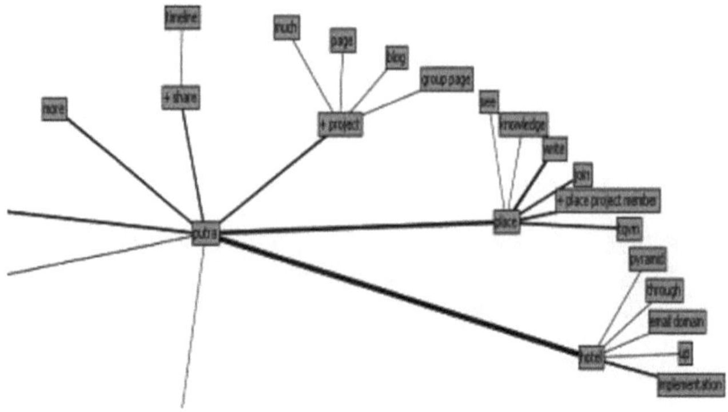

Fig. 5. Concept Map on the Term "ITSSC" and Related Sub Topics

members on these two terms is the highest. Another observation indicated the term "Hotel" was closely related to "Pyramid", "email domain" and "implementation". These connections are consistent because our interview data towards the end of the testing period showed that the text analysis matched the interview findings.

Figure 6 illustrates another significant term, "legal privileges", and its relevant concepts. Since the project is now discussing the legal issues with its clients, conversation between the members are also mostly focused on legal precaution that is of high concern among members in the project. Hence, it can be seen in the concept map that the patterns of this topic and other topics that are well related to legal matters such as "unauthorized", "+prohibit", "liability", "virus damage" and "legal" terms. Furthermore, the thickness of the lines connecting these terms is almost the same, which shows that the frequency of these terms appearing together is almost the same. In addition, as the term "legal" was expanded to the second level, it visually expands to other related terms such as "consent", "companies", "disclosure" and "responsible". The concept maps reveal the conversation patterns on the subject "legal privileges" through topics and sub-topics among the members of the project.

The concept map in Figure 7 shows that "Putra" is another key topic discussed by the team members. The concept map shows that the term "Putra" is closely related to the term "hotel" where the line thickness explains their relationship. And based on the text analysis, the second more relevant term is "place". This shows that most of the related entries are about the network and the knowledge of the network from the terms "join" and "knowledge", as they are clearly highlighted in Figure 7. Another example would be the term "team". As shown in the concept map, the term "team" relates to terms such as "sales", "marketing", "finance", and "purchasing". Based on text posted, it was found that there are few new groups that were just created by the users in this exercise. This clearly shows that the users actually make use of Yammer to create new groups for their own departments for ideas, status and topics of discussion.

Fig. 6. Concept map on the term "Legal Privileges"

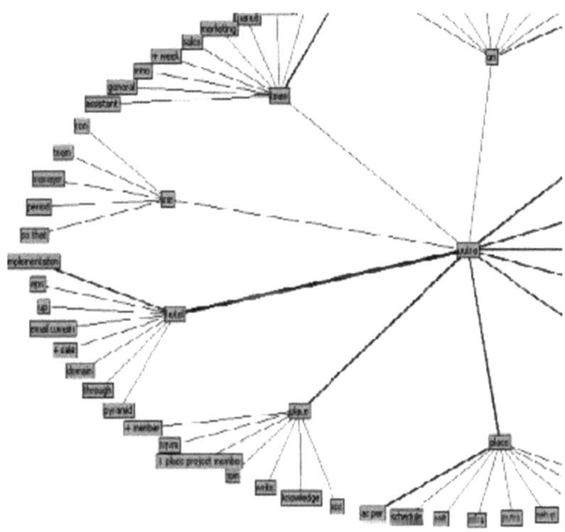

Fig. 7. Concept map on the term "Putra"

5.1 Information Retrieval through Text Filtering

Information retrieval using text filtering was carried out in order to allow extraction of information on specific terms used by the participants. This is very useful in identifying specific information from a large amount of data such as data on social media systems. Based on the updated activity diagram, new findings for the information retrieval perspective are described in Figure 8.

By using the Text Filter (Figure 8), information can be easily retrieved. Therefore, through the Interactive Filter Viewer, the communication topics related to the author can be discovered. As shown in Figure 8, when terms such as "implementation" and "server" are entered as the retrieving criteria, the document on the screen shows all the text entries which contain terms with author detail presented visually. Furthermore, the software also shows the 'Relevance' column which indicates how relevant the term is to the entries. Based on the output in Figure 8, it shows that one of the respondents, Benny Leong, has the highest number of occurrences of these terms in his entries in Yammer. Therefore, it is believed that in the project, Benny Leong is working very closely with server implementation.

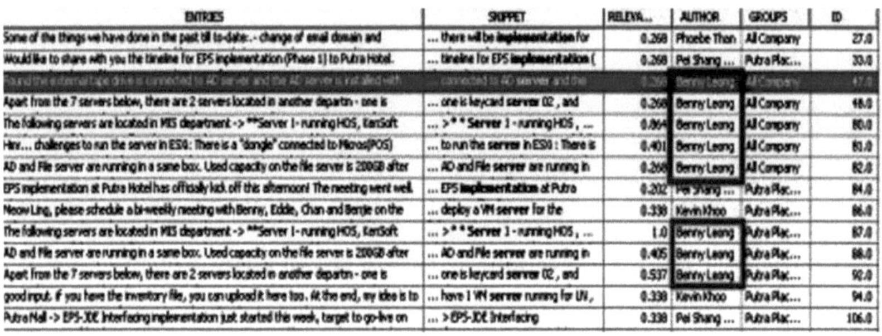

Fig. 8. Retrieving an author based on terms

6 Task Categorizations and Fit Analysis

IP, Fun and Wagner [18] and Du and Wagner [8] pointed out that a clear set of social networking functions help to improve knowledge creation and sharing in a technology-mediated environment. Based on the data collected from our interviews, we found that different categories of tasks required a different set of functions for carrying out day-to-day tasks which involved plenty of knowledge creation and sharing activities. Analysis of the interview content also identified a set of task categories that are carried out by the project members of the team. The set of activities identified in each task is shown in Table 2. Table 2 is a set of non-exhaustive task categorizations identified from the interviews conducted with the members of the project.

Table 2. Tasks-task categories

Tasks or activities of tasks	Task categorization
Software design	Creative
Software documentation	Detail
Debugging	Creative
Programming	Creative
Customer support	Mechanical
Documentation	Mechanical
Schedule project	Creative
Administer project	Routine
Administer people resources	Routines

Based on the ‘Task Categories’ in Table 3, a common set of non-exhaustive functions used by each task category is also identified.

Table 3. Task category characteristics-technology features

Technology functions	Task categorization			
	Creative	Detail	Mechanical	Routine
Content management tools	X			X
Community building tools	X	X	X	X
Time structuring	X	X	X	
Search by category	X	X	X	X
Commentary	X	X	X	X

The fit between different task categories and functions is tabulated in Table 3. From Tables 2 and 3, it can be concluded that the type of knowledge contributed and shared by participants to carry out different categories of tasks needs different functions. There may be some common functions that all may use, such as “Search by category” and “Commentary”. However, “Content management tools” and “Time structuring” are used only by some tasks.

7 Analysis of the Fit of Task Categories and Web 2.0 as the Knowledge Sharing System

The interview content and documentation obtained from the project team provide more accurate relationships between categories of tasks and technological functions that one uses in daily activities. These activities range from ‘change of font for a field or a label on a data entry screen’ to a complex task like ‘rewrite a commission calculation routine’. It is virtually impossible to compile all the activities and the most effective approach would be to group these tasks into ‘task categories’. By relating each ‘task category’ to each group of technological features, a high level relationship will be revealed. Based on these relationships, knowledge activities using a social networking system could further be investigated. The study of the fit of task categories and Web 2.0 functions for knowledge sharing can be deepened as more companies of different trades participate.

8 Analysis on Yammer Microblog Content

Outcomes of text analysis provided a number of useful insights on the microblogs posted by the project members. Concept maps were used to illustrate the most and least communicated topics among employees. Evidence of knowledge exchange activity is shown through employee collaboration. Knowledge contributions from authors are also analysed and identified; this highlights staff engagement on the Yammer social networking platform. As the project is almost at its completion stage, the discussion was found to have focused on legal issues. Therefore, the term "license" and "+server" were found to yield the highest weight and frequency respectively. The text analysis findings matched the outcomes of the interview content; that is, the licensing issue of the project. This has evidently shown that objectives in this project have been accomplished. First of all, engagement from collaboration and communication is strong. Secondly, knowledge mined from posts is generated. Lastly, use of Web 2.0 functions to facilitate knowledge activities for employees of different task categories is shown. In short, the findings have shown that the project members do make use of Yammer to share knowledge on the progress of their project. Although the testing period was short and the data maybe insufficient, the findings show that information posted are mostly project related. Evidence also highlight that microblogging is useful for knowledge sharing within a company and if it is given more time than in this exercise and more participants actively involved in using the system, then findings can be more generalized.

9 Microblogging for Enterprise Education

The use of a microblog system for higher education institutions has been very successful. Nauman and Suku [24] investigated the adoption of Twitter in an Australian higher education institution using Davis's [25] Technology Acceptance Model (TAM) to predict Twitter usage. Their findings suggested that information sharing using Web 2.0 is encouraged but it is more about enjoyment and social presence and not merely about how useful or easy-to-use a technology is. However, exploring enterprise education using microblogs is still fairly limited in terms of research reviewed. For example, Chelmis and Prasanna [26] suggested that learning in an enterprise setting shows that users with strong local topical alignment tend to participate in focused interactions, whereas users with disperse interests contribute to multiple discussions, broadening the diversity of participants. Riemer and Richter [27] explored communication patterns in a team that adopted Enterprise Microblogging. Their findings show that contextual differences and an open communication platform impact on user appropriation. They suggest that decision makers need to vest trust in their employees to use microblogs for productivity in corporate environments for learning purposes. Studies show that there are some moderately successful cases in enterprise education using microblog systems for knowledge sharing; but some still highlight barriers in their implementation besides needs to consider elements such as religion, culture and education systems. Using microblog systems for enterprise education through knowledge sharing has had some small successes but it is still an area that needs more research study.

10 Conclusion

Findings suggest that microblog activities exhibit acceptable levels of engagement and communication patterns among Yammer users. Text analysis highlighted terms with the highest frequency and weight which inform important issues that are most communicated among participants in the project. It is also shown that knowledge is exchanged between knowledge workers on these topics. Findings showed that participants use microblogs to share expertise; hence, the Web 2.0 tool is a useful tool to collaborate, communicate and share knowledge at the organizational level. The fit between different Web 2.0 functions and different categories of tasks has facilitated effective sharing and exchanging of knowledge. In future studies, findings can be generalized when organizations of different trades and different cultural and educational backgrounds from different countries can be studied.

References

1. Smith, G.: Social Networking and the Transfer of Knowledge. The Electronic Journal of Knowledge Management 7(1), 165–178 (2009)
2. Yamamoto, S., Kanbe, M.: Knowledge Creation by Enterprise SNS. The International Journal of Knowledge, Culture And Change Management 8(1), 1–14 (2008)
3. Yang, S.J.H., Chen, I.Y.L.: A social network-based system for supporting interactive collaboration in knowledge sharing over peer-to-peer network. International Journal of Human-Computer Studies 66, 36–50 (2008)
4. Kaiser, S., Müller-Seitz, G., Lopes, M.P., Cunha, M.P.: Weblog-Technology as a Trigger to Elicit Passion for Knowledge. Organization 14(3), 391–412 (2007)
5. Kim, H.N.: The phenomenon of blogs and theoretical model of blog use in educational contexts. Computers & Education 51, 1342–1352 (2008)
6. Gu, L., Wang, J.: A Study of Exploring the "Big Five" and Task Technology Fit in Web-based Decision Support Systems. Issues in Information Systems, X(2), 210–217 (2009)
7. Klopping, I.M., McKinney, E.: Extending the Technology Acceptance Model and The Task-Technology Fit Model To Consumer E-Commerce. Information Technology, Learning, and Performance Journal 22(1), 35–48 (2004)
8. Du, H.S., Wagner, C.: Learning with Weblogs: An Empirical Investigation. In: Proceedings of the 38th Annual Hawaii International Conference on System Sciences (2005)
9. Alejandro, C.S., Urena, J.D.F., Sanchez, R.C., Gutierrez, J.A.C.: Knowledge Construction Through ICT's: Social Networks. In: World Conference on Educational Multimedia, Hypermedia & Telecommunication, vol. 1-9, pp. 2330–2337 (2008)
10. Coakes, E.: Storing and sharing knowledge, supporting the management of knowledge made explicit in transnational organizations. The Learning Organization 13(6), 579–593 (2006)
11. Bausch, P., Haughey, M., Hourihan, M.: We Blog: Publishing Online with Weblogs. Wiley Publishing, Indianapolis (2002)
12. Zhong, N., Li, Y., Wu, S.-T.: Effective Pattern Discovery for Text Mining. IEEE Transactions on Knowledge and Data Engineering 24(1), 30–44 (2012)
13. Mailvaganam, H.: Evolution of Analysis – Microsoft's NetScan and Project Aura (2005), `http://www.dwreview.com/Data_mining/Microsoft_netscan.html` (retrieved June 3, 2011)
14. Marylene, G.: A Model of Knowledge-Sharing Motivation. Human Resource Management 48(4), 571–589 (2009)
15. Palmisano, J.: A Motivational Model of Knowledge Sharing. Handbook on Decision Support Systems 1, 355–370 (2008)
16. Zigurs, I., Buckland, B.K.: A Theory of Task/Technology Fit and Group Support Systems Effectiveness. MIS Quarterly 22(3), 313–329 (1998)

17. Hsu, C.L., Lin, J.C.C.: Acceptance of blog usage: The roles of technology acceptance, social influence and knowledge sharing motivation. Information & Management 45, 65–74 (2008)
18. Fun, I.P., Wagner, R.K., Weblogging, C.: A study of social computing and its impact on organizations. Decision Support Systems 45, 242–250 (2008)
19. Kaiser, S., Kansy, S., Mueller-Seitz, G., Ringlstetter, M.: Weblogs for organizational knowledge sharing and creation: A comparative case study. Knowledge Management Research & Practice, 120–130 (2008)
20. Ras, E., Avram, G., Waterson, P., Weibelzahi, S.: Using Weblogs for Knowledge Sharing and Learning in Information Spaces. Journal of Universal Computer Science 11(3), 394–409 (2005)
21. Yu, T.-K., Lu, L.-C., Liu, T.-F.: Exploring factors that influence knowledge sharing behavior via weblogs. Computers in Human Behavior 26, 32–41 (2010)
22. Maruping, L.M., Agarwal, R.: Managing Team Interpersonal Processes Through Technology: A Task-Technology Fit Perspective. Journal of Applied Psychology 89(6), 975–990 (2004)
23. Goodhue, D.L.: Development and Measurement Validity of a Task-Technology Fit Instrument for User Evaluations of Information System. Decision Sciences 29(1), 105–138 (1998)
24. Nauman, S., Suku, S.: Adoption of Twitter in higher education – a pilot study. In: Proceedings Ascilite 2011, Hobart, TAS, pp. 1115–1120 (2011)
25. Davis, F.: Perceived usefulness, perceived ease of use and user acceptance of information technology. MIS Quarterly 13(3), 319–339 (1989)
26. Chelmis, C., Prasanna, V.K.: An empirical analysis of microblogging behavior in the enterprise. Social Networking Analysis Mining 3(3), 611–633 (2013)
27. Riemer, K., Richter, A.: Tweet Inside: Microblogging in a Corporate Context. In: 23rd Bled eConference eTrust, Implications for the Individual, Enterprises and Society, pp. 1–17 (2010)

An Exploratory Study on the Use of Knowledge Management System and the Employees' Perception on Organisational Knowledge Sharing and Reuse

Angela Siew-Hoong Lee and Tong-Ming Lim

Sunway University, Malaysia
angelal@sunway.edu.my

Abstract. Interest in adopting new digital platforms among Malaysian companies to share, collaborate, crowd source and reuse (both internally and externally) knowledge has recently been on the rise. Challenges persist, however; organisational, people and technological factors are not always easily adapted in well-planned implementation strategies [1, 2, 3]. This research studied the implementation of Practice of Knowledge Management (POKM) that is currently used in an information technology (IT) shared services company. The research findings highlighted that the technological, people and organisational factors affect differently knowledge workers at the junior, middle and senior levels. The findings also highlighted that the POKM quality is stable and organisation of the content is rated well. However, POKM has a poor response time and search capability. Hence, the content is difficult to locate, but most participants agree that knowledge in the POKM is useful for their day-to-day job, accessible anytime and anywhere. The user interface of POKM is not very easy to use, with a weak set of functions and features. And users are not very satisfied with the efficiency and effectiveness of the systems. However, employees are satisfied with the ease of access, download and reuse of knowledge. Most users agree that POKM is a new knowledge acquisition enabler. Innovative ideas and tasks can be accomplished more efficiently. Lastly, users agree that POKM enables knowledge sharing and creation.

Keywords: Knowledge sharing, knowledge reuse, perception, knowledge workers, POKM.

1 Introduction

In an ever-changing economy, the advancement of technology has demanded many companies to constantly evolve themselves to be more competent global players. The number of companies that rely heavily on Internet technology to carry out their day-to-day business operations has increased in leaps and bounds. Advanced web-based systems have become an important part of organisational strategy. It is generally agreed that the key that keeps organisations always ahead of their competitors is to transform themselves into knowledge-centric organisations. Most organisations acknowledge that successful knowledge creation and sharing culture is the key asset

D. Passey and A. Tatnall (Eds.): KCICTP/ITEM 2014, IFIP AICT 444, pp. 205–218, 2014.

of these organisations. The new culture of organisations today is to nurture Community of Practice (CoP) in these organisations to make full utilisation of their knowledge. Therefore, it is important to carry out research in a case study company which has started to use a Knowledge Management System (KMS) to understand factors that cause such efforts to succeed or fail.

In this research, an information technology (IT) shared services company was chosen to participate in this project. The objectives of this project were to investigate information such as difficulties and benefits experienced by employees in the process of implementing and adapting a KMS system. This information will then be used to formulate problem statements for the subsequent phase of the research work. Based on the interviews conducted with employees of the case study company, it was found that the KMS utilisation had been drastically decreased even though tremendous effort had been invested in it. The low KMS usage had not met the objectives of the company. These objectives included increasing knowledge sharing among employees and intensifying organisational communication among employees in the company by riding on the advanced IT automated system currently being implemented. At the stage when research was carried out, each employee was given a set of Key Performance Indicators (KPI): usage of KMS for communication and knowledge sharing. This made usage of KMS a mandatory activity for the employees. This may not have been a good method to encourage usage of KMS as it might result in poor information quality. If the knowledge in the KMS is not very useful, employees will not bother to read or share it. The knowledge-related activities among employees were so poor that the amounts of collaborative communication and knowledge sharing among employees created concerns for the top management.

The objectives of this research comprised the following set of goals:

i. To study the usage of KMS among employees.
ii. To investigate the use of the Knowledge Based Management System (KMS) towards improving job performance through innovative ideas.
iii. To thoroughly understand the KMS benefits, the perception of the system, motivators and barriers among employees.

Currently, the KMS system in the company does not see much knowledge sharing among employees. This project tried to understand factors that motivate employees to accept the KMS as the IT automated tool to improve their productivity rather than a system for use as an information repository only. Therefore, this research used both qualitative and quantitative approaches to collect data to provide a more comprehensive understanding of the KMS implementation in the company.

2 Literature Review

- A KMS manages knowledge and facilitates knowledge sharing among employees in companies. For companies that view knowledge as an important asset, they recognise that if KMS is used effectively, they can be benefited. Shannak [4] described components that constitute a Knowledge Management System (KMS) and highlighted how Knowledge Management System (KMS) performance could be measured.

The research works conducted by Shannak [4] and Davenport *et al.* [5] identified four categories of activities in a knowledge management project. They are: creating knowledge repositories; improving knowledge access and transfer; enhancing a knowledge environment; and managing knowledge assets. Therefore, it is essential that a knowledge management system fulfils these criteria as stated in these four categories.

By creating knowledge repositories, the organisation can capture and store their knowledge, documents and information; hence, easy access occurs. Furthermore, if there is any turnover of employees, the knowledge captured could be useful for the new employees to effectively take on the job [6].

The second category [7] of the activity is to improve knowledge access and transfer. It is about knowledge transfer between employees within a company. This is a complicated process, as different people have different areas of knowledge. To find the perfect substitute to transfer knowledge is tedious. Therefore, in a company, it would be best to have a Community of Practice (CoP) where people with similar interest are grouped together. The ease of accessibility to the required information is very important. If the KMS contains low quality information, it will provide poor quality information to the users, which may not be very useful for their work. Therefore having good categorisation and classification of topics in a KMS is necessary.

Another area that constitutes a Knowledge Management System (KMS) is the knowledge environment. An organisation should enhance its knowledge environment if it wishes to nurture a knowledge creation and sharing environment for all its employees. A suitable environment provides the right ingredients so that employees are more innovative and willing to share their knowledge. To ensure use of KMS in a knowledge-sharing culture is a long term effort, employees must be receptive to culture sharing in a company. Senior employees need to facilitate a useful knowledge management process.

The last category which constitutes a Knowledge Management System (KMS) would be managing knowledge as an asset. Organisations should consider knowledge as an intangible asset which could be transformed into innovative ideas that could improve the company's overall performance. As most companies are moving toward a knowledge-centric organisation, proper knowledge management and use of knowledge is as important as any other organisational agendas. The companies therefore should focus their attentions on the improvement of creation, sharing and utilisation of knowledge. As knowledge management has become an agenda of the highest priority in a company, factors that could intensify the knowledge activity in companies for better profits and productivity are challenging tasks.

3 Methodology

This section presents activities that were designed as part of the research to solicit data as input to understand and answer questions of interest. Firstly, company documents were examined and studied. This was followed by a series of interview sessions. These interviews were conducted to further understand the background information and comments of the interviewees based on a set of questions given to them one week before the actual interview. These interviewees are chosen across all the departments. Each department has at least three (3) candidates, consisting of a junior, mid rank and senior staff member. The interviews were recorded and an interview report was produced. Finally, a questionnaire survey was conducted. The design of the questionnaire was based on the data solicited from the initial document and interview outcomes. The questionnaire was prepared and a pilot test conducted on a group of selected employees. In this paper, the focus is on the outcomes of the questionnaire results after data cleaning, data consolidation, and analysis. The design of the questionnaire was based on several successful instruments as described in studies conducted by Shannak [4], Ong *et al.* [7], Lee *et al.* [8], Ali *et al.* [9], Wu *et al.* [10], Seonwoo *et al.* [11] and Brink [12].

A total of 57 employees of the case company took part in the questionnaire survey. These employees were from five departments (sales and marketing, business solutions, infrastructure service and computer operations, application development and IT process management) and of different levels of seniority in the company. The questionnaires were given out randomly to the employees. The survey was conducted to gain a better understanding of employees' perceptions towards the KMS and their satisfaction level of the system. Due to commercial and confidential reasons, the name of the company and the actual identity of the employees are not revealed.

Prior to the questionnaire survey, a short write-up and briefing on the survey's objectives were given to the employees. The objectives of this survey were to better understand the existing KMS and to find out possible improvements of the current KMS system from various aspects such as functionality and social network capabilities from systems such as Yammer or Facebook. In this exercise, employees were required to fill in general information such as job type and position level. No names were required as the survey was done anonymously so that confidentiality was kept.

The questionnaire was divided into four parts and consisted of a total of 102 questions. The first part consisted of four questions and they were simple dichotomy questions. These questions asked about employees' perceptions of the existing KMS as well as their main usage of the system. Questions asked also included the purpose of using KMS, the type of user that they grouped themselves into and the people they interacted with most through KMS. The next part of the questionnaire survey attempted to ask the employees to rate themselves. Responses for each question were rated from strongly agree (given a value of one) to strongly disagree (given a value of five). This set of questions examined different aspects of the KMS such as the KMS quality, KMS content quality, KMS interface, KMS functions, KMS user satisfaction, perceived KMS benefits, KMS system use, trust, KMS security, organisational issues, extrinsic and intrinsic reward that might affect employees' use of the system. This provided a better understanding of the employees' perception towards the existing KMS system.

In the design of the questionnaire instrument for this research, a set of questions was designed to investigate the future improvements of the KMS. A total of 13 questions were designed to collect responses from the employees. All these questions were used to collect opinions on the features of enhancement of the current KMS system. In this exercise, the evidence of the interview content was validated, to indicate whether employees had a strong desire to adopt social media systems as a replacement to the current system. Lastly, the survey looked at how the employees rated the overall KMS technology in terms of functionalities, flexibility, convenience and reliability. These questions enabled the employees to express their opinions by rating various aspects of KMS as very excellent, excellent, fair, poor or very poor. In short, the design of the questionnaire basically covered all the issues to validate the employees' interview responses.

4 Empirical Analysis

In this section, the findings from the questionnaire survey are thoroughly analysed. The responses from the employees were collected and analysed to understand the employees' perceptions of the KMS, willingness to share knowledge, readiness to adopt an enterprise microblogging system. Based on the questionnaire survey, responses from 37 out of the 57 employees in the company were collected. The response rate was 65%. The process of collecting responses from the participants was quite time consuming due to their busy work schedule.

Figure 1 shows the types of KMS users in the company. From the 37 respondents, 32 of them use the KMS in their work. Five respondents do not utilise the KMS at all. It was clear that some employees' jobs do not require them to use KMS at all. From responses collected, 54% of the respondents are moderate users, 24% are light users and 8% are heavy users. The responses compiled found that employees in the IT shared services company are made up of a large population of 'moderate' knowledge users. The low percentage of 'heavy' knowledge user type has raised the concern of the management, considering this is a knowledge-driven organisation where knowledge is created, used, exchanged and shared on a daily basis. Based on Figure 1, it can be seen that 86% of the employees make use of the KMS to a certain level or extent.

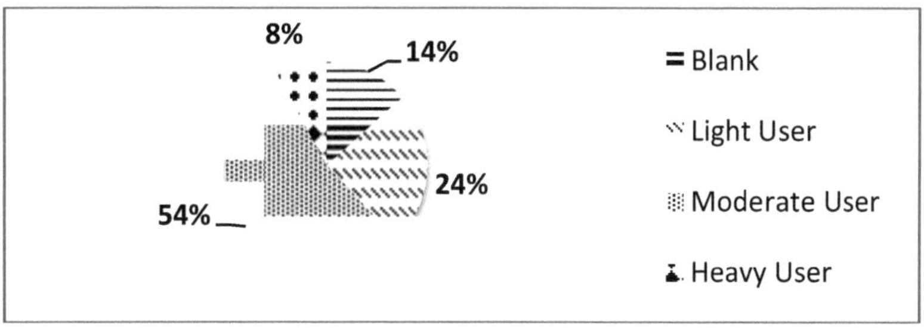

Fig. 1. KMS user types

The KMS quality outcomes shown in Figure 2 indicate another area that provides insight on how employees perceive the system. In terms of KMS quality, a number of questions were asked and analysed. As the chart shows, most of the respondents chose 'Agree' to all the quality related questions. The numbers of positive responses are more than the negative responses. Therefore, it can be deemed that the quality of the KMS is quite good. However, the negative responses from some of the respondents that chose 'disagree' or 'strongly disagree' on the quality of the KMS should not be neglected and these indicate a need for improvement. KMS quality can be a rather serious factor that affects adoption and trust toward the use and confidence in the system. More careful and detailed study may be helpful in this respect.

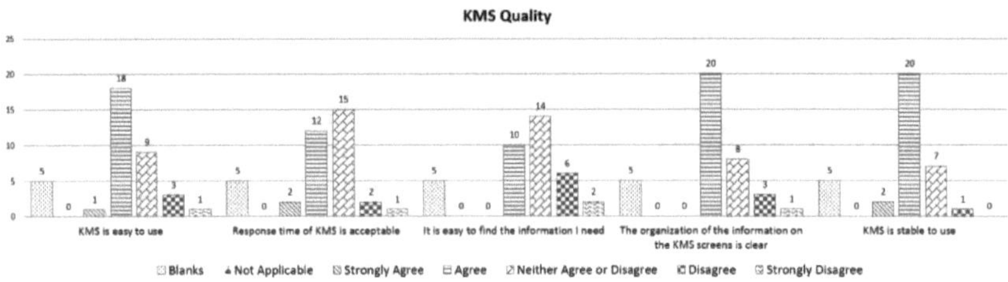

Fig. 2. KMS quality

Another area of interest is the KMS content quality where most of these respondents agree that the KMS content is useful to them. They agree that the KMS is important and helpful to their work; the system is accessible anytime and anyplace as well as the recommended solutions in the KMS being useful. In term of searching capabilities, the KMS is still lacking. In Figure 3, respondents clearly indicate that on average they agree that the KMS is quite easy to use. A total of 11 respondents chose 'agree'. The numbers of respondents who chose 'disagree' and 'strongly disagree' are much higher compared to other responses. Hence, it is believed that the KMS search and retrieve capabilities still need further improvements.

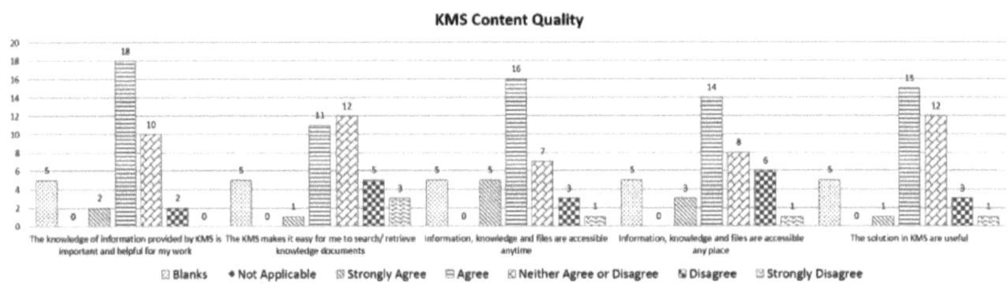

Fig. 3. The KMS content quality

Figure 4 tabulates the responses about the design of the KMS interface. Only a small number of respondents disagree and strongly disagree on the user-friendliness of the system interface. This shows that the system is quite user-friendly. The responses of the question on the functions and capabilities from the respondents are examined and analyzed. The responses show that there is still room for improvement in the KMS. The KMS can incorporate more and better functions and capabilities that

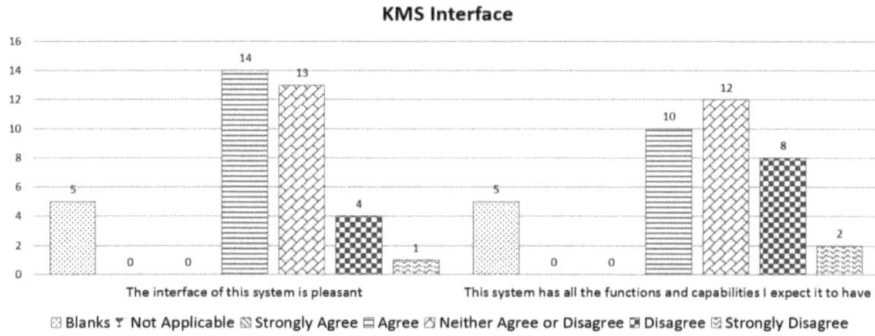

Fig. 4. The KMS Interface

suit user needs. Hence, the interface is a potential research area that the researcher can work on.

In Figure 5, the KMS functions are generally acceptable to the respondents in terms of their usage for knowledge networking, knowledge sharing and knowledge creation. All three questions in this area received positive feedback, as most of the respondents rated 'agree' as their answers. Based on the analysis, it is shown that the respondents have not fully utilised all the KMS functions as they should.

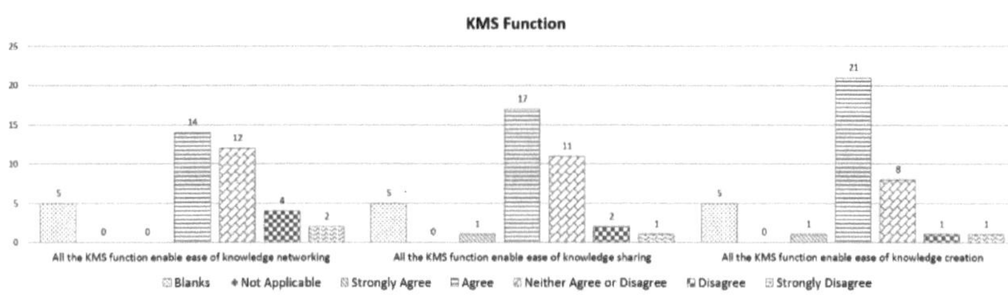

Fig. 5. The KMS functions

In term of user satisfaction, Figure 6 shows the satisfaction level of KMS users in terms of KMS efficiency, effectiveness, ease of access, ease of download and knowledge reuse. The figure shows the majorities are satisfied with ease of access, ease of download and knowledge reuse, whereas for KMS efficiency and effectiveness, the majority of the respondents tend to remain neutral or 'blank'. This message shows that the efficiency and effectiveness of the KMS may need some detailed study. Choosing 'blank' or ignore this question could have multiple hidden messages from the users.

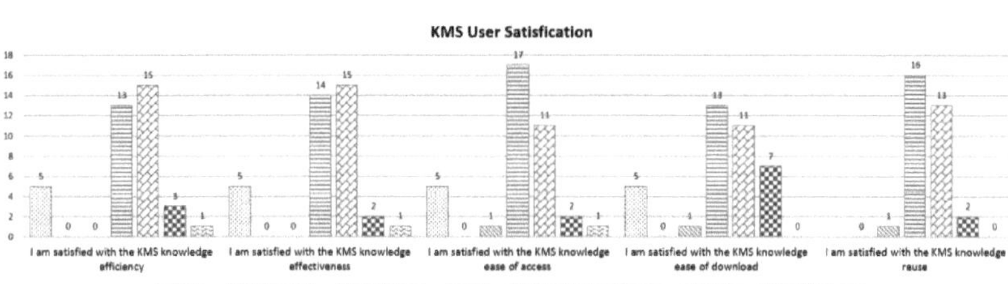

Fig. 6. User satisfaction towards the KMS

Figure 7 shows perceived KMS benefits. This area examines what the user benefited from the KMS's perspectives. Responses of the three questions were analysed. The first question attempted to find out how KMS helped the users in acquiring new knowledge and innovative ideas. The second question asked about how the KMS helped users effectively manage and store knowledge and the last question examined how the KMS helped users to accomplish tasks more efficiently. Based on the respondents' answers, the majority of the respondents agreed that the KMS helped them, with 17 respondents agreeing to the first question, 19 respondents to the second and 15 respondents to the third question. Across these three questions, it shows that most users use KMS to manage and store their knowledge.

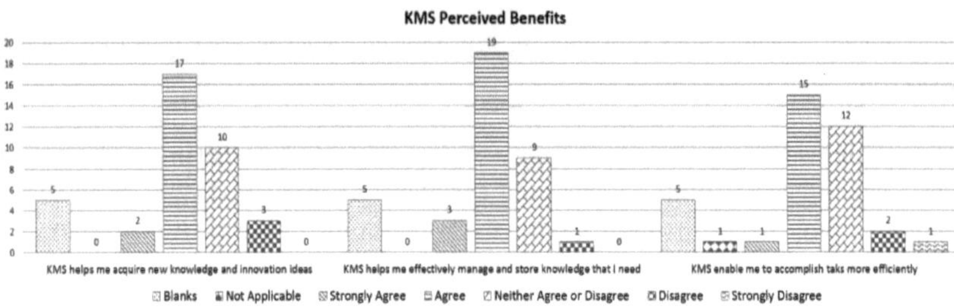

Fig. 7. Perceived KMS benefits

The uses of the KMS according to responses from employees are depicted in Figure 8. The questions on how the users actually used KMS to make decisions, record knowledge, communicate knowledge and information with colleagues, share general knowledge or sharing specific knowledge were asked. The figure shows that a very large majority of the participants chose 'agree' to all of the questions except for the question on the use of KMS to make decisions. Therefore, most users use the KMS to record and maintain their knowledge, communicate knowledge and information with colleagues, sharing general and specific knowledge.

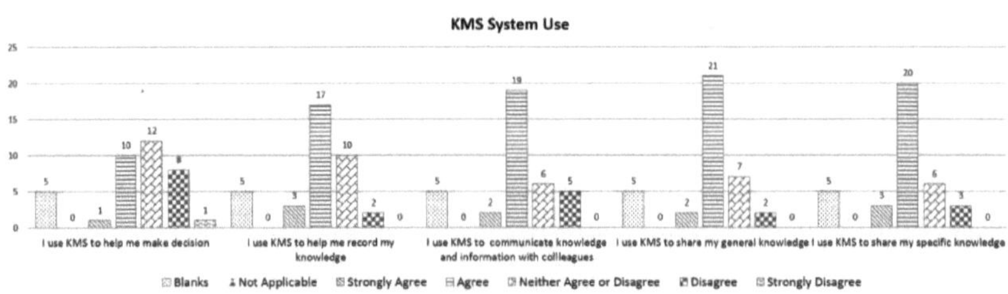

Fig. 8. System use by the respondents

Another question in the survey was about future improvement of the KMS, which required the respondents to comment and provide data on the kind of improvements that could be introduced to the KMS. Based on these responses, future improvements and a potential new system may be introduced to the current system and the company respectively. Figure 9 shows that 22 respondents 'agree' that having more people actively involved to contribute knowledge on the KMS would be more fun. Most respondents agree that the system should provide more and better functions. Most respondents choose a 'watch-and-see' attitude before making a comment. Due to lack of exposure and experience on the new platforms, these respondents expressed that only if they had tried the new platforms would they want to respond to these questions. Therefore, most of them chose to remain neutral.

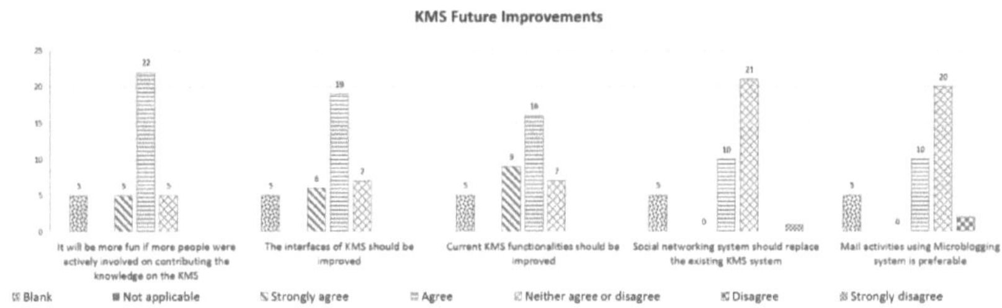

Fig. 9. KMS future improvements

The quantitative approach provides a quick and precise reflection on how employees' respond toward questions asked in the survey exercise. In the survey, respondents also provided some comment on their perceptions of the KMS. Some of the comments that the researcher should take into consideration, summarised as follows, are:

- Poor organisation of the information in the system.
- Inability to offer search features like Google or Bing.
- Need to spend more time to know more about the KMS.
- Depositing articles into the KMS in order to fulfil the monthly quota as part of their KPI has resulted in poor content quality and deviation from knowledge sharing objective set by the company.

These four issues raised by the respondents should be taken into consideration seriously so that the KMS can be improved. In terms of organisation of knowledge and search features, there is still much room for improvements. However, the last issue above, about knowledge material deposited into KMS in order to fulfil the monthly quotas, is certainly a critical issue. The Community of Practice (CoP) in the company with respect to useful knowledge sharing practice is rather poor and weak. This is indicated by the fourth point in the remarks compiled from the participants, where the knowledge sharing being practiced among knowledge workers is driven by the quota set by the company. Hence, the objectives of the knowledge sharing has been deviated; as such, the desire for knowledge sharing practice outcome is poor. This shows that the KMS has not been properly used and the culture of knowledge sharing is still poor. Therefore, it is crucial that the employees change their mind-set to actually make use of the KMS for the purpose of knowledge sharing instead of just merely depositing articles that are not very relevant.

5 Research Findings: Analysis and Discussion

One of the objectives of this research is to study the perception of the usage of the KMS in the case study company towards improving the company's productivity and discovering new innovation from knowledge in the KMS. Currently the system usage is poor. The system is merely used as a referencing system on policy, transactional documents, procedures and other 'new' knowledge articles. As described in Nonaka [13], Aranda-Corral et al. [6], Parameswaran et al. [14, 15], knowledge activities in a full knowledge conversion model such as socialisation, externalisation and combination are essential in a company. The information within the system is now very messy. Searching for specific information is difficult and tedious as employees dump information into the system in order to fulfil their monthly quota currently.

Therefore, through this study, the problems with respect to the existing KMS system are identified. By identifying these problems, the employees and the company are able to plan areas that need to be improved. In order to improve the company's productivity and to discover knowledge for innovation, the quality of the information shared within the KMS needs to be increased and these issues need to be properly managed.

Another objective of this research was to study the current KMS and the employees' perceptions towards the KMS. Based on the survey conducted, the findings were documented. In order to have better understanding of the current KMS performance, the Categorization Matrix of Performance Indicators discussed by Shannak [4] was used as the basis for the KMS analysis. For this study, not all the indicators were used. The research instrument examined a set of relevant indicators in this phase. The measurement from the matrix were handled in two ways, through the log in the database and by conducting surveys. However, in this research, only the survey instrument was used, therefore the indicators which required logging into the database as the source was not used. For the survey measurement, the results were gathered from findings in the form of charts from the preliminary questionnaire survey. Table 1 shows the proposed Categorization Matrix of Performance Indicators, separated into three major focus areas – process, human, and IT - where each area has its own domains and performance indicators. Firstly, in the process focus area, one of the domains is on the quality of knowledge. The performance indicators focus on the extent the employees consider the knowledge in the KMS useful and reusable. This can be seen in the KMS content quality (Figure 2) which shows that a high number of users agree that knowledge information provided by KMS is important and helpful to their work and most of them also agree that finding solutions using KMS is useful. Another performance indicator to be examined is the aspect of work efficiency due to new routines.

Table 1. Proposed Categorisation Matrix of Performance Indicator [4]

Focus Area	Domain	Performance Indicator	Source

Process	Quality of Knowledge	• To what extent the employees:
		  • consider knowledge in databases useful
		  • re-use knowledge
		• Number of returning users in databases
			• Survey
			• Log in database

	Efficiency due to new routines	• Number of:
		  • calls to support function
		  • hours spent with external experts, per month
		  • employees participating in this survey
		• To what extent the employee:
		  • experience saved time in finding the correct information/competence due to using the databases
		  • consider increased number of orders connected to solutions/success stories
			• Survey
			• Log in database

	Incentives	• Number of distributed incentives	• Manager
	Knowledge Contributor	• Occupational title of the Contributor • Business Unit, where the Contributor is working	• Log in database

Human	Knowledge Sharing Attitude	• To what extent employees feel:
		  • comfortable reusing solutions/contributions
		  • comfortable sharing their knowledge in order to help others
		  • that they save time by using knowledge databases in their daily work
			• Survey

	Knowledge Sharing Activities	• Number of hours the employees participate in workshops/seminars/networks or other activities, per month	• Survey

	Use of Participation in Activities	• To what extent employees consider that participation in activities generates:
		  • new relations/contacts
		  • experience and more contributions in databases
			• Survey

	Awareness	• To what extent the employees feel they have been provided with sufficient:
		  • information/education for:
		    ○ the new routines and work procedures
		    ○ the new databases
			• Survey

IT	Active Involvement	• Number of users
		• Number of:
		  • accesses in chosen area, per user
		  • returning users in databases
		  • solutions contributed, per user
		  • success stories contributed, per user
		  • lessons learned contributed, per user
		  • best practices contributed, per user
		  • other contributions, per user
		• Number of employees who have registered as a member
			• Log in database
			• Survey

	Knowledge Structure	• Number of communities in databases • Number of topics in communities in databases • Number of taxonomies in databases	• Log in database

	Usability	• To what extent the employees consider:
		  • the databases to be user friendly
		  • help-instructions in the databases being sufficient
		  • it easy finding colleagues with the correct competence
			• Survey

This is viewed from the extent to which employees experience time saving when finding correct information in the KMS. Our findings show that the current KMS still has issues in helping users to find the correct information in a short span of time.

The human factor was another key performance indicator examined in this research. From the survey results, the KMS user satisfaction (Figure 6) among employees was high. Findings also indicated that most employees agreed that the knowledge in the KMS was reusable and they mostly had no issue in sharing knowledge. In the perceived KMS benefits in Figure 7, it shows that a high number of respondents agreed that the current KMS helped them to efficiently manage and store knowledge and also helped them to accomplish tasks more efficiently. In the analysis on the KMS system use, it shows that most employees used the KMS to record knowledge, communicate knowledge and information with colleagues, share general knowledge and share specific knowledge. However, in terms of decision-making, not many respondents had used the KMS for this purpose.

From the analysis, it shows that most of the respondents make use of the KMS. This shows that the employees of the company are quite actively involved in using the KMS. The last part of this study was on the usability of the KMS; that is, how user-friendly the KMS is. Based on the KMS interface responses shown in Figure 4, 14 out of the 37 respondents thought that the interface was pleasant whereas 13 remained neutral. This showed that there is still room for improvement for the interface of the KMS.

In conclusion, based on the analysis and findings from the survey, the results show that the current KMS's overall performance indicators are still high when compared to the three areas specified in the categorisation matrix. The KMS still fulfils most of the criteria. However, based on the staff perceptions towards the KMS, improvement still needs to be made, especially in the search function to allow better search capabilities and also in the system interface. In addition, the quality of information shared also needs to be improved so that it could help co-workers. Motivation from upper management and commitment of employees is needed to ensure information and knowledge shared is used and useful.

6 Organisational Knowledge Sharing and Education

The use of KMS in education has helped teaching professionals to reap benefits such as sharing of richer resources, appreciating teaching experiences and cross-learning of good practice. This allows improvements in teaching techniques and the quality of teaching delivery. However, findings presented by Petrides *et al.* [16] and Sohail *et al.* [17] also highlight that the journey of knowledge sharing in education comes with challenges too. From the perspective of organisational knowledge sharing, lessons learned and problem solving techniques exchanged and shared among knowledge workers help to educate and improve the quality and productivity of work delivered by knowledge workers. By being able to identify motivators, barriers and better understanding of the perception of KMS, knowledge sharing is an enabler that can educate employees to improve their delivery in organisations.

7 Conclusions and Future Research Plan

In conclusion, Knowledge Management Systems (KMS) are useful for retaining tacit and explicit knowledge which are hidden within employees. KMSs are able to store, access and share among co-workers within companies. However, if a KMS is not being fully utilised, it would defeat its purpose and end up being a waste of company resource. Thus, motivation from the top management, and dedication and commitment from the employees are essential to ensure the on-going use of the system. For future research, the plan is to enlarge the research scope by considering a comparison of the characteristics (unit and organisational level) of the intended subjects and the respondents as well as increase the number of participating companies so that data collected will not be too thin.

References

1. Kulkarni, U.R., Ravindran, S., Freeze, R.: A Knowledge Management Success Model: Theoretical Development and Empirical Validation. Journal of Management Information Systems 23(3), 309–347 (2007)
2. DeLone, W.H., McLean, E.R.: Measuring e-Commerce Success: Applying the DeLone & McLean Information Systems Success Model. International Journal of Electronic Commerce 9(1), 31–47 (2004)
3. Nattapol, N., Peter, R., Laddawan, K.: An Investigation of the Determinants of Knowledge Management Systems Success in Banking Industry. World Academy of Science, Engineering and Technology 47, 588–595 (2010)
4. Shannak, R.: Measuring Knowledge Management Performance. European Journal of Scientific Research 35(2), 242–253 (2009)
5. Davenport, T.H., Long, M.D., Beers, M.C.: Building Successful Knowledge Management Projects (1997), `http://Www.Providersedge.Com/Docs/Km_Articles/Building_Successful_KM_Projects.Pdf` (retrieved August 27, 2014)
6. Aranda-Corral, G.A., Borrego-Díaz, J., Jiménez-Mavillard, A.: Social Ontology Documentation for Knowledge Externalization. In: Sánchez-Alonso, S., Athanasiadis, I.N. (eds.) MTSR 2010. CCIS, vol. 108, pp. 137–148. Springer, Heidelberg (2010)
7. Ong, C.-S., Lai, J.-Y.: Developing an Instrument for Measuring User Satisfaction with Knowledge Management Systems. In: Proceedings of The 37th Hawaii International Conference on System Sciences, Hawaii, HI (2004)
8. Lee, C.-L., Lu, H.-P., Yang, C., Hou, H.-T.: A Process-Based Knowledge Management System For Schools: A Case Study In Taiwan. The Turkish Online Journal of Educational Technology 9(4), 10–21 (2010)
9. Ali, T., Murali, R.: Knowledge Management Obstacles In Malaysia: An Exploratory Study. Public Sector ICT Management Review 3(1), 15–20 (2009)
10. Wu, J.-H., Wang, Y.-M.: Measuring KMS Success: A Respecification of The Delone And Mclean's Model. Information & Management 43, 728–739 (2006)
11. Seonwoo, K., Changyong, L., Yongtae, P.: The Implementation Framework of Knowledge Management System For Successful Knowledge Management: A Case Of R&D Supporting KMS. IAMOT (2006)
12. Brink, P.V.D.: Measurement of Conditions for Knowledge Sharing. In: Proceedings of the 2nd European Conference on Knowledge Management, Bled, Slovenia, pp. 1–16 (2001)
13. Nonaka, I.: Organizational Knowledge Creation. The Knowledge Creating Company (1997)

14. Parameswaran, M., Whinston, A.B.: Research Issues in Social Computing. Journal of the Association for Information Systems 8(6), 336–350 (2007)
15. Parameswaran, M.: Social Computing: An Overview. Communications of the Association for Information Systems 19, 762–780 (2007)
16. Petrides, L.A., Nodine, T.R.: Knowledge Management in Education: Defining the Landscape. Institute for the Study of Knowledge Management in Education (2003), http://iskme.path.net/kmeducation.pdf (retrieved August 27, 2014)
17. Sohail, M.S., Daud, S.: Knowledge sharing in higher education institutions: Perspectives from Malaysia. VINE 39(2), 125–142 (2009)

Digital Skills for Those in Transition – Where Next

Don Passey

Centre for Technology Enhanced Learning,
Department of Educational Research, Lancaster University, Lancaster, UK
d.passey@lancaster.ac.uk

Abstract. How do digital technologies support life transitions? This chapter will provide an overview, accommodating findings presented within the previous six chapters, and highlighting areas for future research. In this context, it is clear that different learning landscapes allow for different learning approaches and enable uses of sometimes specific digital technologies. In learning contexts, a "formal curriculum offers a core range of subject needs; the informal curriculum provides opportunities for these to be developed in another context and with the support or involvement of parents, family or friends; and the non-formal curriculum provides opportunities for young people to work in teams and groups on authentic problems and products" ([1], pp. 200-201). There are implications for developing effective uses in the future that relate to supporting learners in different life transitions. An analysis of individuals in a specific life transition, and the importance of uses of digital technologies and associated digital and soft skills in a learning setting will be offered.

Keywords: Digital technologies, learning landscapes, informal, formal and non-formal learning.

1 Introduction

From evidence presented in the six previous symposium papers, a number of key questions can be considered:

- How and under what conditions do digital technologies and skills enable a stabilising or positive impact upon life transitions?
- What associated skills are concerned in developing social and cultural capital, integrated or developed alongside these digital skills?
- Do digital skills enable individuals to survive situations by empowering and enabling of change rather than just responding to it?
- What is the potential of digital technologies to support life transitions, in relation to recommendations about what needs to happen next?

In taking our understanding further, and in developing appropriate practices to support lifelong learners in the future, there is a clear need to explore these research questions in the context of life transitions and the roles that digital and associated soft skills play in: employment; training; and school settings. Within these settings there is a need to explore different life transitions, which might build further from: an

D. Passey and A. Tatnall (Eds.): KCICTP/ITEM 2014, IFIP AICT 444, pp. 219–230, 2014.

employment transition that aims to strengthen business effectiveness and efficiency through knowledge sharing developments; training transitions concerned with major employment shifts (from ex-armed forces to civilian employment); transitions concerned with major social shifts (from non-employment to employment); or school to college transitions (across a key secondary to tertiary phase). Our understanding in these fields has been considered in previous chapters in the context of emerging research from local, regional, national and international perspectives.

2 Implications for Research Approach and Methods

A starting point, and perhaps a fundamentally important starting point in considering research questions about those in life transitions, is to explore some of the implications for research approach and methods. What is clear from the previous papers in this section is that different research methods have been used when exploring related research questions and issues. These have spanned:

- Organisational case studies (see [2, 3]), where the case study is based in a single organisation, and methods to gather evidence included questionnaires and interviews.
- Individual case studies (see [4]), where the case study is based at an individual level, where evidence is gathered through observation and semi-structured interviews.
- Individual ethnographic case studies (see [5]), where the case study is based at an individual level, where evidence is gathered at multiple times through observation, discussion and ethnographic immersion.

There is distinction here of approach and methods for gathering evidence that align with perceptions and demands of structure and complexity (or level of transition difficulty, perhaps). When individuals are within a formal organisation (like a company or a school), the structure may be considered formal, with the life transition not being considered highly complex or difficult, so organisational case studies may be considered appropriate. When individuals are within a formal organisation (such as a school), and the structure may be considered formal, but life transitions are considered in some way potentially complex or more difficult, then individual case studies might be considered to be more appropriate. These approaches and methods would fall within the more traditional case study approaches described by Yin [6] or Stake [7]. Of note, perhaps, the use of digital frameworks to identify digital skills, such as those presented in an earlier chapter in this section [8], also aligns well with this form of research and development. But, when individuals are within an informal organisation (such as a mentoring or counselling group), and where life transitions are considered potentially complex and difficult, then individual ethnographic case studies might be considered more appropriate and necessary. These approaches and methods would fall within the literature described by Mead [9] or Fetterman [10].

Clearly there are potential implications arising, both with regard to the nature of the evidence that is gathered, and the way that evidence may be used. Using questionnaires and interviews might suggest that a positivist view of the evidence is being considered; that there is a way to consider the evidence in terms of a quantitative concern leading to an overview. On the other hand, using individual and ethnographic case studies, where interviews, observations and an ongoing trail of evidence is captured over time, suggests that there is need to accommodate interpretative concerns; these ways are focused on qualitative concerns that allow individual needs within specific contexts to be understood quite clearly. Even considering this small number of studies suggests a need to consider fundamental elements of research approach that accommodate:

- Increasing complexity of the situation at an individual level (the needs and characteristics of the individual become as important, if not more so, than the organisational and structural concerns).
- Increasing difficulty with handling life transitions (where the need for understanding the role of context and surroundings, and the building of trust, becomes paramount).

3 Using a Framework to Explore the Key Research Questions

This chapter does not attempt to answer all of the key research questions in every life transition context that might occur. Some of the research questions are certainly the focus of studies reported in previous papers. These papers identify the dimensions within the framework of factors influencing life transitions [11], although there is an important addition to consider within the motivational dimension highlighted by one of the previous paper authors, Rogers [12] - adaptability. The dimensions and elements of the framework can be represented in tabular form (see Table 1).

It is possible to use this framework as a means to identify, for any particular life transition in any given context, those elements that are considered important. Importance can be related in a number of ways:

- For the individual themselves.
- For those who are concerned with the transition and supporting that individual.
- For those where digital technologies have the potential to support the individual.

To exemplify this approach, the example of individuals in difficult life transitions, for ex-armed forces personnel moving to civilian employment, is taken (discussed further in [5]). In Table 1, elements considered to be important are shown with ticks in the three right-hand columns. It should be noted that this coding is based on experience of the author from current evidence gathered:

- A – important for the individual themselves.
- B – important for those who are concerned with the transition and supporting that individual.
- C – important for those where digital technologies have the potential to support the individual.

Table 1. Framework to consider factors influencing life transitions

Dimension	Elements	A	B	C
Digital	Concerned with the digital technologies that are accessible to the individual		√	√
	Those that can be used	√	√	√
	Those chosen for use by the individual and those supporting them, such as social network structures			
	For what purpose	√	√	√
Learning	The importance of learning continuity		√	√
	Ways of learning rather than the 'content' of learning		√	√
	How to develop shifts in learning	√	√	√
	The importance of information as well as communication	√	√	√
	Having appropriate accurate and useful information about the transition	√	√	√
Social	How trust, shared understanding, reciprocal relationships, common norms and cooperation are handled	√	√	√
	Considering the roles of the home as well as the formal learning environment	√		
	Integrating concerns of those around the individual	√		√
	Considering how support might work within a given situation	√	√	√
	The levels of support that might be accessible		√	√
	Providing links	√	√	√
	Building social and cultural capital	√	√	√
	Knowledge sharing skills	√	√	√
Temporality	When and how often difficult life transitions emerge		√	√
	How long they are felt to be likely to persist		√	√
	The roles trust, shared understanding, reciprocal relationships, common norms and cooperation play in various aspects of temporal communities	√	√	
	Thinking ahead and being aware of shifts and opportunities	√	√	√
	Having time to build up relationships	√	√	√
	Developing an appropriate time plan	√	√	√

Table 1. (*continued*)

Dimension	Elements	A	B	C
Motivational	The importance of the concept of adaptability	√	√	√
	The roles of interests and attainment, improving self-esteem and confidence	√	√	√
	The importance of qualifications, or demands from those in 'authority'			
	Accommodating age and purpose	√	√	√
	The ways that the individual develops over time	√	√	√
	The importance of opportunities to gather, reflect and discuss	√	√	√
	The roles of identity, agency and structure, adjusting, identifying available assistance, and collaboration as needed	√	√	√
Affective	The role of attitudes	√	√	√
	Whether developing new friendships is important		√	√
	Getting initial contact and 'footholds'	√	√	√
	Gaining initial experience	√	√	
	Being aware of behaviours and emotions	√	√	√
Contextual	The concern with continuity, or the importance of discontinuity	√		√
	The role of context or setting	√	√	√
	Concerns with new routines or organisation	√	√	√
	Being involved in systems that are 'simple' rather than 'complex'	√		
	Being aware that systems do themselves change			
	Being aware of the implications of formal, informal and non-formal settings	√	√	√
	Whether situations are based on team and problem-solving needs or more formal classroom needs	√	√	√
	Being aware of increasing external factors, and those who become 'significant others' over time	√	√	√

What is clear from the pattern identified in Table 1 is:

- The role of those supporting individuals in life transitions is fundamentally important; they are concerned not only with elements associated with individuals in transition, but with additional elements too.
- The role of digital technologies in supporting individuals in life transitions appears to be high.

4 Extending the Roles of Digital Technologies in Supporting those in Life Transitions

Using the analysis in Table 1, it is possible to identify ways that digital technologies might be further used in supportive practices. These additional ways are outlined in

Table 2. In this example, the support provided by digital technologies would involve uses of either an online chat facility, or texts or emails. There is a width of literature that indicates how such support has been and can be developed in educational settings, through either mentor [13] or less formal 'connector' roles [14].

Table 2. Considering ways digital technologies might support individuals in life transitions

Dimension	Elements	Ways digital technologies might be used by supporters
Digital	Concerned with the digital technologies that are accessible to the individual	Finding out what digital technologies individuals can access
	Those that can be used	Finding out what they use
	For what purpose	Finding out what individuals use the digital technologies for
Learning	The importance of learning continuity	Using approaches to match previous learning
	Ways of learning rather than the 'content' of learning	Exploring how to learn with the digital technologies
	How to develop shifts in learning	Highlighting ways different approaches might support the individual
	The importance of information as well as communication	Sending pertinent details and information updates
	Having appropriate accurate and useful information about the transition	Eliciting regular feedback from the individual
Social	How trust, shared understanding, reciprocal relationships, common norms and cooperation are handled	Eliciting ongoing online discussions that broach these concerns
	Considering the roles of the home as well as the formal learning environment	Asking about and discussing these points as appropriate
	Integrating concerns of those around the individual	Asking about roles of others and discussing these
	Considering how support might work within a given situation	Discussing possible roles and responsibilities initially and later
	The levels of support that might be accessible	Describing how often support might be provided
	Providing links	Sending links of potential use
	Building social and cultural capital	Exploring and highlighting this concern in an ongoing way
	Knowledge sharing skills	Supporting a wider network involvement

Table 2. (*continued*)

Dimension	Elements	Ways digital technologies might be used by supporters
Temporality	When and how often difficult life transitions emerge	Raising this appropriately
	How long they are felt to be likely to persist	Monitoring this issue
	The roles trust, shared understanding, reciprocal relationships, common norms and cooperation play in various aspects of temporal communities	Encouraging, asking about and highlighting these issues at appropriate and regular points
	Thinking ahead and being aware of shifts and opportunities	Encouraging feedback and generation of overviews of plans
	Having time to build up relationships	Offering regular positive online interactions
	Developing an appropriate time plan	Discussing a time plan and monitoring this regularly
Motivational	The importance of the concept of adaptability	Bringing in discussion of this need
	The roles of interests and attainment, improving self-esteem and confidence	Gaining ideas of interest, and feeding back positively about aspects of these
	The importance of qualifications, or demands from those in 'authority'	Asking about and discussing these points as appropriate
	Accommodating age and purpose	Relating to a 'close' companion
	The ways that the individual develops over time	Monitoring what is happening, and sharing what is being developed
	The importance of opportunities to gather, reflect and discuss	Agreeing regular feedback
	The roles of identity, agency and structure, adjusting, identifying available assistance, and collaboration as needed	Raising these and discussing them as appropriate over time
Affective	The role of attitudes	Monitoring these from interactions
	Whether developing new friendships is important	Gauging the importance of this when interacting
	Getting initial contact and 'footholds'	Providing contacts and opportunities
	Being aware of behaviours and emotions	Monitoring these and discussing them over time

Table 2. (*continued*)

Dimension	Elements	Ways digital technologies might be used by supporters
Contextual	The concern with continuity, or the importance of discontinuity	Picking up this point and discussing as appropriate
	The role of context or setting	Monitoring and discussing
	Concerns with new routines or organisation	Bringing up and considering ways to accommodate this need
	Being involved in systems that are 'simple' rather than 'complex'	Breaking down needs into steps that can be identified and handled
	Being aware that systems do themselves change	Raising this point for discussion
	Being aware of the implications of formal, informal and non-formal settings	Raising and discussing this concern as appropriate
	Whether situations are based on team and problem-solving needs or more formal classroom needs	Highlighting these points and discussing them as appropriate
	Being aware of increasing external factors, and those who become 'significant others' over time	Highlighting these and discussing the importance of individuals and their roles

From details in Table 2, it is clear that communicative forms of digital technologies (chat facilities, texts, or email, for example) are likely to be vitally important if digital technologies can be used to support not only those who are in life transitions that they find difficult, but also those who are supporting them. However, while these details are suggestive, their use in practice within these situations needs to be trialled and explored.

Some studies have demonstrated that individuals who are experiencing life difficulties can gain from use of communicative as well as information technologies. For example, Dangwal and Sharma [15] reported that women in sheltered homes who had experienced violence engaged with digital technologies, and these supported both recreational and educational purposes, enabling them to develop wider interests. In a school-based context, Blood et al. [16] identified impacts of handheld devices on completion of learning activities and on planning of tasks for learners with negative attitudes. However, some studies have indicated the importance of considering the selection of digital technologies that will specifically address the needs of particular groups (e.g. Schinke, Fang, Cole and Cohen-Cutler [17] considered this in the context of supporting adolescent girls from minority ethnic groups involved in alcohol abuse). So, while this paper has considered the ways that a framework might be used to explore how digital technologies might support those in life transitions, it is clear that it is important that each context is considered separately, so that appropriate digital technologies can be implemented, according to user and purpose.

In this context it is worth considering how the frameworks considered by Cranmer [4] might offer an indication of the forms and ranges of digital skills that individuals in life transitions supported in ways indicated in Table 2 might need. Table 3 uses the Institute for Prospective Studies framework [18] to detail some of the range of digital skills needed, based on details in Table 2.

Table 3. Likely range of digital skills needed by individuals in ex-armed forces to civilian employment life transitions (Source of dimensions and elements: [18])

Dimension of digital competence	Elements	Digital competencies needed by those in the life transition
Information management	Identify, locate, access, retrieve, store and organise information	Identify, locate, access, retrieve, store and organise information
Collaboration	Link with others, participate in online networks and communities, interact constructively	Link with others, participate in online networks and communities, interact constructively
Communication and sharing	Communicate through online tools, taking into account privacy, safety and netiquette	Communicate through online tools, taking into account privacy, safety and netiquette
Creation of content and knowledge	Integrate and re-elaborate previous knowledge and content, construct new knowledge	Integrate and re-elaborate previous knowledge and content
Ethics and responsibility	Behave in an ethical and responsible way, aware of legal frames	Behave in an ethical and responsible way, aware of legal frames
Evaluation and problem solving	Identify digital needs, solve problems through digital means, assess the information retrieved	Identify digital needs, assess the information retrieved
Technical operations	Use technology and media, perform tasks through digital tools	Use technology and media, perform tasks through digital tools

The analysis in Table 3 suggests that while individuals could be supported through uses of digital technologies in difficult life transition situations, the range of digital skills needed by those individuals may be high. Whether individuals already have these digital skills and competencies, or how their development might be accommodated, is a question that cannot be readily answered at this time.

5 Conclusions

At the outset of this chapter, and at the outset of the papers in this section, four key research questions were posed:

- How and under what conditions do digital technologies and skills enable a stabilising or positive impact upon life transitions?
- What associated skills are concerned in developing social and cultural capital, integrated or developed alongside these digital skills?
- Do digital skills enable individuals to survive situations by empowering and enabling of change rather than just responding to it?
- What is the potential of digital technologies to support life transitions, in relation to recommendations about what needs to happen next?

From the evidence presented in the seven papers in this chapter, it appears that a number of conclusions can be drawn, relating to these questions:

- Digital technologies and skills can enable a stabilising or positive impact upon life transitions for some individuals. However, the applications are not necessarily widely used with groups in life transitions, and it appears that the more difficult or complex the transition, the more specific the application of the technology might need to be.
- Associated skills concerned in developing social and cultural capital, integrated or developed alongside digital skills, have been identified in the framework shown in Table 1. How these skills are developed in association with digital skills is not identified in the studies reported here, however. It is also clear that individuals might need quite high levels of digital competencies in order to benefit from forms of online support that might help them in difficult life transitions.
- Certainly individuals can survive situations by their being empowered and enabling of change rather than just responding to it. However, the role of the digital skills and technologies appears to be at a support level rather than having a direct influence, and the roles of adept supporters in enabling change in these circumstances is also highlighted.
- There appears to be a wider potential for digital technologies to support life transitions, but trials and research in this field are at a fairly early stage.

While it is possible to identify a range of important life transitions, and while it is possible to identify a framework through which to look at factors that are involved in and that influence ways individuals are able to move through those transitions, it is clear that there are important factors to consider in taking research further in this area:

- Appropriate selection and choice of research approach and methods to gather evidence that will be pertinent not just to the research outcome, but beyond that outcome for the individuals and those who support them.
- Matching of digital technologies to the needs of those in any specific life transition context.

- Awareness and facility with the uses of digital technologies so that appropriate communication and informational interactions can be used by all concerned.
- Development of appropriate interventions that focus on and support the factors that influence that transition.

Although those in life transitions may well be supported by appropriate uses of digital technologies, there are clearly many perspectives yet to be explored in order to gather relevant evidence to fully consider and focus wider application in this area.

Acknowledgement. My particular thanks are due to Paul Davies, a colleague in the Centre for Technology Enhanced Learning in the Department of Educational Research at Lancaster University who has undertaken the research work with those making life transitions from ex-armed forces to civilian employment that has informed this and the previous chapter I contributed to this book. My thanks also to the Research Support Office at Lancaster University who funded the life transitions research reported in this paper.

References

1. Passey, D.: Inclusive technology enhanced learning: Overcoming Cognitive, Physical, Emotional and Geographic Challenges. Routledge, New York (2013)
2. Lee Angela, S. H., Lim, T.-M.: An Exploratory Study on the Use of Knowledge Management System and the Employees' Perception on Organizational Knowledge Sharing and Reuse. In: Passey, D., Tatnall, A. (eds.) KCICTP/ITEM 2014. IFIP AICT, vol. 444, pp. 205–218. Springer, Heidelberg (2014)
3. Lim, T.-M., Lee Angela, S.H.: Using "Yams" for enterprise knowledge sharing among knowledge workers from the perspective of a task categorisation-knowledge sharing systems fit. In: Passey, D., Tatnall, A. (eds.) KCICTP/ITEM 2014. IFIP AICT, vol. 444, pp. 190–204. Springer, Heidelberg (2014)
4. Cranmer, S.: Digital skills and competencies in schools. In: Passey, D., Tatnall, A. (eds.) KCICTP/ITEM 2014. IFIP AICT, vol. 444, pp. 165–177. Springer, Heidelberg (2014)
5. Davies, P.: Difficult Life Transitions: Learning and Digital Technologies - Discussion Paper and Preliminary Literature Review. Lancaster University, Lancaster (2014)
6. Yin, R.: Case study research: design and methods. Sage, Thousand Oaks (1994)
7. Stake, R.: The art of case study research. Sage, Thousand Oaks (1995)
8. Leahy, D., Wilson, D.: Digital skills for employment. In: Passey, D., Tatnall, A. (eds.) KCICTP/ITEM 2014. IFIP AICT, vol. 444, pp. 178–189. Springer, Heidelberg (2014)
9. Mead, M.: Coming of Age in, Samoa. Penguin, London (1971)
10. Fetterman, D.: Ethnography step by step, 2nd edn. Sage, Thousand Oaks (1998)
11. Passey, D.: Life transitions, learning and digital technologies- common threads and conceptions. In: Passey, D., Tatnall, A. (eds.) KCICTP/ITEM 2014. IFIP AICT, vol. 444, pp. 139–149. Springer, Heidelberg (2014)

12. Rogers, C.: Digital Skills and Motivation in Young People in Transition. In: Passey, D., Tatnall, A. (eds.) KCICTP/ITEM 2014. IFIP AICT, vol. 444, pp. 150–164. Springer, Heidelberg (2014)
13. Salmon, G.: E-moderating: The Key to Teaching and Learning Online. Kogan Page, London (2000)
14. Kotowski, M., Dos Santos, G.M.: The role of the connector in bridging borders though virtual communities. Journal of Borderlands Studies 25(3-4), 150–158 (2010)
15. Dangwal, R., Sharma, K.: Impact of HiWEL learning stations on women living in shelter homes. British Journal of Educational Technology 44(1), E26–E30 (2013)
16. Blood, E., Johnson, J.W., Ridenour, L., Simmons, K., Crouch, S.: Using an iPod Touch to Teach Social and Self-Management Skills to an Elementary Student with Emotional/Behavioral Disorders. Education and Treatment of Children 34(3), 299–322 (2011)
17. Schinke, S.P., Fang, L., Cole, K.C., Cohen-Cutler, S.: Preventing Substance Use Among Black and Hispanic Adolescent Girls: Results From a Computer-Delivered, Mother-Daughter Intervention Approach. Substance Use and Misuse 46(1), 35–45 (2011)
18. Ferrari, A.: DIGICOMP: A Framework for Developing and Understanding Digital Competence in Europe. Institute for Prospective Technological Studies, Seville, Spain (2013), `http://ftp.jrc.es/EURdoc/JRC83167.pdf` (retrieved August 30, 2014)

Key Competencies and School Management

Digital Storytelling and Key Skills: Problems and Opportunities

Monica Banzato

Department of Linguistics and Comparative Cultural Studies,
University of Ca' Foscari - Venice, Italy
banzato@unive.it

Abstract. This paper presents a pilot study conducted at the University Ca' Foscari – Venice, in Italy, in which a group of pre-service secondary school teachers explored the use of digital storytelling through workshops. The aim of this study was to determine the key skills that teachers employ in the production of DS. To this end, the study investigated in detail: the stages of Digital Storytelling (DS) perceived as difficult; the key skills that teachers are able to develop in their use of DS; the obstacles that may prevent the use of DS in schools. Although teachers have recognized the positive value of DS on the pedagogical and educational levels, the sample shows some resistance to using it at school, not so much due to the lack of technical competence, but for institutional reasons such as time constraints, access to technical equipment and curriculum demands.

Keywords: Key digital skills, pre-service teachers, digital storytelling, obstacles.

1 Introduction

Over the past decade, several studies have shown how the new generations are increasing the hours they spend daily in communicating and sharing digital information, now averaging more than 7½ hours a day [1]. Their digital practices have kept up with changing fashions: if years ago, students chatted, blogged and downloaded music and video, today they tweet and employ social media apps to share photos, video and artwork on sites like YouTube and Flickr. However, the digital experiences of this generation are not in themselves informative of their critical awareness of being able "to harness human curiosity, the ability to listen, and seek diverse knowledge in the context of integrated information spaces, constant sharing, public identities, and low barriers to production" [2]; or to "personalize content and reorganize it in a fashion that best allows them to make sense of a topic, and to share it with peers" [3].

The school sector has a responsibility to enhance students' formal and informal learning and to ensure their acquisition of digital literacy [4], conceived as the ability to "access content, analyze and evaluate the messages, create presentations, reflect on findings, and work together in collaborative environments" [2].

D. Passey and A. Tatnall (Eds.): KCICTP/ITEM 2014, IFIP AICT 444, pp. 233–246, 2014.

Teachers today are required to be capable of promoting digital literacy and key digital competences [5, 6], including designing authentic learning environments and experiences. In fact, "it is essential to prepare technologically proficient teachers that are able to provide the learning opportunities that facilitate students' use of technology to construct knowledge and to communicate in the networked world we live in" [7].

Digital Storytelling (henceforth DS) is considered one of the educational methods that allows both significant promulgation of digital literacy [8, 9] and development of strategic skills for twenty-first century training [10, 11]. "Digital storytelling allows the creation of innovative learning experiences, supported and extended by the application of user contributed content Web 2.0 technologies, empowering teachers' abilities to communicate and integrate technologies into the curriculum" [12].

Seeking to harmonise technological advancements with developments in education, many scholars [8, 13, 14, 15] have suggested that DS represents an ideal combination of technology-integrated learning and social constructivist principles. The social constructivists suggest the importance of students' collaborative learning through using digital tools in educational activities within an authentic environment [16, 17], where learners are engaged in constructing and reconstructing their knowledge and beliefs in collaborative ways [18]. In the constructivist learning framework [19, 20, 21, 22], knowledge is not simply transmitted from teacher to student but is actively generated and constructed by the students through social interactions with their physical, social, and technological environment [23, 24]. DS creates an ideal synergy between digital learning environments (i.e. learning management system [LMS], blogs, wiki etc.), technological tools, software (i.e. video editor, audio editor, etc.), and educational objectives (in different subjects, from scientific to humanistic fields) which can facilitate the co-construction of knowledge among students.

However, it is essential to prepare teachers who have completed their pre-service courses and are capable of incorporating their own digital experience in authentic pedagogical pathways. In this manner, teachers should become capable of creating learning opportunities which facilitate the construction and sharing of knowledge with and through multiple channels of information.

Nevertheless, training teachers to employ innovative methods is not a road without obstacles, as beliefs, perceptions, attitudes, experiences and well-established practices, combined with the narrow constraints in which teachers operate (e.g. ministerial programs, organization of schools) can influence positively or negatively the adoption of new ways of learning. This paper aims to answer three basic questions: 1) What are the strengths and weaknesses of DS as perceived by teachers? 2) What are the key skills that teachers would be expected to utilise in DS? 3) What obstacles prevent teachers from employing digital narration in class?

The results presented here are derived from an investigation undertaken at Ca' Foscari University, January - May 2013. This research project was undertaken among the participants in a pre-service course, which aimed to instruct teachers in techniques for employing open digital resources and DS. From the 211 participants, 48 teachers of humanities subjects were chosen to participate in a pilot study. As part of the pre-service course, a laboratory for the creation of DS was setup, in which the participants shared in the processes of creating and producing finished DS products on the Moodle platform. The completed DS products were utilised to stimulate self-reflection on the methods and professional practices, with the aim of collecting the perceptions of the participants: a) as students, who learn through innovative methods employed in ICT (Information Communication Technology); b) as teachers, who reflect on the key skills that they need to put into practice; c) as reflective practitioners [25], who wish to integrate proven practices with new ones.

The creation of digital stories was also aimed at improving teachers' comprehension and faith in the utility and efficacy of employing ICT in their teaching practices.

2 Digital Storytelling and Key Skills

There are several definitions of "Digital Storytelling". From a technical point of view, DS can be defined as the task of telling a story through digital media. The product is a short narrated video (amateur, not professional, usually no longer than five minutes) in which there are music, pictures, drawings or videos, and a voice track. The DS can be shared among a small group or among the great community of the internet by such means as posting it on YouTube (or as Open Educational Resources [26, 27, 28]). The creation of a DS requires the development of multiliteracies, the ability to communicate fluently through traditional and new media, as well as the ability to access, analyze and evaluate the huge amount of network information to create an individual video that weaves, in an original and personal manner, narrative text and vocalisation, images, and sounds. DS can be used in educational activities at all grade levels, up to tertiary education and beyond.

According to Lambert [29], DS should be defined by the presence of seven elements: 1. Point of View: the author begins with his own point of view; 2. A Dramatic Question: the author poses a question (or a problem) which will be answered by the end of the work; 3. Emotional Content: the author gives emotional force to the initial question in order to highlight the problem he/she is addressing; 4. The Gift of your Voice: the author tells the story in his own voice, in order to personalize the work and to help the listener understand the narrative; 5. The Power of the Soundtrack: the author selects music or other sound effects in support of the plot; 6. Economy: the author designs a brief narrative. Facts must be used to give flavour to the story, not to overwhelm the viewer with excess information; 7. Pacing: the author decides on the pace of the story (slow or fast).

DS can be employed for various purposes: to inform, to demonstrate or to communicate a personal vision. "The topics that are used in Digital Storytelling range from personal tales to the recounting of historical events, from exploring life in one's own community to the search for life in other corners of the universe, and literally, everything in between" [8]. It can be used in several ways: it could be created by teachers as a media resource to present an argument and form the subject of classroom debate, or it might be created by the students themselves, individually or in groups. "DS puts technology in the students' hands and stimulates research skills and creativity" [12].

According to Porter [30], "For students to be effective communicators in the 21st century, they need to be sophisticated in expressing ideas with multiple communication technologies, not just the written word". Digital Storytelling is an application of educational technology which uses almost all of the skills that students are expected to have in the 21st century [31]. This proposition is affirmed by Robin, who states [8]: "This creative work provides students with a strong foundation in what many educators have begun calling 21st century Literacy, Digital Age Literacy or 21st Century Skills". According to Robin [8], DS develops four key skills: "Digital literacy: the ability to communicate with an ever-expanding community to discuss issues, gather information, and seek help; Global literacy: the capacity to read, interpret, respond, and contextualize messages from a global perspective; Technology literacy: the ability to use computers and other technology to improve learning, productivity, and performance; Visual literacy: the ability to understand, produce, and communicate through visual images; Information literacy: the ability to find, evaluate, and synthesize information".

3 Pre-service Teachers and Digital Storytelling

A review of the literature reveals an increasing interest regarding the use of DS in the initial training of teachers. For example, Yerrick et al. [32] analyse the use of digital video editing as a significant method to encourage meaningful reflection on the part of teachers. Their research focuses on the impact of DS on the beliefs of pre-service teachers, concentrating, in particular, on teachers' understanding of children's thinking and their own teaching experience. Barrett [33, 34] argues that the use of DS by teachers "is a highly motivating strategy that allows them to make concrete and visible observations about their own practices". His research has investigated the convergence of "student engagement, reflection for deep learning, project-based learning and the adductive integration of technology into instruction". Tendero [35] examines the use of digital storytelling as a means by which teachers have the opportunity to develop multiple points of view for the analysis of their own beliefs. Li [36] conducted an exploratory research project on the usefulness of the use of DS to build an e-portfolio, by means of reflection and self-assessment of the learning process. The researcher found "a useful tool in the enhancement of teaching and learning new literacies in today's technology enriched environments". Heo [37] examined the effects of the experience of DS in pre-service in terms of "teachers' self-efficacy towards educational technology". In addition, this study examined the professional arrangements of the teachers involved, including the opening of a shift to technology education, the degree of availability in the development of educational technologies and the willingness to work beyond the contractual hours of work for the integration of technology into teaching practices at school. Dogan and Robin [38] examined the educational impact and obstacles of DS in the classroom, among a group of pre-service trained teachers. Kearney [39] examined the potential role of DS in pre-service training, focussing on teachers' construction of e-portfolios. He also investigated digital storytelling as "a support for self-reflection during teacher training". Kearney [39] noted that "digital stories can help address the problem of reflection being perceived by students as over-used and that students can use new media to initiate reflective processes in compelling ways". He affirms that further research should be conducted on the use of DS in pre-service, which he defines as "a crucial but underdeveloped area of research into teacher learning".

4 Background and Research Methodology

The pilot study took the approach of case studies, collecting and processing qualitative and quantitative data. The information, collected through two questionnaires, interviews and digital storytelling produced by the pre-service teachers in the workshop, is set out below:

1) The first questionnaire, used at the beginning of the laboratory, allowed the gathering of data on computer skills, the use of video and narrative methods in teaching practice.
2) The second questionnaire, which was used at the end of the workshop, allowed the collecting of information on the strengths and weaknesses of DS as perceived by teachers from two different perspectives: a) as a student, the stages of DS perceived to be difficult; b) as a teacher, the key skills that teachers were able to implement/develop in their DS projects; c) in general, what obstacles might prevent the use of DS in classrooms.
3) The interviews, conducted to triangulate the survey data 1 and 2, were carried out in oral form, throughout the laboratory, and transcribed at the end of the laboratory. The interviews provided further, accurate information on issues that surveys 1 and 2 could not investigate. This work allowed the identification of a sufficient number of significant interviews (about 80% of the participants in the laboratory).
4) DS video products were also useful for the collection of data on key competences of teachers and the educational use of DS.

Given that digital storytelling is a relatively new teaching method in the Italian context and that there are no available data, this study provides information on the attitudes of humanities teachers: (1) regarding the use of basic technology by those with experience of DS methods; (2) on key skills that this sample of in-service teachers are able to implement with DS; and (3) obstacles that may prevent the use of innovative methods and technologies in schools.

The limitations of this study are: a) the sample size (48 participants), although representative, only covers one sector of higher education, humanities (the sciences are absent); b) the sample comes mainly from the north-east of Italy and therefore covers a limited portion of the country; c) the short time frame in which the study took place (five months) limited observations to the period of the workshop and it has not been possible to verify de facto the impact of the data collected. In fact, although a portion of the sample was contacted six months after the end of the workshop, the number of respondents was not enough to form a significant sample.

5 Results

5.1 Sample of Teachers

The study was conducted on a sample of 48 humanities teachers, of which 60% (28) were females and 40% (19) were male. A total of 77% (37) of the sample declared an average experience in secondary schools of 4.7 years for females and 3.8 years for males, an average of 4.2 years. Only 22% (11) declared themselves new graduates without significant teaching experience.

5.2 Survey Results 1

The first questionnaire was distributed at the beginning of the workshop and had the following objectives: (a) to collect data on the computer skills needed to create a video (in particular, the use of Audacity and MovieMaker or another software editor for audio and video); (b) to explore whether teachers had previously employed narrative methods in their teaching practices in the classroom, not necessarily related to the use of technology; c) to determine whether the sample had previously used video in class.

Regarding (a) their knowledge of the software, 95% (46) of the sample declared that they had never used Audacity (though 70% - 34 - claimed to know other software for audio recording), while 45% (22) claimed to have used MovieMaker, 4% (2) iMovie (Apple), and 2% (1) other editing software (Adobe Premiere, Final Cut).

In response to the question (b), if they had already used narrative practices in teaching, 77% (37) of the participants said they had not specifically used narrative methods in the classroom before the workshop on DS. Based on interviews conducted on the sample, it appears that there is broad interest in narrative methods, especially after knowing DS and having enjoyed this opportunity.

The question (c) about using videos in the classroom produced the following results: 87% (42) replied, “I have used videos produced by others”; 6% (3) said, “I have created digital video”; no teacher selected the answers, “I edited videos produced by others”, “I created videos with colleagues” (collaboratively constructed video), or “I assigned my students to create a video as a task”.

From this preliminary analysis, it appears that the use of video is present in the teaching practices of this sample, together with other materials. However, it appears that the members of this sample did not have digital experiences of creating, editing and sharing video (“user generated content”). Furthermore, narrative methods (whether digital or otherwise) do not seem to be widespread in this sample. Finally, the analysis of the sample data does not reveal previous experience of digital storytelling or of other educational activities that merge the narration with multimedia languages (such as video) and sharing them on the internet.

5.3 Survey Results 2

The second survey was conducted at the end of the workshop, after the teachers had experienced all the stages of DS and finished their video. This phase of the survey was aimed at gathering information to identify:

a) the stages of DS perceived as difficult;
b) the key skills that teachers are able to develop in their DS project;
c) the barriers that may prevent use of DS in the classroom.

5.3.1 Perceptions of Teachers on Educational and Technical Phases of DS

Despite the fact that satisfaction about DS was a high 4.6 on a 0-5 scale and that very positive comments were made by the participants in the interviews, teachers reported some difficulties during the development of DS.

The main difficulties at the technical level are represented by the voice-audio recording (81%, 39) and video editing (90%, 43). From the interviews it emerged that the Audacity software is considered to be a good product, compared to other open software, although slightly more complex.

Reported difficulties were not related to use but in determining the right location to record the voice (i.e. to have audio narration of high quality and loud enough to be heard clearly) or hardware-related (lack of a good microphone or sound card) and also the ability to make meaningful the use of their voice (prosody, intonation, etc.). In this case, the teachers felt it would be interesting to promote a workshop on "reading aloud" or "theatre", in order to make the reading similar to expressive acting.

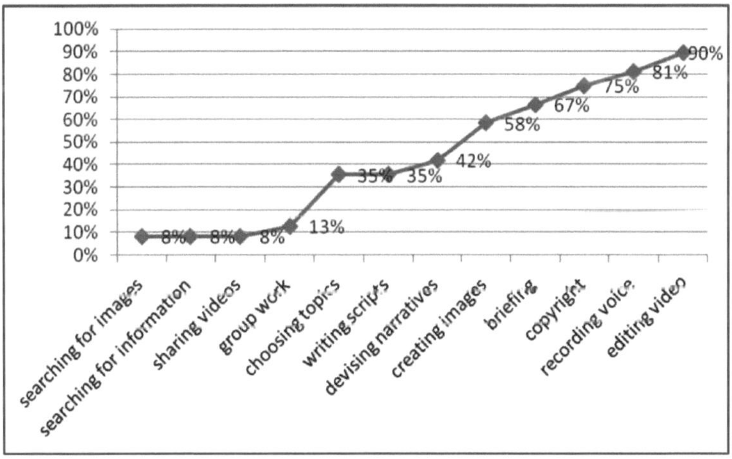

Fig. 1. Stages of DS considered the most critical are those with higher rates

The video editing was an issue for the majority of the sample (90%, 43). From a technical point of view, teachers complained that MovieMaker is not stable software: at times, it suddenly stops working and, as a result, the video editing can be lost. Video editing was perceived by teachers to be interesting, but the synchronization of audio-voice, audio-music, subtitles, video and images requires a lot of time, and the results are not always satisfactory.

Work groups were considered a strength in creating DS and the majority of the participants preferred to work in this mode (only 2 people, out of 48, chose to work individually). However, teachers identified other difficulties, such as: the phase of the initial briefing (67%, 32) was costly in terms of time, since the participants had to know each other and decide how to organize and manage the various stages of the work. The conception of storytelling (42%, 20) and the choice of topics (35%, 17) also took time, but these moments were regarded positively as creative and stimulating learning. However the "rendering of words into images, or images into words" required long reflection.

The phase of researching images and videos was much appreciated by teachers, while the creation of the images was difficult for 58% (28) of the sample. This is due to two reasons: (a) some participants believed that they did not have sufficient skills with photography and video; and (b) they considered that they had not had enough experience translating "words into images" and "images into words". During the interviews, it was possible to capture another critical aspect, which is the copyright of some images (75%, 36), the teachers often had to find ways to avoid violating copyrights (DS requires that sources from which information is derived, whether text or images, be cited). The sharing of video products in the Moodle platform was much appreciated, because the teachers could examine the videos of other colleagues (who provided new ideas and solutions for their own work) and discuss educational issues in the forum. However, only one group decided to publish its products on YouTube. For some teachers, the process of writing was critical (35%, 17), for two reasons: (a) some teachers indicated that they preferred description and explanation of topics rather than narration; (b) others noted that DS requires that scripts be written very concisely.

5.3.2 Key Skills for Teachers

Teachers were asked: "what are the key skills that your DS project develops in students?" At the beginning of the course, when DS was introduced, the teachers were presented with a list of 12 competencies developed by the American National Standards, NETS-S, and 21st Century Skills [9]. To this list were added three more digital skills related to the production of user-generated content that are well suited to video DS (sharing videos, creating community, using Creative Commons). Here follows a summary of a brief description of the key competencies.

"1. Cognitive Apprenticeship: practicing real-world work of digital communication;
2. Creativity and Inventive Thinking: creating multi-sensory experiences for others;
3. Higher Order Thinking Skills (HOTS): going beyond existing information to add personal meaning and understanding;
4. Enduring Understanding: by telling the story of what you know and understand for others, authors deepen their own self-meaning of the topic;
5. Visual Literacy: using images to show, not tell, the narrative story;

6. Technical Literacy: mastering the craftsmanship of applying the technology tools to create powerful communication, not to just use the tools, but to mix and dance the media into illuminated understandings;
7. Information (Media) Literacy: thinking, reading, writing, and designing effective media information;
8. Effective Communication: reading and writing information beyond words;
9. Multiple Intelligences and Learning Styles: addressing not only the opportunity for students to use their preferred mode of learning and thinking, but also enabling them to practice the effective use of all modalities;
10. Teaming and Collaboration: growing skills through practiced opportunities to co-produce group projects;
11. Project Management Mentality: challenge for students to practice time management of complex, involved tasks to successfully meet deadlines modelling real-world tasks;
12. Exploring Affinity: when students create meaningful, engaged work, they discover themselves as successful learners" [9].
13. Community: Use DS to create a learning community;
14. Sharing: share DS with the class, the school and wider community;
15. Using Creative Commons: respect the copyright and the resources utilised.

To answer this item of the questionnaire, teachers had to attribute scores to each of the 15 competencies presented (Very Important, Important, Some Importance, No Importance) according to the degree of importance they attributed to creation of DS by participants. Figure 2 shows the results.

The skills considered "very important" were: 2. Creativity and Inventive Thinking, selected by 69% (33) of the sample; 3. HOTS, 85% (41); 4. Enduring Understanding, 89% (43); 7. Media and Information literacy, 90%; 8. Effective Communication, 95% (46); 10. Teaming and Collaboration, 95% (46); 12. Exploring Affinity, 77% (37); 15. Use Creative Commons, 95% (46).

The skills considered "important", but not fully exploited in their DS projects, were: 1. Cognitive Apprenticeship, 48% (23); 5.Visual literacy, 66% (32); 6. Technical Literacy, 33% (16); 12. Sharing videos, 77% (37); 13. Community, 85% (41).

From the interviews, it appears that skill 1. Cognitive Apprenticeship, did not receive much attention because the participants were mainly focused on curricular issues, topics covered by ministerial programs (i.e. poems, prose, novels, writers, etc.) or topical issues (such as racism, drugs, autobiographies, etc.).

In the end, most of the projects designed by the teachers' DS did not provide links to organizations outside school. Competence 5. Visual Literacy is considered important, but teachers feel they do not have the visual skills, which could instead be developed by colleagues who teach art (most of the sample were teachers who teach Italian literature). Competence 6. Technical Literacy is considered important, but nevertheless the software used for DS is considered basic and therefore it is not thought that DS is technically difficult. The majority of teachers prefer to share the student video with the class or with the school, but they prefer not to publish their videos on the internet (12. Sharing videos).

The interviews show the following concerns: when teaching underage students, teachers have to face a heavy bureaucratic practice to get the necessary permits and this becomes expensive in terms of time and commitment. This is linked to competence 13. Create Community, which was intended as a class and/or school community, not the wider territorial community or the internet community.

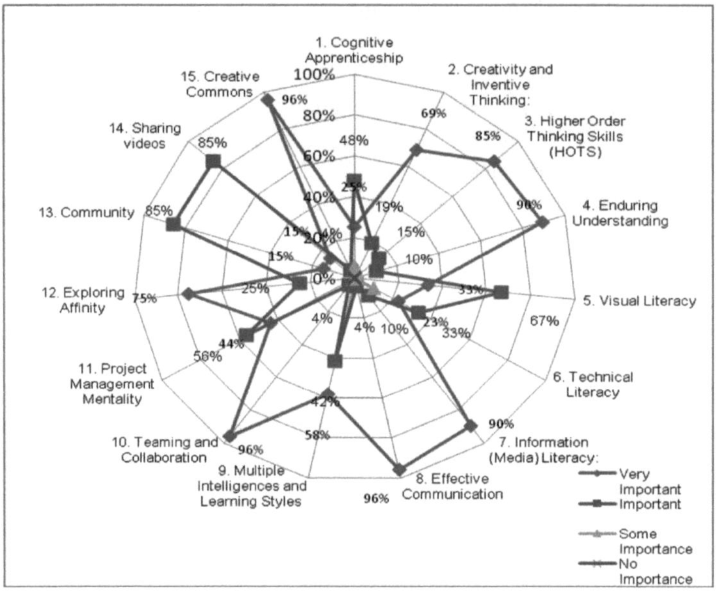

Fig. 2. Stages of DS considered the most critical are those with higher rates

5.3.3 Obstacles to Teachers' Use of DS

Participants were asked what obstacles might hinder the use of DS in their classrooms. Their responses were divided into three categories - "issues of time", "issues of curriculum" and "access to the technologies" - which had been identified as the major obstacles to the use of DS in schools by 95% (46) of respondents.

The interviews showed that teachers complain of having only a few hours a week in order to develop DS. In addition, they were concerned about having to carry out the topics required by ministerial programs (curriculum) to deadlines that the time-consuming development of DS might interfere with. The situation is also complicated by the difficulty of access to computer laboratories. This sample stated that in the schools there is only one classroom with computers, but it must serve all classes. For this reason, teachers need to book the computer laboratory, consistent with the needs of other colleagues, and its availability is not always sufficient for the needs of their educational activities. From the teachers' responses it appears that the hardware and software are often not up-to-date and the technical staff is not always available to solve technical problems. Here are some typical participants' answers:

Interviewee #13 stated: "The critical points are the few hours that we have in high school for teaching. This makes it difficult to devote myself entirely to DS; very often schools do not have up-to-date computer labs and this fact is not of secondary importance; finally, the absence of technical staff discourages the tackling of digital work".

Interviewee #8 stated: "The critical issues are related to the time required for a DS project. The ideal would be to propose it as an extracurricular activity, given the limited time in the morning devoted to school. Knowledge of how to use software needed for DS is not guaranteed: it would therefore be useful to have a course specifically for teachers and students. The computer labs are a critical point: they are not always available and the hardware is not quite up to date".

Interviewee #43 stated: "Among the most problematic situations in the context of the tradition of Italian public secondary schools is probably linked to the spread of multimedia technologies. The difficulty of making a DS video lies mainly within the limits of available hours for my subject (written and oral tests, programming to complete and large classes). There is insufficient time leftover to teach and employ video and audio editing programs".

6 Discussion and Conclusion

The results show that this sample of teachers is in a phase of transition from traditional literacy to digital literacy. There are still many obstacles to overcome which seem less dependent on resistance by teachers but more linked to external constraints (lack of time, ministerial programs, access to technology), as highlighted in the previous section (5.3.3). The results reveal that:

(a) Pre-service teachers show openness and curiosity for innovative methods such as DS. They demonstrate a good familiarity with the technology, although they have only moderate confidence in the integration of the production of DS video in teaching, even if narrative is considered to be a very interesting and productive methodology.

(b) Although these teachers appear familiar with the basic digital technologies, from their answers it emerges that they are resistant to the more advanced practices of web 2.0, such as creating, participating in, and sharing videos on social networks (i.e. YouTube, Vimeo, etc.). The sample appears more inclined to share videos in a protected environment, such as a class group or school. It seems that this choice is due not so much to lack of confidence in the practice of web 2.0, but the perceived need to avoid the bureaucracy required for publication of materials produced by minors on the internet.

(c) This result is also reflected in the selection of the key competences considered important by teachers in their DS projects. It emerges from the interviews that this sample is aware of the potential of DS for the developing of a set of key competencies for digital literacy in teaching and learning. However, if some key competencies are selected above others, this is due less to diffidence or lack of digital skills in the practices of creating and sharing of materials, but results from deliberate choices to avoid logistical or bureaucratic problems of (e.g. authorizations for minors, access to technology) or for reasons of time.

(d) This result is confirmed in the last questionnaire, which investigates what are the obstacles that prevent the use of DS in the classroom. The responses concentrate with great intensity on logistical problems (such as lack of equipment, obsolete computers or insufficient numbers of computer laboratories, as well as hardware and software problems and lack of technical support). They also cite the lack of available time (some stages of DS take a long time to be realized, such as group work, sharing, audio recording, video editing) and the limits due to ministerial programs (i.e. teachers, while recognizing the validity of the method, are under pressure to finish the annual program on time). DS also encounters bureaucratic obstacles, such as requests for permission to publish student work on the internet or to conclude agreements with institutions outside the school or community if the videos are to be open for viewing by the outside world. The interviews reveal that one solution might be for DS to be developed outside of the curriculum hours; however, if DS is used in curricular hours, its structure should be simplified or reduced. Teachers would need the support of school administrators, where these types of activities are encouraged and facilitated.

Finally, in Italy, we would need to profoundly revise the current curriculum of the secondary schools, which is still too rigid to apply learning processes that arise from the nature of digital work, as well as continue to provide substantial support for the training of teachers, and enable them to have enough time to explore the potential of digital storytelling and its uses in the classroom. In fact, the workshop on DS at the university was not without its difficulties: given the high number of teachers who attended the course and the few hours granted to realize their DS projects in the laboratory. However, the collaborative approach of the participants led to positive results and has allowed the realization of this pilot study on the potential of DS in learning.

References

1. Kaiser Family Foundation: Generation M2: Media in the lives of 8-18 year-olds. Henry J. Kaiser Family Foundation, Menlo Park, CA (2010)
2. Hobbs, R.: Digital and Media Literacy: Connecting Culture and Classroom. Corwin Press, Thousand Oaks (2011)
3. Lessig, L.: Remix: Making Art and Commerce Thrive in the Hybrid Economy. Penguin, New York (2008)
4. Mihailidis, P., Cohen, J.: Exploring Curation as a core competency in digital and media literacy education. Journal of Interactive Media in Education (2013), `http://www-jime.open.ac.uk/jime/article/viewArticle/2013-02/html` (retrieved February 16, 2014)
5. Gilster, P.: Digital Literacy. Wiley Computer Publishing, New York (1997)
6. Buckingham, D.: Media Education: Literacy, Learning and Contemporary Culture. Polity Press-Blackwell Publishing, Cambridge (2003)

7. Coutinho, C.P.: Web 2.0 tools in pre-service teacher education programs: An example from Portugal. In: Remenyi, D. (ed.) The Proceedings of the 7th European Conference on e-Learning, pp. 239–245. Academic Publishing Limited, Reading (2008)
8. Robin, B.R.: Digital Storytelling: A Powerful Technology Tool for the 21st Century Classroom. Theory Into Practice 47(3), 220–228 (2008)
9. NETS-T: The ISTE- International Society for Technology in Education, 2008 Report (2008), http://www.iste.org/Content/NavigationMenu/NETS/ForTeachers/2008Standards/NETS_T_Standards_Final.pdf (retrieved February 16, 2014)
10. European Commission: Communication from the Commission to the European Parliament: The Digital Agenda for Europe - Driving European growth digitally. Brussels, 18/12/2012, COM(2012b) 784 (2012). Commission of the European Communities, Brussels, Belgium (2012)
11. European Commission: Europa 2020 una strategia per una crescita intelligente, sostenibile e inclusiva. Commission of the European Communities, Brussels, Belgium (2010)
12. Coutinho, C.P.: Storytelling as a Strategy for Integrating Technologies into the Curriculum: An Empirical Study with Post-Graduate Teachers. In: Maddux, C.D., Ginson, D., Dodge, B. (eds.) Research Highlights in Technology and Teacher Education 2010, pp. 87–97. Society for Information Technology and Teacher Education (SITE), Chesapeake (2010)
13. Sadik, A.: Digital Storytelling: A meaningful technology-integrated approach for engaged student learning. Educational Technology Research and Development 56(4), 487–506 (2008)
14. Di Blas, N., Paolini, P., Sabiescu, A.: Collective digital storytelling at school as a whole-class interaction. In: Proceedings of IDC 2010, New York, NY (2010)
15. Yang, Y.-T.C., Wu, W.-C.I.: Digital storytelling for enhancing student academic achievement, critical thinking, and learning motivation: A year-long experimental study. Computers & Education 59(2), 339–352 (2012)
16. Koohang, A., Riley, L., Smith, T., Schreurs, J.: E-Learning and Constructivism: From Theory to Application. Interdisciplinary Journal of E-Learning & Learning Objects 5(1), 91–109 (2009)
17. Neo, M., Neo, T.K.: Students' Perceptions In Developing A Multimedia Project Within A Constructivist Learning Environment: A Malaysian Experience. TOJET: The Turkish Online Journal of Educational Technology 9(1), 176–184 (2010)
18. Vygotsky, L.S.: Mind in society: The development of higher psychological processes. Harvard University Press, Cambridge (1978)
19. Kanuka, H., Anderson, T.: Using constructivism in technology-mediated learning: Constructing order out of the chaos in the literature. Radical Pedagogy 1(2) (1999), http://www.radicalpedagogy.org/Radical_Pedagogy/Using_Constructivism_in_Technology-Mediated_Learning__Constructing_Order_out_of_the_Chaos_in_the_Literature.html (retrieved February 16, 2014)
20. Tam, M.: Constructivism, instructional design, and technology: Implications for transforming distance learning. Educational Technology & Society 3(2), 50–60 (2000)
21. Jonassen, D.H., Carr, C.S.: Mindtools: Affording multiple knowledge representations for learning. In: Lajoie, S.P. (ed.) Computers as Cognitive Tools, vol. 2, pp. 165–196. Lawrence Erlbaum Associates, Mahwah (2000)
22. Wheatley, G.H.: Constructivist perspectives on science and mathematics learning. Science Education 75(1), 9–21 (1991)
23. Fosnot, C.T.: Constructivism: A psychological theory of learning. In: Fosnot, C.T. (ed.) Constructivism: Theory, Perspectives, and Practice, pp. 8–33. Teachers College Press, New York (1996)

24. Prawat, R.S.: Constructivisms, modern and postmodern. Educational Psychologist 31(3/4), 215–225 (1996)
25. Schön, D.: The reflective practitioner: How professionals think in action. Basic Books, New York (1983)
26. OECD: Giving knowledge for free: The emergence of Open Educational Resources. OECD, Paris, France (2007)
27. UNESCO: 2012 Paris OER Declaration. 2012 World Open Educational Resources (OER) Congress. Unesco, Paris, (2012)
28. Banzato, M.: Barriers to teacher educators seeking, creating and sharing open educational resources: An empirical study of the use of OER in education in Italy. In: 15th International Conference on Interactive Collaborative Learning, ICL (2012), doi:10.1109/ICL.2012.6402105
29. Lambert, J.: Digital Storytelling: Capturing Lives, Creating Community, 3rd edn. Digital Diner Press, Berkeley (2009)
30. Porter, B.: DigiTales: The Art of Telling Digital Stories. DigiTales StoryKeepers, Sedalia (2004)
31. Jakes, D.: Standards-proof your digital storytelling efforts. TechLearning (2006), http://www.techlearning.com/story/showArticle.jhtml?articleID=180204072 (retrieved February 16, 2014)
32. Yerrick, R., Ross, D., Molebash, P.: Too Close for Comfort: Real-Time Science Teaching Reflections via Digital Video Editing. Journal of Science Teacher Education 16(4), 351–375 (2005)
33. Barrett, H.: Storytelling in Higher Education: a Theory of Reflection on Practice to support Deep Learning. In: Society for Information Technology and Teacher Education International Conference 2005, pp. 1878–1883. Association for the Advancement of Computing in Education, Charlottesville (2005)
34. Barrett, H.: Digital Stories in ePortfolios: Multiple Purposes and Tools (2006), http://electronicportfolios.org/digistory/purposes.html (retrieved February 16, 2014)
35. Tendero, A.: Facing Your Selves: The Effects of Digital Storytelling on Teacher Education. Contemporary Issues in Technology and Teacher Education 6(2), 174–194 (2006)
36. Li, L.: Digital Storytelling: Self-Efficacy and Digital Literacy. In: Reeves, T., Yamashita, S. (eds.) Proceedings of World Conference on E-Learning in Corporate, pp. 2159–2164. AACE, Chesapeake (2006)
37. Heo, M.: Digital Storytelling: An empirical study of the impact of digital storytelling on pre-service teachers' self-efficacy and dispositions towards educational technology. Journal of Educational Multimedia and Hypermedia 18(4), 405–428 (2009)
38. Dogan, B., Robin, B.R.: Implementation of Digital Storytelling in the Classroom by Teachers Trained in a Digital Storytelling Workshop. In: McFerrin, K., Weber, R., Carlsen, R., Willis, D.A. (eds.) Proceedings of Society for Information Technology & Teacher Education International Conference 2008, pp. 902–907. AACE, Chesapeake (2008)
39. Kearney, M.: Investigating Digital Storytelling and Portfolios in Teacher Education. In: World Conference on Educational Multimedia. Hypermedia and Telecommunications, Honolulu, HI (2009)

Effect of Principals' Technological Leadership on Teachers' Attitude towards the Use of Educational Technologies

Cevat Celep and Tijen Tülübaş

Kocaeli University, Turkey
tijenozek@hotmail.com

Abstract. In today's world of technology, integration of Information and Communication Technologies (ICT) into education has become crucial. However, without teachers' genuine efforts, it does not seem possible to effectively integrate technology in classroom practice. Teachers' positive attitude towards educational technologies is considered to be essential for the integration of technology into teaching and learning. Research has also shown that principals' technology leadership could be correlated with teachers' integration of educational technology into classroom teaching. This study aims to explore the effect of secondary school principals' technological leadership on teachers' attitude towards educational technology. Data regarding principals' technology leadership were collected using the "Technology Leadership Scale" developed by Sincar in 2009, and data regarding teachers' attitudes towards educational technology were collected using the "Attitude Towards Educational Technology Scale" developed by Pala in 2006. The statistical analysis has revealed that principals' technological leadership had little effect on teachers' positive attitude towards the use of educational technologies and did not have a significant effect on their negative attitude.

Keywords: Technological leadership, educational technology, secondary school.

1 Introduction

In today's world of technology, integration of Information and Communication Technologies (ICT) into education has become crucial in government programs [1] so that the members of modern societies can manage and use excessive information to solve complicated problems and to cope with the evolving demands of the information age. In the emerging knowledge society of our age, educating individuals to be capable of gathering and using information fast and effectively has become a priority for educational institutions. That is why the integration of available technologies into educational processes and the effective use of technological resources has gained importance.

Integration of technology in education has become important in education not only in developed countries but also in developing countries [2]. As a developing country,

D. Passey and A. Tatnall (Eds.): KCICTP/ITEM 2014, IFIP AICT 444, pp. 247–258, 2014.

The Ministry of Education in Turkey has made great efforts and supported major financial investments to integrate ICT into teaching and learning environments. Such projects as e-school, e-registration, e-personnel, e-teacher, the EBA (Education and Informatics Network) and FATIH (Movement of Enhancing Opportunities and Improving Technology) projects have been started to this end. In the scope of the FATİH project, a huge sum of money (800 million Turkish Lira (TL) in 2012 and 1.4 billion TL in 2013) has been invested in developing hardware for schools, distributing tablet personal computers (PCs) to all teachers and students, enabling electronic resources for classroom use, improving Internet connection at schools, developing a technology-friendly curriculum and organizing training events for the teachers and administrators [3]. However, without teachers' genuine efforts, it does not seem possible to effectively integrate technology in classroom practice. Teachers' positive attitudes towards educational technologies are considered to be essential for the integration of technology into teaching and learning. Teo states that teachers are the key players in the integration of technology into education, and highlights the importance of teachers' efficient and appropriate use of technology in maximising teaching and learning [4]. In addition, research shows that teachers' will and competencies in using technology are closely related to their attitude towards educational technologies, which in turn has a great influence on the integration of technology in classroom practice [5, 6, 7, 8, 9, 10].

Leadership is considered to be one of the most influential factors on the practices at school [11]. Anderson and Dexter state that "all of the literature on leadership and technology acknowledges either explicitly or implicitly that school leaders should provide administrative oversight for educational technology" [12]. There is some research which supports this view, stating that technology leadership has a significant influence on teachers' technology use [13, 14, 15, 16]. However, there is some other research which highlights that teachers' beliefs, competencies and perceptions regarding the use of technology could determine their use of technology in class and leadership might not be as influential on their attitude as expected [4, 17, 18, 19, 20]. The review of the literature reveals some controversial findings about the influence of school principals' technology leadership on teachers' attitudes towards educational technologies.

2 The Principal as a Technology Leader

According to Dougherty et al., a technology leader "enables others to effectively and successfully use, manage, assess, and understand technologies of the designed world" [21]. As a technology leader, a school principal needs to understand and be capable of using recent technologies. More importantly, a technology leader should understand and manage the changes brought by the technological advancements as well as supporting the teaching staff through developing their confidence in and capabilities of using technology at school [22].

The literature on the qualities of a technology leader mainly indicates four aspects [23, 24, 25]: *human-centeredness; communication and cooperation; vision;* and *support*. Being human-centered means that decisions and practices at school are centered on the needs and expectations of school staff. In other words, technology leaders show regard to ethics, justice and equity in technology use as well as being vigilant about the issues related to technology use [24]. Another factor that affects technology leadership is interpersonal and communication skills [14, 25, 26, 27, 28, 29]. Technology leaders need to be able to use technology to carry out their own duties and to communicate with others [12]. Chang et al. even state that interpersonal and communication skills are much more important for technology leaders than having technological expertise, because they cannot convey this expertise without these skills [23]. Another important quality of a technology leader is being visionary and establishing a vision at school that fosters the integration of technology in education and receives support from all the stakeholders [12, 28, 29, 30, 31, 32]. Ross and Bailey state that vision is essential to give school staff direction and guidance for the proper integration of technology into classroom practice [33]. Supporting teachers in understanding and using technology, providing necessary hardware and software and being a model for the efficient use of technology is another significant characteristic of a technology leader [12, 34, 35, 36].

Recently, numerous studies have been done about the attitudes of school principals towards technology and their technological leadership qualities [22, 37, 38, 39, 40, 41, 42, 43]. However, many of these studies do not focus on the effect of these qualities on teachers' attitudes towards integrating technology into teaching processes. Moreover, the review of the literature shows some controversial findings regarding the effect of technology leadership on teachers' attitude towards the use of technology. Therefore, studies investigating the relationship between these two constructs might shed light on the future discussions regarding the issue.

This study aims to explore the effect of secondary school principals' technology leadership on teachers' attitude towards educational technology and the way they use technology at school. As mentioned earlier, there are not enough studies in the literature that examine the effect of principals' technology leadership on teachers' attitudes towards educational technology. This study is considered to contribute to the literature in this respect. Furthermore, findings of the study could shed light on regulations regarding the integration of technology into education.

3 Teachers' Attitude towards Technology

Teachers' attitude towards technology is considered to be a key factor in integrating technology in classroom interaction [2, 4, 8, 17, 18, 44, 45, 46]. Huang and Liav state that implementation of technology depends on the positive attitude towards it rather than the state of technology at school [45]. Teo points out the fact that teachers' positive feelings towards the use of technology would reinforce their intentions to use it [4]. Davis et al. state that teachers' behavioral intentions to use technology are determined by their attitudes towards it [18].

In the literature, mainly three theories are mentioned in order to explain teachers' use of technology: the Technology Acceptance Model (TAM) [17], the Theory of Planned Behaviour (TPB) [47] and the Unified Theory of Acceptance and Use of Technology (UTAUT) [44]. TAM specifies perceived usefulness, perceived ease of use, attitude towards use and behavioral intention to use technology. According to TPB, teachers' behavioral intentions to use technology are shaped by their attitude towards technology, subjective norms (that is, the extent to which people important to the teacher think the use of technology is important and beneficial) and teachers' perceived behavioral control regarding technology use (that is, their perception of how easy or difficult it would be to use technology). In addition to these theories, Christensen and Knezek developed the model of Will Skill Tool [8]. The model postulates that teachers' will, skill and access to technology tools are necessary to integrate technology in classroom instruction. Common to all these theories or models is the importance of teachers' attitude towards the use of educational technologies. As pointed out earlier, teachers are the key players in integrating technology into actual classroom practice and it seems impossible without teachers' positive approaches to the use of educational technologies.

4 Method

This is a relational descriptive study that aims to determine the effect of school principals' technology leadership on teachers' attitude towards educational technologies. The universe of the study comprises 320 teachers working at secondary schools in Tekirdağ, Turkey. Questionnaires were distributed to the whole universe and 255 questionnaires were returned. Three of the questionnaires were incomplete, so they were not included in the analysis. The remaining 252 questionnaires were included in the analysis. One hundred and thirty-two (52.4%) of the participants were female and 120 (47.6%) were male. Twenty (7.9%) of the participants were aged between 21-30 years, 104 (41.3%) were aged between 31-40 years, 102 (40.5%) were aged 41-50 years and 26 (10.3%) were aged over 51 years. Eighty-eight (34.9%) of the participants teach physical sciences (mathematics, physics, chemistry, biology), 90 (35.7%) teach humanities (literature, geography, history, philosophy, psychology), 62 (24.6%) teach languages (English and German) and 12 (4.8%) teach fine arts.

Data regarding principals' technology leadership were collected using the "Technology Leadership Scale" developed by Sincar [24]. The scale has four factors (human-centeredness, communication and interaction, vision and supportiveness) and the Cronbach's Alpha was .98. Data regarding teachers' attitude towards educational technology were collected using the "Attitude towards Educational Technology Scale" developed by Pala [48]. The scale has two factors (positive and negative) and the Cronbach's Alpha for the positive attitude factor was .95 and Cronbach's Alpha for the negative attitude factor was .84. Cronbach's Alpha shows the internal consistency of a scale and indicates the reliability of the scale used in the research. Scales are usually required to have a reliability of .70 or more. Thus, scales used in this research can be accepted as reliable.

5 Discussion

This study aimed to analyze the effect of technology leadership on secondary school teachers' attitudes towards the use of educational technologies in classroom practice. First, teachers' attitudes towards educational technology use and their perceptions regarding school principals' technology leadership were analysed using descriptive statistics. Then, the effect of perceived technology leadership on teachers' attitudes towards educational technology was analysed using a regression test.

5.1 Teachers' Attitudes towards the Use of Educational Technologies

The results of the analysis showed that teachers have positive rather than negative attitudes towards the use of educational technologies. The results of the statistical analysis can be seen in Table 1.

Table 1. Teachers' Attitudes towards Educational Technology

	N	$\overline{X}$	SS
Positive Attitude	252	3.964	0.611
Negative Attitude	252	2.285	0.565

According to the results of the analysis, it can be said that teachers have positive attitudes towards technology use in class. According to Davis's theory of TAM [17], perceived ease of use affects perceived usefulness and, as a result, the attitude towards use. Teo states that facilitating conditions such as providing technology tools might have a greater effect on teachers' use of technology than the behaviours of school principals [4]. As mentioned earlier, in the scope of the FATIH project, schools have been provided with interactive whiteboards and projectors as well as computers and Internet connection. As such, teachers have been provided with a large amount of free and ready-to-use electronic resources within the EBA (Education and Informatics Network) project. All these developments might have increased teachers' perceived ease of use and this might have increased their positive attitude towards the use of educational technologies.

However, it should also be noted that the findings show teachers have some levels of negative attitudes towards educational technology use. These teachers seem to believe that technology could hurt teachers' discipline in class. They also indicate that use of educational technologies could not be appropriate for testing purposes and could not be suitable to teach some subject areas.

These findings might suggest that teachers are influenced by traditional beliefs about teaching and testing which usually focuses on teacher-centeredness. Ertmer et al. [1] suggest that technology be placed in the hands of students and they should be supported to use technology to communicate, collaborate and solve problems using more complicated thinking skills. A student-centered approach and a collaborative classroom environment are considered to be a prerequisite to the effective use of technology in class [1, 49, 50, 51, 52, 53, 54]. In addition, it might be considered that teachers are not well informed about the use of educational technologies for testing purposes and student-centered education. This idea could be supported by teachers' answers to two questions asked on the data collection form. The first question was about whether they received any training about the use of technology in class. Two hundred and twenty-four (88.9%) of the participants indicated that they received in-service training. However, 146 of these participants have only attended one training event within the scope of the FATIH project. With this project, it was aimed to build interactive whiteboard systems at schools and to connect this system with tablet PCs which were distributed to teachers and students for free. At the beginning of the 2013-2014 school year, teachers were trained about the use of these interactive whiteboards. One hundred and four of the participants have indicated that they attended courses on the use of Microsoft Office programs and web page design. As a result, it can be seen that teachers only received training on how to use some technological devices rather than ways of integrating educational technologies into education processes. In addition, during the data collection period, teachers complained that the Internet connection was not offered effectively. They also noted that the scope of in-service training courses regarding the integration of technology was not enough in terms of content and length.

Two hundred and thirty-four (92.9%) of the research participants noted that they used educational technologies in class. However, 118 of these participants stated that they only used the interactive whiteboard in classroom interactions and 44 indicated that they used the Internet to do research while they prepared lessons or examinations. Seventy-six of the teachers using interactive whiteboards indicated that they used it to show videos or visuals, 62 reported using it at the presentation stage of the lesson, 30 to do extra tests and exercises, 28 to make the lesson more enjoyable, and 8 to use time more efficiently. These findings show that providing an interactive whiteboard for every classroom affected the integration of technology in classroom instruction. However, it should be noted that teachers need to be offered more training on using interactive whiteboards in a way that leads to a more student-centered education process.

5.2 Perceived Technology Leadership of School Principals

Analysis of the data regarding teachers' perceptions of school principals' technology leadership showed that school principals demonstrate a good level of technology leadership ($\overline{X}$ =3.39). However, the finding indicates teachers partially agree that their school principals are technology leaders, which might mean that they have higher expectations from their school leaders as a technology leader.

Table 2. Perceived Technology Leadership of School Principals

	N	$\overline{X}$	SS
Human-centeredness	252	3.42	0.75
Support	252	3.40	0.84
Communication and cooperation	252	3.35	0.75
Vision	252	3.34	0.78
TOTAL	252	3.39	0.73

As technology leaders, school leaders according to teachers (see Table 2) seem to be human-centered and supportive. Compared to these two dimensions, they seem to be less visionary, communicative and cooperative, which indicates that school leaders might not be as future oriented as expected in promoting the use of technology at school. Also, they might not be using technology efficiently for better communication with school staff and stakeholders. However, developing a schoolwide shared vision for technology and involvement of the stakeholders in the enabling and development of necessary technological structures are considered to be a priority for an effective technology leadership [12, 29, 31]. Therefore, it is important that school principals try to understand the direction and trends of technology development and maintain a clear technology vision as well as having necessary interpersonal and communication skills to convey this understanding and vision to the stakeholders.

5.3 Effect of Technology Leadership on Teachers' Attitudes towards the Use of Educational Technologies

Although school principals are considered to be good technology leaders, this seems to have little effect on teachers' attitudes towards educational technology (see Table 3). In other words, it can be said that teachers have a positive attitude towards using technology in class regardless of principals' support as a technology leader.

In addition, technology leadership does not have a significant effect on teachers' negative attitudes towards educational technologies. In other words, teachers' negative attitudes towards technology use in classroom practice seem to be related to some other factors rather than technology leadership. Teachers' negative attitudes towards educational technologies might be related to some background factors such as technology infrastructure [12], teachers' beliefs about teaching [1] or teachers' beliefs about technology [17, 46].

Table 3. Effects of Technology Leadership on Teachers' Attitudes towards Educational Technology

	B	SE	β	T	p
Constant	3.305	0,178		18,516	0,000
Technology Leadership	0.195	0,052	0,232	3,776	0,000

Dependent Variable: *Positive Attitude*

F=14. 259 **R=0.232** **R^2=0.054** **p < .01**

	B	SE	β	T	p
Constant	2.527	0,169		14,952	0,000
Technology Leadership	0.071	0,049	0,092	1,462	0,145

Dependent Variable: *Negative Attitude*

F=2.137 **R=0.092** **R^2=0.008** **p > .01**

Teo indicates that teachers' intentions to use technology could be much more related to perceived ease of use and perceived usefulness rather than technology leadership of school leaders [4]. He also points out that the environment in which teachers use technology could be more important than the support of school principals. Robert and Handerson state that teachers might depend on their sense of professional duty and personal interest to integrate technology in education rather than an institutional mandate such as a school principal [19]. Another reason why technology leadership did not have a considerable effect on teachers' attitudes towards technology could be linked to the centralist organisation of the educational institutions in Turkey. In other words, the centralised management system in Turkey does not give much autonomy to school principals, especially in terms of finance and resource acquisition. Therefore, the Ministry of Education is considered to be responsible for providing technology tools and promoting the use of technology at schools. That is why the recent initiatives taken by the Ministry might have been more effective than school principals' technology leadership on teachers' attitudes towards technology. Similarly, as Ajzen states in the theory of planned behaviour [47], subjective norm, that is, the extent to which people important to the individual think the behaviour should be performed could influence teachers' attitudes towards technology use. In our study, teachers could have regarded the Ministry as their subjective norm and the recent focus of the Ministry on the use of technology might have resulted in their positive attitude towards the use of technology.

Analysis of the dimensions of technology leadership demonstrated that being supportive and visionary has more influence on teachers' positive attitude towards educational technologies (see Table 4). In other words, school principals who are

Table 4. Effects of Technology Leadership Dimensions on Teachers' Positive Attitudes towards Educational Technology

	B	SE	β	T	p
Constant	3.361	0.177		19.042	0.000
Human-centeredness	0.176	0.050	0.216	3.495	0.001
	Dependent Variable: *Positive Attitude*				
	F=12. 216	**R=0.216**	**R^2=0.047**	**p < .01**	
Constant	3.387	0.157		21.544	0.000
Support	0.170	0.045	0.233	3.783	0.000
	Dependent Variable: *Positive Attitude*				
	F=14.308	**R=0.233**	**R^2=0.054**	**p > .01**	
Constant	3.411	0.174		19.514	0.000
Communication and Cooperation	0.165	0.051	0.202	3.258	0.001
	Dependent Variable: *Positive Attitude*				
	F=10.616	**R=0.202**	**R^2=0.041**	**p > .01**	
Constant	3.368	0.165		20.442	0.000
Vision	0.178	0.048	0.229	3.715	0.000
	Dependent Variable: *Positive Attitude*				
	F=13.800	**R=0.229**	**R^2=0.057**	**p > .01**	

future-directed about the use of technology at school, who can follow and share technological developments with school staff and who can improve facilities and offer opportunities for the integration of technology might help develop a positive attitude towards technology use at school.

As Ross and Bailey state, technology leaders should provide teachers with a vision which directs and guides the integration of technology into education [33]. Inkster notes that creating a vision regarding the use of technology by both teachers and students is a significant indicator of a principals' technology leadership [29]. Bailey highlights the importance of providing access to technology resources and increasing opportunities to acquire these resources as well as pointing out the significance of providing service and technical support in schools [31]. Our findings support these ideas from the literature, although the effect of technology leadership seems to be inconsiderable.

6 Conclusion

A review of the literature demonstrates controversial findings on the effect of school principals' technological leadership on teachers' attitudes towards technology. Although many researchers indicate the importance of leadership in the effective integration of new technologies in teaching and learning [13, 14, 15, 16], there are some researchers that suggest teachers' perceptions regarding technology could be more influential in their use of technology [4, 17, 18, 19, 20].

The findings of our study support the second view, in that technology leadership had a little effect on teachers' positive attitudes towards technology use, and did not have a significant effect on their negative attitudes. This is considered to be the result of recent initiatives taken by the Turkish Ministry of Education, especially the FATİH project. In the scope of the FATIH project, schools are provided with interactive whiteboards and projectors as well as computers and Internet connection. As such, teachers are provided with a large amount of free and ready-to-use electronic resources. These developments might have increased teachers' perceived ease of use and this might have increased their positive attitudes towards the use of educational technologies. In addition, the centralised management system of education in Turkey could be another reason why school principals' technology leadership did not have a significant influence on teachers' attitudes towards technology. As a result of this management system, the Ministry of Education is in charge of providing technology tools and promoting the use of technology at schools. Therefore, the recent initiatives taken by the Ministry might have been more effective on teachers' attitudes towards technology. Similarly, teachers' could have regarded the Ministry as their subjective norm rather than school principals, and the recent focus of the Ministry on the use of technology might have resulted in their positive attitudes towards the use of technology.

Although teachers were found to have a positive attitude towards educational technologies, there are still teachers who are cautious about using technology in classroom interactions. In addition, our investigation revealed that teachers are trying to use technology in a way that supports their traditional teacher-based views of teaching. However, it is highlighted in the literature that effective use of technology in teaching and learning requires a student-centered approach to teaching [52, 55]. Therefore, teachers should be offered courses where they can find the opportunity to adopt new approaches to teaching to integrate technology more efficiently into classroom practice. Moreover, rapid technological changes require on-going training for teachers so that they can develop more advanced skills and knowledge on the use of educational technologies. In short, teacher professional development should be central in the management of technology integration into education processes.

Further empirical and theoretical work seems to be necessary in order to understand the role of school principals as technology leaders as well as to identify factors that affect the attitude of teachers towards educational technologies. The use of technology in education has become significant globally and also culture is considered to be influential in the use of technologies [56]. Therefore, further studies could be conducted to compare the use of educational technologies in different countries and cultures.

References

1. Ertmer, P.A., Ottenbreit-Leftwich, A.T., Sadık, O., Sendurur, E., Sendurur, P.: Teacher beliefs and technology interaction practices: A critical relationship. Computers & Education 59, 423–435 (2012)
2. Agyei, D.D., Voogt, J.M.: Exploring the potential of the will, skill, tool model in Ghana: Predicting prospective and practicing teachers' use of technology. Computers & Education 56, 91–100 (2011)
3. MEB: (2014), http://www.fatihprojesi.com/?pnum=9&pt=PROJE%20B%C4%B0LE%C5%9EENLER%C4%B0 (retrieved on February 20, 2014)
4. Teo, T.: Factors influencing teachers' intention to use technology: Model development and test. Computer & Science 57, 2432–2440 (2011)
5. Woodrow, J.E.: The influence of programming training on the computer literacy and attitudes of preservice teachers. Journal of Research on Computing in Education 25(2), 200–218 (1992)
6. Ross, T.W.: Research, development, and validation of a principal's handbook for implementing technology based learning methods in information-age school. Doctoral Dissertation, Kansas State University, Manhattan, KS (1993)
7. Myers, J.M., Halpin, R.: Teachers' attitudes and use of multimedia technology in the classroom: Constructivist-based professional development training for school districts. Journal of Computing in Teacher Education 18(4), 133–140 (2002)
8. Christensen, R., Knezek, G.: Instruments for assessing the impact of technology in education. Computers in the Schools 18(2), 5–25 (2002)
9. Morales, C.: Cross-cultural validation of the will, skill, tool model of technology integration. Doctoral Dissertation, University of North Texas, Denton, TX (2006)
10. Marshall, G., Cox, M.: Research methods: Their design, applicability and reliability. In: Voogt, J., Knezek, G. (eds.) International Handbook of Information Technology in Primary and Secondary Education. Springer, New York (2008)
11. Hoy, W.K., Miskel, C.G.: Educational administration: Theory, research, and practice, 9th edn. McGraw-Hill, New York (2013)
12. Anderson, R.E., Dexter, S.: School Technology Leadership: An Empirical Investigation of Prevalence and Effect. Educational Administration Quarterly 41(49), 49–82 (2005)
13. Aten, B.M.: An analysis of the nature of educational technology leadership in California's SB 1274 restructuring schools. Doctoral dissertation, University of San Francisco, San Francisco, CA (1996)

14. Murphy, D.T., Gunter, G.A.: Technology integration: The importance of administrative supports. Educational Media International 34(3), 136–139 (1997)
15. Hughes, M., Zachariah, S.: An investigation into the relationship between effective administrative leadership styles and the use of technology. International Electronic Journal for Leadership in Learning (2001), `http://ucalgary.ca/iefll/volume5/hughes.html` (retrieved January 4, 2014)
16. Deryakulu, D., Olkun, S.: Technology leadership and supervision: an analysis based on Turkish computer teachers' professional memories. Technology, Pedagogy and Education 18(1), 45–58 (2009)
17. Davis, F.D.: Perceived usefulness, perceived ease of use, and user acceptance of information technology. MIS Quarterly: Management Information Systems 13, 319–339 (1989)
18. Davis, F.D., Bagozzi, R.P., Warshaw, P.R.: User Acceptance of Computer Technology: A Comparison of Two Theoretical Models. Management Science 35(8), 982–1002 (1989)
19. Robert, P., Henderson, R.: Information technology acceptance in a sample of government employees: A test of the technology acceptance model. Interacting with Computer 12, 427–443 (2000)
20. Hayytov, D.: Eğitim Yöneticileri Teknoloji Liderliği Yeterlik Algıları ile Öğretmenlerin Teknolojiye Yönelik tutumları Arasındaki İlişki. Dissertation, Gazi University, Ankara, Turkey (2013)
21. Dougherty, J.L., Mentzer, N.J., Lybrook, D.O., Little-Wiles, J.: Philosophical Perspectives on Technology Leadership. In: Wang, S., Hartsell, T. (eds.) Technology Integration and Foundations for Effective Leadership. Information Science Reference, Hershey (2013)
22. Akbaba-Altun, S.: Okul yöneticilerinin teknolojiye karşı tutumlarının incelenmesi. Çağdaş Eğitim 286, 8–14 (2002)
23. Chang, I., Chin, J.M., Hsu, C.: Teachers' Perceptions of the dimensions and Implementation of Technology Leadership of Principals in Taiwanese Elementary Schools. Educational Technology & Society 11(4), 229–245 (2008)
24. Sincar, M.: İlköğretim Okulu Yöneticilerinin Teknoloji Liderliği Rollerine İlişkin Bir İnceleme (Gaziantep İli Örneği). Dissertation. İnönü Üniversitesi Sosyal Bilimler Enstitüsü, Malatya, Turkey (2009)
25. Chang, I.: The Effect of Principals' Technological Leadership on Teachers' Technological Literacy and Teaching Effectiveness in Taiwanese Elementary Schools. Educational Technology & Society 15(2), 328–340 (2012)
26. Roy, D.: Educational technology leadership for the age of restructuring. The Computing Teacher 19(6), 8–14 (1992)
27. Bailey, G.D., Lumley, D.: Technology staff development programs. A leadership sourcebook for school administrators. Scholastic, New York (1994)
28. Jewell, M.J.: The art and craft of technology leadership. Learning and Leading with Technology 26(4), 46–47 (1998)
29. Inkster, C.D.: Technology leadership in elementary school principals: A comparative case study. Doctoral Dissertation, University of Minnesota, Minneapolis, MN (1998)
30. Cory, S.: Can your district become an instructional technology leader? The School Administrator, Special Issue, 17–19 (1990)
31. Bailey, G.D.: What technology leaders need to know: The essential top 10 concepts for technology integration in the 21st century? Learning & Leading with Technology 25(1), 57–62 (1997)
32. Bridges, J.W.: Principal influence: Sustaining a vision for powerful new forms of learning using technology. Doctoral dissertation, University of California, Los Angeles, CA (2003)
33. Ross, T.W., Bailey, G.D.: Technology-based learning: A handbook for teachers and technology leaders. IRI/Skylight, Arlington Heights, IL (1996)
34. Robinson, B.: Technology leadership in the English educational system: From computer systems to systematic management of computers. In: Kearsley, G., Lynch, W. (eds.) Educational Technology: Leadership Perspectives. Educational Technology, New Jersey (1994)

35. Kinnaman, D.E.: What it really means to integrate technology. Technology & Learning 14(8), 130–141 (1994)
36. Ford, J.I.: Identifying technology leadership competencies for Nebraska's K-12 technology leaders. Doctoral Dissertation, University of Nebraska, Lincoln, NE (2000)
37. Can, T.: Bolu orta öğretim okulları yöneticilerinin teknolojik liderlik yeterlilikleri. The Turkish Online Journal of Educational Technology 2(3), 94–107 (2003)
38. Cerit, Y.: Küreselleşme sürecinde ilköğretim okulu yöneticilerinin nitelikleri. Abant İzzet Baysal Üniversitesi Eğitim Fakültesi Dergisi 4(8), 1–11 (2004)
39. Akbaba-Altun, S., Gürer, M.D.: School administrators' perceptions of their roles regarding information technology classrooms. Eurasian Journal of Educational Research 33, 35–54 (2008)
40. Helvacı, M.A.: Okul yöneticilerinin teknolojiye karşı tutumlarının incelenmesi. Ankara Üniversitesi Eğitim Bilimleri Fakültesi Dergisi 41(1), 115–133 (2008)
41. Karadağ, E., Sağlam, H., Baloğlu, N.: Bilgisayar destekli eğitim: İlköğretim okulu yöneticilerinin tutumlarına ilişkin bir araştırma. Uluslararası Sosyal Araştırmalar Dergisi 1(3), 251–266 (2008)
42. Seferoğlu, S.S.: İlköğretim okullarında teknoloji kullanımı ve yöneticilerin bakış açıları. Akademik Bilişim, 1–6 (2009)
43. Hacıfazlıoğlu, Ö., Karadeniz, Ş., Dalgıç, G.: Eğitim Yöneticileri Teknoloji Liderliği Standartlarına Ilişkin Öğretmen, Yönetici ve Denetmenlerin Görüşleri. Kuram ve Uygulamada Eğitim Yönetimi 16(4), 537–577 (2010)
44. Venkatesh, V., Morris, M.G., Davis, G.B., Davis, F.D.: User Acceptance of Information Technology: Toward a Unified View. MIS Quarterly 27(3), 425–478 (2003)
45. Huang, H.M., Liaw, S.S.: Exploring users' attitudes and intentions toward the web as a survey tool. Computers in Human Behavior 21(5), 729–743 (2005)
46. Meelissen, M.: Computer attitudes and competencies among primary and secondary school students. In: Voogt, J., Knezek, G. (eds.) International Handbook of Information Technology in Primary Secondary Education. Springer, New York (2008)
47. Ajzen, I.: The Theory of Planned Behavior. Organizational Behavior and Human Decision Processes 50, 179–211 (1991)
48. Pala, A.: İlköğretim birinci kademe öğretmenlerinin eğitim teknolojilerine yönelik tutumları. Celal Bayar Üniversitesi Eğitim Fakültesi Sosyal Bilimler Dergisi 16, 179–188 (2006)
49. Hadley, M., Sheingold, K.: Commonalties and distinctive patterns in teachers' integration of computers. American Journal of Education 101, 261–315 (1993)
50. Becker, H.J.: How exemplary computer-using teachers differ from other teachers: implications for realizing the potential of computers in schools. Journal of Research on Computing in Education 26, 291–321 (1994)
51. Dexter, S.L., Anderson, R.E.: USA: A model of implementation effectiveness (2002), `http://edtechcases.info/papers/multicase_implementation.htm` (retrieved September 20, 2013)
52. McCain, T.: Teaching for tomorrow: Teaching content and problem-solving skills. Corwin, Thousand Oaks (2005)
53. Judson, E.: How teachers integrate technology and their beliefs about learning: Is there a connection? Journal of Technology and Teacher Education 14, 581–597 (2006)
54. Andrew, L.: Comparison of teacher educators' instructional methods with the constructivist ideal. The Teacher Educator 42(3), 157–184 (2007)
55. Means, B., Olson, K.: Technology and Education Reform. Office of Educational Research and Improvement, Washington, DC (1997)
56. Gullivan, M., Srite, M.: Information technology and culture: Identifying fragmentary and holistic perspectives of culture. Information and Organisation 15, 295–338 (2005)

Creating Knowledge Sharing Culture via Social Network Sites at School: A Research Intended for Teachers

Cevat Celep, Tuğba Konaklı, and Nur Kuyumcu

Kocaeli University, Umuttepe Campus, 41380, Kocaeli, Turkey
celep@kocaeli.edu.tr

Abstract. Social networks, like forums, friendship sites, music sharing sites etc., are gaining importance in a quickly changing world. They are also becoming a current issue on the agenda of an 'education' sector who wants to be harmonized with the changing world. Social networks which students admire make educators think about how a speedy, pervious and structured Internet could be used in an educational concept besides its entertaining aspect. Activating these features of social networks may clear away the obstacles of a knowledge sharing culture which originated from existing organization concerned with the individual and technology in educational organizations. This research aims at investigating which functions of Internet are preferred by educators and recommends what can be done to develop a knowledge sharing culture via social networks at school. Data have been gathered from 13 teachers via semi-structured and open-ended questions. The instrument used in this study was the interview. The data were coded and transformed into categories. The results showed that teachers mostly use the social networks Facebook, YouTube and Google+.

Keywords: Social networks, knowledge sharing culture, teachers, content analysis.

1 Introduction

Social network lexically means "individuals (partnerships and roles in rare situations) that are connected to each other with one or more social relations, and thus form a social bond" [1]. These relational bonds can include affinity, communication, friendship, and authority. Social networks likewise establish a virtual "community" and act together, share ideas, produce solutions, and undertake similar studies.

Networks in an educational sense support change and sustainability of change. Social and professional networks connected by users via the Internet get connected to each other through interaction, relation and shared information and with time this transforms into professional support [2].

The first website examples fitting the social networking definition were "Classmates.com" (in 1995) and "SixDegrees.com" (in 1997). Whereas Classmates.com particularly offered a way to find ex-classmates, SixDegrees.com offered profile making and friends, listing opportunities to users [3].

D. Passey and A. Tatnall (Eds.): KCICTP/ITEM 2014, IFIP AICT 444, pp. 259–264, 2014.

Social network services can be defined as web pages that collect beneficial information online, share it with others and provide an environment to communicate with other people. Social networks such as "MySpace", "Facebook", "Hi5" and "Cyworld" enable their users to interact with other people with similar interests by participating in groups or creating groups [4]. Another social network system is the blog. Blogs are websites that can be updated regularly and display text entries in reverse chronological order (the most recent entry first) and cover text, images, news, etc. [5]. In contrast, the wiki is composed of web pages that allow users to edit them as they wish. It is a free environment where all individuals can reach and change information on any subject. Facebook, the most popular social network, is known as the social network used by students most [6].

Generally, social network services are based on friendship, affinity, interests and activities. However, this is not the only function of social network services. These networks enable individuals to share information, establish and develop relations, etc. Social network websites enable people working inside and outside of organizations to communicate with their colleagues. Cooperation, by utilizing social networks, provides opportunity to exchange information between education implementers and information producers (universities). Even though social networks are used in an informal manner, they bear the potential to be used to support teaching and learning activities. Besides providing more apparent identities for class discussion socially, social networks can host several learning styles inside and outside of a class by communicating with users in a more individual manner [7]. Social networks have properties such as developing student and teacher communication abilities, expanding participation, strengthening peer support, and enabling cooperation based learning [8]. Social networks can improve student learning, enable interactions between school-student and student-student relations, increase access of students with regards to lessons, improve writing skills of students, and these networks can be integrated into lessons easily [9]. Social networks form an environment where teachers participating associate their personal and professional identities and teachers also use Facebook groups so as to form a teacher network and cooperate [10, 11].

Children and young people gain basic skills and competencies necessary for schools and work places on their own by interacting with popular culture [12]. Social networks can be used for digital media sharing among students, asking questions, sharing lesson-related resources, creating study groups and communicating with classmates [13].

Knowledge sharing among individuals is defined as a process which covers exchange of knowledge with other individuals so as to make them understand, adopt and use it [14]. It is very crucial in knowledge sharing that knowledge comes out of one source and reaches a certain target. This is the way knowledge sharing distinguishes itself from knowledge transfer. Knowledge sharing behaviour includes the highest contribution to organizational activity and covers individual behaviours of working people such as sharing existing work knowledge, competencies and experiences with other employees [15].

Technological facilities such as Internet and social network websites play an important role in strengthening collaboration between new members and experienced members [16].

While many traditional web applications focus on the delivery of content, social networks such as blogs, wikis, and podcasts focus on social connectivity and since these instruments are managed with participation and interaction of users, it is stated that they highly support knowledge sharing and collaboration necessary for social and active learning [17].

2 Method

This research is designed with a qualitative method and aims at determining at which level and with which purposes social networks are used by teachers in their knowledge sharing with their administrators and managers, students, other colleagues and parents. To this end, a semi-structured interview form that included open-ended questions was applied to a working group consisting of 13 teachers. The population of the study consisted of randomly selected teachers working in primary schools in the İzmit/Kocaeli district. The data obtained were examined through content analysis.

3 Discussion

Teachers who participated in this study stated that they mostly used social networks "to share knowledge and resources with educators". It was found that teachers widely prefer social networks such as Facebook, Google+ and e-school. E-school is an information management system prepared by the Ministry of Education enabling duplex communication particularly with parents. Teachers who follow policy makers, trade unions and government bodies on Twitter and establish contact with them, use e-blogs in order to create diaries for lessons.

Teachers pointed out that administrators and managers widely preferred Facebook in announcing school events and in-service training programs, developing project cooperation, reminding about the times of school meetings, discussing regulation amendments, and enlightening teachers and students about social issues. Teachers stating their administrators and managers did not use social networks noted that this stemmed from not trusting an informal environment, not delivering the content quickly and accurately, manipulation of knowledge, thinking of possible misuse of information due to virtual environments, and open characteristics of social networks.

Teachers explained that they mostly used social networks to share school activities and information regarding education and assessment processes. Apart from that, YouTube was the social network preferred by all of the teachers included in the study due to its educational videos that were used in lessons. Teachers share contents by loading course content, quizzes, homework, study forms, videos, and Microsoft (MS) PowerPoint presentations in the groups they create with their students on Facebook, Wikispace and Google +. One of the obstacles of a knowledge sharing culture teachers try to establish in schools is students' lack of knowledge and desire to use social networks effectively.

Teachers indicated that they share files, records, audio-visual materials relating to lessons, and also establish networks in the preparation phase for assessment tools and share materials with their colleagues via social networks such as Facebook, Google + , and Twitter. Teachers also point out that lesson plans, materials, working papers, MS PowerPoint presentations, etc. prepared in collaboration with district schools are shared through Wikispace and additionally, seminar and training announcements among teachers are communicated through social networks. Schools create virtual networks where best practices are shared, by sharing photographs of school activities on Instagram. It is known that discussion groups are formed among teachers to discuss the future of the profession, improvement of conditions and sharing of up-to-date information in various forums. Teachers admit that they particularly benefit from social networks in knowledge sharing with colleagues living a long distance away and social networks are indispensable for them.

The teachers who participated in the study stated that they especially use e-school in knowledge sharing with parents. However, leaving aside the social networking function of e-school, they also expressed they use e-school as an announcement system that reports academic success, absenteeism and disciplinary status of students to parents. Most of the teachers do not deem it appropriate to share information with parents on Facebook. They prefer e-school since it is secure software and accessed with personal passwords whereas Facebook makes data accessible for everyone. Teachers think that parents should not know about their personal ideas and private life; this can lead to prejudices in parents. Besides, teachers put forward that knowledge sharing with parents on social networks can draw them into lazy practice and diminish their physical presence in schools and thus school-family collaboration will dwindle. Especially as the teachers received reactions by parents when they share visuals on Facebook belonging to students, they prefer not to share information on students or activities through these social networks. However, some teachers emphasize that knowledge sharing on such social networks increases a sense of belonging about their schools for each stakeholder.

4 Conclusion

Generalizing the use of social networks among teachers is crucial in terms of rendering education processes more up-to-date and functional. Considering that students use technology in more effective and beneficial ways than teachers, the outcomes of creating a knowledge sharing culture through social networks by the teachers keeping up with these trends will favourably affect education processes in schools.

As a result of this research, it is seen that the knowledge sharing through social networks is limited mostly in parent-teacher relations. In order to increase this sharing, parents should be informed of social networks and their consciousness should be raised to the harmlessness of secure knowledge sharing. Moreover, it is understood from responses of teachers that teachers do not limit knowledge sharing for the purpose of education; they are concerned with sharing their personal information and thus they are afraid of change in the attitude of parents towards them.

Disapproval of knowledge sharing on social networks by administrators, managers and parents can be associated with organization culture. The bureaucratic structure of institutions and the formality of actions and procedures in Turkey do not match up with the informal nature of social networks.

Teachers should limit their knowledge sharing on social networks only to "educational" matters. In this way, preferring to use social networks in their sharing of knowledge with parents will not harm their private lives.

This study is a descriptive study demonstrating the creation process of a knowledge sharing culture by teachers through social networks. It is important in terms of highlighting the need for delivering solutions to the challenges in the process; it is one of the rare qualitative studies conducted on this subject.

References

1. Marshall, G.: Sociology Dictionary. Science and Art Press, Ankara (1999)
2. Hargreaves, A.: Sustainability of educational change: The role of social geographies. Journal of Educational Change 3(3-4), 189–214 (2002)
3. Boyd, D.M., Ellison, N.B.: Social network sites: Definition, history, and scholarship. Journal of Computer Mediated Communication 1(1), 210–230 (2007)
4. Kwon, O., Wen, Y.: An empirical study of the factors affecting social network service use. Computers in Human Behavior 26(2), 254–263 (2010)
5. O'Reilly, T.: What is web 2.0: Design patterns and business models for the next generation of software. Communications & Strategies 65, 17–39 (2007)
6. Biçen, H., Çavuş, N.: The most preferred social network sites by students. Paper presented at World Conference on Educational Sciences (WCES), İstanbul, Turkey (2010)
7. Ellison, N.B.: Introduction: Reshaping campus communication and community through social network sites. In: Salaway, G., Caruso, J.B., Nelson, M.R. (eds.) The ECAR Study of Undergraduate Students and Information Technology, pp. 19–32. EDUCAUSE Center for Applied Research, Boulder (2008), http://net.educause.edu/ir/library/pdf/ers0808/rs/ers08082.pdf (retrieved February 26, 2014)
8. Lepi, K.: 25 ways teachers can integrate social media into education (2012), http://edudemic.com/2012/07/a-teachers-guide-to-social-media/ (retrieved February 17, 2014)
9. Ajjan, H., Hartshorne, R.: Investigating faculty decisions to adopt web 2.0 technologies: Theory and empirical tests. Internet and Higher Education 11, 71–80 (2008)
10. Mazman, S.G.: Sosyal ağların benimsenme süreci ve eğitsel bağlamda kullanımı. Unpublished master's thesis, Hacettepe University, Ankara (2009)
11. Saunders, S.: The role of social networking sites in teacher education programs: A qualitative exploration. In: McFerrin, K., et al. (eds.) Proceedings of the Society for Information Technology and Teacher Education International Conference, pp. 2223–2228. AACE, Chesapeake (2008)

12. Jenkins, H.: What is learning in a participatory culture? (2009), http://henryjenkins.org/2009/05/what_is_learning_in_a_partic ip.html (retrieved February 17, 2014)
13. Yuen, S.C.Y., Yuen, P.: Web 2.0 in education. In: Conference Proceedings of the Society for Information Technology, pp. 3227–3228 (2008)
14. Ipe, M.: Knowledge sharing in organizations: A conceptual framework. Human Resource Development Review 2(4), 337–359 (2003)
15. Yi, J.: A measure of knowledge sharing behavior: Scale development and validation. Unpublished PhD dissertation, Indiana University, Bloomington, IN (2005)
16. Lave, J., Wenger, E.: Situated learning: Legitimate peripheral participation. Cambridge University Press, Cambirdge, ProQuest Digital Dissertation (UMI No. 3204302) (1991)(retrieved February 17, 2014)
17. Ajjan, H., Hartshorne, R.: Investigating faculty decisions to adopt Web 2.0 technologies: Theory and empirical tests. Internet and Higher Education 11, 71–80 (2008), doi:10.1016/j.iheduc.2008.05.002

The Effect on School Operations of the Use of School Management Software in Victoria

Christopher Tatnall[1] and Arthur Tatnall[2]

[1] Hurstbridge Primary School, Melbourne, Australia
Tatnall.Chris.D@edumail.vic.gov
[2] Victoria University, Melbourne, Australia
Arthur.Tatnall@vu.edu.au

Abstract. In this paper we will discuss the effects on schools in Victoria, Australia of use of the various school management systems provided by the Education Department, and the difference the use of this software has made to school operations. To better appreciate this, using a case study methodology, we will look at the use of these systems in a primary school in metropolitan Melbourne. The Victorian Education Department provides a raft of software for various administrative tasks in its schools and these are described in the paper. The goal of the paper, however, is to analyse the difference these management systems have made to the operation of the case study school and other schools in Victoria, compared with pre-computer manual systems.

Keywords: Educational management systems, schools, Victoria, applications.

1 Introduction: Schools in Victoria

The Commonwealth of Australia is a federation of six states and two territories each having a considerable degree of independence. Constitutionally, school education is the responsibility of state governments [1, 2] and each state may approach school education in a rather different way. This paper will look explicitly at school education in the State of Victoria.

The Department of Education and Early Childhood Development (DEECD) is responsible for school education in Victoria. As this Department has had various names over the years, for the purpose of this paper when we refer to the 'Education Department' this should be taken to mean DEECD (or any other previous titles of this Department). The Victorian school education system comprises 2,236 schools: 1,529 government schools, 486 Catholic schools and 211 independent schools. This paper deals only with government schools. The 2,236 government schools have 554,683 students and 40,965 teaching staff [3]. Government schools in Victoria are, within a Government stipulated total budget, largely self-governing.

Every school needs to store large quantities of data relating to administrative matters concerning individual students and groups of students. These data are collected from many formal and informal sources including: student enrolments, early years' interviews, observational surveys, running records, other formal testing and

D. Passey and A. Tatnall (Eds.): KCICTP/ITEM 2014, IFIP AICT 444, pp. 265–277, 2014.

notes [4]. Over the last 25 years, many different computer systems have been used around the State for school management purposes, some of the school's own design or purchased directly by this school, others provided by the Education Department. It is only those currently provided by the Education Department that are discussed in this paper.

2 Research Case Study: Hurstbridge Primary School

Case study research is a commonly used qualitative approach in Information Systems (IS) [5, 6] and as IS research topics commonly involve the study of organisational systems, a case study approach is often quite appropriate. This case study involves the detailed examination of the use of school management software in a single primary school [7, 8, 9] and its main concern is with the detail and complexity of the case, which it treats as a bounded system. The purpose of this case study is not so much to describe the various educational management systems used in schools in Victoria, but to look at their use at Hurstbridge Primary School, in outer metropolitan Melbourne, and how it has changed the way that school operations are undertaken [10].

The case study research undertaken involved interviews with the principal, assistant principal, several teachers and the school office staff. It also involved examination of documents, reports and websites as well as detailed observation of relevant school operations.

Hurstbridge Primary School is situated in the semi-rural town of Hurstbridge, 32 kilometres north-east of Melbourne. The picturesque setting of the newly constructed school, completed in 2005, is set amongst the gum trees along the Diamond Creek and provides a magnificent environment for members of the school's community. The school comprises two main wings, a library and computer laboratory, art room, music room, instrumental music rooms, after-care room, hall, science and Italian room.

In 2014, the staffing profile consisted of a principal and assistant principal, three leading teachers, 16 classroom teachers and many specialist teachers.

The principal indicates that Hurstbridge Primary School is proud of its student learning outcomes that are above or at the Victorian State level according to the Victorian Essential Learning Standards and National Assessment Program – Literacy and Numeracy (NAPLAN) testing results (see section 3.5). The staff are highly focused and committed to raise this bar even further, providing excellent opportunities for their children.

The school have many different programmes to cater for children of all levels. The 'Eagles' programme provides students with enrichment and extension activities outside of things already done in the classroom. 'Eagles' operates each week and students from grades 2 to 6 (7 to 11 year olds) have an opportunity to be involved. Students are selected based on their lower than average academic results and groups change each term. 'Eagles' programs are currently offered in English, mathematics, music, computing, art and music. They also offer support programmes at each year level, a reading intervention programme in the junior school (6 to 9 years of age) and corrective reading in the upper school (9 to 11 years of age).

Students have the opportunity to attend a number of specialist classes each week, which are currently offered in music, physical education, art, library, computers and Italian.

The school leadership team runs the school operations, staffing, curriculum and budgeting. The leadership team consists of the principal, assistant principal and leading teachers. Victorian schools receive a budget to run their school each year. This budget is based on the number of enrolments in the school. From this budget the school has to pay staff, purchase resources, run curriculum programmes and pay the bills. The school leadership team needs to look at this budget and plan appropriately to ensure that they have sufficient funds to cover all the operations of the school, ensuring they do not run into a deficit.

3 School Management Software in Victoria

There are two categories of application software used in Victorian schools: curriculum applications and administrative applications. To keep these separate, schools have two entirely separated and unconnected networks:

- A Curriculum Network, accessible by teachers. This can be accessed throughout the school using either Ethernet or Wi-Fi connections.
- An Administration Network that is accessible only to school management and school administrative office staff, but not to teachers. The Administrative Network is accessible only via an Ethernet connection at specific locations.

3.1 CASES21

In the early 1980s a newly elected Victorian Government found that it was not possible to gather consistent financial data from all its government departments, as each had its own accounting system [11]. This meant that the government was unable to draw up a balance sheet for the State of Victoria as a whole, and as a consequence, it quickly decided to set up accounting standards that would be used by all government departments, and to institute a centralised accounting system [12]. In the case of the Education Department, with the aim of making schools more centrally accountable, this system *imposed* an unalterable chart of accounts, which for small primary schools was seen as unnecessarily complex. Birse [11] suggests that "*the system was definitely not set up to empower schools. It was fairly imposed, and from that point of view they got it wrong*".

The result was CAAS [13] where the development philosophy placed emphasis on an integrated database management system: "*All school records should be part of an overall construct where a general information system comprising students, staff, assets, facilities and financial data is readily available to school-based personnel to assist in the administrative process*" [14]. CAAS was designed to be used with Microsoft (MS) Disk Operating Systems (MS-DOS) and a later version became known as CASES. Since that time CASES has been through several different versions culminating in the Computerised Administrative System Environment in Schools (CASES21) which is now used in all government schools in the State.

CASES21[1] provides support to government schools for administration, finance and central reporting (back to the Education Department). CASES21 runs on a MS Windows personal computer (PC) within the school and is claimed to have been designed to be easily modified to meet evolving school business needs. It currently has two main modules:

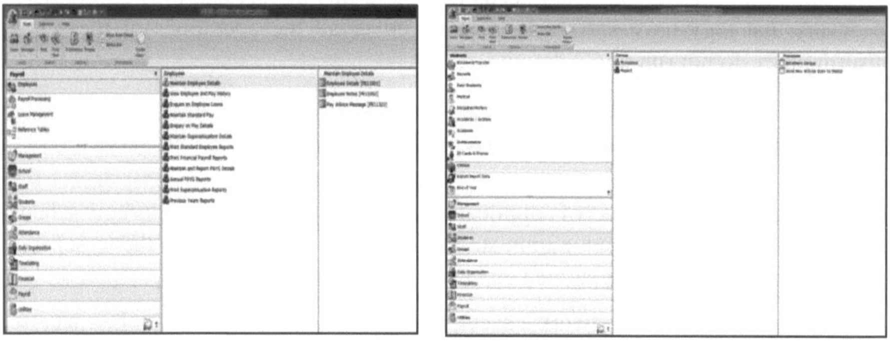

Fig. 1. CASES21

- **Administration Module:** Student and family records, photographs, enrolments and census; Student medical records, welfare, accidents and sick bay; Attendance; Student achievement, incidents, discipline and merit; Activities, excursions, home groups and houses; Staff records and photographs; Daily organisation and calendar; Timetabling; School details, management, council and parents' clubs.
- **Finance Module:** Payroll, staff records and leave for school-level employees; Student, family and sundry debtors; Creditors; Asset register; Budgets; Reporting; End-of-year and end-of-financial year [15].

The use of CASES21 is mandatory for all government schools, and all school data are stored on site but automatically backed up online remotely by the Education Department. This means that the Education Department can create its own reports from any of the school's data and the school does not need to send it anything. Within the school, CASES21 is used by school management and office staff with no direct teacher access. CASES21 is linked to most other management systems within the school and to the Education Department.

3.2 School Maintenance System (SMS)

Audits of all (government) schools are carried out each financial year by the Education Department to determine the maintenance needs of each of their buildings.

---

[1] CASES21 is a customised version of the Maze school software system, marketed commercially by CIVICA.

Based on priority considerations, it then determines works to be included in its maintenance programme and the prioritised data are loaded onto the School Maintenance System (SMS) in order to assist with its State-wide maintenance and infrastructure planning [16]. SMS is accessed online and linked to CASES21.

At the school level, SMS is used to assist with buildings and facilities, property management, repairs and urgent works. At Hurstbridge Primary it is used mainly by the assistant principal and the school office staff. As SMS works online the Education Department is always easily able to see the school's spending patterns and to check to see that the cost of all maintenance, repairs and urgent works is within the school's global budget. An important feature of SMS is for tracking urgent works, which is done automatically.

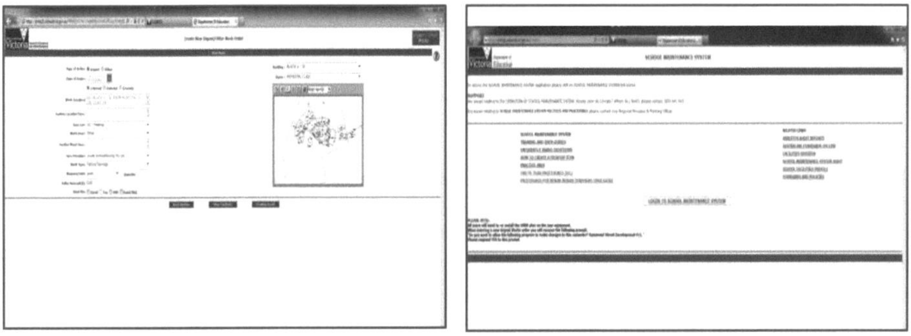

Fig. 2. School Maintenance System (http://prms21.eduweb.vic.gov.au/home/)

3.3 EduPay

While selection and appointment of teaching and administrative staff is done at a school level, the Education Department manages the payment of all salaries. The Department's human resources (HR) and payroll system – EduPay - is web-based and designed to enable viewing of up-to-date leave and salary information. It also allows school teaching and administrative staff to access their pay-slips, apply for leave and to view and update their contact and banking details [17]. It also is linked to CASES21.

Recruitment and position advertisements are done via the EduPay website. Schools list their new teaching jobs and openings over the weeks on the EduPay website and then this is transferred to the Education Department 'Recruitment on Line' website. This system provides the only way in which teachers can apply for new positions. The way that this is done is that the teacher writes a job application, taking care to take note of the selection criteria, and then upload this as a portable document format (PDF) onto the EduPay website. EduPay then automatically sends emails to prospective applicants to tell them whether they have been shortlisted, not shortlisted, or successful. If they are successful, then EduPay sends out their employment contract.

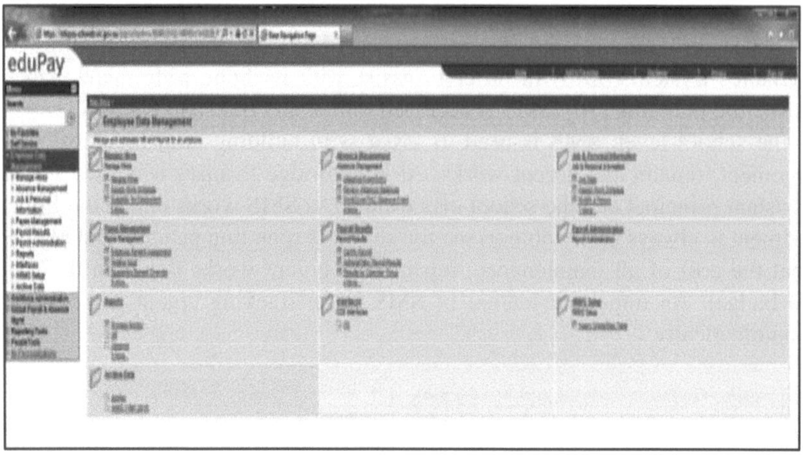

Fig. 3. EduPay (http://www.education.vic.gov.au /hrweb/pages/resources/edupay.aspx)

3.4 Program for Students with Disabilities (PSDMS)

PSDMS has been designed for use by schools to provide information about support processes associated with funding applications, eligibility evaluations and budget reporting for students with physical and intellectual disabilities. This program provides funds for teacher aids to assist these students, and not for facilities or equipment. PSDMS also is linked to CASES21.

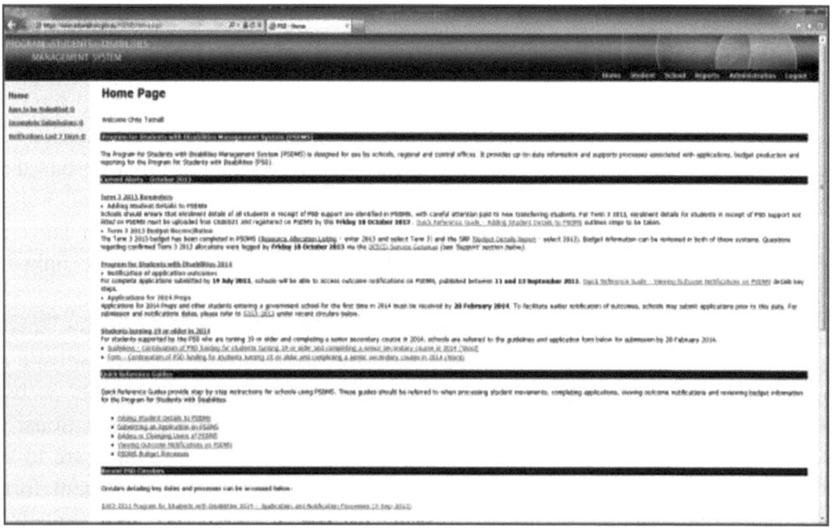

Fig. 4. Program for Students with Disabilities (http://www.education.vic.gov.au/school/principals/finance/Pages/swdsystems.aspx)

3.5 Student Performance Analyser (SPA)

Student Performance Analyser (SPA) is a web-based tool intended to assist schools to *analyse, display, store and communicate* student performance and assessment data. SPA has been designed to produce a number of '*sortable* reports' to provide interpretation and monitoring of the progress of students, either individually, in groups, or by the whole school. It calculates the amount of '*value added learning*' against the Australian Curriculum and shows where students are performing in relation to the curriculum. SPA stores student data continually, allowing creation of an on-going profile history of each student.

SPA is provided to its schools by the North-West Region (in which Hurstbridge Primary School is located) and not by the Education Department for all schools. Its use is completely voluntary and not in any way mandated by the Education Department. Within the school each teacher enters their own class results onto a spreadsheet (or something similar) and then later uploads them to SPA. Student details can be downloaded from CASES21 and all teachers have access to this system.

As well as internal school testing, results from the NAPLAN testing can also be entered into this system. NAPLAN is an annual assessment for all Australian students in Years 3, 5, 7 and 9 (i.e. at ages 8, 10, 12 and 14 years) and is intended primarily to test reading, writing, spelling and numeracy [18]. When all the NAPLAN results have been collated by ACARA (the National Curriculum Authority) they are sent to each school from where they can be uploaded into SPA. This enables results' analysis and a comparison to be made between this school and other local schools, a given type of school, or all schools.

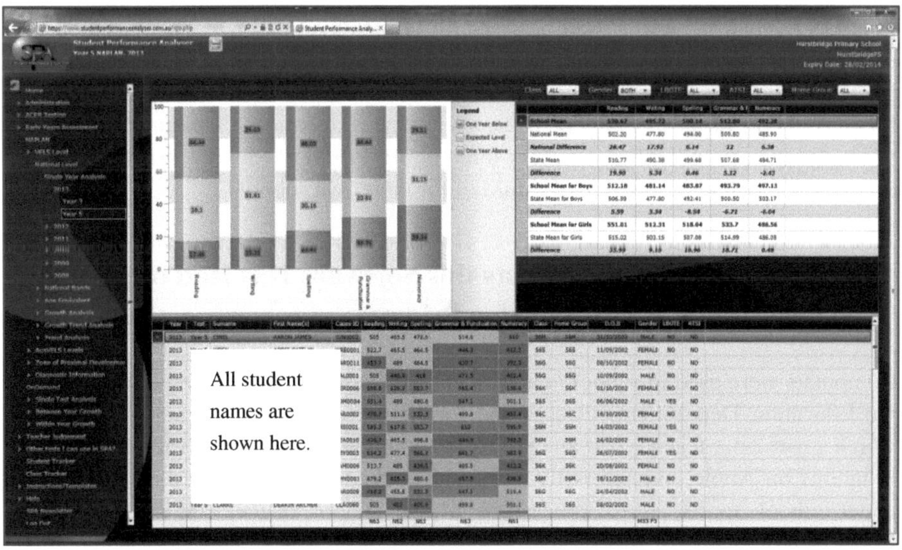

Fig. 5. Student Performance Analyser (https://www.studentperformanceanalyser.com.au/spa/)

3.6 QuickVic

This system allows student reports to be created by teachers. It is essentially a MS Access database and is accessible for use by teachers, school management and office staff. In the first instance, student details are downloaded from CASES21, then each teacher enters reports for each student in their class. The system then allows reports for each student to be printed and sent to each parent. Data is school-based (local) and not online, but is uploaded to CASES21 twice each year.

3.7 Ultranet

The Ultranet was designed as a web-based system to support delivery of curriculum, online teaching and learning and sharing of knowledge across all Victorian government schools [19, 20]. It began its service to all Victorian government schools in September 2010. It had many of the features found in a business extranet in that it was closed to people outside the Victorian Government school community and required a username and password to gain access, but with over 500,000 users it was a good deal larger than most business extranets. The Ultranet's intended users were school teachers, as well as school students and their parents, all of whom would be issued with usernames and passwords.

The Ultranet was potentially an innovative technology that could have provided value to the Victorian education system, but for a variety of reasons [20] it was not successful and was discontinued at the end of 2013.

3.8 EduMail

This MS Exchange email system is based on MS Outlook. Each teacher has their own email address provided by the Education Department. Bulletins are sent weekly from the Education Department to the school management, which then uses the system to forward these to each individual teacher. The Education Department does not normally contact individual teachers directly via EduMail. School management has access to the management side of EduMail for their own school.

4 An Analysis of the Effects this Software Has Had on School Operations at Hurstbridge Primary

Computers were used in school management applications in some schools long before the Education Department released the forerunner of CASES21. Some schools, in which a particular teacher had an interest in computing, used teacher-designed BASIC programs on Apple computers for things like scheduling and recording information about school sports, word processing in the school office, for assistance with timetabling and for listings of students in each class. These were very much single school applications, but by the mid-1980s the Education Department began to show an interest in using computers for administrative purposes. In a letter to the Director

General from the State Computer Education Centre in May 1985, possible applications for the use of computers in school administration were listed as: word processing, student records, accounting, timetabling/scheduling (in post-primary schools mainly), inventory, ordering/budgeting and library [21]. A 1986 report by the newly-formed Schools Administrative Computing Unit (SACU) noted that a large number of schools used a variety of hardware and software in school administration and that: "*The general lack of uniformity in respect of systems, both software and hardware, prompted the development of the schools' accounting system*". It went on to say that: "*The proposed increase in responsibilities for school administrators will result in the need to provide management information to school councils and school communities to facilitate accordant analysis of school operations*" [22 :4].

There is no member of staff currently at Hurstbridge Primary who remembers how school administration was carried out in the 1980s, but it is unlikely that the school then made any use of computers for this purpose.

4.1 CASES21

Thus, before CASES, many schools made no use of computers for school administration and those that did make some use of computers did so in a fragmented un-coordinated way. For administrative details of schools' financial and other data, the Education Department had to reply on typed (or sometimes handwritten) reports, make telephone calls and gain information from visits by school inspectors. CASES21 made a fundamental difference to this.

Apart from assisting schools with some administrative tasks, perhaps the biggest difference made by the introduction of CASES21 was the flow of information back to 'Spring Street' – the location of the Education Department. It is now very easy for someone in Spring Street to obtain details of the finances, enrolments, teachers, students and maintenance requests for any school in the State.

Financial matters are now handled by office staff in the school, but the Education Department has online access to all these data at any time. Use of CASES21 makes the task of handling finance, record keeping and enrolments by the school very much easier.

4.2 School Maintenance System (SMS)

Before introduction of this fairly new system, purchase orders to a contractor for any school maintenance tasks had to be handwritten at the school and then sent off to CASES21 for Education Department approval. Now, after the school has set up the system with contractor names and other details, when maintenance is needed, it sends an order to the contractor and also enters this directly into CASES21 where all the data is stored remotely. The school office staff then just pay the bills from CASES21, making it easy for the school to track spending.

This system is also used for routine inspections and occupational health and safety issues. Once set up, the system remembers dates for checking and ordering of these inspections. Use of this system has made these school administrative tasks a good deal easier.

4.3 EduPay

For quite some time teachers have been paid by direct bank transfer rather than by cheque. Before the EduPay system, teachers were sent payslips each fortnight with information about their pay, leave etc. All this information is now provided online. Whether this is better is a matter of personal opinion: some teachers are happy with this, others would prefer a printed payslip rather than having to go online to check.

4.4 Programs for Students with Disabilities (PSDMS)

The school has found that the system's provision of information about support processes associated with funding applications, eligibility evaluations and budget reporting for students with physical and intellectual disabilities is a big improvement on doing this by hand.

4.5 Student Performance Analyser (SPA)

Prior to the introduction of this program, each teacher tended to keep their own student assessment data, in some cases in a spreadsheet and in other cases on paper. Now at Hurstbridge Primary, student details can first be downloaded from CASES21. Each teacher then enters their own class results onto a spreadsheet and then later uploads them to SPA. The system has made analysis simpler with its *sortable* reports that can interpret and monitor student progress. Comparisons can be made between individual students, classes, cohorts, boys/girls, or the whole school. (SPA provides information only for this school and no comparison can be made with other schools, and unlike most of the other systems, data is stored within the school and the Education Department does not have direct access to this.)

4.6 QuickVic

Before introduction of this system, some student reports were handwritten by teachers and others were typed, in some cases on a typewriter but more recently using MS Word. In those times, one paper copy of each student's report had to be sent to their parents and another kept in a file at the school. The school duplicate had to be created either by using carbon paper, sensitive paper, or by photocopying. Copying and filing the reports was thus a large administrative burden on the school.

Now, student details are first downloaded from CASES21. Each teacher then enters results and reports for each student in their class on their own (local) computer before uploading them to the school server, from where summary data is available to school management. This system is not online but later the results, but not the reports, are uploaded to CASES21.

One criticism of computer-generated reports like this, sometimes heard from parents and teachers, is that these are nowhere near as personal as the old handwritten reports. This is a difference, but whether positive or negative is a matter of opinion.

4.7 Ultranet

Use of the Ultranet could potentially have made a significant difference to the way the school operated, but this is no longer the case as the Ultranet was discontinued at the end of 2013.

4.8 EduMail

Almost everyone, of course, now makes use of email, whether they use it for work or at home, and teachers are no different. The system provides each teacher with their own email address and in addition to these individual staff accounts, the school also has its own email account. While at one time in the past the Education Department used to communicate with schools and teachers via 'The Victorian Education Gazette' printed monthly, in more recent times a summary weekly bulletin was provided by fax. Now everything is sent to the school by email.

5 Conclusion

What difference to school management and to teachers have these new systems made at Hurstbridge Primary School? The answer is that they have made a great deal of difference. Very little administrative output is now handwritten, with some purchase orders being an exception. This has made a quite dramatic change in the way that the school office operates, and has changed the roles and tasks of office staff. The old cash books are gone and there is now no need for office staff to count or balance cash: office staff jobs are very different. Much more access to data is now available and reports can easily be generated for each subject budget (which was very difficult in the past) and for any other account. This provides more easily accessible information, to both teachers and school administrators. All accounts and bills are settled by electronic payment and parents pay any school fees via BPAY (an Australian electronic bill payment system). This makes quite a difference at the parent-school interface.

Office work is now easier and more interesting, but more computer knowledge than before is needed. Computerised school management systems have radically changed the way that the school handles its administrative matters, and this has considerably affected teachers, school administrators, office staff and parents.

References

1. Tatnall, A.: The Growth of Educational Computing in Australia. In: Goodson, I.F., Mangan, J.M. (eds.) History, Context, and Qualitative Methods in the Study of Education, pp. 207–248. University of Western Ontario, London (1992)

2. Tatnall, A., Davey, B.: Reflections on the History of Computer Education in Schools in Victoria. In: Tatnall, A. (ed.) Reflections on the History of Computing. IFIP AICT, vol. 387, pp. 243–264. Springer, Heidelberg (2012)
3. Department of Education and Early Childhood Development: Statistics for Victorian Schools (2014), http://www.education.vic.gov.au/about/department/Pages/factsandfigures.aspx (retrieved August 25, 2014)
4. Tatnall, C., Tatnall, A.: Using Educational Management Systems to Enhance Teaching and Learning in the Classroom: an Investigative Study. In: Tatnall, A., Okamoto, T., Visscher, A.J. (eds.) Knowledge Management for Educational Innovation. IFIP, vol. 230, pp. 75–82. Springer, Heidelberg (2007)
5. Orlikowski, W.J.: CASE Tools as Organizational Change: Investigating Incremental and Radical Changes in Systems Development. Management Information Systems Quarterly 17(3), 1–28 (1993)
6. Alavi, M., Carlson, P.: Review of MIS Research and Disciplinary Development. Journal of Management Information Systems 8(4), 45–62 (1992)
7. Merriam, S.B.: Case study research in education. Jossey-Bass, San Francisco (1988)
8. Stake, R.E.: Case Study Methods in Educational Research: Seeking Sweet Water. In: Jaeger, R.M. (ed.) Complementary Methods for Research in Education, pp. 253–265. American Educational Research Association, Washington, DC (1988)
9. Yin, R.K.: Case Study Research, Design and Methods, 2nd edn. Sage Publications, Newbury Park (1994)
10. Hurstbridge Primary School: Hurstbridge Primary School: Imagine, Believe, Achieve (2014), http://www.hbridgeps.vic.edu.au/ (retrieved August 25, 2014)
11. Birse, J.: Victorian Administrative Computing Unit, Melbourne, Australia. Taped interview (1994)
12. Tatnall, A.: Information Technology and the Management of Victorian Schools - Providing Flexibility or Enabling Better Central Control? In: Barta, B.Z., Telem, M., Gev, Y. (eds.) Information Technology in Educational Management, pp. 99–108. Chapman & Hall, London (1995)
13. Schools' Administrative Systems Development Unit: Computer Aided Administrative System - STAGE 1 - Staff and Students (Version 1.3). Ministry of Education Victoria, Melbourne, Australia (1987)
14. Directorate of School Education: Computerised Administrative Systems Environment in Schools - MS-DOS desktop computer hardware specifications. Victorian Government, Melbourne, Australia (1993)
15. Department of Education and Early Childhood Development: CASES21 (2012), http://www.education.vic.gov.au/management/ictsupportservices/cases21/functionality.htm (retrieved August 25, 2014)
16. Department of Education and Early Childhood Development: School Maintenance System (2013), http://prms21.eduweb.vic.gov.au/home/ (retrieved August 25, 2014)
17. Department of Education and Early Childhood Development: Human Resources: EduPay (2013), http://www.education.vic.gov.au/hrweb/pages/resources/edupay.aspx (retrieved August 25, 2014)
18. Australian Curriculum Assessment and Reporting Authority: NAPLAN (2011), http://www.nap.edu.au/ (retrieved August 25, 2014)

19. DEECD: Ultranet (2011), `http://www.education.vic.gov.au/about/directions/ultranet/default.htm` (retrieved August 25, 2014)
20. Tatnall, A., et al.: The Ultranet: an eGovernment Project Management Failure? In: Wigand, D.L., et al. (eds.) 26th Bled eConference, eInnovations: Challenges and Impacts for Individuals, pp. 32–47. Organizations and Society, Bled (2013)
21. State Computer Education Centre: Some thoughts on computers in School Administration. Ministry of Education, Melbourne, Victoria, Australia (1985)
22. Schools Administrative Computing Unit: Recommended Computing Systems for Administration in Schools. Ministry of Education, Melbourne, Victoria, Australia (1986)

An Information Service to Act in Binomial 'Monitoring–Improvement' of Educational Performance in Portugal: Three Focus Group Studies to Explore the Concept

Antonio Castro and Delfina Soares

Centro ALGORITMI, Department of Information Systems, University of Minho, Portugal
antonio.castro@algoritmi.uminho.pt,
dss@dsi.uminho.pt

Abstract. This paper presents an analysis of a focus group discussion, which was carried out to collect information about the need, utility, and value that can be associated with the existence of an information service aimed to support educational leadership activities. The service intends to support leadership in monitoring and improvement of school performance and activities. To check the perceptions of school actors about the existence of this kind of service and to identify perspectives that would add value to the director's community, three focus group discussions were held in three different Portuguese country regions (Algarve, Lisbon, and Porto). The groups were designed to include a maximum of six school directors that tend to be representative of each region. The duration of group discussions ranged from one hour and ten minutes to one hour and thirty minutes. To stimulate discussion, a roadmap with eleven questions was prepared. The group discussions were audio recorded, transcribed and analysed. This paper details the design and preparation of the focus group activities and presents a reflexive discussion on the data collected.

Keywords: Focus groups, IT education management, educational IT leadership.

1 Introduction

A huge penetration of Information Technologies (IT) in schools has been witnessed over the last decades. This has produced significant benefits, reported in many scientific studies and technical reports such as 'Technological modernization of education in Portugal Diagnostic Study' [1], 'Technological Modernization of schools' [2], 'OECD/CELE review of the secondary school modernization in Portugal' [3] and 'The Implementation of the Technological Plan for Education in Portugal, a School Perspective' [4]. Despite all the benefits pointed out, it is our conviction that currently available IT in schools is not adequately used to its full. In this project, it is advocated that IT can be adequate in terms of supporting bigger benefits, specifically at the monitoring and improvement level of school activities and performance. The existence of an information service could be useful, therefore. A

D. Passey and A. Tatnall (Eds.): KCICTP/ITEM 2014, IFIP AICT 444, pp. 278–288, 2014.

technologically-based information service that: i) collects; ii) stores; iii) analyses; and iv) reports data interacting in IT school management ecosystems, in order to produce new knowledge, may substantially contribute to school performance work. This research project has been working on the description and specification of such an information service.

Information services are information technology (IT) based services that perform functions involving some form of information processing that is of some value in a market or society sector. The essence of the information service (the concept) that is explored in this research project encompasses the following aspects: (i) collection (as automatically as possible) of information from schools and its storage in information repositories following data warehousing approaches; (ii) processing of this information, using business intelligence technology, with Key Performance Indicators (KPIs) in analytical engines; (iii) providing reports and search facilities; (iv) providing reports and search facilities to support benchmarking analysis to leadership groups.

- To check the school director's sensitivity (or any other executive board individual) to the acceptance and functionalities of this kind of information service, three focus groups (FGs) were prepared to discuss these needs. The focus group discussion was selected because it allows interaction among the multiple actors and the emergence of multiple and complementary perspectives [5]. Discussing different perspectives may lead to unexpected findings. Moreover, in terms of research perspectives, the model is open and does not impose any circumscribed opinion, taking richness into the process from unclogging single opinion. This openness of approach allows wide opportunity to comment, expose ideas, and share experiences. Besides providing qualitative and circumscribed information to the research, the use of focus groups also allowed the creation of a set of contacts and connections with interested stakeholders for this research project.
- Three focus groups were conducted. Each focus group involved a maximum of six individuals, all of them with school direction responsibilities. The discussions were located in three different regions of Portugal (Porto, Lisbon and Faro), in March 2013.

2 Group Constitution

The process started with a directed and personalised invitation addressed to each school board (the group that directs the business of the school). The invitation sent included: i) a brief description of the research project; ii) the place and date where the discussion would take place; iii) the goals or the focus of the discussion; and iv) a presentation of the research project, its context and a presentation of the research center with some of its work. Every discussion group gained individuals from different places in the region. Up to six confirmations were accepted for each group, representing diversity and heterogeneity from the regions. The event in Algarve happened in Faro, the most representative city in the region, which received school directors from cities of Vila Real Santo António, Albufeira, Portimão and Lagos.

The second focus group was run in Lisbon and involved directors from the cities of Lisbon, Paço de Arços, Algés, Sintra, Peniche and Santarém. The latter focus group took place in Porto and involved directors from Maia, Oliveira do Bairro, and Porto cities.

To make up the groups, there was collaboration from the technological partner in this project. The partnership considers technical issues and access to schools as well. The invitation was sent to school direction boards that at least use software management. Each board agreed to participate, indicating an individual who would be present.

The topics of the discussion were carefully prepared [6] and sequenced. Preparation included experiences gained so far, to cover topics, components and ingredients considered in context. These experiences covered: i) the six Portuguese governmental programmes for IT in education and results to date; ii) the autonomous approach in some schools contracted by the government; iii) the commercial option versus ministerial offer for software management; iv) IT strategic alignment policies to educational projects; and v) Key Performance Indicators used in different domains, such as the Portuguese educational system and the Organisation for Economic Co-operation and Development (OECD). Closing the discussion, a review was shared, to identify and clarify the approach taking and discussed in each matter. The goal and discussion achievement do not look for consensus, in getting collective decisions. Rather, the success of the discussion success was measured through collecting qualitative information arising from participants' opinions. These results were solicited through open questions and procedures where the participants felt absolutely free to choose the form of their response, orally or in mien.

3 Session Planning

After the groups had been identified, each session was carefully prepared. They were planned to work through three different sessions: i) open session, to introduce the researcher and the project, ask for permission to record the discussions and give acknowledgment for been present. This session was meant to put the participants at ease, afterward ii) the discussion session, included initially some introduction questions to introduce the elements helping participants to respond freely, some other questions focusing on the key aspects and the kernel of the discussion, and finally some challenges were cast and inducements proposed. Finally, the iii) closure session, during which final acknowledgements were addressed, notes were taken and backups records were made. The conduct of the FG included a pilot phase. It was planned to take about one and a half hours. During this pilot, special attention was given to the quality and sequencing of the questions to be used. It was assumed that answers and individual questions may use an estimated time that would not correspond if answered in-group; a set of eleven questions was defined.

The focus group activities ran in a participant school, equidistant from all participants. There were an invitation to those schools, who all readily agreed.

4 The Questionnaire Roadmap

To prepare the discussion, a pilot with questions was designed for each of the different sessions, and some rules were imposed. The first rule to develop the discussion was to establish that dichotomous questions and ‘Why’ questions were to be avoided, in order to maintain focus. For each theme for discussion, a range of context slides was used to provide support for the discussion and to propitiate and facilitate discussions between the participants. In total, the eleven questions were allocated across the three sessions as follows:

- *Open questions*: With dual intention, to put participants at ease and develop affinities between group actors. They were asked about professional skills and the length of time in their job. It was intended that there should be a quick answer and it should be done in a factual way, for example – ‘director of school ... with x professional years in the job’. Thus, questions were applied like:

  Q1: Who is the oldest group member? What kind of work have you been doing over this time?
  Q2: How wide is the gap between the oldest and the youngest school director? What differences can you report happening across that time period?

- *Introductory questions*: questions that introduce general topics for discussion and provide participants the opportunity to reflect on past experiences and their connections with topics involved. These issues are not critical to analysis, but also were intended to promote the discussion around IT and education management.

  Q3: With the governmental IT programmes shown in the slide, which one is most prominent in your mind, and what values have these programmes brought to your school?
  Q4: How was the IT investment leveraged? Both the school and governmental ones?

- *Transition Questions*: These questions pave the way to the core issue. The questions also drive the participants to the research problem and the research questions.

  Q5: How can IT contribute to support the educational service?
  Q6: Is it possible for IT to have more influence in school performance? How?
  Q7: What has been done and what remains to be done in terms of annual activities planned at this moment?

- *Key questions*: In this session issues considered were essential to the research. The contribution and acceptance about significance of information services, in terms of additional helpful functionalities, was discussed. Collective reflections answered were encouraged; also in this category analyses of time invested were considered without restrictions. The followed questions were asked:

Q8: How is your school positioned now, in terms of ministry goals? If you are on target, how do you measure it?

Q9: Are outcomes this academic year aligned with your expected goals for this present year? When deviations occur, how long do these take to be diagnosed?

Q10: Supposing your management software supports the entire school flow process, for what proposes should stored school data be accessible? Should it be shared with other schools? Should it contribute to aggregated information in terms of global knowledge?

Q11: Is there any value to leadership and school governance afforded by aggregated information? For example, what benefits can be found when collectives work with other schools? Will there be any advantage in linking leadership and knowledge in between?

- *Final questions*: The questions raised here close the discussion and allow a reflection on materials discussed. These questions remained open and depending on each group were:

  Brief questions - If the discussion was considered to have achieved its goals, a brief summary of the essential issues was stated in two or three minutes; then the discussion was closed, highlighting favourable findings and considering: 'Are these the essential matters discussed here? Does someone want to add something else?"

  Final question – If the discussion was not considered to have achieved its goals, strategic points were revisited, and discussed briefly before making final acknowledgments to participants and to the host in particular.

5 Results

The analytical space was organised to look for ideas that could be of particular interest to the project and to identify key concepts [7]. The elements reported from direct group speech transcriptions were divided into two groups – favourable and unfavourable elements to the service exposed. The key ideas formed or developed through group discussions are listed here without using any priority criteria:

A. Provisioning aggregate information from schoolwork.
B. The facility to build effective school networks
C. Availability and facilitation of electronic process exchange between schools.
D. Performance schoolwork monitoring, individually and in aggregated mode.
E. Providing another intelligence element, a driver to schools' extra activities available in the market.
F. Broad consent to software management through commercial platforms and not as a unique solution to all schools.

These points, retained from discussions as key concepts and ideas, were developed during the discussions, sometimes from discussion, sometimes from an idea launched.

To substantiate the description in each idea, some excerpts from the transcripts for each key idea in the discussion follow:

Idea A: Provisioning aggregate information from schoolwork

To collect information from schools, and to store it in a huge repository to allow different kinds of aggregate reports, is a base concept from this project. This idea was not opened in the discussion to explore the concept, but just to ascertain acceptance. The idea was well accepted, as schools have already been targeted for deep scrutiny, from different parts of society. Therefore they can discuss information independently. Most participants showed willingness to take part and contribute to this experience.

Idea B: Building bridges between leaderships to facilitate effective school networks and develop a community of practice

How schools organise relationships between themselves was a matter discussed but while avoiding undue concern. Building affiliation between schools is difficult so this facility is seen as useful to this project. There are movements and associations taking place, but they have a geographical constituency. This element can add value to the service being developed here; it happened unexpectedly, emerging the first time in the Algarve group discussion. The matter emerged by an alternative interpretation of electronic exchange, where an individual in the group observed and pronounced that there could be further exchange of information and electronic files, and said “... for example... it also happens with temporary student exchanges in the programme exchange... - … our school takes and sends groups with a German school... I think it is a two year exchange programme... because they want to learn Portuguese language and it is part of a contract to stay for a week in Portugal...” Then someone suggested “… broadcasting this event should be useful...” This idea does not mean the availability of a direct contact between schools, but a space used by schools as support for exchanges and extra-curricular activities. A space where stakeholders can share events and activities – from accommodation to normative assessment, describing the activity itself, the service can be useful if it has a feature that allows exchange of events and activities between schools.

Idea C: Use the ‘service’ as a facilitator to student processing for inter-exchange

Facilitating inter-exchange processes in digital format was an idea that gathered wider support. It was introduced into the discussion in the Algarve group. This idea received wide acceptance due to procedural volumetric transfer needs concerning students between schools. Extending the concept, and if possible making it more comprehensive using the concepts of interoperability, it was an idea that should be represented further, although the focus in this research project is not to support operations in and in-between schools, but to connect leadership and knowledge.

Idea D: Collecting information to monitor

This key idea is the dominant concept of the information service presented; to monitor to improve. In discussion groups, the moderator launched the idea not directly but openly in an attempt to steer the discussion into a confluence of ideas. Some contributions emerged in discussion.

Initially, the group discussion held in the Algarve was resistant to some elements, to available information from schools in the form of databases. It was clear that this point was 'well spoken', for safety in terms of individual rights and guarantees, need to be ensured by the National Commission for Data Protection (CNPD). In the Lisbon discussion group, the position was the opposite and indicated willingness to provide details since all issues need to be raised by the CNPD. Some examples from the Lisbon discussion group stated: "... no problem... these are administrative data, we live in a republic, free, and democratic... It is necessary to have guarantees protecting data, which is personal, that must be protected.... about the administrative data there is an obligation to school administration to provide them to whom they are entitled.... and they do not need to prove they are entitled... or that the constitution that wants to oversee the actions of public administration is calling... I learned this from a judgment about commission access to official documents.... by a question released many years ago because a parent asked me.... – Please, I would like to know the name, qualifications, professional experience of all teachers of my son.... and [he] said to me, look I 'm a doctor, I am a surgeon and everyday I make medical surgical interventions, and it does not bother me that someone will ask what is the curriculum... this is a right that is accessible to everyone.... therefore the education of my children is no less important than what I do... I was surprised... I made an appointment with the National Commitment Administrative Data, and they sent me the judgment... after... twenty days... with six or seven pages that said... so... everything is nominative, where you live, phone number and so on... I'm not authorised to give it to anyone and I have to manage according to that... Everything that is personal but is not relevant... the situation in their career, the teacher can gain the Masters degree but never gave me anything to put in the biographical record... But his name was entered with the qualification he gained at the Masters level and due to this he has been repositioned in his career... administrative data and the judgment given that ended in the constitution have to provide all those who have an interest in them... and then he wrote... interest is very generic, every citizen has the right to see the acts of the public administration, it is a constitutional right and just tell the citizen to view them... this has to be provided... Therefore more than monitoring it is to investigate to help to enter the market, to create wealth, to help to be more effective and evolve... therefore no one can deny that data."

This matter is delicate and sensitive. There exists some resistance to providing databases even with guarantees. Ensuring CNPD assumptions would enable the gaining of schools' agreements to provide their databases in order to develop a prototype planned in this research project. Because this is a sensitive and critical point, it was always repeated at the end of the discussions, in the review time.

Idea E: Availability of another support element, provider of extra-curricular activities to meet different needs. This element should be bi-directional, into and from the 'service'

This idea appeared tenuously in the Algarve group. It was then validated and complimented by other groups. Its acceptance by representative individuals, gave an indication of the strength that this kind of functionality could provide in terms of information and adding value to the service. This element appears to suggest acting as facilitator and a networker between schools and institutions who for some reason maintain a relationship of interest with certain schools in particular and education globally. On the school side there exist interests in all institutions that provide activities that can collaborate and contribute to the construction of informal learning. From the institution side, there is sometimes difficulty in gaining access to a plurality of schools, across geographic and activity diversity. Thus the validity of an element like this in the 'information service' may act as a 'hub' to approach stakeholders, and make available extra-curricular activities. These activities support construction skills for learners and other ones that may be identified by the elements of interest in the remaining educational community (teachers, aides, parents and administrators).

An illustrative example from the discussions driving this idea, is cited here from an extract from the Algarve group discussion: "... And further down the line, be able to find activities that already have results to help in accomplishing certain goals... taking for example study visits, dedicated activities from universities or pedagogical organisations such physics labs." These were followed soon after by positive reinforcements from other individuals, such as "That should be interesting" and from another individual form Vila Real "Of course... ", or an Albufeira individual "That should be good!... And share examples between schools that have already tried and worked fine." The group argued about the same examples as in this case, with two individuals saying: "Being able to have a list for example... the fifth year, in history discipline... this and this and this... sixth year, in geography discipline... this and this and this..." to complement with a Lagos individual: "but note that the north of the country have more offers with a set of institutions and information that is well crafted.... there is a greater tradition in exchange between institutions and schools."

It was felt that this possibility could provide links to generate social value, well-being and organisational economic performance for the educational establishment and give return to the institutions that provide these activities. This is an element where everyone can gain benefits.

Idea F: Broad consent for a school free selection of a software management platform

The concern about selection of software management providers was a point where there was intensive discussion in all groups, mainly on two themes, history on the one hand and selection between commercial providers or the Ministry provider on the other. There was a consensual discussion about the history of software providers. The same did not happen when it was necessary to discuss the option of providing a commercial provider versus a ministerial provider. In historical terms, almost all participants identified their first providers as 'JPMAbreu', 'Prodesis' and 'Truncatura', just naming the most referenced from the last decade. There was also a big concordance about a provider lifecycle up to this time. About providers, two forces dominated the discussions: preferences for commercial providers; and preferences for a unique provider that must be ministerial. The defenders of a unique ministerial provider for management software argue that it would be better for schools

Table 1. Favourable and unfavourable elements to the exposed service

Favourable elements	Unfavourable Elements
FAV1: There is no universal system for administrative and pedagogical management, with capacity to collect data from different platforms of the education system, and return this information to schools and stakeholders.	UNF1: Hindrance to cover all school processes, pedagogical and administrative ones.
FAV2: Schools feel great pressure due to the accountability of their work by parents, the media, local and national authorities.	UNF2: Technological pedagogic support adapted to school mission and global measures is missing.
FAV3: Each school produces academic result analyses every trimester.	UNF3: A lack of habit in using the technology in collaborative work.
FAV4: All elements identified an evolution and benefits in the introduction of government programmes for IT in education.	UNF4: Regulatory changes require updates and incur costs.
FAV5: There is a richer technological environment in schools.	UNF5: Evolution and maintenance is absent in platforms used.
FAV6: There is a legal need to produce internal evaluation.	UNF6: Small market.
FAV7: All groups agree positively to have a community of practice to share and connect experiences.	
FAV8: It is necessary to monitor targets for each educational project, by identifying variances and methods to measure outcomes.	
FAV9: Wide preferences to choose software management freely according to school needs.	
FAV10: Lifecycle of IT governmental programmes in education and technologies.	

essentially for two reasons: i) they do not have any responsibility in that process; and ii) every school has to use the same management software. The defenders of commercial providers for management software argue that they can change when they decide usefully, and it improves competitiveness between providers of management software.

Still on this matter, there was a relevant contribution from the Lisbon focus group discussion that is important to share. A school director with extensive professional experience said with conviction about the end of the first cycle software that was used led to 'market dry up'. Explained prospectively, software vendors have a period of expansion in license sales, but they are then forced to create structures where programmers become burdens when the new school market has all been served. This justifies their need only to sell 'upgrades', which became unsustainable to the companies, he said. This was also in his view, a strong reason to have a single software vendor. Defenders of commercial options, with some irony and humor, compared the option with the selection of the 'one book' (movement regime of the 1950s and 1960s, which required all schools in the country use the same textbooks).

This matter, for a single ministerial supplier or free appeal to the market, despite not fracturing any group opinion did not lead to consensus. There were different individuals who identified with each of the two options; those who defended the unique solution were in the large minority coinciding with their time in service, and experiences.

Principal elements were identified in focus group discussions. Some may be useful to the project and some might go forward to consider in future work. For the analyses, a second iteration from the discussion records classified strengthening and weakness factors as well. These two characteristics were identified and grouped – favourable elements and unfavourable elements to service viability (defined in Table 1).

6 Reflections and Conclusions

The information service studied in this research project intends to act essentially in two domains: i) aggregate information from diverse schools and classification of information with an analytical engine supported by KPI parameters: and ii) develop a community of practices, connecting leadership groups, knowledge and educational stakeholders.

Performing focus groups with professionals with expertise gave important constructs to consolidate the research. Interacting with school directors, together across the country, conducted in different representative country regions, developed important elements. Some participants expressed their willingness in providing school information and becoming a partner in this research project. This evidenced the advantage that can come through from using focus groups and the interactivity afforded. The acceptance and curiosity aroused by the exposed service and discussion succeeds, generating interest in collaborative work and getting access to independent knowledge.

The use of focus group discussion as a technique was a particularly useful tool, showing useful paths and understanding to fulfil the research need. The discussion allowed school directors' views about evolutionary paths of IT in education and its strategic importance to emerge.

It is also important to refer to limitations found in this process. The moderation of the discussion was done by the researcher, which may have influenced the way the discussion proceeded. The peer interaction led to some inefficiencies in sharing results, led to some difficulties in discussion (essentially when they spoke simultaneously), inefficiencies in individual discussions (discourse drift) taking into discussion irrelevant purposes outside the context, losing precious time and forcing a considerable direction on the discussion. Another difficulty related to the analyses of results. The interaction between group elements in the discussion brought forward comments that deserved to be interpreted. Finally a closing limitation experienced, was advice about group constitution that could be brought to the analyses through different perspectives.

Despite the limitations pointed to in the last paragraph, the decision to undertake focus group discussions proved to be a good option, considering the richness of the perceptions and opinions shared by the educational stakeholders during the discussions, and not least gaining a privileged introduction to schools from across the country. Discussions have led principally to two outcomes: key ideas useful to the service; and the validation of the service itself, and favourable and unfavourable aspects identified. The priority was to identify possible ambassadors to the project. An ambassador needs to be available to participate, providing information and contributing to refine the project.

The needs for benchmarking, by levels and accessible to school directors, with independent data from schools, was presented in all discussions. Another relevant outcome was the need for availability to share school information for such a project. Other relevant aspects achieved were the availability of building bridges to decrease distances between schools, direction boards and projects.

It is recognised that the selection of focus group discussion, as a tool to collect and search for additional information into this research project, is not a perfect tool and there were some limitation. However, all the discussions were achieved and were successful, and the focus group discussions demonstrated benefits and were assuredly a good option to deal with such different sensitivities raised by the different school directors.

References

1. GEPE: Modernização tecnológica do ensino em Portugal. Estudo de Diagnóstico. Minitério da Educação, Lisboa, Portugal (2008)
2. Gabinete de Estatística e Planeamento da Educação: Modernização Tecnologica das Escolas. Ministério da Educação, Lisboa, Portugal (2008)
3. Blyth, A., Almeida, R., Forrester, D., Gorey, A., Hostens, G.: Modernising Secondary School Buildings in Portugal. OECD Centre for Effective Learning Environments (CELE), OECD, no place of publication (2009)
4. Castro, A., Santos, L.: Implementation of the Technological Plan for Education in Portugal, a School Perspective. In: Tatnall, A., Kereteletswe, O.C., Visscher, A. (eds.) ITEM 2010. IFIP AICT, vol. 348, pp. 75–85. Springer, Heidelberg (2011)
5. Morgan, D.L.: Focus group. Annual Review of Sociology 22, 129–152 (1996), http://www.jstor.org/stable/2083427 (retrieved August 31, 2014)
6. Krueger, R., Casey, M.: Focus Groups: A Practical Guide for Applied Research. Sage Publications, Thousand Oaks (2000)
7. Krueger, R.A.: Analyzing and reporting focus group results. Sage Publications, Thousand Oaks (1998)

Educational Stakeholders and Key Competencies

Key ICT Competencies within the European Higher Education Area

Javier Osorio and Julia Nieves

Universidad de Las Palmas de Gran Canaria, Spain
javier.osorio@ulpgc.es

Abstract. The recent incorporation of Spanish universities in the European Higher Education Area (EHEA) has produced fundamental changes. In a short period of time, universities have moved from a system focused on the professor and accumulating knowledge to one focused on the student and acquiring competencies. This new setting presents a challenge to educational managers about how to effectively organize the development of these types of competencies. One of the most important competencies for students' preparation to enter the job market is the use of Information and Communications Technology (ICT). This paper examines the key competencies in university education and their relationship with competencies in the use of ICT. To do so, first, two European studies are outlined, followed by one study at the national level, and finally a more local study is described. The results show that the socio-economic context determines to a certain degree which educational competencies must be developed in university education. Moreover, the ICT competencies are acquired more effectively if they are combined with other educational competencies valued by the job market. The study ends with a section on implications for the educational management of ICT.

Keywords: Competencies, ICT competencies, EHEA.

1 Introduction

The implementation of the European Higher Education Area (EHEA) has produced a significant transformation in the teaching-learning approaches used in Spanish public universities. In a relatively short period of time, university education has gone from being based on memorizing contents to being based on developing skills and competencies. It has evolved from instruction focused on the figure of the professor as the source of knowledge to a system where the student becomes the protagonist in his/her learning process, while the professor takes on a secondary role of support or guidance. Some tension has been experienced by professors and students during this transition. Both collectives have had to adapt to a new environment, in many cases after being accustomed to other methodologies or work methods for many years. The natural inertia often reflected in resistance to change became evident in Spanish universities. At times, both professors and students have tacitly limited themselves to merely transforming the terminology, while maintaining the essence of the old teaching-learning systems [1].

D. Passey and A. Tatnall (Eds.): KCICTP/ITEM 2014, IFIP AICT 444, pp. 291–305, 2014.

One of the main changes imposed by the new situation involves assimilating and understanding the concept of competencies. The term competency has been widely addressed in the educational literature [2, 3]. A competency can be defined as the skills or knowledge acquired in a certain area [4]. The EHEA framework has developed qualification guidelines for developing homogeneous competencies in the universities of the different member countries. The purpose was to adopt a common terminology and establish a set of competencies that can be considered general, and that, in the current socio-economic context, must be developed by all students in higher education.

One of the most frequently mentioned competencies in the different reports elaborated for higher education is the one related to the use of information and communications technology (ICT). There is widespread agreement that students in higher education must show that they have skills in this domain. However, although they highlight the importance of this competence, relatively few studies have addressed which specific ICT skills should be developed in higher education, beyond merely knowing the main steps in operating an electronic device for a certain purpose.

The different actors in the educational process often have a vision of ICT competencies that is limited to their use, without considering aspects related to their link to other educational competencies. ICT has a transversal nature; that is, its existence makes sense as far as it supports and facilitates a more efficient or competitive way of performing activities and processes that lead to value generation. ICT competencies should, at the same time, make it possible to develop other competencies, so that the students reinforce their capacity to develop skills in certain specific areas, such as team work, leadership, problem-solving, etc., using the potential that ICT offers [5].

Therefore, within Spanish universities' process of incorporation into the EHEA framework, this paper analyzes the competencies that internal and external agents to the university consider fundamental in guaranteeing the success of the educational process. For this purpose, it reviews recommendations and studies of a general nature in the European setting, as well as a specific study in the Spanish context. Finally, the paper examines a medium-sized Spanish public university, showing the results of a questionnaire completed by business management students on the use of ICT tools. The objective was to find out whether there was a relationship between students' rating of ICT and the development of other educational competencies. The results, although not generalizable, can offer a sort of guide to managing the development of key ICT competencies in the educational setting.

The paper begins with a review of the EHEA. Next, it presents a summary of some topics related to competencies in the educational setting, followed by a description of different studies related to the competencies that should be developed in higher education. Then the results are presented from a 2013 study about the perceptions of business management students from a Spanish university about the interest in the use of ICT in their knowledge field. Finally, some recommendations are proposed for making ICT competencies compatible with other educational competencies.

2 Conceptual Framework

2.1 The European Higher Education Area

The June 1999 Bologna Declaration opted for the creation, by 2010, of a European higher education area that would be compatible among all the signing countries. At the same time, it was supposed to be competitive, offering a high level of attraction for European students and those from other continents. The European education ministers determined six lines of action in Bologna, and three more were added in May 2001 in Prague:

1. Adoption of a system of easily readable and comparable degrees.
2. Adoption of a system essentially based on two main cycles (undergraduate and postgraduate studies).
3. Establishment of a system of credits.
4. Promotion of mobility.
5. Promotion of European cooperation in quality assurance.
6. Promotion of the European dimensions in higher education.
7. Promotion of lifelong learning.
8. Support to higher education institutions and students.
9. Promotion of the attractiveness of the European Higher Education Area.

The guidelines would have to be refined to offer universities and higher education institutions in the signing countries a set of well-defined rules to assure homogeneity in the structure of higher education programs. The Bologna Declaration was an important landmark because it represented the will of the signing countries to advance in the construction of a common educational framework that would facilitate the free circulation of professionals through all the European Union countries. Thus, based on this framework, employers could know and compare the competencies acquired by the professionals they wanted to hire, regardless of their country of origin. However, although agreement on higher education was reached by the European Union and other neighboring areas, it has not yet been possible to create a common structure for primary and secondary education.

In order to develop the strategic lines established in the Bologna Declaration, a pilot study was carried out called "Tuning educational structures in Europe", launched in the year 2000, through the joint work of representatives from a large group of European universities [6]. Some of the objectives proposed were the establishment of a system of homogeneous and comparable degrees, the adoption of a system based on two cycles (undergraduate and postgraduate studies), with another one for specializing in research, and the establishment of a credit system as a reference to measure and compare the student's personal work during his/her training process. The project was designed to determine the generic and specific competencies students should acquire in different first and second cycle disciplines in a series of thematic areas: business studies, educational sciences, geology, history, mathematics, physics and chemistry. In sum, the competencies describe the learning results, that is, what a student knows or can demonstrate after completing a stage in his/her learning process.

The competencies act as frames of reference for elaborating and evaluating study plans. Their purpose is to allow flexibility and autonomy in the elaboration of curricula, while introducing a common language to describe the study plans of the diverse higher education degree programmes. To draw conclusions from the Tuning project, questionnaires were elaborated that were filled out by 7,125 graduates, professors and business owners in 16 European countries.

2.2 Dublin Descriptors

After the publication of the first conclusions of the Tuning Project, the Dublin descriptors were published. They consist of a set of generic competencies that make it possible to differentiate the skills and knowledge the students should have developed at the end of each cycle in the framework of studies adapted to the EHEA. They were defined by a group of international experts who called themselves the Joint Quality Initiative (JQI) and published their conclusions in 2004 [7]. Five sets of criteria were established that would develop in different ways depending on the study cycle considered:

1. Acquiring knowledge and understanding.
2. Applying knowledge and understanding.
3. Making informed judgements and choices.
4. Communicating knowledge and understanding.
5. Capacities to continue learning.

The sets of criteria are not exhaustive; instead, they are skills that must be developed at each higher education level, but to different degrees. They include: (i) the most basic, which is called the short cycle within the first cycle and refers to studies that take about 2 years; (ii) first-cycle studies, also called bachelor's degrees, with a duration of 3 to 4 years; (iii) second-cycle studies, which take 1 to 2 years and correspond to the master's degree; and, finally, (iv) third-cycle studies, or doctorates, with an estimated duration of 3 years. The Dublin descriptors are compatible with the agreements reached in the Tuning project. They complement and develop the definition of the competencies established in this project.

3 The Role of ICT Competencies in the EHEA

As explained above, the competencies represent a dynamic combination of knowledge, understanding, skills and abilities. In the area of ICT, the development of competencies is the key to establishing standards that make it possible to measure the degree of adaptation to educational objectives. Clearly and coherently defining competencies is extremely important for facilitating the educators' task. The ICT field is constantly evolving, with technologies that emerge and then become outdated in very short periods of time. The life cycle of all the ICT-related products is, on average, shorter than that of any other technology [8]. For this reason, the students' acquisition of fundamental knowledge and skills that are not dependent on the ICT available at any given time becomes a continual challenge for educators in this field.

In this sense, reports like the Tuning project or the Dublin descriptors do not shed much light on which competencies must be developed in the specific area of ICT. The Tuning project explicitly establishes the development of skills in the use of information and communications technologies as a generic competence. That is, the importance of this tool is recognized, leaving more precise description for a second level the specific ICT competencies that must be acquired depending on the students' degree programme. In the first phase of the Tuning project, specific competencies were identified for each subject, reaching certain areas that were later broadened in new phases. The specific ICT competencies identified were the following:

- Art History: No specific competencies in ICT use.
- Business: (a) identify and operate adequate software; (b) design and implement information systems.
- Chemistry: Skill at using modern computer and communication techniques applied to chemistry.
- Earth Sciences: No specific competencies in ICT use.
- Education: Ability to make use of e-learning and to integrate it into the learning environment.
- History: Ability to use computer and Internet resources and techniques for elaborating historical or related data (using, for example, statistical or cartographic methods, or creating databases).
- Linguistics: No specific competencies in ICT use.
- Mathematics: (a) ability to use computational tools of numerical and symbolic calculations for posing and solving problems; (b) knowledge of specific programming languages or software.
- Nursing: Demonstrate the ability to use modern technologies to assess and respond appropriately to patient/client need (for example through telenursing, multimedia and web resources).
- Physics: Be able to perform calculations independently, even when a small [personal computer] PC or a large computer is needed, including capacity to utilize or develop computation systems or programmes for information processing, numerical calculus, simulation of physical processes, or control of experiments.

As can be observed, some subjects do not have specific associated competencies in the use of ICT, and others are quite generic, in spite of being specific competencies. This information, although limited, offers a certain guide about what skills should be developed by the students. In order to examine the relative importance awarded by different agents to acquiring competencies in the use of ICT, reference will be made to two studies at the national and local levels. These studies, although reflecting the situation of only one country and area, can be quite useful.

4 Importance Given to ICT Competencies

Coinciding with the beginning of the implementation of the EHEA in Spain, a report by Accenture was published on the professional competencies of Spanish university graduates [9]. The purpose of this study was to find out the perceptions of the three most important agents in professional training and development, that is, companies, professors and students. The objective was to contrast the competencies that companies' human resources departments valued most in hiring professionals with what the professors thought the graduates should have. The students were the third element to be contrasted, through the identification of the competencies they value most. In all, 398 questionnaires were evaluated. Table 1 organizes the 16 most valued competencies the three types of agents were asked to rate, regarding their importance in the professional realm. Few significant differences can be seen in the ratings of some of the competencies, while in others the differences are noteworthy. This is the case with knowledge of a second language, which the students rated in last place for their professional activity compared to the opinion of the professors (8th place) and the human resources managers (5th place).

However, regarding the importance given to ICT competencies, the gap between graduates and firms was smaller (7th and 6th places, respectively), compared to the opinions of the professors, who rated it in 10th place.

Table 1. Competencies defined by the Tuning Project according to the priority given to them by different agents in a national study. Source: adapted from Accenture [9]

	ACADEMIC	COMPANIES	GRADUATES
1	Determination and perseverance in the tasks given and responsibilities taken	Determination and perseverance in the tasks given and responsibilities taken	Ability to evaluate and maintain the quality of work produced
2	Ability to adapt to and act in new situations	Ability to adapt to and act in new situations	Ability to plan and manage time
3	Ability to communicate both orally and through the written word in first language	Interpersonal and interaction skills	Interpersonal and interaction skills
4	Ability to evaluate and maintain the quality of work produced	Ability to evaluate and maintain the quality of work produced	Ability to adapt to and act in new situations
5	Ability to plan and manage time	Ability to communicate in a second language	Ability to identify, pose and resolve problems
6	Ability for abstract thinking, analysis and synthesis	Skills in the use of information and communications technologies	Determination and perseverance in the tasks given and responsibilities taken
7	Interpersonal and interaction skills	Spirit of enterprise, ability to take initiative	Skills in the use of information and communications technologies

Table 1. (*continued*)

	ACADEMIC	COMPANIES	GRADUATES
8	Ability to communicate in a second language	Ability to communicate both orally and through the written word in first language	Ability to work autonomously
9	Capacity to generate new ideas (creativity)	Ability to plan and manage time	Ability to communicate both orally and through the written word in first language
10	Skills in the use of information and communications technologies	Ability to search for, process and analyse information from a variety of sources	Ability to search for, process and analyse information from a variety of sources
11	Ability to work in a team	Ability for abstract thinking, analysis and synthesis	Ability to work in a team
12	Ability to work autonomously	Capacity to generate new ideas (creativity)	Ability for abstract thinking, analysis and synthesis
13	Ability to identify, pose and resolve problems	Ability to identify, pose and resolve problems	Capacity to generate new ideas (creativity)
14	Ability to search for, process and analyse information from a variety of sources	Ability to work autonomously	Ability to motivate people and move toward common goals
15	Spirit of enterprise, ability to take initiative	Ability to motivate people and move toward common goals	Spirit of enterprise, ability to take initiative
16	Ability to motivate people and move toward common goals	Ability to work in a team	Ability to communicate in a second language

This report was limited to indicating that ICT is considered a necessary requisite for obtaining a job with a university degree and that the perception of firms' human resources departments is that computer use has improved considerably in recent years.

In addition, continuing within the Spanish territory, in 2009 a study was conducted on the most valued competencies in the specific socio-economic setting of Gran Canaria Island [10]. This study was sponsored by the Social Council of Las Palmas de Gran Canaria University. The Social Council is an organization that controls the university's functioning, and it is made up of a representation of social collectives and public institutions. The purpose of the study was to identify the priorities in the professional competencies of the graduates of this university, to find out whether they differed from those included in the Accenture report. The justification for the study was the possibility that the priorities regarding the most valued competencies for the professional activity would be different in these specific environmental conditions. Gran Canaria Island is located 1,300 kilometres from the Spanish coast; it has a population of 850,391 inhabitants [11] and a surface area of 1,560 square kilometres. It has a specific socio-economic situation stemming from its distance from the European continent and the fact that its economy is mainly based on the services sector and more specifically, on tourism. The study was carried out using questionnaires sent to firms and local trade unions. The questionnaire was responded to by 45 human resources managers with people with university degrees as members of their staff and by 44 trade union representatives with jobs in firms and public organizations on the island. The questionnaire was sent to the trade union representatives due to the vision this collective could have of the professional setting, given that, although forming part of it, they might value the competencies differently from the way the human resources managers would. As in the Accenture report, the initial references were the 32 competencies identified in the Tuning project. Of these 32 competencies, the 16 most-valued ones were selected. Table 2 shows the results obtained, organized by priorities given to the different competencies evaluated. This table identifies those competencies for which there is agreement between the national and local reports on the responses to the questionnaires filled out by the firms (local trade unions representatives' responses are also compared with national managers' ones).

Table 2 Competencies defined by the Tuning project according to the priority assigned by different agents in a study on Gran Canaria [10]

	COMPANIES	Coincidence	UNIONS	Coincidence
1	Determination and perseverance in the tasks given and responsibilities taken	Yes	Ability to apply knowledge in practical situations	No
2	Ability to apply knowledge in practical situations	No	Knowledge and understanding of the subject area and understanding of the profession	No
3	Spirit of enterprise, ability to take initiative	Yes	Ability to communicate both orally and through the written word in first language	Yes
4	Capacity to generate new ideas (creativity)	Yes	Capacity to learn and stay up-to-date with learning	No
5	Interpersonal and interaction skills	Yes	Ability to identify, pose and resolve problems	Yes

Table 2. (*continued*)

	COMPANIES	Coincidence	UNIONS	Coincidence
6	Capacity to learn and stay up-to-date with learning	No	Ability to work in a team	Yes
7	Ability to work in an international context	No	Ability to plan and manage time	Yes
8	Ability to be critical and self-critical	No	Skills in the use of information and communications technologies	Yes
9	Ability to make reasoned decisions	No	Ability for abstract thinking, analysis and synthesis	Yes
10	Knowledge and understanding of the subject area and understanding of the profession	No	Ability to adapt to and act in new situations	Yes
11	Skills in the use of information and communications technologies	Yes	Ability to evaluate and maintain the quality of work produced	Yes
12	Ability to act on the basis of ethical reasoning	No	Ability to design and manage projects	
13	Ability to work in a team	Yes	Determination and perseverance in the tasks given and responsibilities taken	Yes
14	Appreciation of and respect for diversity and multiculturality	No	Ability to make reasoned decisions	No
15	Ability to adapt to and act in new situations	Yes	Ability to act on the basis of ethical reasoning	No
16	Ability to identify, pose and resolve problems	Yes	Capacity to generate new ideas (creativity)	Yes

The table shows that the similarity between the 16 most-valued competencies in the two reports was about 50% in the case of the firms and 63% for the trade unions, which implies certain variations in the different perceptions on a national report compared to a local one. Regarding the position occupied by competence in handling ICT, the respondents from the firms put it in 11th place, while those belonging to trade unions put it in 8th place. For this competency, the differences between the three agents interviewed was not significant.

5 ICT Competencies: What Are They?

As can be observed, both the reports and the agents participating in the aforementioned studies coincide in highlighting the importance of acquiring competencies in ICT. Traditionally, ICT competencies have been defined as the ability to use the computer, peripheral equipment, operating system and software [12]. Among the set of skills mentioned, it is understood that handling software refers to the use of applications related to basic tasks (e.g. office automation and browsers), as well as specific applications depending on the user's professional field. This vision of the ICT competencies has possibly become one of the most widely extended in the area of higher education. Currently, in the majority of the higher education institutions, when students begin their university studies, it is assumed that they have competencies in the use of the computer, peripheral equipment and the operating system. Based on this premise, it is common practice for university professors to require the students to know how to use the specific software related to the subject they teach. This type of learning has the obvious advantage of bringing the students closer to knowing and handling tools that they will probably use in their professional lives. On the other hand, from the point of view of the professors, they can argue that they collaborate to develop a skill, the use of ICT, which is considered important in studies on higher education [13].

However, this approach reiterates the model frequently repeated in higher education, according to which the teaching of a discipline is fragmented in subjects that are taught in an unconnected way. This means that the students acquire very specific knowledge and skills, but they do not develop the capacity to understand the interactions among them, losing the global view. Teaching specific software applications for each subject in an isolated way from other subjects can only strengthen the effect of fragmentation of knowledge.

As an alternative to this teaching approach, there is an argument for the usefulness of developing competence in using ICT by relating it to other learning competencies. This proposal would involve developing competencies in a combined way, that is, by promoting the development of ICT skills together with one or more of the other competencies proposed in international studies such as the Tuning project. This approach would facilitate the ability to use specific software, which, in turn, would lead to developing competencies such as teamwork, problem-solving, organizing and planning, initiative and entrepreneurship or the capacity to generate new ideas, among others. Obviously, combining capacities is not a simple process, given that certain types of software do not facilitate the development of capacities like those mentioned. However, this limitation can be overcome by integrating the software as part of a broader activity where the objective is not limited to the use of specific software, but rather includes the parallel development of other generic competencies. This proposal undoubtedly involves greater effort on the part of the professor and the students, who would probably have to dedicate more time to performing these types of tasks. The time these two agents have available, as well as other subjects that need the students' attention, can be an important inhibitor of this type of proposal. However, the present study proposes that the students, as leading actors in their own educational process, positively value learning based on competencies that are valued in the job market. Therefore, this paper establishes the following research hypothesis:

University students will more positively rate activities involving the combination of ICT competencies with others of a more generic nature than activities that require the development of competencies focused exclusively on ICT use.

6 Method

To contrast the proposed hypothesis, a questionnaire was given to students in the fourth and last year of the business management study plan. The study plan followed by the students is characterized by the traditional approach of fragmenting knowledge into subjects in the form of isolated compartments. The questionnaire was responded to in May 2013 by the 41 students present in the classroom on the last day of instruction. The subject they were enrolled in was called 'Decision and Simulation Models', an optional subject with a transversal nature. The course highlighted the importance of contemplating a firm's decision-making as a coherent set of decisions that can affect all the functional areas, at the same time that both the short and medium term are considered in the temporal horizon of decision-making. There is an intensive use of simulation models and tools, with the computer playing a key role, which means that all the sessions are carried out in the computer room.

During the 2013 course, the teaching was structured with a competitive business game as the main thread. The students were grouped in teams of 3. The teams competed with each other to obtain the best result on an indicator of the performance of the company they managed. The teams' incentives on this activity were the desire to win and become the best decision-makers in the class, and the chance to obtain up to 5% of the final grade for the best positioned team at the end of the competitive game. Moreover, using the setting proposed by the business game as a reference, as well as the characteristics of the company the students had to manage, the groups were asked to elaborate other activities, all of them based on the use of ICT. All of the activities were related to modelling and decision-making. In summary, the activities requested from the students consisted of:

- Assignment 1: Create a conceptual model, using software for representing conceptual maps, of the functioning pattern and structure of the business game in which the group participates.
- Assignment 2: Construct, using a spreadsheet, a quantitative decision-making support tool that would be useful for making decisions in the company managed by the group in the business game.

Table 3. Link between the proposed activities and the general competencies described in the Tuning Project to develop in higher education

ASSIGNMENT	GENERAL COMPETENCIES
Assignment 1	Ability for abstract thinking, analysis and synthesis Skills in the use of information and communications technologies
Assignment 2	Ability to search for, process and analyse information from a variety of sources Ability to make reasoned decisions Knowledge and understanding of the subject area and understanding of the profession Skills in the use of information and communications technologies
Assignment 3	Capacity to generate new ideas (creativity) Ability to search for, process and analyse information from a variety of sources Ability to make reasoned decisions Ability to work in a team Knowledge and understanding of the subject area and understanding of the profession Ability for abstract thinking, analysis and synthesis Skills in the use of information and communications technologies
Assignment 4	Ability to search for, process and analyse information from a variety of sources Knowledge and understanding of the subject area and understanding of the profession Ability for abstract thinking, analysis and synthesis Skills in the use of information and communications technologies
Assignment 5	Ability to plan and manage time Capacity to generate new ideas (creativity) Ability to identify, pose and resolve problems Ability to apply knowledge in practical situations Ability to make reasoned decisions Ability to work in a team Spirit of enterprise, ability to take initiative Interpersonal and interaction skills Ability to adapt to and act in new situations Ability to motivate people and move toward common goals Skills in the use of information and communications technologies

- Assignment 3: Diagnose the competitive situation of the company being managed in the business game and make a strategic plan for it using software for strategic planning.
- Assignment 4: Model and simulate, using systems dynamics software, the results forecast in any variable (e.g. benefits, personnel, savings, etc.) of one of the strategies proposed by the students for the company in the business game.
- Assignment 5: Manage a virtual company using competitive business game software.

Table 3 shows the link between the proposed activities and the general competencies described in the Tuning project to be developed in higher education. As can be observed, the 5th activity included a greater number of generic learning competencies. Several of these activities were those most highly rated by the students in the results of the Tuning project (see Table 1).

The questionnaire the students were asked to fill out presented a series of questions about the subject. They were asked to rate their level of interest in each of the activities on a 5-point Likert scale. Table 4 shows the means and standard deviation values obtained for the different activities. All the assignments were highly valued. The table shows that the most highly rated activity was the business game (5th assignment). To find out whether the value reached was significant compared to the score obtained for the other activities, a paired t-test was carried out between the business game activity and each of the other activities. The results, shown in Table 5, yielded significant differences at 99% (p-value=0.000).

Table 4. Means and standard deviation values obtained by the different activities

DESCRIPTIVE STATISTICS			
	N	Mean	Std. Deviation
Assignment 1	39	3.5385	.75555
Assignment 2	40	3.9250	.97106
Assignment 3	39	3.8974	.75376
Assignment 4	41	3.2439	1.09042
Assignment 5	40	4.5500	.59700
Valid N (listwise)	33		

Table 5. Paired t-tests between the business game activity and each of the other assignments

PAIRED SAMPLES TEST				
		T	df	Sig. (2-tailed)
Pair 1	Assignment 1- Assignment 5	-6.812	36	.000
Pair 2	Assignment 2- Assignment 5	-3.321	37	.002
Pair 3	Assignment 3- Assignment 5	-4.789	36	.000
Pair 4	Assignment 4- Assignment 5	-7.514	38	.000

These results may well show that the students, aware of the competencies they have to develop to prepare for their entrance in the job market, positively value both the ICT applications that develop specific competencies and those that develop general ones.

7 Implications for the Educational Management of ICT

Managers of higher education face the dilemma of which ICT competencies the students have to develop. There is still some lack of definition about which ICT competencies the students need, not only in their specialized field, but also in light of new issues and requirements in the modern world and in the job market. Throughout this paper we have proposed an approach that would relate ICT competencies with more generic ones associated with the educational process. For this purpose, based on generic competencies defined in highly respected international reports, it is advisable to identify the most relevant ones in the specific socio-economic environment in which the teaching-learning process takes place. Then, people responsible for educational management could propose that ICT competencies be taught under an integrating prism that not only develops specific competencies related to the students' future professional field, but also more general competencies that companies and organizations offering jobs consider necessary in university students' training.

References

1. Gonzalez, J.M., Arquero, J.L., Hassall, T.: The change towards a teaching methodology based in competencies: a case study in a Spanish university. Research Papers in Education 29(1), 111–130 (2014)
2. Stewart, J., Hamlin, B.: Competence-based Qualifications: The Case for Established Methodologies. Journal of European Industrial Training 16(10), 9–16 (1992)
3. Martinez, M., Carrasco, S.: Propuestas para el cambio docente en la Universidad. [Proposal for teaching change at the university]. Octaedro-ICE, Barcelona, Spain (2006)
4. Short, E.C.: Competence reexamined. Education Theory 34, 201–207 (1984)
5. Llorens, A., Llinas-Audet, X., Ras, A., Chiaramonte, L.: The ICT skills gap in Spain: Industry expectations versus university preparation. Computer Applications in Engineering Education 21(2), 256–264 (2013)
6. Gonzalez, J., Wagenaar, R.: Tuning educational structures in Europe. Final Report Phase One. Deusto University, Bilbao, Spain and Groningen University, Groningen, The Netherlands (2003)
7. Joint Quality Initiative (JQI): Shared 'Dublin' descriptors for Short Cycle, First Cycle, Second Cycle and Third Cycle Awards. Draft 1 working document on JQI meeting in Dublin on 18 October 2004 (2004), http://archive.ehea.info/folder?year_selected=4&issued_by=349 (retrieved September 4, 2014)
8. Laudon, K., Laudon, J.: Management Information systems: managing the digital firm, 10th edn. Prentice Hall, Harlow (2007)

9. Accenture: Las competencias profesionales en los titulados. Contraste y diálogo Universidad-Empresa [Graduates professional competencies. Contrast and dialogue University-Companies]. Accenture (2007)
10. Social Council of Las Palmas de Gran Canaria University: Analysis of most valued competencies in the specific socio-economic setting of Gran Canaria Island. Internal working paper (2009)
11. INE: Informe Anual 2012 [Annual report 2012]. Instituto Nacional de Estadistica [Statistics National Institute], Madrid, Spain (2012)
12. Moore, D.: Curriculum for an engineering renaissance. IEEE Transactions in Education 46, 452–455 (2003)
13. Evans, D., Goodnick, S., Roedel, R.: ECE curriculum in 2013 and beyond: Vision for a metropolitan public research university. IEEE Transactions in Education 46, 420–428 (2003)

Learner Differences in the Online Context: Introducing a New Method

Arne Hendrik Schulz[1] and Debora Jeske[2]

[1] Institute for Information Management Bremen, University of Bremen, Germany
ahschulz@ifib.de
[2] Psychology and Communication Technology (PaCT) Lab, Department of Psychology, Northumbria University, UK
debora.jeske@unn.ac.uk

Abstract. The paper introduces an alternative method to analyze different learning styles among students. This method was developed as an alternative to more traditional methods such as hierarchical cluster analysis. The method was tested using a large data set (n = 868) which included participants completing a small e-module in addition to a small number of measures to assess learner characteristics. The resulting log files were analyzed using the new method. Results were similar to those observed using traditional methods. The method provides a new starting point for subsequent analysis and identification of learner differences using other information such as log files from e-learning and Massive Online Open Courses (MOOCs).

Keywords: E-learning, log file analysis, cluster analysis, learner group differences, learning strategies.

1 Introduction

The research about learners in e-learning environments covers many different areas in education, pedagogy, psychometrics and design. A lot of research addresses pedagogic questions like acceptance of tests and materials or the extent to which learners benefit from using digital systems like Learning Management Systems [1, 2, 3]. Determining the needs of different users and learner groups plays a significant role in education as this allows educators, practitioners and designers to respond to and adapt tutor instructions to various learning characteristics exhibited by these groups. This has generated numerous studies on adaptive hypermedia, personalized design and e-learning [4, 5].

The use of trace and log file information to identify different groups of learners and users using various algorithms and analyses allows researchers to examine different behaviors. This approach of identifying different user groups is very helpful when combined with additional behavioral data gathered during online activities. In addition, when we try to understand learning processes, many more variables may come into play. The pace at which we learn and how we navigate is often influenced by various different learner characteristics ranging from prior knowledge, age,

D. Passey and A. Tatnall (Eds.): KCICTP/ITEM 2014, IFIP AICT 444, pp. 306–317, 2014.

motivation, learning preferences to strategies [6]. This means that when we create clusters using log files, we can use these new clusters in combination with additional learner characteristics to better understand cluster differences. These independent variables might inform research in the area of digital competencies which e-learners may lack and hence impact the efficiency with which e-learning tools can support their learning.

1.1 Previous Research

There has been a lot of research on the topic of learner analytics in digital environments, recently summarized under the term learning analytics [7], a subcategory of educational data mining [8, 9, 10]. Chen et al. [11] create a framework for analyzing students' online learning portfolios. They include logon times, logon days, general activity within the system (clicks, duration of studying) and course results (midterm and final) of 162 undergraduate students. Results show that higher online learning activity and more intensive work with online materials leads to significantly better course results and grades. Del Valle and Duffy [12] clustered 59 learners of an "online teacher professional development curriculum". Based on the online behavior (total time online, course duration, average inter-session interval, proportion of time on learning resources, proportion of learning resources accessed, exploration, proportion of time in messenger) the authors extracted 3 user clusters named mastery orientated, task focused and minimal approach. The former two groups can be characterized as being more active within the course; the last group is more inactive, but has the highest self-reported prior knowledge. The more active groups (mastery orientated and task focused) had a higher satisfaction and higher learning effect (self-reported). Lee [13] asked 116 students of a general education course at a Taiwan university to fill out a questionnaire about their online learning perception and styles. Three clusters were extracted and described. One cluster represented students that are highly motivated and adopted deep learning strategies, the second cluster had students that were also highly motivated and tended to adopt deep learning strategies. The last cluster had students with the lowest motivation and adoption of deep strategies. Quinell et al. [14] also found significant differences in the learner styles of first year university degree biology students. There are several other studies researching students' performances and clustering them using self-reported measures [15, 16, 17]. Nevertheless, most of these studies rely only on questionnaires and sometimes on examination and term results or grades. They do not take students' online behavior into account.

1.2 Goals of This Research

In order to capture the learner characteristics of more diverse and broader learners, it will be essential to utilize new tools to analyze patterns and optimize what we learn about our learners. The aims of this paper are therefore to: (1) describe a new method to cluster learners and (2) demonstrate the utility of this method in a large data set of e-learners for which both log files and self-reported learner characteristics had been collected. We focused on variables that had also been included in the examination of learner differences in previous research. We provide evidence demonstrating that the new method performs similarly and as well as traditional cluster analysis.

2 Introduction to the New Clustering Method

All user actions within our developed e-learning model (including content and questions) are logged. This information is used to extract separate user groups based on their systems' usage. We cluster the user using hierarchical clustering technique [18, 19, 20] with Ward's [21] linkage algorithm. The distance between two users is measured via two measures developed by Xiao et al. [22] and Xiao and Zhang [23], named *frequency based measure* and *viewing-time based measure*. Both measures are based on the *cosine angle* [24] and are widely used in the areas of information retrieval [25]. Xiao et al. define a webpage that consists of k different pages $P = \{ p_1, p_2, p_3, \ldots p_k \}$ accessed by n different users $U = \{ u_1, u_2, u_3, \ldots u_n \}$. Frequency based measure takes into account how often pages are visited by the users, while the viewing-time based measure considers the amount of time each user is spending on different pages. Therefore, let $acc(p_k,u_i)$ be the number of times user u_i is accessing page p_k and let $t(p_k,u_i)$ be the time t the user u_i spends viewing page p_k. If a user is not accessing a page (and is not spending any time on that page) each measure will be 0.

The similarity of two users, according to the frequency based measure, is calculated using the following formula:

$$sim\_fb(u_i,u_j) = \frac{\sum_k (acc(p_k,u_i) \cdot acc(p_k,u_j))}{\sqrt{\sum_k (acc(p_k,u_i))^2 \cdot \sum_k (acc(p_k,u_j))^2}}$$

$\sum_k (acc(p_k,u_i))^2$ is the squared sum of the access times of all accessed pages by user $u_{i/j}$ and $\sum_k (acc(p_k,u_i) \cdot acc(p_k,u_j))$ is the product of all accesses done by both users. If both users access the same pages and have identical accesses on all visited pages, their similarity will be 1. If they do not visit any common pages at all, their similarity will be 0.

The viewing-time based similarity of two users is calculated using the following formula:

$$sim\_vt(u_i,u_j) = \frac{\sum_k (t(p_k,u_i) \cdot t(p_k,u_j))}{\sqrt{\sum_k (t(p_k,u_i))^2 \cdot \sum_k (t(p_k,u_j))^2}}$$

$\sum_k (t(p_k,u_i))^2$ is the sum of the squared viewing times of all visited pages by user u_i and $\sum_k (t(p_k,u_i) \cdot t(p_k,u_j))$ is the product of all viewing times visited by both compared users. The interpretation of the results is straightforward. We combine both algorithms and weight them. Weighting is needed as the frequency based measure may not bring up the best results, due to the fact that many users visited each page of the e-module once only: the users had a mean of 19.4 page visits (sd = 4.1). Compared to the 18 pages the e-module consisted of, there seems to be not a big variety among the users. Therefore, we weight the viewing-time based measure with .85 and the frequency based measure with .15. The final measure has the following formula and will be referred to as *cosine similarity*:

$$sim(u_i, u_j) = 0.15 \cdot sim\_fb(u_i, u_j) + 0.85 \cdot sim\_vt(u_i, u_j)$$

The idea of both algorithms is that users with similar interests have a common "footprint" in the log files. Using the frequency based measure, this means that they will have the same numbers of accesses of common pages [cf. 26]). Using the viewing-time based measure assumes that the same interests are reflecting in the same viewing times. Furthermore, this measure is indirectly taking into account more hidden variables like literacy (affecting the viewing time). Both algorithms do not measure sequence of the pages. The e-learning modules are linear which does not need such a feature.

3 Application of the New Method

In the next step, we wanted to apply the new method to a data set of e-learners for which we also had log file information. As shown above, we took the number of page visits for the *frequency based measure* and the visiting time per page for the *viewing-time based measure*. If a user had multiple page visits, the viewing times were summed up.

The test material was a small e-module featuring five short chapters on team development. Participants had to complete a number of short test questions. Following this, participants completed a set of items to assess their learning characteristics.

3.1 Self-reported Variables

The questions included demographics, prior knowledge about the topic and about e-learning in general, as well as questions about the self-reported measures (discussed further below). These were accessed via a questionnaire that had to be answered before the module itself.

Deep and surface learning strategy: deep versus surface processing refers to learning styles that capture how learners utilize diverse learning strategies to come to a specific goal [27]. Deep and surface strategies were identified using three items which were inspired by subscales produced by Biggs et al. [27]. An example item for deep strategy is: "When I am interested in a topic, I spend additional time on trying to learn more information about it". An example item for surface strategy is: "I tend to learn more than is necessary" (reverse-coded). So this learning difference helps to detect the amount of effort that individuals invest into learning about a topic, that is, either in-depth or superficially. The response options ranging from (1) "never or only rarely true of me" to (5) "always or almost always true of me".

Serialist learning preference: serialists can be labeled "operation learners" with a more pronounced bottom-up approach [6, 28]. These individuals tend to focus on the immediate or local aspects. They have a narrower focus, oftentimes emphasizing the details and the way to success rather than trying to achieve a larger overview. Serialists learn in a linear and sequential fashion which goes hand in hand with an emphasis on memorizing facts for reproduction, emphasizing product in order to construe logical arguments and simple hypotheses [29]. Serialist processing is often contrasted with holist processing. Holists tend have a more global strategy and wider focus on several aspects [28]. This also means they like to focus on numerous topics simultaneously, emphasizing the use of numerous sources in order to elaborate on information and seek patterns amongst facts. These aspects lead to more generalized descriptions and higher level comprehension, but potentially at the expense of individual detail. In all three datasets, serialist preference was measured using 7 items. An example here is: "I deal with a new topic as thoroughly as I can first time around". The response options ranged from (1) "strongly disagree" to (5) "strongly agree".

Prior knowledge: we also asked participants one item each about their prior knowledge with e-learning modules and the topic of the e-module. Knowledge about e-learning was assessed using four answering options: (1) I have a lot of experience with e-learning; (2) I have some experience with e-learning; (3) I have very little experience with e-learning; and (4) I have no prior experience with e-learning. The four answering options asked about topic familiarity as follows: (1) I was very knowledgeable; (2) I was quite knowledgeable; (3) I knew a little; and (4) I didn't know anything about it. All answers were reverse-coded, so that more knowledge corresponded with higher scores.

All items measuring learning strategies and preferences were summarized to provide a mean-centered composite for each scale. All scales featured a reliability coefficient above .7.

3.2 Participants and Procedure

Participants were students at a distance-learning institution in Germany. They were offered opportunity to participate in exchange for obtaining research credit (N=686). We collected information about participant sex and age. Participants were between 17 and 63 years old (M=32.62, SD=9.27), the most frequent age (mode) indicated was 28 with a mean of 32.6 years (SD = 9.2). About one fifth were female (n = 145). Male participants were slightly younger (M = 32.3 vs. M = 33.6). A t-test provides no significant difference (t-value = 1.402, degrees of freedom = 218.441, p-value < 0.16).

Data collection took place in spring 2013. In total, 686 participants completed both the test and the questionnaire. Missing and incomplete information reduced the number to 669 participants.

4 Results of the Analysis

We first examined the given cluster solutions. Scree plots and dendrograms led us to a four cluster solution. In the next step, we conducted descriptive statistics and correlations of the measures (Table 1). Finally, we examined user clusters based on log file information obtained from all learners during the e-module. In the final step, we examined how the clusters we identified using log files, and how they differed in terms of their learner characteristics.

4.1 Cluster Results

The visualization of the clustering process in the dendrogram indicated four possible solutions, between two and four groups of classifications. A scree plot indicated a three cluster solution. A four cluster solution leads to a higher distance between the clusters (.099 versus .109) and a lower within-group distance (.171 versus .169). Possible distances range from 0 to 1 as the calculated distances have the identical range. Additionally, the average silhouette width indicator [30] suggests a four cluster solution (.251 versus .239). The average silhouette width ranges from -1 to 1. The absolute value is interpreted. Additionally, the fourth generated cluster in the four cluster solution (split from cluster 2 in the three cluster solution) shows a better silhouette than the non-split cluster 2 in the three cluster solution, Therefore, we decided to use a four cluster solution.

4.2 Descriptives for Self-report Measures

Descriptive statistics about the self-reported measures show that the users selected response options in the middle of the five-point scale with higher average scores for deep strategy processing and serialist preferences (see Table 1). The prior knowledge was above average for both variables with a slightly higher value for prior e-learning knowledge (and a lower standard deviation).

Table 1. Summary of self-reported measures (N=669)

Variable	Scale	Mean	SD
Deep strategy	5	3.52	0.85
Surface strategy	5	2.98	0.95
Serialist preference	5	3.57	0.67
Prior topic knowledge	4	2.90	1.12
Prior e-learning knowledge	4	3.07	1.07

The correlation matrix reveals that knowledge and behavior are almost uncorrelated and mostly not significant. Prior topic knowledge and prior e-learning knowledge have a weak correlation ($r = .17$, $p < .001$). Deep strategy and surface strategy has a moderate and negative correlation as expected ($r = -.51$, $p < .001$). In addition, surface strategy and serialist preference correlate negatively ($r = -.18$, $p < .001$). For more details see Table 2.

Table 2. Correlation of self-reported measures

	Deep Strategy	Surface Strategy	Serialist preference	Prior topic knowledge	Prior e-learning knowledge
Deep strategy	1				
Surface strategy	-0.51***	1			
Serialist preference	0.02	-0.18***	1		
Prior topic knowledge	0.03	-0.02	0.07	1	
Prior e-learning knowledge	0.06	-0.08	0.06	0.17***	1

Note: Pearson Correlation - $p < 0.05$ = *; $p < 0.01$ = **; $p < 0.001$ = ***

4.3 Learner Differences

The cluster sizes were big enough to test them for significant differences related to the following characteristics: age, surface strategy, deep strategy, prior knowledge (according to the e-module topic and e-learning in general) and serialist learning preference. Additionally, we included the time used in the e-module and the number of page visits in the analysis. Covariates were gender and age (where age was not a dependent variable).

The results of the analysis of variance suggest significant group differences in relation to the prior e-learning knowledge of the participants in the different clusters, their level of serialist learning preferences and the amount of time used (see Table 3). A number of other differences appear relevant as a means to differentiate the clusters from one another. The findings are summarized in Table 3.

Table 3. Analysis of cluster differences

	Cluster 1 Mean	Cluster 2 Mean	Cluster 3 Mean	Cluster 4 Mean	ANCOVA
Age	33.03	31.10	33.72	31.06	$F(3.663)=1.103$, $p=.347$
Deep strategy	3.53	3.49	3.48	3.88	$F(3.663)=1.949$, $p=.120$
Surface strategy	2.99	2.98	2.90	3.01	$F(3.663)=.194$, $p=.900$
Serialist preference	3.49	3.62	3.60	3.78	$F(3.663)=2.954$, $p=.032$
Prior topic knowledge	3.22	3.27	3.35	2.97	$F(3.561)=5.383$, $p=.001$
Prior e-learning knowledge	3.01	2.77	2.66	2.47	$F(3.632)=2.218$, $p=.085$
Page visits	19.36	19.47	19.05	19.00	$F(3.662)=.306$, $p=.821$
Total time	374.77	460.98	349.49	514.16	$F(3.662)=16.088$, $p<.001$

Figure 1 also visualizes how the four clusters compare in terms of the learning-relevant characteristics (deep strategy, surface strategy, serialist preferences, and prior learning.

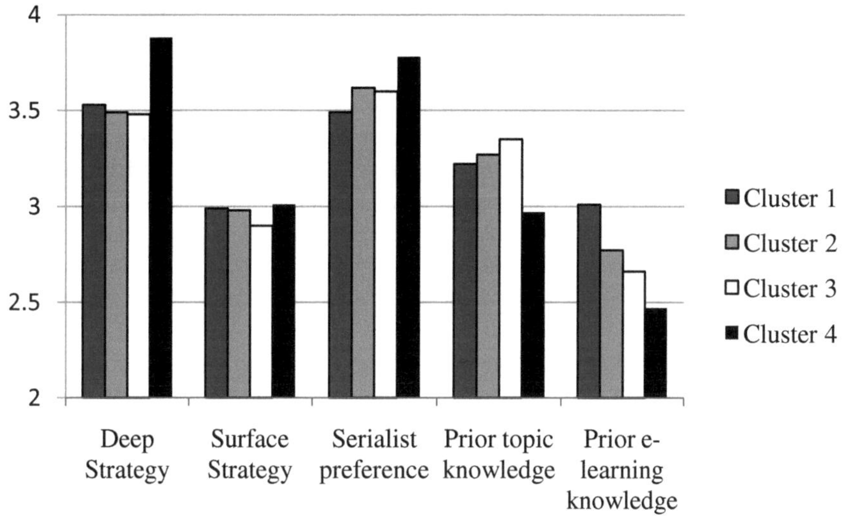

Fig. 1. Visualized cluster differences

In order to label the three clusters of e-learners coherently, we decided to label the clusters first and foremost based on their level of prior knowledge as e-learning *experts* (those with the highest prior knowledge), e-learning *users* (with average prior knowledge) or e-learning *novices* (with low prior knowledge). All clusters featuring high serialist learning preferences were labeled as *sequential*, as in very orderly, and those with low values on this variable as *superficial* e-learners. All clusters featuring high scores in terms of their surface strategy approach were considered as *surface* e-learners. We focused on the significant differences only.

We consider Cluster 1 as *disengaged but knowledgeable e-learning experts*. The assigned users have the highest e-learning knowledge (3.01 out of 4), but only average knowledge about the topic compared to other clusters (3.22 out of 4). They also exhibit the lowest serialist preference compared to other clusters (3.49 out of 5) and appear to be more disengaged (superficial in their approach). They spend a relatively low amount of time in the small e-module overall compared to other groups. High e-learning experience might have led to greater disengagement with the e-module. In addition, their tendency to work in a less sequential and detail-oriented manner led to less time spent in the module.

Individuals in Cluster 2 are *engaged and knowledgeable e-learning users*. They appear to have average topic knowledgc (3.27 out of 5) and e-learning experience (2.77 out of 5, hence users, not experts). They show a more pronounced serialist preference (3.62 out of 5). They have, however, invested quite a lot in learning as they also spend more time in the e-module than two out of the four clusters. This suggests that average experience and greater orientation to detail also increases learning time.

Cluster 3 seems to include *disengaged but very knowledge e-learning users*. They have the highest familiarity with the topic (3.35 out of 4), but average familiarity with e-learning (2.66 out of 4). They have serialist preferences similar to those of Cluster 2 (3.60 out of 5). At the same time, this cluster spends the least amount of time on the e-module. This suggests that while they are detail-oriented, higher familiarity with the topic may lead to a more disengaged learning process.

Cluster 4 includes the *engaged but not very knowledgeable e-learning novices*. This group has very limited e-learning experience (2.47 out of 4) and limited topic knowledge (2.97 out of 4). At the same time, this group includes the individuals with the strongest serialist preference. They will diligently study the materials, and take longer than individuals from other clusters. The novelty of the topic and e-learning in addition to their detail-orientation (via serialist preference) may explain why they are more engaged with the materials.

Our clusters suggest that prior knowledge can help to explain cluster difference in terms of time dedicated to the e-module learners are studying. Learning characteristics such as serialist preferences (detail orientation and sequential processing) may play an additional role when trying to explain cluster differences, especially in relation to the amount of time that individuals will invest in a task.

4.4 Performance of the Cosine Similarity

We also examined the type of clusters obtained using the Euclidean distance [31] instead of the cosine angle, again applying Ward's linkage method in the hierarchical cluster analysis. The results are largely identical, resulting in four clusters that showed similar learning differences. An analysis of variance using four clusters revealed several significant differences, in relation to prior knowledge (e-learning and topic), serialist learning preference and age.

Whereas the results were quite comparable, we observed two differences. First, the clusters computed with the Euclidean distance were more equally distributed, resulting in two clusters with about 210 cases each and two further clusters including 116 and 132 cases, respectively. The generated clusters using the cosine similarity are significantly unequally distributed, resulting in two big clusters (281 and 291 cases) and two small clusters (65 and 32 cases). Secondly, and more importantly, the goodness of fit between the two dissimilarity measures is significantly different. We computed the *Average Silhouette Width* [32] for both solutions. The Silhouette Width compares the dissimilarity between within-cluster cases and without-cluster cases for each case. The value has a range from -1 to 1, where 1 stands for a perfect fit of that case into its designated cluster. The Average Silhouette Width is the grand mean over all cases. Kaufman and Rousseeuw [30] define all values below 0.25 as not suitable ("no structure found"). Values between 0.26 and 0.5 are being considered as having a weak structure, values between 0.51 and 0.7 are seen that a reasonable structure has been found and values above 0.7 stand for a strong structure.

The Average Silhouette Width of the solution defined by the Euclidean distance was 0.04. This solution indicates that the solution did not result in a meaningful structure. One bigger and one smaller cluster also had Average Silhouette Widths values below 0. The two remaining clusters showed a weak structure (0.27 and 0.37). The clusters generated by the cosine similarity led to a better detection of the underlying structure. The Average Silhouette Width value was 0.26, which means that the cosine similarity helped to detect evidence of a weak structure. One big cluster had an Average Silhouette Width value of 0.53 ("reasonable structure found") while one small cluster had a width of 0.32. The values of the two remaining clusters ranged from -0.05 up to 0.04. This means that the structure still cannot be regarded as being meaningful, but the algorithm shows a better solution than the Euclidean distance.

5 Discussion

The results of the new method suggest that we can obtain differentiated cluster profiles by considering both log files and self-report data together. The new method presents an alternative to hierarchical clustering, which resulted in similar results. The advantages of the new method are as follows: first, the algorithms we used were developed for the application in web-based digital systems; additionally, we combined two measures to include both the time spent on every page and the number of single page accessed by each user; and finally, our analyses showed that the cosine similarity had a better detection of the underlying structure than the Euclidean distance. Xiao et al. [22], Xiao and Zhang [23], and Kumar et al. [33] developed more algorithms to compare users. Some of these algorithms include the users' path and can lead to better cluster solutions. In fact, due to the linear structure of the e-module, these algorithms were not needed, but could be implemented easily if needed.

In conclusion, we believe that the combination of new methods and more data can aid future learning analyses aimed at detecting digital competencies and personalization opportunities. Most of the research tends to focus on the needs of younger learners. However, given the importance of lifelong learning, future users are likely to show increased demographic and skill diversity. As learners become more differentiated in terms of their past learning (prior knowledge), age and various related skills (digital competence), it becomes more appropriate to include these variables in order to consider their influence. This development also suggests that learners will start from different baselines. New methods such as the one we introduced will provide the means to consider such differences and characteristics and address these potentially in personalized and different tutoring - so as to improve performance for all users across the board and to increase user satisfaction and optimize the learning experience [34, 35].

References

1. Concannon, F., Flynn, A., Campbell, M.: What campus-based students think about the quality and benefits of e-learning. British Journal of Educational Technology 36, 501–512 (2005)

2. Garrison, D.R.: E-Learning in the 21st Century: A Framework for Research and Practice. Routledge, New York (2011)
3. Selim, H.M.: Critical success factors for e-learning acceptance: Confirmatory factor models. Computers & Education 49, 396–413 (2007)
4. Brusilovsky, P.: Adaptive Hypermedia. User Modeling and User-Adapted Interaction 11, 87–110 (2001)
5. Hsiao, I.-H., Brusilovsky, P.: Motivational Social Visualizations for Personalized E-Learning. In: Ravenscroft, A., Lindstaedt, S., Kloos, C.D., Hernández-Leo, D. (eds.) EC-TEL 2012. LNCS, vol. 7563, pp. 153–165. Springer, Heidelberg (2012)
6. Jeske, D., Backhaus, J., Stamov Roßnagel, C.: Evaluation and revision of the Study Preference Questionnaire: Creating a user-friendly tool for nontraditional learners and learning environments. Learning and Individual Differences 30, 133–139 (2013)
7. Greller, W., Drachsler, H.: Translating Learning into Numbers: A Generic Framework for Learning Analytics. Educational Technology & Society 15, 42–57 (2012)
8. Baker, R., Yacef, K.: The state of educational data mining in 2009: A review and future visions. Journal of Educational Data Mining 1, 3–17 (2009)
9. Dyckhoff, A.L., Zielke, D., Bültmann, M., Chatti, M.A., Schroeder, U.: Design and Implementation of a Learning Analytics Toolkit for Teachers. Educational Technology & Society 15, 58–76 (2012)
10. Romero, C., Ventura, S.: Educational Data Mining: A Review of the State of the Art. IEEE Transactions on Systems, Man, and Cybernetics, Part C (Applications and Reviews) 40, 601–618 (2010)
11. Chen, C.-M., Li, C.-Y., Chan, T.-Y., Jong, B.-S., Lin, T.-W.: Diagnosis of students' online learning portfolios. In: Frontier. In: 37th Annual Education Conference-Global Engineering: Knowledge Without Borders, Opportunities Without Passports, FIE 2007, p. T3D–17. IEEE (2007)
12. Del Valle, R., Duffy, T.M.: Online learning: Learner characteristics and their approaches to managing learning. Instructional Science 37, 129–149 (2009)
13. Lee, S.W.-Y.: Investigating students' learning approaches, perceptions of online discussions, and students' online and academic performance. Computers & Education 68, 345–352 (2013)
14. Quinnell, R., May, E., Peat, M.: Conceptions of Biology and Approaches to Learning of First Year Biology Students: Introducing a technique for tracking changes in learner profiles over time. International Journal of Science Education 34, 1053–1074 (2012)
15. Richardson, J.T.E.: Mental models of learning in distance education. British Journal of Educational Psychology 77, 253–270 (2007)
16. Sparks, R.L., Patton, J., Ganschow, L.: Profiles of more and less successful L2 learners: A cluster analysis study. Learning and Individual Differences 22, 463–472 (2012)
17. Wade, S.E., Trathen, W., Schraw, G.: An Analysis of Spontaneous Study Strategies. Reading Research Quarterly 25, 147–166 (1990)
18. Everitt, B.S., Landau, S., Leese, M., Stahl, D.: Cluster analysis. Wiley, Chichester (2011)
19. Hastie, T., Tibshirani, R., Friedman, J.: The Elements of Statistical Learning: Data Mining, Inference, and Prediction. Springer, New York (2011)
20. Liu, B.: Web data mining: exploring hyperlinks, contents, and usage data. Springer, Berlin (2011)
21. Ward, J.H.: Hierarchical Grouping to Optimize an Objective Function. Journal of the American Statistical Association 58, 236–244 (1963)

22. Xiao, J., Zhang, Y., Jia, X., Li, T.: Measuring similarity of interests for clustering web-users. In: Proceedings of the 12th Australasian Database Conference, pp. 107–114. IEEE Computer Society, Washington, DC (2001)
23. Xiao, J., Zhang, Y.: Clustering of web users using session-based similarity measures. In: Proceedings of the 2001 International Conference on Computer Networks and Mobile Computing, pp. 223–228 (2001)
24. Tan, P.-N., Steinbach, M., Kumar, V.: Introduction to data mining. Pearson/Addison-Wesley, Boston (2010)
25. Grossman, D.A., Frieder, O.: Information Retrieval: Algorithms and Heuristics. Springer, Dordrecht (2004)
26. Xu, B., Recker, M.: Teaching Analytics: A Clustering and Triangulation Study of Digital Library User Data. Educational Technology & Society 15, 103–115 (2012)
27. Biggs, J., Kember, D., Leung, D.Y.P.: The revised two-factor Study Process Questionnaire: R-SPQ-2F. British Journal of Educational Psychology 71, 133–149 (2001)
28. Ford, N.: Learning Styles and Strategies of Postgraduate Students. British Journal of Educational Technology 16, 65–77 (1985)
29. Ford, N.: Cognitive styles and virtual environments. Journal of the American Society for Information Science 51, 543–557 (2000)
30. Kaufman, L., Rousseeuw, P.J.: Finding Groups in Data. An Introduction to Cluster Analysis. Wiley, Hoboken (2005)
31. Deza, M.M., Deza, E.: Encyclopedia of Distances. Springer, Dordrecht (2013)
32. Rousseeuw, P.J.: Silhouettes: A graphical aid to the interpretation and validation of cluster analysis. Journal of Computational and Applied Mathematics 20, 53–65 (1987)
33. Kumar, P., Krishna, P.R., Bapi, R.S., De, S.K.: Rough clustering of sequential data. Data & Knowledge Engineering 63, 183–199 (2007)
34. Facca, F.M., Lanzi, P.L.: Mining interesting knowledge from weblogs: a survey. Data & Knowledge Engineering 53, 225–241 (2005)
35. Mobasher, B., Cooley, R., Srivastava, J.: Automatic personalization based on Web usage mining. Communications of the ACM 43, 142–151 (2000)

Online Free School Meals as a Cloud-Based Solution: Three Case Studies of Its Use in England

Alan Strickley

Cria Technologies, United Kingdom
alan.strickley@criatech.co.uk

Abstract. Online Free School Meals (OFSM) was a transformational programme supported by the Department for Education (DfE) in England. The full process is documented by Strickley[1]. Whilst the use of the system can be judged an overwhelming success, most Local Authorities (LAs) have stopped short of the full web-based system in which parents can apply directly via an online form as a result of the perception of negligible cost benefits created by a lack of technical expertise, scarce resources and server and development costs. The paper describes how these issues were overcome by developing a generic cloud-based solution. The paper looks at the general structure of the solution and examines the experiences of three types of user: an academy consortium, a single school and a large LA to illustrate adoption, implementation, usage and benefits. It concludes that a cloud-based system is cost effective by removing much administration and as a result of lowering the stigma of applying can result in an increase in applications. This has resulted in financial advantages for schools and LAs.

Keywords: Free school meals, stigma, eligibility checking service, cloud, online.

1 Background

The provision of free school meals (FSM) for children within England and Wales requires that the parent/carer provides evidence that they are eligible, based on a number of criteria. From April 2012 these criteria concerned children whose parents were in receipt of certain support payments [2].

The online free school meals (OFSM) programme was supported by the Department for Education (DfE) and implemented by Connect Digitally in England and Wales in 2010. The full process, documented in Strickley [1], consisted of a web portal which, based on the three criteria of surname, date of birth and National Insurance number (NINO) or National Asylum Support Service (NASS) reference number, can check if a parent/carer qualifies for the entitlement of FSM for their children.

The process is performed using a system called the Eligibility Checking System (ECS) which matches the three criteria against data held in three central government databases, namely, the Home Office, the Department of Work and Pensions (DWP)

D. Passey and A. Tatnall (Eds.): KCICTP/ITEM 2014, IFIP AICT 444, pp. 318–330, 2014.

and Her Majesty's Revenue and Customs (HMRC). A decision is normally received in seconds.

The new online system removes the paper evidence required to prove eligibility [3] thereby creating efficiencies in terms of time and cost for a local authority (LA), removing the stigma for a parent/carer's application [1,4 ,5] as well as giving quick turnaround of a decision, an audit of continuing eligibility and a free school meal for the child within days of an application. As [1] describes, use of the FSM ECS was quickly adopted by LAs and resulted in large efficiencies for schools and LAs as a result of no longer requiring paper proof of eligibility and through continual audit of those eligible.

However, without moving to the full web enabled stage (Stage 4 as described by Strickley) the system was not as streamlined and stigma-free as might be, due to the parent/carer being required to provide a paper application (although no paper evidence) to the school or LA and the need for the data to be input into the ECS (via the portal) by the LA periodically as a comma-separated value (CSV) file; often generated and stored in a spreadsheet.

At the time of the Strickley paper (2013) only 10 LAs had taken the transformation to the full web-based solution. This was because for an individual LA the costs of developing a web-based service solution were high compared to the added benefits that such a system was perceived to generate (assuming that the technical expertise was available to the LA in the first place, which in smaller LAs might not be the case). These costs could generally be assigned as:

- Designing the web-based public facing form.
- Generating the code for the form and hosting it.
- Developing the web services code to communicate with the ECS.
- Obtaining accreditation for these web service calls from the DfE FSM Support Desk.
- Communicating the eligibility outcome to the parent and school.

Supported by the work done by Connect Digitally with respect to the OFSM programme, an independent development company, Software for Data Analysis (SDA) [6], in partnership with the author, developed a solution for the support of OFSM using web services which would help remove these obstacles of cost and resources and enable the full system to be implemented through the following initiatives:

- Creating a generic web-based public facing form that could be adapted to the look and feel of the LA whilst still keeping the basic structure and functionality.
- Using the same web service calls for every form instance.
- As a result of using the same web service calls for every form instance, achieving accreditation from DfE with very little code change.
- Creating a generic email communication system.
- Developing interoperability with the school management information system (MIS).

In addition, a generic back-office system was created for the LA, school (or both as appropriate) where the eligibility check results could be viewed.

By holding both the application form and the back-office systems on a cloud-based system it was possible, with very little adaptation of the generic model, to give users access to the results of eligibility applications made by parent/carers for their children.

Development began in May 2011 of a cloud-based solution and the initial prototype was available in early 2012 with the first users implementing between May 2012 and April 2013. These early adopters are the subjects of the 3 case studies.

2 Implementation

As explained in the "Background" section, the process was intended to be relatively seamless. This section briefly describes the steps involved in creating a system for any type of user. It also examines the various components of the system.

The system was promoted using existing contacts within LAs using a demonstration system via a dedicated web page [7]. Costs were calculated on the size and status of the user and the number of FSM pupils based on government statistical data, but were tailored to the existing conditions of austerity within the UK at the time such that an "average cost" would be in the region of £5,000 per LA and £500 for a single school as against £15,000 to £20,000 for a bespoke solution [8].

Once agreement was made with the LA, implementation was via the following steps:

- Accreditation from the DfE was sought via the company in partnership with the host LA [9].
- A URL was assigned for the application form and back-office functions.
- A list of schools and user details were supplied by the LA.
- Any existing FSM data were supplied in a format defined by SDA for import into the new system.
- Local Land and Property Gazetteer (LLPG) data were supplied by the LA for the address checker. (Where this was not available a national address checker was available at extra cost.)

Once this was arranged the application URL was given to an LA with an LA back-office and school back-office both accessible via the web. These three components are described in "The components of the solution" section below. In addition, user guides were also distributed.

These processes generally could be achieved within 2 weeks. As described above, the system is cloud-based. Whilst this makes for major efficiencies, with respect to upgrades, bug fixes and speed of implementation, it did cause concerns around security. Hence this next section on "Security" deals specifically with this area.

3 Security

Any system needs to be secure but one that utilises cloud technology has to be more so [10]. The company, SDA, was chosen to provide the highest level of data security and comply with all appropriate regulations and codes of practice. In particular, SDA had extensive experience in providing and managing systems involving the transferring and handling of large quantities of personal data, for example, the DfE's National Pupil Database (NPD) and Key to Success (KtS) service. In addition to working on many projects and services for the DfE, SDA also worked for many other central government, local government and non-departmental public body organisations.

Only trained SDA staff, with experience of handling personal data, were permitted to access the OFSM system. All SDA staff were cleared to Baseline Personnel Security Standard and had Enhanced Disclosure and Barring Service (DBS) clearance.

The SDA servers are located in one of TelecityGroup's [11] data centres in London. TelecityGroup is the leading operator of network-independent data centres in Europe and all of their data centres are certified to the ISO 27001:2005 (Information Security Management) standard and have Payment Card Industry Data Security Standard (PCI DSS) accreditation. Physical access to the data centre is controlled by biometrics and access card and the centre is fully staffed for 24 hours every day of the year.

Intrusion detection mechanisms (both within the OFSM domain and between the OFSM domain and connected networks) were in place to identify potential attacks. The OFSM service also has mechanisms in place to detect suspicious activity and to identify suspected multiple applications. Information security events were reported through appropriate management channels as quickly as possible. Management responsibilities between SDA and the LA were established to ensure quick, effective and orderly response to information security incidents. The OFSM service also incorporated reliable user authentication, including measures concerning password strength, renewal and re-use. Audit logs, recording the activities of all users, exceptions and information security events, were produced to assist in future investigations and access control monitoring.

4 The Components of the Solution

The OFSM system consisted of two major elements: the public facing application form and a back-office which collated the results of the application for schools and LA.

4.1 Application Form

The application form was a generic transactional web form which consisted of 5 major sections.

- Home screen: General information and the choice to start a new application or amend an existing one (requiring a unique reference and applicant's date of birth).

- Declaration: A screen explaining the general requirements for eligibility, including legal and essential information such as privacy notices and data protection information.
- Parent/carer: Details of the parent/carer making the application (or for whom the application for eligibility is being made). In particular the legal surname, date of birth and NINO or NASS reference numbers as these are used in the eligibility checking process. In addition, address information, relationship to the child and email address are collected.
- Child: Details of the child/children including their current school. The school is essential so that the application can be seen by the appropriate establishment.
- Submit: Submission of the information above, to the ECS, with electronic declaration of accuracy to ensure due diligence against fraudulent applications.
- End: Almost instantaneous outcome of eligibility check is given to the applicant together with next steps. In addition, an email (if address supplied) is sent to the applicant and at the end of each day the school is sent an email to inform them that there are new eligibilities in their back-office system.

Upon completion of the form the result is stored in the cloud database and is viewable through the LA and school back-office functions.

4.2 School Back-Office

The school back-office is a cloud-based application accessible from any browser that allows the school to examine applications made for FSM eligibility by parents for children in their school. These may be viewed under a series of menu items.

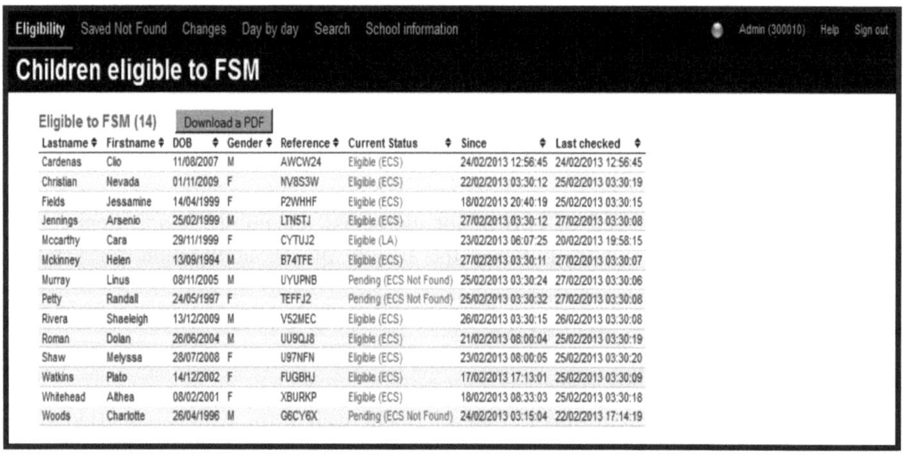
Eligibility Saved Not Found Changes Day by day Search School information Admin (300010) Help Sign out

Children eligible to FSM

Eligible to FSM (14) Download a PDF

Lastname	Firstname	DOB	Gender	Reference	Current Status	Since	Last checked
Cardenas	Clio	11/08/2007	M	AWCW24	Eligible (ECS)	24/02/2013 12:56:45	24/02/2013 12:56:45
Christian	Nevada	01/11/2009	F	NV8S3W	Eligible (ECS)	22/02/2013 03:30:12	25/02/2013 03:30:19
Fields	Jessamine	14/04/1999	F	P2WHHF	Eligible (ECS)	18/02/2013 20:40:19	25/02/2013 03:30:15
Jennings	Arsenio	25/02/1999	M	LTN5TJ	Eligible (ECS)	27/02/2013 03:30:12	27/02/2013 03:30:08
Mccarthy	Cara	29/11/1999	F	CYTUJ2	Eligible (LA)	23/02/2013 06:07:25	20/02/2013 19:58:15
Mckinney	Helen	13/09/1994	M	B74TFE	Eligible (ECS)	27/02/2013 03:30:11	27/02/2013 03:30:07
Murray	Linus	08/11/2005	M	UYUPNB	Pending (ECS Not Found)	25/02/2013 03:30:24	27/02/2013 03:30:06
Petty	Randall	24/05/1997	F	TEFFJ2	Pending (ECS Not Found)	25/02/2013 03:30:32	27/02/2013 03:30:08
Rivera	Shaeleigh	13/12/2009	M	V52MEC	Eligible (ECS)	26/02/2013 03:30:15	26/02/2013 03:30:08
Roman	Dolan	26/06/2004	M	UU9QJ8	Eligible (ECS)	21/02/2013 08:00:04	25/02/2013 03:30:19
Shaw	Melyssa	28/07/2008	F	U97NFN	Eligible (ECS)	23/02/2013 08:00:05	25/02/2013 03:30:20
Watkins	Plato	14/12/2002	F	FUGBHJ	Eligible (ECS)	17/02/2013 17:13:01	25/02/2013 03:30:09
Whitehead	Althea	08/02/2001	F	XBURKP	Eligible (ECS)	18/02/2013 08:33:03	25/02/2013 03:30:18
Woods	Charlotte	26/04/1996	M	G6CY6X	Pending (ECS Not Found)	24/02/2013 03:15:04	22/02/2013 17:14:19

Fig. 1. Eligibility screen

The screen in Figure 1 shows the list of currently eligible children in a school obtained from selecting the menu item Eligibility. The list may be re-ordered by clicking on the appropriate column heading, printed as a screen dump or downloaded as a portable document format (PDF). Additional menu items along the top have the functionality as below:

- Saved Not Found: This menu item allows the non-eligible pupils to be viewed as a single view.
- Changes: This screen shows all of the applications which have changed status in the recent past (e.g. last 5 days).
- Day by Day: This screen displays the new applications and changes, in daily lists, over the recent past (e.g. the last 5 days).

In addition, clicking on the reference (column 5 in Figure 1) brings up a screen containing the complete application data set as shown in Figure 2.

Fig. 2. Application details

Here various functions may be performed such as adding siblings, transferring a pupil's eligibility status to another school using the same system and editing the existing application details.

Figure 3 shows the search menu item through which applications may be searched, based on a single criterion or multiple criteria. In addition, this screen may be used to obtain a CSV file output of the results of the search.

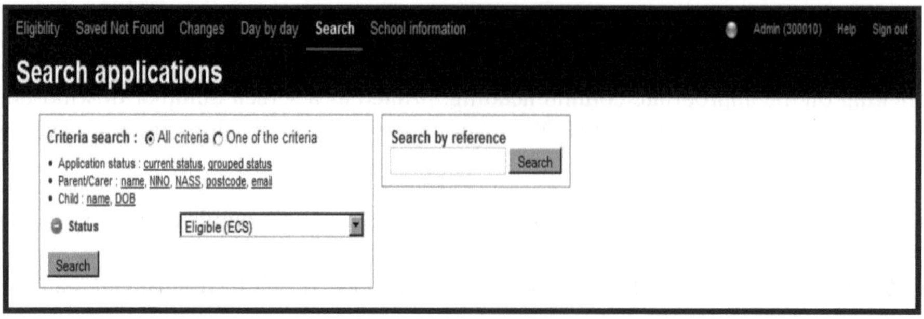

Fig. 3. Search screen

Figure 4 shows the school information screen by which the various administrative functions, such as adding users and changing the school details, may be accessed.

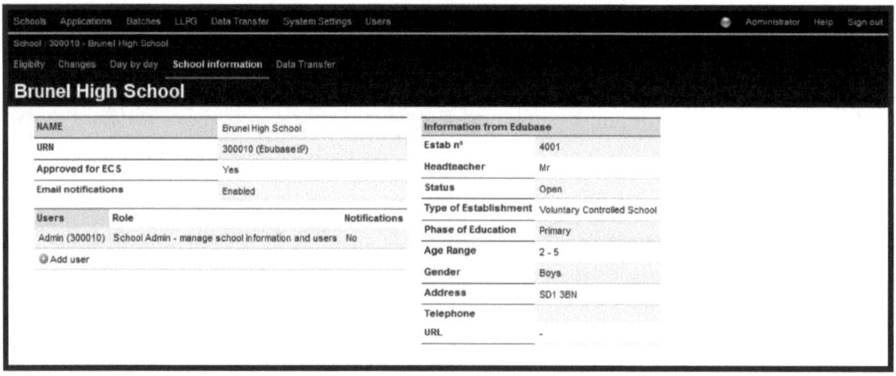

Fig. 4. School information

4.3 LA Back-Office

The LA back-office enables the LA to see all of the applications for schools within its area using the search menu or for a single school if selected from the school's menu. Whilst encompassing all of the usual administrative functions such as user setup, audit frequency, email content, etc., the main function of the back-office is to see the status of applications made. This is achieved under a series of sub-menus as shown in Figure 5.

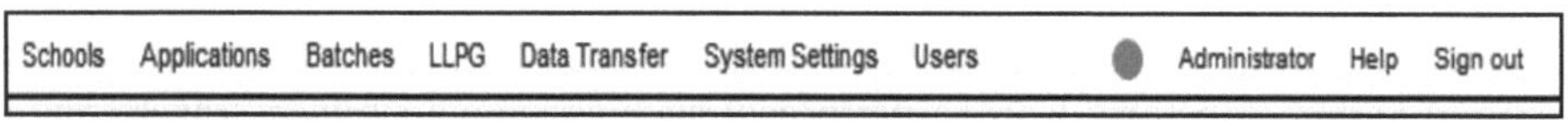

Fig. 5. LA back-office menu

The school back-office is essentially a cut-down version of the LA back-office with a restricted view of the school that the login allowed. A fully functional demonstration version of both the application form and the back-office functions can be found at [7].

5 Research Approach

The purpose of this research was to investigate how effective the introduction of a conceived user-friendly, cost-effective, cloud-based solution for OFSM would be in a variety of school settings. It was decided to look at three distinct groups of users that were using the system: an LA (which included all the schools within the LA); a single school; and a consortium of schools (academies) that were geographically disparate.

Although there are now three large LAs, several single schools and consortia using the system, with as many waiting for implementation to commence, it was decided to focus on the first users of each of the three category types, to give the study early results in what was a very short time period.

The case studies utilised semi-structured interviews with the users (a selection in the case of the LA and consortium, based on availability) and administrators. These were carried out by one of the developers not known personally to the interviewee. In addition, emails received as a result of the process, support calls and statistics before and after implementation were also used.

The interviews asked questions about the system including the user's reasons for choosing the solution, how they previously checked eligibility, advantages and disadvantages of the system, how they rated the system, possible improvements and any additional comments.

Interviews were conducted via telephone following an email request with a preview of the questions above and the option to respond via email; however, none of them chose this option.

These interviews were intended to obtain an evaluation of the system and were open ended to give the users ample opportunities to express their opinions without too much structure or question bias.

6 Case Study One: An Academy Consortium

6.1 Background

The Academy Consortium is a consortium of 18 academies (27 from September 2013) across England from Portsmouth to the Midlands. As an academy is independent of the LA and is directly funded by the government, the group wanted the advantages of an online system that they could use as a consortium of schools that made up the group.

6.2 The How, When and Where

As a result of information from an existing OFSM system user one of the finance directors arranged for the system to be demonstrated to the consortium managing group and a decision was made to pilot the system with one school and after the success of the pilot go for a full implementation across all the schools in January 2013.

6.3 What

A Consortium-branded online form was created with an appropriate universal resource locator (UR)L and back-office systems. The system was rolled out to one school in December 2012 and following the success of this pilot to all the 19 schools in January 2013. From September 2013 a further 9 schools joined the Consortium and are using the OFSM system.

6.4 Result

The initial pilot school had already asked parental permissions to check eligibility on their behalf and where they had consented had given the appropriate details to the school. All of these applications were run through the system in the first couple of weeks. As a result 10 new eligible pupils were identified, resulting in provision of a school meal for these pupils and an extra income as a result of Pupil Premium (an extra amount of pupil-focused funding for children who are eligible for FSM) of around £6,000.

Interviews were carried out with the contact officer, who initiated the system across the academy group and supported the users on a day-to-day basis and considered the software to be "Outstanding". However they did consider that transfer of the data to their school management information system (MIS) would be an improvement.

An interview with a school administrator resulted in the following comment:

"Everyone thinks it's brilliant and has significantly reduced admin [sic]".

7 Case Study Two: A Single Academy School

7.1 Background

This single academy primary school obtained academy status in 2012. Previously part of the LA, the school had been and still was part of the LA's batch ECS service which schools could buy into. This would typically involve the school collecting eligibility status data from parents/carers (name, date of birth, NINO, etc.) creating a data file and sending to the LA. The LA would then check this file against the ECS and append with the appropriate result.

However, the school wanted a real-time system that parents could access themselves at any time and would give an instant decision to both parent and school, without having to use the LA as an intermediary.

7.2 The How, When and Where

As a result of networking with a neighbouring LA the school was made aware of the SDA product that would enable the school and citizen to have a faster response and more control over the process. A demonstration of the system was organised on the school office computer in February 2013.

7.3 What

The solution consisted of a transactional web application form customised with the school logos and look-and-feel that was accessed via an appropriate URL/web address. The school's own privacy notices and data protection advice together with any other information were also added.

7.4 Result

The system removed the need for parents to bring personal data into the school allowing them to make applications in the privacy of their own home (or office, internet café, library, etc.) and gave them an instant response. This removes the stigma and the waiting associated with the old system. The school gets an immediate update of eligible pupils allowing them to organise the free meal as quickly as possible as well as accumulating data for Pupil Premium and other FSM-based benefits.

7.5 Conclusion

Although only running the system for a month, through publicity in the school magazine the school had already had 2 new eligible applications which they put down to the ease of use of the system for parents.

An interview with the office manager resulted in the following statement:

"Saves time and cuts down on paperwork and administration".

This was mainly as a result of the self-documenting features of the software and the removal of the need for office staff to examine and make decisions based on the paper evidence supplied.

This was echoed by the office administrator who thought the software was:

"really good... brilliant".

In addition they were impressed by the speed of the online decision (usually seconds) and thought its extension to the area of uniform grants would be helpful.

8 Case Study Three: A L LA

8.1 Background

The LA is a large local authority with over 500 schools and over 17,000 children potentially eligible for free school meals. The LA was already a regular user of the ECS for the batch processing of school meal applications from parents. Written forms from parents were delivered to the schools and passed on to the LA or delivered directly to the LA. Once the results of the application were known, the LA would pass on the data to the schools, usually on a spreadsheet.

8.2 The How, When and Where

The LA wanted to enable parents to apply online, thus reducing the use of paper and keyboard entry at the LA. They wanted to get an immediate result and to notify both the school and the LA at the same time. In addition, they wanted to encourage the use of electronic communications between the parent, the LA and schools and to conduct automatic audits and renewal applications.

Setting up such a service in-house would have made demands on scarce internal resources, involving both staff and hardware, and any new development would have to compete for priority with other critical applications.

8.3 Result

SDA were able to offer an efficient and cost-effective cloud-based solution to the LA; there were minimal start-up costs and a low annual rental charge. The LA was also given a reduced cost for being a regional lead authority.

The LA initially conducted a pilot with four schools to ascertain how the system would work in practice. SDA customised the online application form with the logos and look-and-feel of the LA web site and assisted the LA with their own data protection statement and privacy notices which appear on the initial pre-application screens.

Following a pilot in March 2012, the LA decided to roll out the system to all schools in the LA. The LA supplied legacy OFSM data and contact details for each of its schools and SDA were able to populate the new system with these data. SDA also set up initial user identification data (IDs) and passwords for each school user. Schools were given the URL link to access the application form and the back-office system.

Local Land and Property Gazetteer (LLPG) data were uploaded to enable postcode validation, mapping and address lookup facilities, with none of the ongoing costs usually associated with using commercially available addressing data. The list of participating LA schools is presented to applicants in school selection dropdown menus.

8.4 Conclusion

Because all schools and the LA are essentially using the same database, changes are immediate and visible to all those with rights to view them. Any amendments to how the system functions are done on the cloud by SDA so the LA is relieved of all the system maintenance responsibilities associated with client-based systems.

In all, the system requires minimal LA and school input and runs the OFSM process automatically as far as this is possible. In addition, it gives schools more control over their business and minimises the demands on scarce LA resources.

Despite being the largest user in this research the comments were the most positive of the three. This can be summed up by the quotation below from the catering services manager:

"The new free meal eligibility checking system has improved efficiency and communication between the LA and schools. School Administrators are very happy with the access to real-time information, and it has simplified our LA process, reducing time spent on checks whilst ensuring their accuracy. We now hope that the online route will encourage more parents of children eligible for free meals, to make sure their children have them."

It seems that the simplification of the process and the reduction in time needed to administer it in a larger environment is greater for a larger number of users and particularly in a public service environment. Further studies in other comparable LAs will enable more evidence regarding this.

9 Conclusions

The use of the system described appears to have been an outstanding success based on the evidence collected. Initiating the online system is fairly easy including creating a URL for the establishment and a bespoke application form. Accreditation for web services can be turned around in a week as all the security and web service calls are identical for each system.

The system has the advantage of giving the LA up-to-date information about all applications, removing the need for annual reapplication and performing regular audit at weekly intervals ensuring that the benefit is always available to those who are eligible. However, additional benefits are being recognised. For example, the removal of the stigma of application at the school can increase applications, helping to increase the number of applications from the estimated 200,000 parent/carers [1] who do not currently apply for the entitlement but who are considered to be eligible.

10 Further Work

As more LAs roll out the system there will be greater data to make comparative studies of the system's usage, effectiveness in terms of increasing eligibility application and overall user satisfaction. This will form the basis of a more quantitative study in the future.

The addition of early year's entitlement for 2-year-olds based on FSM eligibility further increases the scope of an eligibility checker and this is currently in development.

FSM eligibility is also used as a trigger for summer schools (additional tuition for pupils when they move between primary and secondary schools). The effects on academic performance as a result of this extra teaching and learning will be interesting, although, of course, these need to be tempered against the reported advantages [11] of receiving regular nutritious meals themselves.

The system can be used within England and Wales as they have the same criteria for FSM; however, it is considered that given the cooperation from the appropriate government that the principles could be extended to the rest of the UK or beyond through the use of a similar middleware solution connecting central databases to a public portal in a secure way.

References

1. Strickley, A.: Data sharing between local and national governments for the benefit of the citizen: Online free school meals as a transformational project. In: Passey, D., Breiter, A., Visscher, A. (eds.) ITEM 2012. IFIP AICT, vol. 400, pp. 107–118. Springer, Heidelberg (2013)
2. Children's Food Trust: Free school meals: why don't all parents sign up? Findings from a survey of parents in England. Children's Food Trust, Sheffield (2013)
3. Department for Education: Eligibility Criteria (2013), http://www.education.gov.uk/schools/pupilsupport/pastoralcare/a00202841/fsmcriteria/ (retrieved August 29, 2014)
4. Storey, P., Chamberlin, R.: Improving the take up of free school meals. DfEE Research Report 270 (2001), http://dera.ioe.ac.uk/4657/1/RR270.pdf (retrieved August 29, 2014)
5. Granville, S., Staniforth, J., Clapton, R.: Investigating Local Authority procedures for identifying and registering children eligible for free school meal entitlement. Scottish Executive (2006), http://www.scotland.gov.uk/Resource/Doc/157044/0042264.pdf (retrieved August 29, 2014)
6. SDA: Home page (2013), http://www.sda-ltd.com/ (retrieved August 29, 2014)
7. SDA: OFSM home page (2013), https://www.cloudforedu.org.uk/ofsm/ (retrieved August 29, 2014)
8. Connect Digitally: Frequently asked questions for web services. Department for Education, Sheffield (2013)
9. DfE: FSM system integration guide. Department for Education, Sheffield (2010)
10. Wyld, D.C.: Moving to the cloud: An introduction to cloud computing in government. IBM Centre for the Business of Government, Hammond, LA (2009)
11. Telecity: Home page (2013), http://www.telecitygroup.com/ (retrieved August 29, 2014)
12. DfE: Evaluation of the free school meals pilot: Impact Report. National Centre for Social Research, London (2013)

A National Single Indicator for Schools in England: Helping Parents Make Informed Decisions

Alan Strickley, John Bertram, Dave Chapman, Michael Hart, Roy Hicks, Derek Kennedy, and Mark Phillips

Software for Data Analysis Limited, London, UK
alan.strickley@sda-ltd.com

Abstract. With an ever-increasing measurement of pupil and school performance and presence of resultant statistical tables and indicators, parents are faced with a sometimes overwhelming plethora of data and information when monitoring the performance of their children's present or prospective school. The authors are part of a company that has developed a parent/carer-accessible site to attempt to address issues and needs for parents/carers. Anecdotal evidence indicates that a single portal where parent/carers can find all the relevant data about schools in England would be an invaluable tool for monitoring and choosing a school. It was decided that such a site would be built around a National Single Indicator (NSI). The indicator is formed from an amalgam of expected progress measures: the main threshold level; pupils' average points score; and the value added measure. By changing the weight attributed to each of these measures, the website allows parents to modify their relative importance according to the value they place on them. This dynamically alters the overall result to give users their own "personal indicator", which means they can compare schools in a list tailored to their own specification.

Keywords: School performance tables, national single indicator, Ofsted, NSI, parents.

1 Introduction

The data held in schools and shared with local and central governments in England has increased since the advent of computerised Management Information Systems (MISs) in the 1970s up until the current time [2]. In particular this has concerned:

- Electronic replacement of the admissions' register [3].
- Electronic recording of attendance [3].
- The National Curriculum [4].
- Electronic examination entry and results [5].
- End of Key Stage (age-related) entry and results [6].
- Common transfer file (an interoperable file format used to transfer selected pupil data when that pupil moves from one school to another) [7].
- Pupil level census (a central government electronic return by all schools which includes selected individual personal and performance data about pupils) [8].

D. Passey and A. Tatnall (Eds.): KCICTP/ITEM 2014, IFIP AICT 444, pp. 331–345, 2014.

With an increase in parental access to school admission procedures and the coordinated admission process which includes equal preferences [9], the choice of school is seen as a critical factor. With much of the data about schools being available in the public domain, school selection has become an important social and political concern within England at secondary and more recently at primary levels.

Data about schools is available in a plethora of formats and locations, from league tables (ranking of schools by government-agreed rating measures), attendance levels, Key Stage (age-related) results and value added from central government, the British Broadcasting Corporation (BBC) and newspapers are amongst those that publish this information [10,11,12,13]. For many parents the information is disparate and often in a format that is confusing and complex to understand (as supported by [14]).

A decision was made by the authors to compile all of the available data from the various sources (but mainly the Department for Education in England - DfE) into a website which could be accessed by the public to help choose a new school or evaluate the performance of existing ones. The site would be underpinned by a fundamental value which was defined as the National Single Indicator (NSI) for each school. This would have a value (A-E) together with a less granular star rating, calculated on a set of key performance criteria (described in the next section) but could be fine-tuned by the user adjusting the weightings for each of these criteria. The result was the School Performance Tables [15] website which is described in detail later in this paper.

This paper looks at the basis of the NSI for schools, the fundamental design of the web interface, together with initial user reactions and considerations for further work.

2 Background

Performance tables have been published by the DfE [11], and its previous incarnations, since 1992 for Key Stage 4 (KS4) (aged 14 to 16 years) and 1996 for Key Stage 2 (KS2) (aged 7 to 11 years). The main aims of publication were to assist parents and carers in selecting schools for their children and to encourage school improvement by providing objective indicators against which schools' performance could be measured.

The current performance tables provide over 200 separate data items per school from which interested parties are expected to make judgements. This may be well within the capabilities of local government authority staff and others familiar with education performance data, but for parents and carers it can be a daunting task.

The aim of the National Single Indicator (NSI) is to provide a simple, but robust, method for parents and carers to be able to view schools' relative performance without needing to view multiple screens of data and without having to perform offline calculations.

It is important to note that the NSI does not aim to be a tool to aid school improvement – there are many available tools for this purpose and much expertise in schools, local authorities and support organisations focuses on this issue. As it stands, the NSI does not integrate with school MISs in any way; however, the option for schools to add context-sensitive information onto the site is a feature that will be added in the future.

The NSI is a single indicator describing school performance at KS2 and KS4. The indicators at both of these Key Stages are closely aligned, sharing expected progress, value added and average points scores as common components and differentiating only on the key indicators used to assess performance of Level 4+ (average expected attainment) at KS2 and 5A*-C (expected public examination attainment) at KS4.

The components at KS2 or KS4 (average points score, value added and expected progress) are given equal weighting with a default, notional, value of 2. This value can be varied between 0 and 4 in increments of 1 according to personal choice, or perceived importance, that users place on it. For example, it may be that a parent places more store by a school's ability to "add value" to their children's education than the school's performance measures.

3 What Data Are Used for the National Single Indicator?

The developers intended the NSI to be a well-rounded and justifiable indicator of a school's performance. This section explains how the indicator is calculated. The NSI is based on the following base components.

3.1 Key Stage 2

The following performance indicators are taken from the DfE's published Performance Tables data [11] (where the precise definitions of each may be found):

- Progress measure, comprising:
    - Percentage of pupils making at least 2 levels of progress in a nationally prescribed mathematics test.
    - Percentage of pupils making at least 2 levels of progress in a nationally prescribed reading test.
    - Percentage of pupils making at least 2 levels of progress in teacher assessment of writing.
- Percentage of pupils achieving Level 4 or above (where Level 4 is the average expected standard) in reading and mathematics tests and teacher assessment of writing.
- Average points score.
- Overall value added measure (a single measure of the added value that the school has provided).

3.2 Key Stage 4

The following performance indicators are taken from the DfE's published Performance Tables data [11] where the precise definitions of each may be found:

- Progress measure, comprising:
    - Percentage of pupils at the end of Key Stage 4 achieving the expected level of progress between Key Stage 2 and the national General Certificate of Secondary Education (GCSE) examination in English.
    - Percentage of pupils at the end of Key Stage 4 achieving the expected level of progress between Key Stage 2 and GCSE mathematics.
    - Percentage of pupils achieving 5 or more A*-C (or equivalents (the national expected standard) including A*-C in both English and mathematics GCSEs.
- Value added measure based on the best 8 GCSE and equivalent results (a single measure of the added value that the school has provided).
- Total average (capped) points score per pupil (an average value based on the best 8 GCSE results for each pupil in that school).

3.3 Calculation Methodology

In generating a NSI, the following exception classes apply (i.e. no NSI score is calculated or provided) and are allocated as follows.

- New school: no results data are provided in the Performance Tables, so it is unclassified – as a New School.
- A school without data in one or more of the measures: will normally be either an independent school or a school with very small cohort numbers, so it is unclassified – with Insufficient Data.
- Special school: schools where all (or the vast majority) of pupils have special educational needs and cannot fairly be compared to mainstream schools, so it is unclassified – as a Special School.

For schools not allocated an exception class, the following general methodology is used for both Key Stage 2 and Key Stage 4:

- Normalised scores are calculated: each of the performance measures described in sub-sections 3.1 and 3.2 above is normalised to provide a score between 0 and 1. This is done by taking the actual values and calibrating them into a single scale from 0 to 1.
- Weightings are allocated for the purposes of calculating the NSI: each of the 4 main performance measures is given equal weighting. For the component measures of the main progress measure, equal weighting has been given to English and mathematics.
- A single indicator score is calculated: an NSI score is calculated by multiplying each normalised score by its respective weighting and then divided by the sum of the weightings (4 for the NSI).
- A single indicator band is calculated: the mean and standard deviation of NSI scores are determined. An NSI band is allocated depending on the number of standard deviations from the mean of each individual NSI score.

- Single indicator ranking within the band is calculated: for each ranking, the minimum and maximum normalised scores for each of the performance measures are determined and, consequently, the score range. Each NSI score is allocated an NSI ranking within each NSI band based on the difference between NSI score and the band's minimum score and that difference's proportion of the score range.

The final NSI is either: (a) an exception class; or (b) NSI band plus NSI ranking, represented as a value A to E, augmented by a finer graduation of 1 to 5 stars, each with quarterly intervals (i.e. quarter, half and three-quarter star shadings).

Whilst there continue to be arguments and discussions regarding the validity of the performance tables and the individual indicators used [16, 17], such arguments are for the DfE to address. The NSI is provided on the basis that the DfE and Ofsted (the school performance inspectorate) consider the performance tables and individual indicators to be valid and fit for purpose.

As part of the pre-launch evaluation of the site, a large sample of 1000 schools was selected, and their NSIs compared to the individual performance measures. The result of this testing showed a very accurate match in most cases indicating that the algorithm used in the calculation of the NSI was producing its intended outcome.

4 Design of the School Performance Website

The website – www.schoolperformancetables.com – is intended to be a simple, straightforward means of comparing schools, at both primary (KS2) and secondary (KS4) levels by means of a single indicator. It goes further in being the first such site to provide a search facility that can offer a user-defined set of given subjects beyond the core curriculum. In addition, it will offer schools the option of subscribing to the site, allowing them to both advertise and brand their school and also provide commentary and context to the performance data presented.

In common with the intention to provide a simple and straightforward experience, the site attempts to be intuitive to navigate, with the minimum amount of information necessary to convey a given point, and that information to be provided, for the most part, graphically. More complex information, where absolutely necessary, (such as the description of how our indicators are generated), is available through links. In addition, the site is mobile reactive, enabling a better experience for the increasing number of smartphone and tablet users. It, therefore, differs in look and approach from the traditional performance tables delivered by the DfE. Plenty of clean space and economical instructions prevail, as opposed to dense sets of data and exhaustive instructions and guidance.

4.1 Home Page

Figure 1 shows the home page, which is the one that parents will be directed to from any external link. It is considered that parents and schools will be the main users of the site. Therefore, three main search criteria are invoked for the initial search, these being name, place and Key Stage. In addition, a subject search has been added for secondary schools.

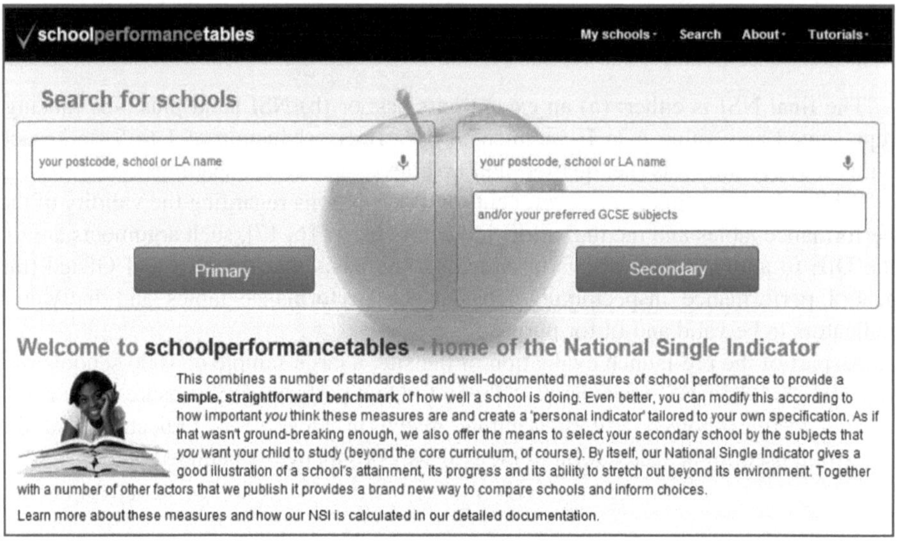

Fig. 1. Home page

The school search box is versatile, allowing multiple postcodes, abbreviated school names, regions etc., to be included. The subject search box allows for any of the examination board subjects to be input. This is designed to be particularly useful where a user requires a particular subject or specialism to be available at a school. The types of searches are illustrated in the Tables 3 to 6 below.

Table 1, below, shows how the program interprets various postcodes and names from the home screen.

Table 1. Search for schools using a postcode or name

Postcode or school name	Results of search
se1 1xw	Displays a list of all schools with distances from that postcode
se11xw	Displays a list of all schools with distances from that postcode. Note that the postcode need not contain a space
se1	Displays a list of schools within SE1
albion school	Displays a list of schools that match this name. Note that it is not case sensitive
Collège Français Bilingue de Londres	Displays the school with this name
waltham forest	Displays a list of schools in Waltham Forest LA

For schools in a local authority (LA), it is possible to enter a postcode (for example, a home postcode); the schools will be listed in order of distance (see Table 3).

Table 2. Postcode and LA search

Postcode or LA name	Displays
se1 1xw southwark Lewisham	Displays all schools in Southwark and Lewisham, with distances from the postcode se1 1xw

Table is a useful feature that lets you search for schools by subjects taken at GCSE. This is only available as a search for secondary schools.

Table 3. GCSE subject search

Law, Polish, Spanish and Statistics	Displays all schools where these subjects have been taken at GCSE

Table shows how to combine the school search and subject search so that, for example, it is possible to find out the nearest school offering preferred subjects at GCSE, or find out all schools in a local authority that offer them.

Table 4. Postcode, LA and GCSE subject search

se1 1xw (school search box) Law, Polish, Spanish and Statistics (subject search box)	Displays all schools where these subjects have been taken at GCSE by distance from se1 1xw

The results of a search take the user through to the "Summary Page", comprising five tabs as shown in the next sub-section.

4.2 Summary Page

Fig 2 shows the summary page based on search criteria.

This summary page shows schools selected, together with their NSI (and less granular star rating incorporating quarter stars as described in section 3.3), the postcode, distance in miles and yards (from the search post code; blank if no postcode given), age range, primary or secondary phase, intake gender, school type and religious orientation. From this screen a new search may be initiated, or by selecting the appropriate checkboxes next to the school name, a subset of the list may be generated for comparison purposes.

Clicking on the school name takes the user to the NSI screen as shown in the "NSI" sub-section. Clicking on the various tabs gives more comparative information as described later.

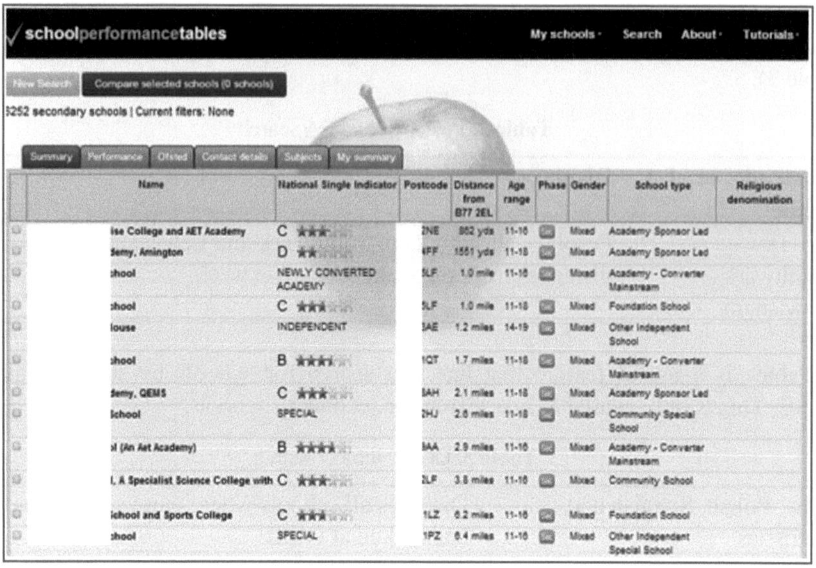

Fig. 2. Summary page

4.3 Performance Tab

Figure 3 shows the performance components screen which gives the ability to "weight" the various indicator components described in the "NSI" section according to the importance individuals place on them. The "dials" are set at the median value of 2 by default.

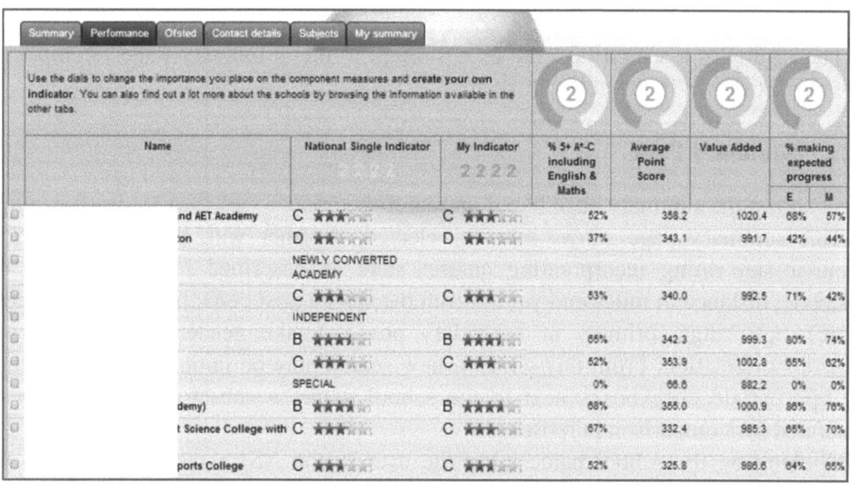

Fig. 3. Performance tab

The "dials" above each of the performance indicators (as described in the NSI sub-section) allow the user to weight each, resulting in a value in the "My Single Indicator" column. Fig. 3 shows an example where the user has selected "% Level 4+ in reading, writing and mathematics" as the only and full weighted indicator. This makes a significant difference to the NSI for some of the schools shown.

4.4 Ofsted Tab

Clicking on the Ofsted tab shows the selected schools' most recent inspection results in terms of overall, teaching, achievement, behaviour and leadership scores. Clicking on the inspection date takes the user to the appropriate full inspection report at the Ofsted website.

4.5 Contact Details

The contact tab displays the various contact details of the school: address; telephone number; and website unique resource locator (URL) are included on this screen. Clicking on the website address takes the user to the school website.

4.6 Subject Tab

Clicking on the subject tab gives the current subjects offered at GCSE. Note that if a primary school search is chosen, then this tab will not be available.

4.7 My Summary

Fig. 4 shows the "My Summary" tab which enables the user to put their data into a single screen.

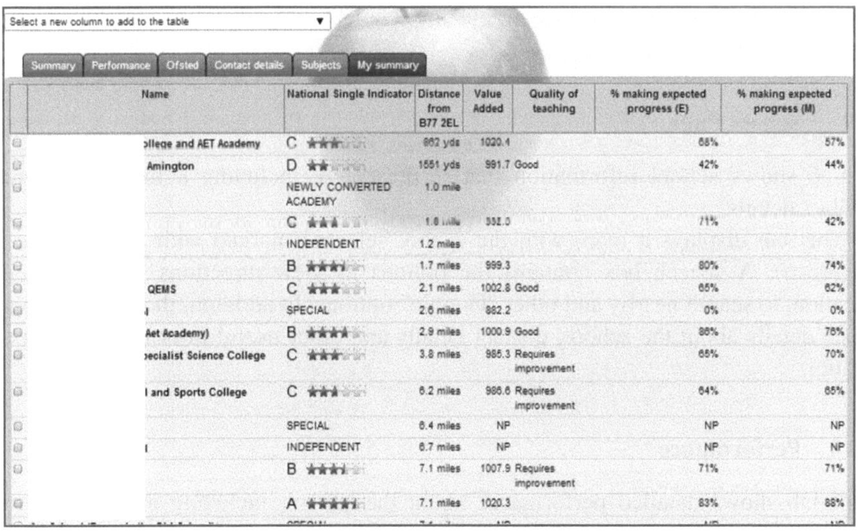

Fig. 4. My summary tab

By using the dropdown menu, various columns may be added, which will contain data shown from the tabs described in the previous sub-sections. For example, performance data, Ofsted information, contact details, subjects etc. may be appended to the right of the NSI column.

4.8 National Single Indicator

Fig. 5 shows the NSI screen for the school selected from the summary screen.

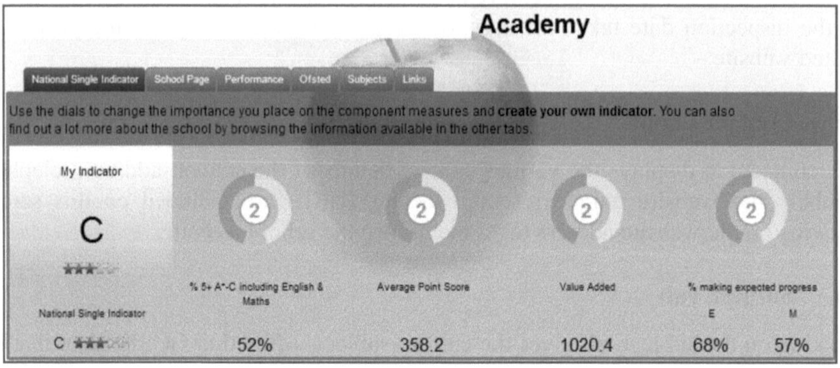

Fig. 5. NSI tab

This screen gives the breakdown of the NSI for the school with the individual percentages below the weighting "dial". The percentage making up expected progress is split into the component parts, reading, writing and mathematics. As with the performance tab (Fig. 3) these "dials" may be moved to change the weightings which create the NSI.

4.9 School Page

Fig. 6 shows school information that is presented, including a map and various contact details.

This tab displays a map, with the school selected marked with a "pin" ('A' in Figure 6). A speech box contains the options to view directions from a specific location, to search nearby and other "Google" options. In addition, the screen displays basic details about the school, contact details and other useful information about the school.

4.10 Performance

This tab shows detailed performance about the school, including numbers on roll, number of free school meal (FSM) pupils, and Key Stage information pertaining to the school.

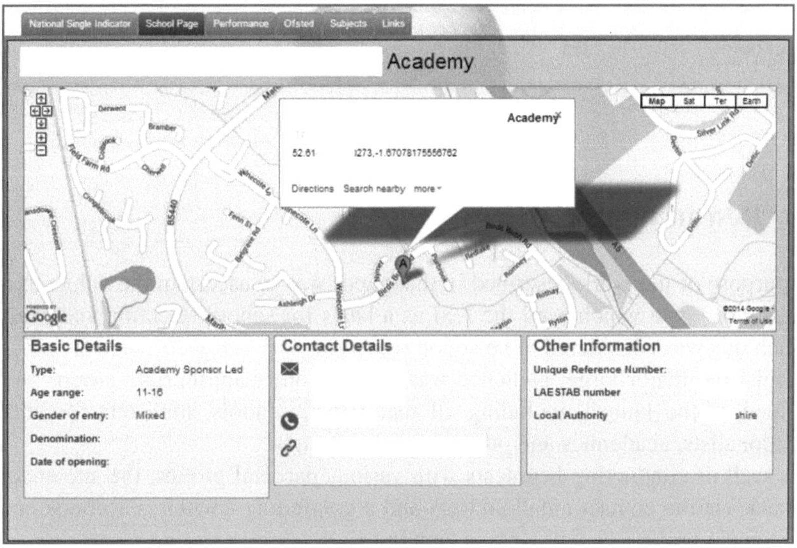

Fig. 6. School page

4.11 Ofsted

This tab shows the Ofsted information about the single school selected which gives details about the latest Ofsted inspection such as Overall Effectiveness and summary of the key findings for parents and pupils. This is a more detailed view than the information presented in section 0.

4.12 Links

The links tab shows useful links that are pertinent to the evaluation of the school, such as DfE performance tables, DfE statistics about the area, Office for National Statistics about the neighbourhood statistics, school details from the national database EduBase, Ofsted parent view and Ofsted inspection reports.

4.13 Menu

Fig. 7 shows the menu system that is available at the top right of all screens. These have the following functions:

- My schools: brings up a list of schools that have been selected by the user from the comparative screens.
- Search: returns the user to the main search page as shown in Fig. 1.
- About: gives details and documentation about the single indicator.
- Tutorials: help and advice on using the website.

Fig. 7. Menu

5 Research Methodology

The purpose of the work described in this paper was to ascertain the value, usage and feedback of a site which used the NSI as a basis for school selection and evaluation. As such this was considered to be action research.

Whilst the major target audience was parents, other appropriate groups were also informed of the launch, including all maintained schools, ministers for education, educationalists, academics and other interested parties.

As well as conducting beta tests with various parental groups, the site encouraged feedback via the contact email address and a continuing Twitter, Facebook and other social media promotional process is ongoing.

All responses were welcome in order to include every possible feedback and this, together with statistical data collected from the web site, will enable a more complete evaluation to be documented.

6 Results So Far

The site launched on schedule on 23rd January 2014. The quotation below offers an example of the type of responses received as a result of all maintained school head teachers being informed of the launch.

> *"The idea of a single, graded indicator, applied to a school, is nonsensical. Schools are complex and multifaceted, and cannot be reduced to a single grade. What is the point of doing this?" Primary Headteacher*

This reply does not surprise. Schools do not like the idea of league tables or performance measures particularly when they do not score highly and for the reasons given in the quotation and accepted by the authors. However, these measures are currently the only available data that parents can use to judge a school by and the NSI attempts to make a simplified indicator that can then be used to look at more detailed information about the school. Indeed, if a parent were to look at the league tables available in much of the media, then finding more information would be a considerable task. A less critical view from a secondary school tends to support the view that a simplified approach has merits.

> *"It certainly is a very interesting idea and I have to applaud your desire to "to cut through the noise and get to the point." Deputy Headteacher, Secondary School*

A quotation showing a different perspective follows. Parents are not necessarily expert in statistics and although the NSI is not a complete picture of a school's performance it does act as a benchmark for parents to begin their evaluation.

> *"This is a really useful tool for parents to help them selecting their children's school. It is easy to use and informative." Parent of a child applying for a place in September 2014*

Another very encouraging comment, which confirmed the testing applied, regarding the reliability of the NSI and the general usability of the website, follows.

> *"I have checked the schools' website against the local schools here and I would say that it is very clear and helpful: it also ties in with what I know about these schools." Professor of Education*

The Open Data Institute [18] is a key body encouraging and fostering the use of openness and transparency in data and information. Their endorsement of the underlying principles of the website follows.

> *"interesting and highly relevant example of good practice in the data meets education sphere." Open Data Institute (ODI)*

Other comments have noted the speed that the results are generated in real time when adjustments are made to the various weightings of the components of the NSI. This was achieved even though the developers worked to very tight timescales and complex design specifications.

The site has received 5,157 visits since its launch, peaking at 1,713 on a single day, with an average 265 per day. These figures are expected to increase exponentially as word of mouth and publicity expands the user base.

Since the launch of the website, the government has indicated its intention to require schools to present "easier-to-understand" [19, 20] information on its performance and a group consisting of the Association of College and School Leaders (ACSL), National Association of Head Teachers (NAHT), United Learning and PiXL (an online resource company for schools) are intending to launch a new performance site in the autumn of 2014 [21, 22, 23]. It would seem that others, including the government, feel that the current system is over complex and confusing for users.

7 Future Work

It is intended to enable schools, parents and other appropriate persons or bodies to add contextual information to the site that will help put the information into perspective. It is also hoped to add more information such as admissions policy, more detailed performance measures supplied by the school, behavioural data, homework policies, etc. The creation of an application for smart telephones is also a possible development with the added advantage of possible funding by users. Funding for the site is to be considered and such options as advertising and premium versions are to be considered.

Feedback from schools, parents and other relevant establishments is to be closely monitored as will the use of the site. These will feed back into the future developments and structure of the site.

References

1. SDA: Home page (2014), http://www.sda-ltd.com/ (retrieved August 31, 2014)
2. Strickley, A.B.: An evaluative study of the use of management information systems in Birmingham primary schools. VDM Verlag, Saarbrücken (2009)
3. DfE: Amendments to school attendance regulations (2014), http://www.education.gov.uk/schools/pupilsupport/behaviour/attendance/a00223868/regulations-amendments (retrieved August 31, 2014)
4. DfE: The national curriculum (2014), http://www.education.gov.uk/schools/teachingandlearning/curriculum (retrieved August 31, 2014)
5. AQA: Home page (2014), http://www.aqa.org.uk/ (retrieved August 31, 2014)
6. DfE: Key Stage 2 (2014), http://www.education.gov.uk/schools/teachingandlearning/assessment/keystage2 (retrieved August 31, 2014)
7. DfE: CTF information (2014), http://www.education.gov.uk/researchandstatistics/datatdatam/ctf (retrieved August 31, 2014)
8. DfE: School census information (2014), http://www.education.gov.uk/researchandstatistics/stats/schoolcensus (retrieved August 31, 2014)
9. DfE: School admissions code (2014), http://www.education.gov.uk/aboutdfe/statutory/g00213254/school-admissions-code-2012 (retrieved August 31, 2014)
10. BBC: Home page (2014), http://www.bbc.co.uk/news/education-11950098 (retrieved August 31, 2014)
11. DfE: School performance tables (2014), http://www.education.gov.uk/schools/performance/ (retrieved August 31, 2014)
12. Guardian: School league tables (2014), http://www.theguardian.com/education/school-tables (retrieved August 31, 2014)
13. Daily Mail: League tables (2014), http://www.dailymail.co.uk/news/article-400873/How-school-college-fares.html (retrieved August 31, 2014)
14. Dearden, L., Vignoles, A.: Schools, markets and league tables. The Journal of Applied Public Economics 32(2), 179–186 (2011)
15. SDA: School performance tables (2014), http://www.schoolperformancetables.com/ (retrieved August 31, 2014)
16. Goldstein, H., Leckie, G.: School league tables: what can they really tell us? Significance, 67–69 (2008), http://eprints.ncrm.ac.uk/545/1/league%20tables%20critique.pdf (retrieved August 31, 2014)

17. Goldstein, H., Spiegelhalter, D.J.: League tables and their limitations: statistical issues in comparisons of institutional performance. Journal of the Royal Statistical Society. Series A (Statistics in Society) 159(3), 385–443 (1996)
18. Open Data Institute: Home page (2014), http://theodi.org/ (retrieved August 31, 2014)
19. DfE: Parents to be given key information on schools' performance (2014), https://www.gov.uk/government/news/parents-to-be-given-key-information-on-schools-performance (retrieved August 31, 2014)
20. DfE: Publishing performance measures on school and college web sites (2014), https://www.gov.uk/government/consultations/publishing-performance-measures-on-school-and-college-websites (retrieved August 31, 2014)
21. United Learning: Education profession unites to publish performance tables (2014), http://www.unitedlearning.org.uk/News/TabId/92/ArtMID/476/ArticleID/162/Education-Profession-Unites-To-Publish-School-Performance-Tables-.aspx (retrieved August 31, 2014)
22. NAHT: Education profession unites to publish performance tables (2014), http://www.naht.org.uk/welcome/news-and-media/key-topics/inspections-and-accountability/education-profession-unites-to-publish-school-performance-tables/ (retrieved August 31, 2014)
23. PiXL: School performance tables (2014), http://www.schoolperformancetables.org.uk/ (retrieved August 31, 2014)

Author Index

FSC
www.fsc.org

MIX
Papier aus verantwortungsvollen Quellen
Paper from responsible sources
FSC® C105338

If you have any concerns about our products,
you can contact us on
ProductSafety@springernature.com

In case Publisher is established outside the EU,
the EU authorized representative is:
Springer Nature Customer Service Center GmbH
Europaplatz 3, 69115 Heidelberg, Germany

Printed by Libri Plureos GmbH
in Hamburg, Germany